Beyond The Secret
Dr. Louis Turi, M.D.U.S.

Startheme Publications LTD
Copyright 2007 by Dr. Louis Turi

Editing by Samantha Turner and Laurie Shafer
Cover and some interior illustrations by Madeline Rosenstein

ISBN: 0-9745209-3-4
Published by Startheme Publications Ltd.
4411 N. 23rd St. Phoenix AZ 85016
Tel: (602) 265-7667 - Fax: (602) 265-8668
Email: Dr. Turi@cox.net

Visit our websites:
www.drturi.com
www.myspace.com/drturi
www.cherrytap.com/drturi
www.globalenquirer.com/
Email dr.turi@cox.net

Printed in the United States of America

Table of Contents

"The Greatest Secret of All is Discovering One's Celestial Identity"

---Dr. Turi

Letter From the Author

Special thanks are given to all my great friends and family, faithful clients, students, and readers from all over the world. Also, I wish to thank all the numerous open-minded journalists and hosts of radio and television programs.

I am grateful to all of those spiritual men and women who have helped me to enlighten their audiences with my spiritual gift. I appreciate all those souls who have guided and supported my work. In their common efforts to alleviate man's suffering, they have all become vital participants in the understanding of the human experience. All of you have been invaluable in furthering my gift, and I am infinitely grateful for allowing me to pass on my spiritual gift to the world.

This book was started in 1995 and reflects my personal life experiences and my own definition of the "Universal Code" and how it shapes the human experience. Imagination has no limits and there is nothing you cannot be or achieve. Powerful emotion is the essential fuel needed for liberating and channeling the subconscious' miraculous creative forces.

There is so much more behind this physical world and its rigid rules. One must relentlessly investigate all options of what it means to be an immortal soul confined into a physical envelope and acknowledge the extraordinary. One must also never forget that the fine key of wisdom comes from rich experiences and can only bring about constructive transformation. The possibility exists for each and every one of us to reach and enjoy the best of both the physical and spiritual worlds. Conventional disciplines such as traditional psychology, psychiatry, conventional science, and religious doctrines tend to eradicate the inexplicable; but with time, the truth will always prevail.

This stimulating work will act as a pathfinder to help you to uncover some of the answers that God enslaved every one of us to search for. This avant-garde material is quite controversial and could be construed as unrealistic by some young souls. In no way would I purposely try to convert anyone to my personal belief system. "Beyond the Secret" is simply a sensible approach to the extraordinary and a testament of my own spiritual essence. My findings are based upon all of my spectacular life's adventures and the decision to accept my theories is solely yours. By reading this book I trust you to ascend to a much higher level of awareness and raise your own vibrations. My mission is to help you to recognize the possibility of UFOs and become more attentive of the Universal Mind. With this book, I am offering you a stairway to the "Universal Code" and the opportunity to swiftly draw upon your subconscious' creative forces to your advantage.

It is through acceptance and supreme wisdom that an advanced soul will guide and heal others. This honorable aspiration is a reality to some human beings who share an intrinsic mission with extraterrestrials, mankind's fate, and God's will. Only a few privileged select souls will be allowed to undergo such staggering and unyielding UFO encounters. It is because of those imposed experiences that I now perceive, comprehend, use, and teach the "Universal Code"; thus, speaking the dialect of the Gods. Anyone can master the hieroglyphs of the Universe and unleash a mighty power that can be used for the well being of all. True wisdom is the golden door to the miraculous wonders of the archetypal realm of consciousness.

Like the great Prophet Nostradamus I was born in Provence, France. Following my fourth UFO abduction in 1991, I was compelled to master the "Universal Code" and practice it as the great Seer used to do. Over five hundreds years ago no computers or watches were available and I made a full job to bring back intuition and symbolism against a modernized mathematically oriented jargon. This work involves the essence and channeling of the Great Prophet's spirit and his eternal message to mankind.

Dr. Turi "The Modern Day Nostradamus"

Don't let your disagreement with others become an excuse for hatred or disrespect, instead, sincerely seek to learn from and understand those perspectives that differ from your own. Never forget that ignorance is pure evil and true knowledge is real power.

- Before you devote, explore.
- Before you give up, seek more.
- Before you condemn, investigate.
- Before you talk, listen.
- Before you inscribe, reflect.
- Before you waste, make.
- Before you ask, give.
- Before you spend, accumulate.
- Before your last breath, bestow life.
- Watch your thoughts; they become your words.
- Watch your words; they become your actions.
- Watch your actions; they become your habits.
- Watch your habits; they become your character.
- Watch your character for it will become your destiny.

Once more, thank you for your patronage and trust in my work.

"The future is nothing other than the reincarnation of your thoughts"
-- Dr. Turi

PREFACE

Important Facts About "The Secret"

In 2006, a new sensational movie entitled "The Secret" came out and the production was quite phenomenal, but also significantly incomplete. The movie was also endorsed by Oprah Winfrey and broadcast on her television program. In the overpowering optimistic script, nothing pertaining to the negative manifesto of this Universal Law was exposed or explained in the Oprah show. Realize also, that I do support, understand and even promote not only the "Secret", but also all other Universal laws that make the human experience possible.

However, the question remains after watching this well-produced movie, what will you be able to do or accomplish with it? 'The Secret" is an overwhelmingly inspired production, skillfully shaped by wise and talented souls. However, like anything left unfinished, it can cause more detriment than improvement in the long run. Another important law well demonstrated in the movie is that we tend to attract what we fear the most. I do acknowledge the true value and purpose of the show and all the well-spoken wise participants, but there is much more about the Universal Laws and their interaction with a multitude of unforgiving celestial rules. This book is designed to point out the facts, entertain, and educate the reader at the same time. Many people are in total denial and expect riches and fast results with minimum efforts, but common sense dictates otherwise. I think it's only fair to teach both sides of the law that draws miracles, and to make people aware of the cosmic regulations that interact with the subconscious creative forces.

It took me years of practice at the Royal School of music in London to learn to play piano. I also wanted to be a pilot and I worked overtime to be able to invest in my dream. It took patience and diligence to learn the many aeronautical laws that allowed me to fly safely and enjoy "being above the world". But all along, other crucial laws were in action. It is by carefully auto-analyzing all dramatic events that transpired in my life that I was able to recognize the subtle "Universal Code" in action.

In this great capitalist country, everyone is out there working hard to make a buck. The "Secret" was not offered for free to the media and rest assured that all participants involved in this production got paid (or should have been) for their valuable expertise and participation. Universal Laws teachings are priceless, really and there is nothing wrong in getting remunerated for a job well done. The dramatic loss of my brother through the negative manifesto of a law which creates events needs to be further investigated. This terrible experience denounces the harmful expression of a particular law. I strongly feel that you should recognize both sides, not just experience the huge uplifting boost from concentrating solely on a supremely positive end. There are spiritual and astrological laws in effect too. I will expose my case as clearly as possible and once you toss this book onto your shelf, you will be the sole judge of my findings.

The fact is; you will get what you pay for in life and you must realize that a cheap service has not much value. You simply cannot learn to fly an airplane (your life) by listening to one hour long CD or DVD - it's just impossible. For example there is a big difference between a 25-cent newspaper horoscope and a $300.00 - 90 minutes taped Full Life Reading that I provide. Or a huge difference between a 60 minutes DVD production "The Secret" and 16 CD's each sixty minutes plus 4 hour-long DVD's (including three of my books) of crucial information on mastering the Universal Code. A full week of intense spiritual teachings is needed to raise your vibration and build any form of Cosmic Consciousness and get "the rest of the secret". The producers of this movie know that the masses are lazy and unwilling to spend time away from sports and or any other form of entertainment. The numbed souls would rather read "Harry Potter" and escape reality with a fictional book, indulge in recreational drugs, watch movies and sports, or simply sleep through life.

My books and teachings are real and demand you to do serious mental gymnastics, while other famous spiritual writers will use a great dose of imagination, cleverly using words such as Angels, God, Jesus or any other deity -- but will not teach you anything solid. They are simply adapting to your needs, using religion, and like "The Secret", giving you another way to deceive yourself with impractical expectations. There are too many other laws at work, you are not aware of yet and this is why you are reading this material. With patience and observation, this book will guide you into the marvel of your god given powers and with discipline you will be able to access the power that you need to bring about all of your wishes.

There is only one hair between Divine information and pure imagination. If you want to fly high, you will have to invest time, money and effort and regardless of how much you read or watch the movie "The Secret", you are not going to take off anywhere fast because you did not put the right effort and time into your search for the truth. The only one who wins is the one who got your cash, and like any McDonald's drive through fast food, it may not necessarily be good for your body, mind, and your spirit! You will have plenty of time to sleep when you are dead. Dreaming is fine, but act now and do something for the world, for the children of tomorrow, and most of all… for yourself! For this is what you were born to do, to grow and to accomplish miracles. Remember, from a small village in France, I came to this great country in 1984 with only $50 in my pocket and I am a true example of success, where my inner wisdom and will brought me the true "American Dream" and all its blessings that I had wished for.

Some parts of the secret reside in your ability to raise your vibrations and understand "The Draconic Law" and how it supports or negates the "Law of Attraction". The same applies with the "Universal Law of the Moon" and her passage through the belt of the Zodiac and how you can productively use her whereabouts to "plant the seed" and safely collect the results in time. This book is loaded with examples that will give you the option to understand, recognize, and use the "Universal Code" and its unlimited power. It's all about energy and energy exerts a pull on everything around you and dictates why a magnet will either attract or reject a metallic object because of its polarity. The "Law of Appeal" involves magnetism and a magnet will not attract a piece of wood. If you are single and looking for love, you can wish this law to bring you a beautiful attractive soul and be in denial forever; if you are overweight or if you smoke cigarettes and this person doesn't. Valuable information on how to build magnetism and become irresistible to everyone is offered later in this book.

You must raise your vibration first and gather enough magnetism; then you will become "attractive" or magnetize the opposite sex. The "Law Of Drawing" will never work in your favor if you do not vibrate at the same level as your own expectations. You may also wish for any law to bring you riches, but if you do not educate yourself on the "Universal Code" or educate yourself on the subconscious creative forces (or sleep all day long), your only chance to get wealthy is to win the lottery and the odds are one in a million. A beautiful healthy body will attract another beautiful healthy body and a non-smoker will resent anyone unwilling to kick the bad habit. There is also such a thing as what science calls chemistry, but it's simply the stars in action. Thus someone born with the planet Venus (love) in Pisces (Universal love) won't really care what you look like. These souls are reluctant to use critical judgment and operate with deep guilt feelings. They make you wonder why a very attractive lady loves a homely guy. The stars don't care about what you look or smell like per says, but as humans, we do.

Take for instance, a weak Pisces lady who marries her drug addicted abusive jailhouse lover. The guilt and strong drive to help, care, and love is stronger than the critical mind and is usually produced by an afflicted Pisces Moon (emotions) and Neptune (deception) in the chart. This book will give you the option to learn a multitude of Universal Laws that will undeniably bring miracles into your life and explain what an infantile science could never provide. This is the story of my life and how the Universal Code played a crucial part in molding my destiny. It is because I went through hell many times and came back alive, that I can expose to the best of my ability what took me a lifetime to assimilate. It is because of my critical work that the children of tomorrow will be able to master and make good use of all celestial regulations. The children of the future will be well aware of the "secret" and spiritually equipped to work in harmony with the Universal Code to bring about peace, love, and respect to humankind. This incredible journey from my dramatic childhood in France, to my highest accomplishments in the USA, will take hold of your soul and will make you wonder or even cry, just because it all really happened…

"There are other universes of multiple dimensions unidentified to our earthly senses, but affluent with superior forces. Behind the cosmic curtain God hides all the answers of all pre-existing things."
-- Dr. Turi

Part 1

Early Life

Pont Saint Esprit

I was born during the late hours of a cold winter night in February. I was raised in a small village named Pont Saint Esprit (the Bridge of the Spirit) in Provence, France. Please keep in mind that all of the following experiences are authentic, and some of them are very dramatic and reflect aspects of my own turbulent life. All of those bygone experiences were the indispensable ingredients I needed to recognize my own conviction of the subconscious power we all possess inside. The purpose of this work is to make you aware of your own creative spiritual essence and to allow you to recognize your ability to control the outcome of your personal existence. Blessed with this knowledge, my only aspiration is for you to realize that this book is a training manual dedicated to better your life. "Your future is nothing else than the reincarnation of your own thoughts" -- and with that you can attract and enjoy a rich and fruitful life.

I also realize that the following stories may be hard to believe for many of you - my credibility will be greatly questioned. I am also sure that some readers may also question my sanity. Well rest assured that I have better things to do than to make myself look like a disturbed schizophrenic abducted by aliens! These are my experiences and anyone has the right to remain skeptical, as this phenomenon is so incredible by its very nature. Nevertheless, I decided to come forth with the truth because I am all about the truth. Realize that we can only relate to each other because of our own experiences, education, and **U.C.I**. or "**Unique Celestial Identity**".

Following four incredible UFO experiences, I was lead by extraterrestrials to master the work of Nostradamus, and to unlock the golden keys of our Universe, which answer the fundamental question of what it means to be human. Since the tender age of seven years old, I have been under extraterrestrial authority, and have been directed to master the cosmic clock. The contents of this book will challenge you to acknowledge the incredible and benefit from all my dramatic experiences since my first UFO abduction. This is the story of my life starting with my first UFO contact. Four times I have experienced the incredible with ETs and their crafts and unless you go through those "encounters" yourself, you can never really comprehend the depth of my emotions. Am I a chosen one? Not at all, or if I am, I don't know it yet.

I am not a walk in; I did not see a far away light or what seemed to be a space ship. I dealt with theses extraterrestrials intelligence face to face in 1957 and for many months as I was growing up, then on August 11, 1971, November 11, 1981 and August 11, 1991. And yes, as incredible as it may sound to you, I was standing less than 30 feet under a solid space ship and spent time inside the saucer itself. Each time these remarkable events took place, I was with a family member -- first with my sister, then my older brother Jo, and then with my ex-wife Brigitte. It was synchronized in this manner by the "force", perhaps to keep my own sanity. Yes, I confirm that ET's and UFO are very real and there are many groups with different agendas. The legacy left by those interstellar visitors is inarguable to those close to me and to all of those people who know me well. The downloading of supra-knowledge and cosmic wisdom upon my psyche took place on August 11, 1991 above the city of Los Angeles and it is absolutely real.

The Universe operates on a tight celestial and logical order where chaos is nowhere to be found. It is icy cold, serene, and infinite. This celestial system is deceivingly lifeless to the young soul's eyes (scientists/astronomers). But all of those rocks (stars) and extraterrestrial inhabitants have a very specific agenda imposed by God's will. Like an engine precisely tuned, the universe is running smoothly and perfectly. Like a piano flawlessly and finely tuned by the creator, it produces an eternal celestial music interacting with the human psyche. To rise to a higher cosmic consciousness and perceive the working of the Universal Mind is a serious challenge. The reality is that: 99% of the people on earth were not born with the celestial tools (planets by location and aspects) to decode the universal dialect of the gods, perceive the universal hieroglyphs, realize the divine manifestation upon mankind, or even conceive any extraterrestrial life.

"A human being is part of a whole, called by us the 'Universe', a part limited in time and space. He experiences himself, his thoughts and feelings, as something separated from the rest--a kind of optical delusion of his consciousness."
--Albert Einstein

My First UFO Experience

Since the tender age of seven years old, extraterrestrial intelligences have interacted and programmed me to convey to you an awareness of the dynamics of our universe and its interaction upon mankind's psyche, influencing to our daily worldly affairs. As I've already said, I was born during a very cold winter night in February in the southern part of France in "La Provence." This small locale is called Pont Saint Esprit or translated in English, "The Bridge of the Spirit." This is the same area in Provence where the famous prophet Nostradamus was born and wrote the renowned "Prophecies".

The village of "Vallis Clara" took a big importance in the 13th century with the construction of the bridge, under the Pont Saint Esprit, or "The Bridge Of The Spirit" to which the town owes its current name. The bridge was built from 1265 until 1309 and in a particularly dangerous place, because of the very fast currents of the Rhone. The bridge measures 919 meters long, it was modified several times during the history and now has 25 arcs. Formerly it was closed in its extremities by fortresses and two towers rose in the middle. For the needs of the navigation, two arcs were replaced by an arc in cast iron in 1854, then by a suspension bridge in 1944 and finally, by an arc in concrete more in accordance with the rest of the bridge. In 1860, the bridge was widened. The story goes that a Saint worked on the bridge and was never seen at payday and when forced to get his money, offered it all to the workers who needed more than he did. Some believe it was Christ himself.

Realize that I have nothing to do with the great Seer, Nostradamus, apart from being born under the same local stars and the fact that I spent years rekindling his divine way of interpreting the stars. As far as extraterrestrials beings invading my early life, no tangible answers or explanations were available in 1957 to my family or myself. I simply knew that "little monkeys" regularly came to visit me in the kingdom of the night. Those small creatures had big menacing black eyes, and I learned years later that this group of ETs are now identified as the "grays" or dignified robots that do all the dirty work. During this time in my life, I could only see and accept them as "little monkeys," and were described as such to my wondering mother the morning after. The first few visits were very dramatic for me; I became literally paranoid with fear and could not be left alone in the dark. After so many years, the rest of the family (seven brothers and sisters) can still recall my awful screams in the middle of the night.

Preceding the encounters, my stepfather built the "bedroom" in the attic to separate the growing boys from the girls, but was originally designed to confine and punish me. I inherited a powerful set of stars or U.C.I. (Unique Celestial

Identity) and as a child I was a handful. Call it ADD or ADHD, but luckily for me, Prozac and Ritalin with its deadly side effects did not exist in those days. Regardless of the daily punishments and physical abuse at school, I was so unruly and such a handful that none of my mother's friends or family members, in any circumstance, would or could take care of me. Only the tremendous patience and soft, loving, and comforting words of my mom would do the trick to calm me down.

All of us at the old house

The updated house (1985) The top right window was the attic and my bedroom then.

13 Rue Saint Antoine, the original statue of the Statue of the Saint was stolen and replaced by a picture.

Before my stepfather made the decision to "alienate" me from the rest of the family, we all dog housed together. My grandfather owned the ripened house, and the old structure suffered tremendous damage during WW1 & WW2 with the German bombings. Grandpa's nickname was "Sardines" (he loved fishing.) Sadly for him, while at war, he lost both of his legs on a mine and with his meager war subsidy, he could not afford to repair the impaired old house. Thus, there were no bathrooms, no running water, and no electricity available to our starving family. I used to go around the baker's house and collect rock solid bread from his trash can and burn some newspaper in some remote areas of the village, to soften it and eat it. For years, hard bread and a spoon of cocoa dropped in boiling water was all mother could afford to feed us with then. Salt, milk, meat and sugar were an unaffordable commodity and not available. Clothes were also collected from the trash or given away by considerate neighbors.

During the icy cold winter, my brother Vincent and I had to burn newspapers and boxes to melt down the ice from the street pump to drink if we were thirsty. We had no bathroom, thus my daily job was to empty the pot of bodily fecal rejects and with eight brothers and sisters it did not take too long to fill it up. During the winter rains, the mighty Rhone river waters rose well above his banks. When the water retired, armed with a broomstick and a fork tied at the tip, we caught many fish trapped in the small pools. Many times we were so hungry that we ignited a fire and cooked the fish right there where we stood. We were masters in using our slings, and crows and other birds of prey, as well as drowned rabbits, were part of the menu.

Years later, my stepfather and all the boys worked hard to restore the patriarchal house. Even at a young age I was very aware of its dilapidation, and wondered how "la veille maison" could still stand, and what should be done to alert the family if it was to crash down on us without notice. The old structure had a noisy soul of its own and seemed to breathe, crack, squeeze and whisper during the depth of a windy night.

In the nocturnal hours, silhouettes and phantoms from the dark corners of the attic were coming alive, all because of the dim streetlight filtering through a dirty broken window. Carrying a small candlelight, I could barely find my way up the long steep stairway but saw enough of my environment in the attic to find my way to a small bed and a hard dirty mattress. A thick weathered filthy blanket was my only option to take on the cold cutting winter night. Undressing was out of question and pajamas were simply a luxury we could not afford. It is in this deplorable setting in my early life, that I would encounter these uninvited, and quite terrifying creatures, night after night.

Myriads of cats were living with us and were my only source of heat during many cold winter nights. Our old house was a paradise for lots of pests, especially for spiders, scorpions, cockroaches, fleas, bats, and especially huge rats. The butcher next door did all the animal slaughtering and meat cutting right from his own house adjoining ours. Before reaching the filthy underground sewer system, all the bloody wastes had to sail by our house through a broken concrete pipe. The floating stinking bloody animal guts and rejected body parts found their way naturally down to the underground city sewer system to the mighty Rhone River. Drawn in by the putrefying blood-spattered smell, huge rats made our house their living ground heaven. Most of the vermin's time was spent eating, fighting each other, and mating all year round. Incidentally, it is because of a Papal order during the Dark Ages that the rat population exploded, and combined with a lack of hygiene, the bubonic plague took millions of lives in Europe. The incredible irony is that the ill-advised ruling Pope of those days ordered the slaughtering of cats all over Europe because of their supposed association with the devil.

Starving neighbors' cats also found our old house a paradise for their hunting and feasting delights. This brawling carnival of cats-and-rats concerto took place every night during my afflicted upbringing. In the 50's, our neighbors had no money for food, let alone money for neutering their cats, so the feline offspring's kept growing each year. I recall those long-gone days with anguish -- they were certainly grueling and demanding on all of us. The possibilities of ingesting contaminated food, or being stung or bitten by innumerable dangerous creepy-crawly creatures was very real and statistically probable.

The old unsanitary house could be described as a wild jungle, harvesting a myriad of crawling pestilence. Wild dogs and cats, bats, crows, foxes, birds of pray, even owls were also common because of the food chain diversity.

I recall our close neighbor; the now departed Laura, nearly losing her unguarded toddler to a monster rat's vicious bites. The soiled pest was especially attracted to the sweet smell of milk on the suckling infant's skin and clothing. Luckily for her the screams, of one of her older children saved the nursling. One of my favorite pastimes with my departed young bother Vincent was to kill as many rats as possible with a slingshot before going to bed.

I often spent some time before dark, hunting for cats to share my bed, mostly to keep me warm during the cold and long winter nights. Sometimes my chase was made easier when a fleeing cat would make its way up to the attic bedroom, carrying a bloody prey in its sharp fangs. It was then in those circumstances, in the winter of 1957, that my first UFO encounter took place. Over the years, I was to experience three more of those astonishing encounters. Each one of these occurrences was simply extraordinary in nature.

The Fateful Night

"Time to go to bed." Mom said. "You have five minutes to go upstairs, and then you must blow out the candle. Also be careful not to set the house on fire," she added. "Yes Mom," was my reply. "Have you seen Grisette, Mom?" I asked her. "No, she just had new kittens and you may not see her for a while," she answered. Grisette was a beautiful tabby cat; she resembled a miniature tiger, constantly rubbing her striped coat on everyone's leg. She was by far my favorite feline friend, and she spent most of the bitter wintry nights curled up purring next to me.

Later during the night, I was deep asleep when I woke to something stroking my foot. I immediately thought it was Grisette wanting to join in my bed for some warmth and affection. First I called the animal, as I wanted her to come closer to the top of the bed. The night was chilly and she was welcome to share some of my precious body heat collected under the blanket. She did not move an inch; instead she gave me a stronger signal that she (I thought) was still there. Quite surprised, I realized that she wasn't making her way to the top of the bed as she always did. Thus, half way numbed, I raised myself on the bed and in the semi-darkness reached for her.

As long as I live, I shall never forget that creepy moment frozen in my mind. That unworldly episode would haunt me the rest of my life. Surprised and horrified, I watched four strange creatures; they were about four feet tall and those creepy "visitors" were staring at me from the bottom of my bed.

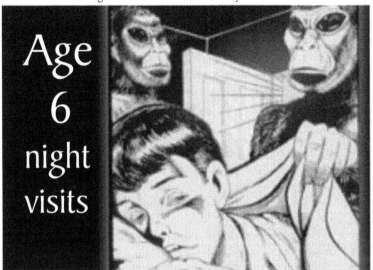

Age
6
night
visits

They were suspiciously looking at me with their large, piercing black eyes, as if they were wondering how to proceed. I was in shock and unable to make a single sound. My throat was tightened in a knot and I felt powerless. I swiftly brought the blanket above my head and hid away under the covers. In spite of the cutting cold, I began perspiring in fear wondering how and why those things were here. I was desperately hoping and waiting for those "visitors" to go away. Finally after what seemed to be an eternity, I slowly pulled the blanket away from my eyes and peeked out into the semi-darkness. To my extreme surprise, one of them seemingly had anticipated my move and stood by the headboard and positioned himself less than an inch from my petrified face. It was too much for me and I simply passed out! The morning after my mom's screams got me out of my "deep sleep".

"Come on Louis get up son, you're going to be late for school!" she yelled from downstairs. In a flash, I painfully recalled the night's awful experience and still panicking, I screamed for rescue. My frightened mother rushed up the stairs and got me out of bed. Crying, trembling, and very upset, through many convulsing thumps, I strafed hard trying to explain to my mother the odd experience I had suffered the night before. "For God sake, what's going on Louis?" she repeatedly said to me. "You had a nightmare? Did something scare you? Tell me, son. Mommy is here now, you're safe." I looked at her for a while, and then asked, "Are they gone?" "Who? What? Let's talk about this downstairs," she said, helping me out of the bed. Still very upset, I described as best as I could the detrimental occurrence, but not surprisingly my mother thought of it as a bad dream. In the following weeks, the situation got worse as the bloodcurdling "visitors" kept coming for me. Nobody could help me understand what was really going on in the attic; I only knew that none of cats, including Grisette, would come upstairs and share the bed with me. The instinctive reluctance of the cats to show up was my only indication to expect another visitation.

Not much information in this little French village in the late 50's was available pertaining to the UFO phenomenon. Especially when the family did not even own a television set or could even afford a cheap radio to expand the limited horizon. The ordeal was an ample part of my upbringing, as the "little monkeys" were looking for or forging a specific curriculum upon my psyche. The nightmarish experiences repeated for months and years to come. My behavior became erratic, my emotions uncontrollable until my recurring screams became too much for the sleeping neighborhood. My mother thought me to be mentally disturbed. On the advice of our local physician, an evaluation on my mental health was planned at the local hospital. My downhearted mother was also informed of the possibility of a nasty side effect involving the still experimental electrical brain shock treatments of those days. She became unsure about the dangerous form of electric therapy and decided to repeal the entire idea and cancelled the meeting. She did not want her son to be an experiment, and in the process my brain never got fried; thus I kept my sanity!

Trying to fix a computer (your brain) with an electrical surcharge of a few thousands volts is the faster way to loose your hard drive (your memory). My mom never graduated from any well-known academic institution, but thank God she was born with lots of common sense and a great intuition to back it all up. She made the vital decision to not let the local doctors experiment on my fragile psyche. I wish all mothers would simply use their intuitional gifts and challenge doctors' prognostics suggesting nefarious drugs prescriptions for their children. Later, following the first initial abductions, I became a little more trustful of the ETs' visitations knowing that I would be perfectly fine the next day. As I grew older, the nightly Alien visitations slowly desisted, but a firm awareness of a close spiritual connection was born. I already knew that I was to meet and deal with them again, somewhere, somehow, sometime.

"Incredible experiences breed incredible people that have incredible things to say"
-- Dr. Turi

Prophetic Dream

I realized that I could make sense not only to my own dreams, but also to many of my friends. Becoming a Clinical Hypnotherapist years later, added more wisdom to my inner spiritual talents. Once, a friend called me wondering about a particular dream and wanting some explanations. In the dream, her boyfriend is talking to her, but his breath is awful, then she walked outside and ran across the street. Her boyfriend is now screaming at her from the porch and she can still smell the hideous odor from her distance. "So what do you think about my dream, Louis?" she asked. "This is a prophetic dream, and tells me that your boyfriend is not exactly building your self-esteem or he's verbally abusive to you," I answered. "Its funny you said that because our relationship is deteriorating real fast, we fight too much" she added. I explained to her that her subconscious was quite clear and to be ready for a new section of her love life. My good actor friend Gary Busey and I are very close and Gary is often on my telephone discussing spiritual matters with me. Once, he asked me to explain a disturbing dream that he had.

"In my dream Louis" He said, "There is a beautiful, very young girl sitting on the grass. I approached her and told her how fine looking she was. I tried to get close to her but she immediately turned vulgar to me and asked me to leave right away." he added. In the dream she told him he was ugly, old, and to leave her alone and Gary was perplexed by her behavior. He continued explaining his dream " I hate you too, and you are ugly too!" he screamed at her. "So what's all this about, Louis?" he asked wondering. I explained to him, that the little innocent girl was a representation of deep need to find true love again and the little girl's response was his fears to never fulfilling it. He was amazed by my findings as usual and thanked me warmly. When you are able to understand the messages from your subconscious, whether it is in your dreams or awakened states, you will greatly benefit from this incredible source of information. Another significant dream took place when I was a child and it declares so much about my involvement with astrology. It was another cold and windy winter night, when I went to bed upstairs in the attic. Grisette my stray cat was already there, she was sitting on the old mattress gazing through the darkness waiting for me.

As always, the wind was making a lingering rumbling sound through the broken window, while the dim streetlight produced a pantomimic shadow movie each night. I was often starving, exhausted, and frozen; my feline friend was a blessing and also a badly needed source of heat. She was a companion and the silent witness to many dramatic nights of dealing with the extraordinary. In the hours of darkness we both swiftly fell into Neptune world of dreams. This was the first prodigious dream I ever had and it was very prophetic in nature. This dream predicated an extraordinary life loaded with astonishing occurrences and gave me a glance of what was to come in the future. I now understand and use omens as I also practice dream interpretations in my Astro-Psychology practice.

First, I saw a mighty Bull dashing towards me head-on with its menacing horns down.

Taurus

I got scared, but the sturdy animal stopped in his tracks and looked at me, straight in the eyes. Dense smoke came out of his large nostrils, and then the magnificent astrological symbol of Taurus (the bull) gave me a reverence by bending on its left knee. His menacing horns did not aim at me but at the ground and after giving me a form of respect, he walked away peacefully.

Then two children came along, a young boy and his sister, they both smiled and waved amicably at me and kept waking following the bull.

Gemini

I just witnessed the symbol of Gemini "the twins" in my dream. Then the "crab" or the sign of Cancer came along walking sideways. No direct message was offered to me by the symbol itself. I looked above in the night sky and saw the most beautiful, clear, cutting Full Moon anyone can ever hope to dream to see. The moon rules the sign of Cancer and depicts emotions and feelings in one's chart.

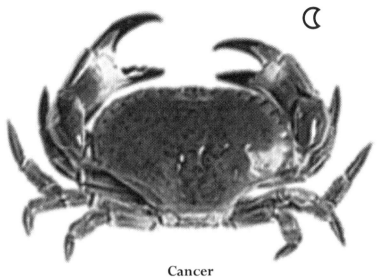

Cancer

Moon

My passion and connection to the Moon is very deep as she rules women in general. I mastered all the secrets of the Moon over the years and her mysterious impact in our lives and to the world at large. My yearly book "Moon Power" is a sure indication of the tremendous and rewarding work that I generate and share with my faithful readers worldwide. Following the sign of Cancer came Leo the lion, enveloped in a majestic golden light.

Leo

In my dream I was afraid, as the Lion looked real with menacing roars, but the powerful king of the beasts turned into my beautiful loving cat "Grisette" for just as he jumped onto me, it turned into Grisette and landed smoothly on my lap. I petted my cat for a while in my dream, then he licked my face and this is when I woke up because of my cat licking my face... In this book "The Rest of the Secret" I simply explain how the subconscious interacts with the Superconscious in time and space and offers you its magical guidance through symbolism, dreams, and omens. This book is a masterpiece of thoughts and dreams transforming into reality. Knowing that the "future is nothing else than the reincarnation of your thoughts" you can only find in your thoughts and your prophetic dreams, your own future's reality. You have been made in the image of God; there is no difference between you and God. If you are aware of it or not, you have inherited the essence of creation itself as you reincarnated on this solid physical world. It all started in the stars, where you came from and as you ascend and raise towards your own godly powers, the ultimate challenge is to realize that as a child of the universe you are a God in training on this world. This work will bring forth your own cosmic consciousness, your own immortality, and your own relationship with the divine.

My Upbringing

Much of my time was spent with my schoolmate Claude. We both were barely 12-years-old. For some unknown reason, and for weeks at a time, we would pretend to speak English. On our way to school and everywhere we happened to be, we were making all sorts of crazy sounds and speaking loud to impress who ever would happen to catch the "English" noise. I am sure many of you pretended to speak a foreign language, but there is no doubt in my mind now that my subconscious knew all about my unusual fate and my unique mission in life. Little did I know that ten years later I would be embarking on the most incredible adventures, first in the UK and then the US, that would change my life forever. Those memories are so old but so fresh at the same time. Why such an impact and such a clarity of reminiscences in this particular time in my childhood? I am not speculating anymore, accepting the incredible chain of events that lead me to where and who I am today. It is obvious the " Law of Attraction" and the subconscious plays a very important part of a child's fate. I strongly recommend you to watch your children at play and catch the hidden message of a unique fate. Incidentally, my friend Claude is still in France, in the same village and never ever thought of changing his uneventful life. There are of course other significant laws that molded my destiny that Claude did not have to deal with. Blame it all on his U.C.I. or (Unique Celestial Identity) for the three years age difference between us changed the stars' pattern and had a lot to do with it.

Life was tough for me then, food was scarce and I had to do anything to survive. I was wild and undisciplined. Finally the school Principal expelled me from the institution at the age of thirteen. It is amazing how uneducated adults and teachers alike are able to negatively carve the delicate psyche of vulnerable children. Born with a tremendous energy (moon in Gemini) my attention span was very limited and my nervous system extremely high. By today's standards, I would be classified as suffering a serious affliction of "Attention Deficit Disorder" or worse ADHD (Attention-Deficit/Hyperactivity Disorder). Luckily for me, the school system in those days did not harbor traditionally educated psychologists prescribing deadly drugs to the children. Thus once again, my psyche was spared and my celestial gifts left undamaged. Contrary to what mundane psychology professes; Astro-Psychology sees these ADD/ ADHD "disorders" more as a potent gift that seems to affect particular souls positively such as Einstein, President Clinton, and myself.

The new medical term ADHD was created by the scientific community and designed to enrich the mighty drug industry. New drugs are constantly being created and following a trained doctor's diagnosis many gifted children are deprived of their natural physical and spiritual "speedy" aptitudes and turned into zombies. In the long run, the drug will negatively affect their natal attitude and life accomplishments. Not only was I born with a nervous Moon in Gemini, but also a powerful Dragon's Head in Aries. The moon denounces my emotional response to life and Gemini is an air sign ruled by Mercury (The Lord of communication). Thus I love (need) to talk and express myself. Thus as imposed by my U.C.I. (Unique Celestial Identity), I had to talk at all the time. Combined with my fiery natal Dragon's Head in Aries (ruled by Mars The Lord of War) and the air element of Gemini, which fueled the fire of Mars, I was simply incapable of controlling my overflowing nervous physical and spiritual energy. Cosmic consciousness is a must for any teacher to really relate to a child's spiritual conception. I had to find any possible way to vent out the intense energy out of my mind and my body. Doing so, I was disturbing the class at all time. Trying to control my hyper active nature, my ignorant teacher relocated me as far as possible from him, right up against the wall. Suffering a serious ear infection (otitis) I could not hear a thing of what he was teaching. He could never understand my bursts of energy and to punish me; he violently smacked my face numerous times, busting my nose, and also made me kneel on a steel ruler for long periods of time.

I really think this bastard was sadistically enjoying inflicting pain to children and he tried very hard to break my young spirit into submission. Nothing he did to control me worked as planned as I still had to get rid of my turbocharged nervous energy. He also tried to confine me under his desk and sat there with his bony knees right in front my bloody nose for hours. That was terrible because after a while in this uncomfortable position, I had to move to let the blood circulate through my painful kneecaps and tortured back and legs. Many times, this vicious teacher would violently and suddenly kick me back to stillness. This may sound unbelievable by today's standards, but this is how things were in the 1960's in French schools. This was probably his own effective deplorable method to get rid of some of the frustration he was probably suffering at home and in his dull life. This is the way things were during those days and I became numb to this daily dose of pain and never complained to my parents or siblings. When the level of Mercurial energy reached the roof, usually during a Full Moon period, my entire nervous system was going literally out of control and I felt like I was about to explode inside. No matter how, I had to find a way expel of some of this boiling steam. I wish my teachers knew more about my U.C.I. and Astro-Psychology methodology, as he could have simply helped me to release some of it by making me running around the school a couple of times. Armed with true knowledge, they certainly could have adopted a less deplorable attitude towards me and other kids.

Instead, this ignorant teacher ordered me to go outside of the warm class and to stand motionless between two huge trees in the playground. There, in the middle of the snow with no jacket against the piercing cold "mistral" wind, I had to withstand arctic temperatures, motionless for hours. This rough treatment did not help me much to fight the poring infectious organism tormenting my contaminated ears; especially when most of the time I was left outside freezing to death with an empty stomach. The pain I experienced from my otitis (in both my ears) was intolerable and Q-tips were not available then. I could only use toilet paper collected from the school bathroom and half burnt dirty matches found in the street. I used these "tools" to dry up the constant flow of infectious discharge, hoping to be able to hear the teacher calling me back to the warm classroom. Then, to make things worse, the abusive School Master saw me standing there and used a truly devastating method of punishment against me. In the privacy of his office with all windows and thick brown curtains tightly closed, he struck me on the face over and over again until I simply passed out. To me it was more relief than pain, because finally I was left senseless to all the mental and physical abuse. I used to wake up wondering where I was and why I was there.

I am still resentful for such a treatment of many children in the 60's; I was far from being alone. Every one of those cowards enjoyed inflicting pain to many kids. Another teacher's favorite abuse was to lift a child from the ground by his own cheeks. Once I saw him treating my now departed younger brother Vincent this way, and the depth of the anger I experienced was just incredible. Like a vicious predator he took such a pleasure inflicting pain to a defenseless 11 year-old child. I promised myself to make him pay for this awful act by taking my revenge on his car. I used a huge nail to mess up the paint and none of his tires were left intact. When my teacher had enough of me, he sent me to another brutal beast teaching the class next-door. This individual took inhumane pleasure in hitting me on the top of my head with his five feet long thick wooden ruler. I saw many stars well before I could learn anything about them! This evil person also enjoyed smashing the tips of my fingers with a steel ruler until the blood gashed out of my nails. Those two fiends joyfully exchanged their methods of punishments to one another. As always I never complained, as pain, suffering, and hardship was a normal part of my juvenile life.

Sadly enough for many other young victims and myself; no one really knew our rights or what was going on inside the private walls of the school, or could even afford an illicit legal investigation. Thus nobody could help me to press charges against these appalling perpetrators. Over the years, I sadly learned that most of these disgraceful treatments got even worse, with many raped orphans stuck in various "helpful and dedicated" French educational religious institutions. It all came to light when my wondering stepfather saw my hands and asked me about my bleeding fingers. He was furious and drove me to the teacher's home to confront him. As expected with any abusers, the coward hid away to avoid a nasty altercation with my big and angry stepfather. Nowadays such a treatment is totally inconceivable but it all happened as such. More dramatic disgusting experiences took place but cannot be divulged in this book. These facts would make you ill and I'd rather fade away and pretend it never happened to me. Sometimes I wonder if today legally protected U.S. children could remotely conceive the pain and suffering I endured as a child in an institution designed to teach love, guidance, and respect to the children.

Finally I exhausted the will and patience of my abusive teacher and fed up with my uncontrollable nervous energy (Moon in Gemini/Dragon in Aries); he fired

27

me indefinitely and sent me to the only English teacher in the small school. I was ordered to copy the entire French dictionary and strongly advised to keep quiet or suffer the consequences. I will never forget when I first entered his grouping, he asked me to stand in front of the class. Facing all the kids. He said, "You see class, Louis is a good example of someone who will never speak English or land a good career in life. He was born to lose and will be a total waste to society." He viciously degraded me in front of all the teens. Luckily for me, even at this tender age my self-esteem was always high and will always remain unquestionable. Fearless of the consequences, I was already making unwise gestures behind his head and the stupefied class couldn't do anything else other than to laugh. Luckily for me the teacher did not see anything and my audacity paid off. I was quite lucky to get away with it, considering the penalties. Unlike physical abuse, words for me are easier to deal with -- thus there were no lasting negative legacy left on my young psyche. Incidentally, nearly thirty years later in one of my trips back home to France from the United States; I was doing some shopping with my mother. I instantly recognized the old English teacher; he was walking around looking for some produce. I could not help myself and approached him and began a conversation. I spoke to him in fluent English.

"Hi Mr. Clap how are you doing? Long time no see. Do you remember me? I am Louis, the kid that would never speak English, that's what you said, remember?" He was perplexed and surprised. To my amazement he never understood a single word that I said. Then amazed, he asked in my native French tongue. "I'm sorry young man, but I don't know you, who are you?" "Don't worry Mr. Clap, it's a long story." I said. The years carved deep lines on his face and I realized how impossible it would be for the old man to recall such a long gone period. As a child I promised myself to punish those teachers and beat them up when I grew up. The revenge and resentment I carried with me for so long dissipated almost immediately while looking at the old man's face. I asked him to wait for me. My mom, who knew the old teacher well, kept taking to him. I went right back to the store and offered him a copy of my yearly Moon Power book and said, "Here, Mr. Clap, this might refresh your memory, and it will help you to not forget your English." I added sarcastically. He looked at me wondering and politely said to me.

"Young man, I do not know who you are, but I hope my memory will come back when I read your book. Good evening Madame Turi and thank you for the book." he added. Like a bad dream in one of the many dramatic chapters of my life, the old man slowly walked away and disappeared into the mist of my peculiar life. Walking back to the car, my curious mother asked "What was all this about Louis?" "Nothing Mom, I just met one of my old teachers and he just brought back sad memories." I said. She felt the depth of my feelings and said with her usual high spirit "I know you went through a lot Louis, perhaps growing up this way has prepared you for special work you are doing in America, son. Don't you worry my boy, that's all in your past now, life must go on!" She gave me a hug and we drove back to the warmth of the house to enjoy her great cooking.

Naughty but Cute

My sister Noelle and I, age 3 and 4

As children, my sister Noelle and I spent days at the pre-school playing all day long, while mother was really busy keeping her seven children clean and healthy. During those days, washing machines of course did not exist and the village's housewives met regularly at the "lavoir".

My now 80 year-old mother

Outside View of "The Lavoir"

This very old structure was built a century ago for the purpose of washing clothes. It was pretty much the equivalent of modern laundry, but without hot water. The cold water is coming from a spring and collected in two small pools. One was used to soap and beat the clothes with a huge wood hammer like tool, and the other to rinse the soap and bleach away. I recall my mother pushing a wheelbarrow on the pebbly pavement, trying hard not to tip off the huge bucket loaded with a mixture of clothing, hot water, soap and bleach. The hard-working ladies struggled to raise large families of seven to fifteen children, as birth control methods were not an option in those days. Most of the time their husbands were busy self-destructing, drinking and smoking in excess, trying hard to erase awful and dramatic WW2 memories. Newspapers and radios were very rare, and washing at the lavoir was their own way to pass on the news and gossip.

Inside View of "The Lavoir"

By looking at the architecture and Mythology the ancients builders must have known about Astrology by representing the face of Neptune and its zodiacal sign Pisces (the two fish).

The Sign of Pisces (the fish)

Neptune (Lord of the Seas)

Old "13th Century "Chapel De L'hospital" facing the "Lavoir"

Once I was on the playground and I saw my mother going past to the "lavoir", so I asked my friend Claude to lift me up the six-foot tall fence. I landed on my butt and ran as fast as I could to join my mother. Something I did so many times before, and both Mom and my teacher knew I was safe and laughed at my crazy actions. A few years later on my way back home from school I heard commotions and screams coming from the old building. To my surprise my younger brother Yves was fighting two other kids who had cornered him there.

As soon as he saw me, an upsurge of power came to him, as the protective big brother had now entered the scene. Unlike Vincent and me, Yves was a bit shy and became the victim of these two particular bullies. The two kids became petrified when they gazed upon me, as my reputation preceded me all over school. I told my brother "OK Yves, give your best shot and show them that you are not scared of them!" I wanted my younger brother to take care of himself, build more faith and self-worth, and fight against his tormenters by himself. He did so brilliantly that day, and earned the respect he deserved by all the other kids in his class. I congratulated him for his courage and was very proud of my little brother for defending himself against two bigger guys.

Myself and my brothers Yves And Daniel

As a kid, I was a huge handful and always at the wrong place, doing the wrong thing. Many times I found myself swimming, climbing, and falling in one of the two old public fountains. This fountain was the *"Rendez Vous"* and the usual meeting place for all the adolescent kids of my generation. A few times "Les Gendarmes", or the police, stopped fights between the village's "bad boys." Later on in my life, I have found myself astral projecting in my dreams and met with my siblings and many of my departed good friends at this fountain.

Don't ask me how I got there

Skinny little devil Louis

Looking like an angel

The Goddess of Navigation
Diane Alias Artemis Sister of Apollo

Losing Dad

I only saw my father for about thirty seconds, in my entire life. I only knew he was very sick and could not visit us. I will always remember this dramatic phase in my life; I was barely eleven-years old, when the schoolmaster entered the class and whispered a few words to my teacher; he then asked me to go outside and meet with the rest of my family. Grandma and mother were waiting for us in a black taxi, trying hard to conceal the tears running down their cheeks. I knew my father was very sick and I saw him for the first time, just a few days earlier.

He spent many years in the hospital trying to recover from tuberculosis. He was very weak and very skinny and could barely breathe. He also found out that Mom had a lover and he was devastated. With eight kids to feed and no money or love, Mother was very vulnerable and she desperately needed help. For years she waited for my dad to get better, but he never did and she knew he would never be the same man again.

My stepfather was a young man and a very hard worker and his assistance was a blessing to my destitute mother. My mother could not afford anything for herself and spent all her time working for her children. She met Daniel by "accident" when my aunt's boyfriend Paul begged her to join them to the only movie theater in the village; she accepted and met with Paul's best friend Daniel and he became my stepfather.

My Father's illness made it impossible for him to be with us or support us and Mother had to endure hell, in so many ways, to raise her large family by herself during and after the war. She was still a fine and beautiful Scorpio magnetic young woman, in need of attention in 1956 when she met Daniel. To this day my mother is still with my step dad after nearly 45 years of marriage. I heard that dad was home and something terrible took place, but because we were so young, no one told us anything else. Years later I found out that my very weak but jealous father escaped the hospital and tried to kill my Mother.

I was innocent and eager to see my father and often asked why he could not be with us. Mom was always saying dad was in the hospital and too sick to join us. I asked her to take me to him, but seeing him in the hospital was impossible because the pulmonary disease he suffered (tuberculosis) was very infectious and he was in quarantine. Rapidly approaching death, he wanted to see his kids and wife for the last time. Under the influence of so much medication, most of his common sense was gone - it took him hours to walk the short distance from the village hospital to the old house, stopping every two or three steps to catch his failing breath. He finally made it to the house and after a terrible struggle; he made it all the way up the long sharp stairway to the first floor where we resided. Grandpa lost both of his legs on a German mine and lived on the ground floor, and on that dramatic day, he was absent.

Imagine my mom's surprise seeing my dad's agonizing face and falling on his knees on the kitchen floor. At first she was in shock, looking at her dying husband, wondering how or why he was there. Then she realized how serious the situation really was because his contagious disease and ran past him to the back of the house where we were playing. She ordered us to come with her immediately -- I never saw my mother's face so scared in my life since that day and I was very young. She tried really hard to contain herself and told us to hold hands and to follow her down the stairs in the street immediately. She knew my Dad could not walk anymore and she felt safe to take us away from him as soon as she could and avoid the contagious killer disease.

I was the last kid on the row and as I passed by the kitchen door I saw Dad sitting on a chair. He was holding his head between his hands trying very hard to keep his balance. I was ecstatic and I screamed, "Daddy, daddy, you finally came back home!" I launched towards him, kicked the door wide open, and jumped on his knees. Mom screamed as loud as she could "Louis come back here right now!" and placed herself between the door and my siblings so no one else would see or run to him. I did not understand why Mom was so petrified and why she would scream so loud for me to come back to her. I was so happy to see my dad and nothing and no one would stop me now. I had no idea of the gravity of the situation and I could care less about his deadly extremely contagious illness.

I only saw him for a few seconds but I will never forget his face. He was so weak trying so hard to breath and did not spoke a single word to me; instead he took my young innocent face in his big hands and cried so many tears. "Why are you crying, Daddy?" I said, "I am so happy to see you Dad, I missed you so much!" He never answered me, maybe to avoid contaminating me with his tuberculosis and more heavy tears were running down his face. Even as a child, I can still see the depth of his gaze and the amount of pain and suffering he was going through. He knew well that was his last time to see his son and he could not even tell me that he loved me.

Then I felt like lifted in the air by a tornado, Mom made sure all my brothers and sisters were safe in the street and rushed up the stairs to the kitchen to take me away. I was crying and kicking, wanting my dad, not realizing the gravity of the situation, then a few minutes later; Grandma arrived and took all of us to her house. Later I heard that Dad tried to kill Mom and that was it. I was wondering why Dad would do such a thing but as a child I had only love to offer to all the people around me. Dad was extremely weak, thus Mother was able to fight him back and her screams alerted the neighbors and one of them ran to the police. The law enforcement arrived with two nurses and took him back to the hospital, where Dad expired only a few days later. The tuberculosis was very advanced and was the result of the war, extreme hardship, and malnutrition which all took their toll on his health. Life in captivity was so severe and many POW liberations came much too late in 1945 from the German concentration camps.

Being so close to my Dad brought some concern to Mom and Grandma. The next day, they took us all to the hospital for a preventive inoculation (BCG) against the serious pulmonary disease highly infectious nature. Even in sickness, my father would never ever put anyone of us at risk. He was driven by despair and the large amount of drugs he ingested for months at the hospital did not help at all. Luckily for us, no one in the family developed the deadly sickness. I can say I am the last one to see my father alive and I wish it had been under better circumstances, but that is just the way it was, dramatic and very painful.

My First Job

The loss of my father marked me terribly and my life did not get better for many years to come. I was busy trying to survive and one of my favorite endeavors was to knock the door of the local bakery, asking for bread or old croissants for grandma's goats and chickens. The baker knew the throw-outs were not for the birds or animals, but for us. The collected bread was has hard as a rock and impossible to chew. I used to lead my siblings to a remote street, sit in circle, and pore a bit of water on the bread and soften it by burning newspapers. We were always starving and collecting and ingesting the throw-outs was very much anticipated.

The bakery owner was a good man and one day by "accident" he saw the fire in the middle of the small street. I realize now, why the next day he asked me if I wanted to help him. He said that I could learn the trade and become a good bread baker. I was delighted, mostly because I would have access to food everyday and gladly accepted the offer. I went home and told Mom about the fantastic deal and she was very proud and happy for me. I had to wake up at 4:00 am everyday and then walk to the bakery in the middle of the cold and dark winter mornings. It felt so good to enter the warm bakery, the smell of freshly baked bread and croissants felt like pure paradise to me. I was finally able to eat as much as I wanted and most of all, bring two loafs of bread home everyday to my family.

My job consisted in keeping the place sanitary, cleaning up the utensils, as well as bringing wet canvasses on top of the oven to dry. Many times I simply passed out and slept for hours in this warm paradise. The owner was a kind, sensitive man and never woke me up. He wanted to bring some relief in my life and those of my siblings. He became the father I never had and on our day off, he used to take me fishing on the bank of the Rhone River. Sadly, he also suffered a terminal disease and he never told me anything and he suddenly passed away. His loving wife felt the tremendous pain I was going through and many times we comforted each other's crying. I was devastated to lose another father and only a few weeks later his widow sold the bakery and moved back to the comfort of her family in another town. The old man was like the father I never had and brought great relief from suffering and privations. May God bless his soul!

Both my biological and surrogate fathers were dead and I missed them very much. I found comfort in the old baker's heart and losing him felt like losing my dad again. I experienced serious depressions for months to come and many times I came back to the long stairs leading to the fishing area where we spent so many happy hours together. I was crying, desperately longing for his love and protection. Each step down to the river brought sad memories and I thought it would be a good place for me to die.

The Stairs of La Place Saint Pierre

I nurtured a subconscious "death wish" for a while and I was determined to impress all my friends by running on the high wall of "Saint Pierre" stairs from one end to the other. The edge is barely a foot wide and in some days impossible to stand against the "Mistral" fierce wind. Luckily for me, my natal Dragon's Head in Aries protected me against violent death.

Close Call

To cope with the loss of our father, the Social Services suggested to my Mother to send us all to a government children's camp vacation for a month, located in the city of Sete in the French Riviera. We rode in a car for the first time on the way to the hospital weeks before to get vaccinated and the idea to ride a bus loaded with kids was exhilarating to all of us. The dedicated social worker brought two boxes of second hand clothes and some shoes and we really enjoyed this special treat. Underwear and socks were a luxury and it felt like receiving Christmas presents.

The "million dollar" picture with our new clothing. I am holding a plastic gun next to my brother Vincent. My "new" shoes came without shoelaces.

I was so excited to get away from home, especially since I had never seen the sea. I also knew that food would be on the table everyday and I did not have to look in the neighborhood trashcans to survive-- at least for a while. All was set for us to go on our first vacation ever, within the next few days. Finally the greatly anticipated day arrived. An old noisy, smoky bus arrived, loaded with many screaming kids. My siblings were scared and shy, but not me. I grabbed my little bag and lead them inside the aged school bus. Mom screamed from the outside, "Louis be nice to everyone and be careful, listen to your 'monitors' and don't fight with anyone." "No, I won't Mom, I promise you, and I'll be good." I answered. She knew me well, especially of my turbo charged "stars" and anticipated trouble for me and surely enough, she was right.

She blew me a kiss through the window and the rasping bus slowly began its two hundreds miles journey down to the Mediterranean coastline. I was all over the place, jumping on the seats and incapable of being still more than a few seconds and soon got myself in trouble with other unruly youngsters. The guardians were teenagers, trying hard to control a bunch of exuberant kids. They caught me a couple of times disturbing the driver and brought me back to my seat but not without some kicking and screaming. Finally the old bus made it to the beautiful French coastline and for the first time in my life, I saw the sea. I was totally mesmerized by the immensity of the Mediterranean Sea. I felt the rejuvenating marine ozone air engulfing my lungs and I sat still for the longest time ever in my twelve young years enjoying this natural show. The weather was just perfect and warm as we arrived at the *"colonie de vacance"*.

We were guided around the facility to what I would now classify as old "barracks". It was paradise to me, because I was told to use the rest rooms anytime and to shower twice a day, a "luxury" we never had at home. I was guided to my bed and told to place all my belongings in the sideboard. I was also told to hurry for my first meal at the refectory. Even though the poorly equipped facility looks more like a communal jail than a resort to nowadays standards, I was in total heaven, just because I also had my own real framed bed and real sheets to sleep in. The first three weeks vacation went by quickly and we all enjoyed walking the one-mile distance to the sea everyday. To me eating and swimming was the best part of the day. We also had snacks at four o' clock each afternoon on the sandy beach, and there was enough food to satisfy my constant hunger. Then two days before the end of my vacation, disaster struck. I was having a great time with some friends playing soccer when one of the bigger boys purposely kicked one of my teammates. The kid fell on the sand, crying in pain I was incensed by this deliberate attack, and simply kicked him back as hard as I could. We started to fight but two of his friends joined him and beat me hard until a supervisor came along and separated us. I managed to defend myself while pinned down on the sand but I received a bad kick on the face, which broke my nose.

My nose was bleeding profusely but I was used to pain, so I simply went to the sea and cleaned my nose with the salty Mediterranean water, something that I should never have done. On the way back the same bullies attacked me again, but I inflicted serious damage to the head of the one that kicked me in the face, with a stone I had picked up on the trail. I knocked him out cold and an ambulance was called to take him to the emergency room. Those days were rough and many of those kids, like me, were also from dysfunctional families and were as wild as me. I was taken to the infirmary, cleaned up, and sent to confinement, away from all the other kids as punishment for fighting.

I knew the end of the "holidays" was close and I was not upset at all to be left alone. The only problem is that I had a broken nose and the untrained infirmary staff never noticed it. The very next day my face was distorted, my eyes were halfway shut, and I suffered a terrible migraine. I could feel the pulse of my heart in my nose and with each beat, accompanied a crucifying pain. I was somewhat accustomed to pain; I fell asleep hoping to feel better the next day. However, I never woke up and ended up in a coma. I woke up in the infirmary two days later and a local doctor was called in. His diagnosis was that I had a broken nose that caused a serious brain infection, which made me comatose. He was chastising the nurses for confining me without proper medical attention. He immediately called for an ambulance to take me sixty miles away to the French Navy base of Toulon, where I was to receive emergency treatment or possibly die within the next few days.

I could not see anything around me but shadows and my head felt like a balloon about to explode. I was screaming in pain and asking for my Mother and the troubled emergency staff reassured me that I would see her soon. I heard lots of commotion around me, as I was rushed to the emergency room. The surgeon loudly declared that he would not operate on me until the infection would be contained. Soon after, I felt like dozens of hands were grabbing and holding me down. I felt the intense pain from a long fat syringe going through my left nostril all the way up to the center of my eyes discharging a large amount of penicillin. I could hear the tissues splitting, as another loaded needle penetrated my other nostril, by the doctor repeating the procedure. I was in agony and really found out what true pain was all about.

The doctor then stuffed both of my nostrils with long white gauze to absorb the infectious discharge. I was put to bed and I was left there, screaming in pain for hours. Intravenous or oral painkillers could not be used at this time for fear of interference with the heavy doses of penicillin. Not knowing if I had allergy to the medication, there is not much the doctors could do to spare me the torture, but just to wait and see. I was in agony, in total darkness and very scared. The pain was so acute, that I could not sleep or eat and to make things worse, I could barely breath. So in the middle of the night, I decided to remove the gauze from my nostrils with my dirty fingers and re-infected my nasal orifices.

The horrified doctors reprimanded me and after reinserting the gazes in my nostrils, they placed me in a room between two young recovering soldiers. My earsplitting screams at night kept the entire hospital awake and forced them to give me some painkiller and sleeping pills. After a few days the infection was finally contained and the surgeon removed the shattered cartilage from my nose. The surgery was quite dangerous and involved some delicate procedure very close to my brain. Finally, after a few weeks I was allowed to go back home and live a normal life. A few years later, my mother told me that the Doctor's prognostic was dreadful. If the infection could not be contained within twenty-four hours, I would have died of brain infection within a week. Incidentally, to this day some people think that I have a boxer's nose.

Turning Really Wild

Losing Dad was terrible for all of us and brought more anger in my life. I was upset at God and wondered why he would take away the people I loved most. I did not like my stepfather either, especially his tough disciplinary actions towards me. I was wild, unruly and my adventurous spirits lead me to other precarious situations, where I could have easily lost my life again and again. My mother has always been religious and many times told me "I found my god and you will find yours". She never imposed her Christian religious views on any of us and instinctively knew not to poison our vulnerable mind with hell or "end of the world" dogmatic biblical folklore. However, in France like the USA the national school system is set to lure all the children to the Christian church and its holy teachings. I was in a spiritual quest and I decided to join the religious "club" and for the first time visited one of the very old church in our small village.

Various Old Churches in The Old City

After school the pious group of children followed the priest to the church next door. I felt like an ant in front of a mountain and I was really impressed by the old imposing structure. However, a very different feeling penetrated me as I walked past the heavy wooden doors. All the religious painting and statues inside had a depressing impact on me. Unlike the warm sunny outside, it smelled bad, felt wet, cold and uninviting inside. I could feel countless years of prayers built by the collective thoughts of innumerable amount of people's pains, drama and sorrow, impregnating the ancient walls.

The smell of incense, the darkness and the huge wooden crucifix, made an ever-lasting negative impact on me. Jesus impelled on a cross and the bloody wounds on his chest would frighten any child - and considering what I had already gone through in my life, it is quite a statement. What a strange disgusting place, I thought. I was expecting angels, love light and a more positive "home" for God. Not a bunch of burial chambers, dark scary tombs, vaults and a burial place for the many religious cadavers collected over the centuries. But what struck me the most, was the dead man on a cross facing me.

Realize, that I was never taught about Jesus or Christianity before then and simply reacted as a pure and innocent child to this frightening environment. This is where the caption, "Because of the explicit pictures, caution is strongly advised for under age children" should apply.

Church Saint Saturnin 15th Century

The old French priest tried really hard to convert me into a nice, loving respectful Christian. He was regularly teaching us prayers and the Rosary, but his stomach-churning breath repelled me. I know it is quite a loathsome thing to denigrate a man of the cloth, but the mixture of red wine, cigarette smoking and bad teeth was simply intolerable and I could not understand the paradox of how such a revolting person could teach me any form of light or purity.

I was much more interested in the old organ which penetrated its sweet symphony deep in my soul. And I especially adored the church bell - It meant school is over, time to go home. I always wanted to climb all the way up to the top of the church's tower and bang that huge bell with a hammer. This old bell was weather broken and did not resonate for many years. With passing time termites consumed much of the wooden stairways to the top of the church and no one would dare going up there to change the ropes and fix the mechanism. Large sections of the staircase were missing and badly consumed by termites. My urge to go up there consumed me but only bats, pigeons and owls could do so.

I made a plan to try the devil and thought that in the house of God nothing bad could happen to me. During a moonless night, I "removed" a few yards of rope and hooks used to haul cement and material from a construction site. I announced the project to a few friends and against all odds made it to the top of the church. I took the heavy hammer from my belt and bang as hard as I could and made the old bell sing after centuries of silence. I was elated and fulfilled; it was a serious challenge and I had to succeed, especially when all the boys a few hundreds feet down, waited to hear the bell. Then I challenged my own self to something I always wanted to do and walked all around the top thin edge. The wind was blowing very hard up there and I could have plummeted to my death, anytime. But, once more I escaped with my precious life, knowing that many angels were right there with me, protecting me in the span of their white wings.

Church Saint Saturnin's Tower

Death Trap

During those days the Rhone River always rushed his tumultuous water. Many years later the French Government built a nuclear facility diverting the mighty River course, seriously reducing the water flow. From my vantage point, on top of the church, I noticed a long man-made tunnel crossing the river starting right from the bottom of the church. My curious mind and adventurous spirit made me wonder where and what could be found in this passageway. I was on again for another interesting adventure.

Fantastic Views of Pont Saint Esprit Bridge (1265/1309)

I enjoyed the full view of the River, the imposing old bridge built by the Romans, the old Citadel and after a couple of hours hanging in ropes, I made my way back safely down to the church floor.

I told my amazed friends about my discovery and I immediately set a plan to uncover the secret corridor. I knew a door leading to the tunnel had to be located somewhere in the church and after many days of searching, we found the door but could not open it -- breaking it was out of question. The pastor would most certainly find out and would murder me in the presence of Jesus, before my time. I deduced that the city underground sewage may lead us to that passage and I was right. I ordered the guys to get flashlights, ropes, tools, our pellets guns and slings in case we encounter bats or rats or whatever imaginary demons could be waiting for us down there. I lead the group of boys deep inside the city underground sewer complex carefully marking the many splitting tunnels with white chalk.

I followed the running putrefied water for a while to a deep drop. Soon we were in pitch the dark. We could hear the rushing sound of the mighty river above. Bats and rats were everywhere and disturbed howls flew above our heads. We walked slowly and carefully stumbling on fallen rocks and rusted ammunitions, open boxes of gas mask, sharp bayonets and skeletons of the French resistance; courageous fighters using the secret passage for clandestine missions against the Germans. We proceeded cautiously deeper inside the damp and warm bowel until we came across a solid rusted steel door.

I wisely asked the guys to walk about fifty feet back and to be ready to run towards the entrance of the tunnel, if needed. I used my heavy hammer, pounding on the old gate's latches, hoping for the mechanism to release its rusted grip. The mighty Rhone River was unusually loud by the door where I was, but I kept pounding on the oxidized gateway. Then to my horror, water started to flush out from the top of the gate. I immediately realized that the tunnel roof had given way behind the door and that we were going to drown like rats if we did not get out of there immediately. The German Air force aimed for the old bridge to cover their retreat, but hit the tunnel and the metal door was the only rusted thing between sure death and us.

I screamed, "Damn, drop all right here! Come on guys, let's get the hell out of here, now, run, run!" We all sprinted back towards the entrance and I knew that the door could not take the river pressure for long and could give way anytime. We had only a few moments to get out of this terrible situation. I never felt death so close in my life, but I was more concerned with Patrick. He was the smallest kid in the pack and he could not run as fast as the rest of us. Soon, I caught up with him, screaming my head off for him to run faster. But he stepped on wet rocks and fell cutting his knees badly but the adrenalin kicked in and bounced back running even faster. Regardless of the eminent danger, I would rather die with him then to leave him behind. I simply could not live with yet another tragedy in my life.

We were nearly two hundred feet if not more, inside the tunnel and still no daylight, just unadulterated darkness. We were all out of breath scared and extremely tired but I kept screaming, "run guys, come on run for your life guys, that door is about to give up don't stop now". The damped stuffed tunnel did not get any ventilation and running was nearly impossible and we were slowing suffocating due to the lack of oxygen. Then my worst fear materialized when I heard a big bang, I knew the door had finally broken and I could hear the tons of water rushing towards us. I could feel the draft pulling us inside the bowel as we approached the last few feet of the tunnel entrance. I knew the higher we would go the more chances we would have to survive the upcoming wave. The awesome power of water could never be so real. My parents always warned me about the dangers of fire, and now I was learning first hand how dangerous water could be.

Then the wall of water hit us in the back and literally spit us outside the tunnel. The boys were lying down wet and exhausted trying hard to catch their breath. I had to keep my leader face intact, so I played it cool, but I was as scared as all the rest of the boys. Patrick broke down in tears, happy and relieved to escape the adventure with his life. I did not need more trouble with my stepfather, so I made the gang to swear silence but a few days later the priest found out about this escapade and while pointing his finger down, he told me "Louis, if you keep this up you will end up in hell and it's very hot down there, and you'll die" he added. Then wondering I innocently asked the priest, "Isn't hell above?"

He responded surprised "why would you say that?" "Well the Sun is very hot, so hell is above not under in the ground - it's quire obvious." I added laughing uncontrollably. He became very upset with me and ordered me not to challenge the bible's teachings ever again. I agreed but asked another question. "What will happen to me when I die?" I asked. He replied "you will become an immortal spirit like the angels, and if you are good on earth, you will go to paradise, and if you are bad you will go to hell and burn forever". I was petrified of his answer, and then I thought it over for a while and asked him another question. "What is the difference between a spirit and an angel?" "None," he said, and I felt better and thanked him. He was perplexed and could not understand why I thanked him and went on teaching more about the gospel. Then I interrupted him again, something I should never have done but I was early in learning the protocols of the Christian church.

He said with a rude tone of voice. "What is it now Louis?" I asked him "Can I burn the wings of an angel with a candle?" He responded really annoyed this time "In the Lords' name why would you ask me such a question? Of course NOT! "Then I hit him with a good dose of rationale by saying. "Well if angels and spirits are the same thing and when I die I become a spirit, then like them I can't burn then?" His face turned red and he screamed, "I told you not to challenge the Bible, you are going straight to hell" and threw the Old Testament in my direction, barely missing my head and then ran after me in the church. I knew I was never going to be a good Christian. I was forever banned from the church and ended up on my little butt outside the old church' steps. I guess my only good experience with Christianity and the church is when I made an old broken bell sing after many years of silence. That old bell has not been heard by anyone since then in my village.

Deep Scars

My early years were very tough, I was destitute but very rich with freedom and I enjoyed the songs of wild birds and the uncontaminated fresh air. Being so close to nature is something I miss everyday, living in a large American city where noise and car pollution is a part of modern life. During those trying days, money was scarce and my stepfather Daniel, my brother Vincent and I were spending much time maintaining our garden on the other side of the Rhone River's rich muddy banks. Growing potatoes, tomatoes, salad and fruits was a cheaper way to survive and the only way to feed a large family. Walking through the thick woods, picking wild berries, nuts, wild asparagus and mushrooms was a daily chore for my brother and I.

The only way to get to the garden was by foot and it took us about three long hours just to get there. Regardless of the weather, we had to cross a mile long old bridge and each arch of the overpass was fitted with a very long steel ladder. Using them to save time was totally against the rules established by our unbending disciplinary stepfather. We still used them and in the process risked our lives each time, as many of the bars were either missing or rusted by the elements and ready to give away under our weight. A couple of times, while using the ladders to save time a couple of bars gave away under me. So I was always first going down, so my younger brother Vincent would be safe following me.

Then one day I convinced my younger brother to save more time and take on the dangerous river's tumultuous currents and swim across it. The picture shown above was taken after the building of a nuclear site in the city of Mondragon just a few miles upstream and the water level of the mighty Rhone is now very low indeed. During those days the river was really large and often overflowed into the low part of the old city. Using the ladders was totally forbidden by my step dad and luckily for us he never found out for if he did, his large hands would have certainly left red imprints in our unruly bottoms. We were both great swimmers, and in the hot summer, the river's cool water felt good, especially when returning home after sweating for many hours working the dirt.

The Old Bridge

The Rhone River

Then one day I convinced my younger brother to save more time and take on the dangerous river's tumultuous currents and swim across it. The picture shown above was taken after the building of a nuclear site in the city of Mondragon just a few miles upstream and the water level of the mighty Rhone is now very low indeed. During those days the river was really large and often overflowed into the low part of the old city. Using the ladders was totally forbidden by my step dad and luckily for us he never found out for if he did, his large hands would have certainly left red imprints in our unruly bottoms. We were both great swimmers, and in the hot summer, the river's cool water felt good, especially when returning home after sweating for many hours working the dirt.

I shall never forget the catastrophe that took place in the garden during the hot summer of 1965 I was only 15-years old. My stepfather wanted to collect water from a well in large drums he brought to the garden. Just a few feet under the rich ground the garden's well gave us all the water we needed from the river. Our task for the day was to cut the top of the drums with a hammer and chisel and fill them up with water. I did not want my brother to hurt himself, so I took upon myself to use the hammer and chisel to cut the three drum tops.

It was a really hot summer day and I worked really hard for a couple of hours, I was very thirsty and the water we brought, was long gone. Then I made the serious mistake to drink some of the rusted water avidly. My stepfather always insisted for us to pump a few gallons and wait for all the murky water collected in the pipe to exit and drink only when the water becomes clear. All would have been fine after a few gallons but my Aries Dragons" Head combined with my speedy moon in Gemini, makes me extremely fast and impatient in all that I did and still do. This was something I would regret drastically, later on.

We still had to position one of the drums under the hand pump and rolled it closer to it. We both pushed and kicked the rolling drum when it suddenly took a sharp left turn in the direction of the crops. I did not want to mess up we worked so hard to grow, so I instinctively tried to correct the direction of the drum with my hands. The rolling drum was like a sharp circular saw and cut both my left fingers right to the bone. I still have the deep scars as a painful memory and recall the agonizing pain and the blood pouring out of my hand. Vincent was petrified watching me helplessly screaming holding my hand tightly.

The wounds were serious and required a few stitches, but I was miles away from home and on the other side of the river. No one was near us, no help was available and the garden was in a very remote area in the woods. I knew I had to do something fast, since I was bleeding profusely. While holding my left hand, I asked Vincent to tear off my T-shirt left on the floor and to tie it tightly around my wrist. I had to control my own panic and think fast to get myself out of this mess. I could not take the shortest way back home swimming. I also had to stop the blood gushing out from my fingers after removing the T-shirt that turned my hand lifeless.

My only option was to take the long way back home, since there was no way I could lift myself up the tall bridge wall with one hand or even use the ladder. Then to make the situation worse while walking, I felt a burning sensation from the inside of my guts. Walking fast circulated the poisonous water I drank earlier through my system and the toxins jammed my kidneys and the intense pain forced me onto the floor, I really felt that death was imminent. I was convulsing and vomiting on the road trying hard to keep conscious, as the pain coming from my insides was intensifying by the second. My horrified younger brother was crying heavily, trying all he could to help me. He held me tight and said "Come on Louis, be strong please, you will be fine -- hang on"'. Little did he understand the gravity of my situation and I passed out by the dirt road. I regained consciousness at home and I heard the doctor telling mom that I had an intestinal infection and my hand had a huge bandage on it. Later on, my brave brother Vincent told me that he dragged me under a tree away from the burning sun, and ran home as fast as he could. He told me he nearly got killed trying to halt cars on the bridge, and finally an old man stopped and both drove back to get me and bring me home. Vincent simply saved my life this day, and God forbid if I was alone, I would not be writing my memories today. It took me a few days to recuperate, but soon I was back on my feet and ready for more crazy adventures. As a kid, I was wild and always looking for "trouble", I had no fears and still love a good challenge. My adventurous spirit brought me both monstrous pain and fabulous satisfactions.

———

Jaws of Death

A few months later while looking for wild mushrooms in the forest Vincent and I stumbled onto two animal traps lost on a trail. Vincent sensed trouble and said "Don't touch this Louis, you are going to get hurt". I never saw or used any traps before and of course I wanted to play with the new toys and as usual did not listen to him. I played with them for a while, and armed with a stick, I unleashed their deadly jaws a couple of times. I was excited in the possibility to catch small game especially when wild rabbits were plenty and ravaging the gardens -- this also meant free tasty food for us.

I did not want anyone to find the location of the traps, so I went deeper inside the woods, set them up and covered them with branches. I marked a few trees along the track with my small hatchet and we took the way back home. We arrived at sunset totally worn out starving and very thirsty. My stepfather suspected something and asked us why we were so late that evening, but Vincent and I knew better than to tell anything about the traps. The next couple of days during daylight we checked the Jaws of Death and again came back home unusually late. My stepfather became very suspicious and I knew soon the truth would have to come to light.

Innocently Vincent mentioned the snares to our youngest brother Yves and of course, he finally asked my mother at the dinner table when we would bring the rabbits home to eat. My stepfather heard Yves' comment, and under pressure Vincent finally told him all about the traps left in the woods. My step dad was furious and after a long series of butt drumming, he ordered me to go back to the woods and remove the traps. He ordered me to bring them back home or stay out until I do. We were about to eat our meager supper consisting of boiling water, a spoon of chocolate powder and slices of bread as hard as cement. It was about 7:00 PM And I was starving but I knew better than to challenge my enraged stepfather and left the dinner table.

Only a few hours ago the weather turned real nasty and I could hear the thunder outside. My concerned mother tried to help me out of this situation saying, "Well its late now, let him do this tomorrow morning". "No! He's got to go right now," my stepfather responded. "I don't care -- he has to learn the hard way!" he added.

I glanced outside through the window it was a pitch dark, rainy and windy evening. I asked if Vincent could join me but my stepfather ordered him not to. I accepted my fate and began the long walk in the direction to the old bridge. I could not take the short cut and swim across as the Rhone River's treacherous current at night and I knew the water level was also rapidly increasing. On my way out, my faithful Labrador Bobby must have felt my despair and happily followed me under the rain. I wanted to take that forced trip as fast as possible and I planned to take one of the dangerous ladders towards the end of the bridge and save myself hours walking. But I did not want Bobby to sit there on the bridge and wait for my return or risk to be killed by a car. Regardless of my orders and a few pebbles thrown at him, Bobby kept following me. Soon the darkness of the night enveloped us and with no flashlight, I was wondering how I would find my way in the woods. The chilly rain was pouring from the sky and I was very cold and starving. I was trying hard to stay on the bridge, holding the wall, battling the freezing cold "Mistral". My wet, light clothing was no match for the piercing wind. I could hear the turbulent Rhone River under me, rushing thought the arches, wondering how high and how fast it would rise out of his bed. In spite of the elements Bobby was still behind me.

After what seemed to be an eternity I reached the end part of the old bridge hoping to find a dry arch. It was pitch dark and I could not see the bottom of the arch and could only trust my luck. I took on the dangerous long skinny steal ladder all the way down.

In the picture under you can barely see some shadows and the ladders landing right in the middle of the large concrete pointed bases. They were designed this way to cut the water tumultuous current as it flows through the arches. The small archways above the concrete footings are designed for the water to flow easily through the bridge when the Rhone River rises above the footings. The trip down was very dangerous and the bridge was very high. Once I reached the bottom of the ladder, I had another fifteen feet of concrete to climb down to reach the ground safely.

The Old Bridge

It was a moonless night and I knew I was safe, as I could not hear the rushing water under the bridge any longer. I could not see the bottom of the arch either, but I trusted my instincts to land on dry ground. I grasped the steel bars and I was about ten feet down the ladder, when Bobby's loud barks and deep howling forced me to return to top of the bridge. In spite of the rain and wind, my dog managed to jump on the tiny wall. I was so scared for him and I did not want him to fall to his death following me.

How am I going to do bring him down with me I thought? I would never forgive myself if my dog I loved so much got killed on the bridge. I made the decision to bring him down with me and took a huge risk that could have easily killed us both. I simply squeezed the dog between my body and the bars of the ladder, and slowly against all odds, made my way down. Bobby's large paws were resting on my shoulders and he must have known not to make a single move or he would crash to his death, over 100 feet down. I prayed that he would not panic during this maneuver. He was now and them licking the water off my face and his warm breath made my cheeks and nose feel alive again.

As expected, in some places the bars were missing, and a couple of them snapped under our weight. But by some miracle, I managed to grab my dog by his fur and hold him steady until I could get my footing back. The rain made the bars very slippery and the raging wind, very hard for me to hold on to the ladder. I finally landed safely at the bottom and I cried in the darkness. It was more of a relieved weeping or an emotional exhales if you will, from having taunted death and lived to tell all about it. Also, since my dramatic UFO abductions, I was really scared of the dark and I was so far from everyone in the middle of nowhere. Bobby was happily licking my face and barking, and this helped me to fight the imaginary demons I saw hiding under the ancient bridge. I made it so far, I thought, but I was worried to be surrounded by water on the wrong arch. But, I was far enough from the rising water, and I did not have to climb back the old ladder and start all over again.

Now I had to take on the fifteen-foot direct drop from the top of the concrete footing - and do this without light. The bridge foothold itself was built on huge pile of sharp rocks. I took a chance again with my dog, I had no other alternative but to lay down on my belly, holding Bobby by his hind legs -- and then dropped him. I heard a loud crash followed by a sharp squeal as he crashed on the rock below but he was all right and barking for me. I felt my way down the long concrete wall, holding on to cracks and trees branches and safely made it to the rocky bottom. Bobby's refined nose found me almost immediately in the dark and we both crawled down rock by rock and made it in one piece to the sandy ground. I had some cuts and bruises, but I was tough and somehow happy to finally be on the other side of the river.

The city's dim lights and the shadow of the old church helped me to locate myself as I walked along the bank of the raging Rhone river. It was still raining and thundering relentlessly and the many strikes of lightning provided me with enough luminosity to make my way towards the woods. I had another mile or so to walk and the river was showing dangerous signs of overflowing. I could not walk safely along its bank any longer and aimed for higher ground. Bobby was running all over chasing rabbits fleeing the growing river but he would respond immediately to my piercing whistle and never wander too far away from me.

After a long walk, I passed the familiar garden and finally reached the edge of the forest. It was very difficult for me to see the deep marks left in some trees leading me to the traps. I was awaiting more lightning to do so, until I at long last I found the exact location. I was exhilarated! Bobby and I made it safely through the woods, and now I could bring the traps back home and be forgiven by my stepfather. Hungry and freezing in the dark, I was concentrating on finding the traps as quickly as possible so that I could go back to the safety and warmth of my home. I knew Mom would not, and could not be sleeping, knowing that I was on the other side of the river. But like all of us, she also knew my stepfather's temper well -- and under no circumstances would she ever challenge him. I sometimes wonder how can parents be so irresponsible with their children but it was a very rough time, where survival took over conscience.

I was crawling on my knees, feeling the ground for the stick and the chain. Then I felt the cold and wet fur of a rabbit's body. The powerful mechanism literally cut it in two. I made sure Bobby was behind me at all times to avoid accidentally stepping on the remaining trap. The other lethal device was placed just a few feet away and I knew it could easily cut my hand off, too. As I was fussing around, the perilous mechanism went off. I heard a crushing slap. To this day, I do not know how or why the device went off and I know for sure I never touched it. I was sitting in the dark, startled so far away from home and I would have certainly have bled to death if the trap had cut my hand.

I took the snares and began my long journey home. Somehow, I felt like I passed a test of some sort, like some aged tribal ritual where I had to show I was a man. The spirits were with me that night and no one but me experienced it. I wanted to prove to my stepfather that regardless of his unwise decision, I would make it safely back home. Daniel a kid himself, he was barely twenty years old then and I realize now his attitude and decisions were far from being wise. Like every one of us life taught him valuable lessons and he is no longer the brute he used to be. Over the years his Aries character changed drastically and he became a real loving and responsible mature person.

I was much too tired to take on the bridge's long ladder again. Instead Bobby and I took the long but safe way back home. It took me all night to make it safely back home. The traps and chains were heavy and I had to stop a few time to relieve my bleeding hands and crushed shoulders. The clouds magically moved away and like a new breath of life, the warm sunlight appeared above the high mountains. As expected, a tired and worrisome Mother was impatiently waiting for her incorrigible son. She was very happy to see me safe and sound and after tipping hard bread into a hot cup of cocoa, I returned to the attic and fell deeply asleep on the small couch. A mixture of drama, courage and luck has always been a part of my early dramatic life and I somehow knew that; all would be just fine at the end, and it was.

Bobby's Death

A few days later, Bobby began to show severe signs of sickness. We were so poor then and we could barely afford food to survive and taking care of a dog humanely was not an option especially with any practicing veterinarians in the village. Armies of pets were eating whatever was available to them in trashcans as well as dead wild animals. A few days earlier, while accompanying me in the woods, Bobby ingested what was left of a rabbit killed by a fox. In the South of France rabbits destroy crops and concerned farmers regularly deposit stale poisonous meat in their lands.

Bobby was in great distress, convulsing and vomiting all over the house. Vincent and I instinctively knew that we were about to lose our beloved fury friend. My stepfather ordered us to get out of the balcony where Bobby was convulsing, wanting to put an end to his misery. He took a broom and swiftly crashed Bobby's skull. We heard the muffled crack echoing all over the house and we felt his soul pass us by. We were very tough then, but we could not hold our tears. We both cried for days, in silence at the loss of our dear pet. This may sound barbaric to the reader, but during those days there was no way for us to deal humanely with Bobby' terminal sickness.

My stepfather Daniel was also trying hard to cover his emotions and own tears, as he loved Bobby dearly. He brought the puppy into the family years earlier as a Christmas present to all of us. This was a very heartbreaking day for the family, but especially for me, as Bobby was always there when I needed him the most. His presence was very comforting in the darkest and coldest moments of my dramatic upbringing. After collecting ourselves we asked Daniel if we could bury the body and he said, "OK, but make sure to be back home by seven o'clock at the latest". Vincent helped me to insert his bloody heavy body into a large bag and we drug it down the long stairway onto a wheelbarrow. We then walked to the *Bois De Sanguin*, a small wooded area about two miles away from the village. We took turns pushing the wheelbarrow along the small road and to the trail leading to the woods. I could not stop seeing Bobby running left and right, sniffing and barking on the same trail for so many years when he was alive. All the while hating God wondering why he was taking away everything that meant so much to me. We made a big cross with some thick branches and buried our dog in the small gully. We both cried on the burial place holding each other's, then all of the sudden, by some mysterious manifestations and for the last time, we heard Bobby's unmistakable barking resonating all over the woods.

A Memorable Christmas

Our family was very poor, but we somehow always managed to have the best and biggest Christmas tree, any kid could ever dream of. My stepfather and I would ride his big motorcycle into the high snowy mountains, looking for the mightiest pine tree we could find. I did not have much protection against the cold or the falling snow and I was holding on to him as hard as I could, to keep from falling of the motorbike and avoid the bitter winds. After what seemed to be an eternity, my little butt was always in a despicable state as we arrived at a remote location. After picking out the best tree, we would cut it down and drag it to the road. Many times, I was ordered to run up the slope and hide behind the brushes to the sound of an approaching car. I don't think any farmer would be happy to find out that we stole a tree on his private property.

My stepfather really did all he could to make Christmas a good time for all of us, and behind his terrible controlling triple Aries fiery temper, there is still a great loving heart. I found out many years later, that he would always be there for me, regardless of the trouble I was in. Once my car died on me over two hundreds miles away from home and he did not think twice to rescue me. This fact helped me to forgive him for the hardship he inflicted on all of us and now as a mature man myself, I realize he was also suffering greatly. Marrying a much older woman at eighteen years of age and trying to raise her seven kids is actually a testament to his will and true character. I know many people who would never ever take the challenge or responsibility to deal with a woman with one single child.

The trip back home was like a clown act at a circus. The tree was joined on the side of the bike, and with the snow-packed road and the never-ending gust of wind, we hit the ground a few times. Luckily, the thick blanket of snow and the low speed saved us from serious injury. We arrived home a few hours later totally wet and frozen to death.

We did not have the luxury of getting toys, but we certainly had a big tree. It was an incredible sight with all the Christmas decorations and lights mirroring in the living room. We were so small and everything appeared to be so big then. This is why it is important to never treat a child as an adult and realize his own tiny world and the impact of your mature words on his fragile immature psyche. I recall my street and home to be huge as a child but so small now, when I return to visit every year or so. Mother was always deeply religious, but she never imposed her beliefs on any of us. She always told me that she found her God, and that I would in time find my own. My mother's way of thinking was truly revolutionary knowing that in every small village religious customs are a very important way of life.

My stepfather was totally against any form of religion, period; he thought they were designed to abuse weak-minded people. He was born with good logic and with an advanced moon in Aquarius and smart enough to realize the nefarious mind–control dogmatic teachings benefited only the religious organizations. This is hilarious when you realize that during the Christmas period adults are taught that Jesus will come back from the heavens to save the world, while children are waiting for Santa Claus to come down the "chimney" with toys. All takes place the same night on December 25th and with time; for both the adults and the children, those religious holidays (and myths) became an intrinsic part of our lives.

"Mythology is what grown ups believe, folklore is what they tell their children, and religion is both."
~ Cedric Whitman

Finally, Christmas arrived and a flying chubby Santa Claus managed to slide through the burning fireplace and safely deposited a few boxes under the tree for all of us. Some ribbons, chocolate and biscuits made the small packages very attractive. We all rushed under the tree looking for our names and grasped our presents. To us, it was a very special holiday because this was the first time we ever got a Christmas present and I was thrilled. We always heard of presents and chocolate but my parents could never afford anything else than the stolen tree, home made decorations and real white candles light.

I tore off the paper and cover of a box bearing Vincent and Louis' names and inside was two silver cowboy guns. My goodness, we were in paradise and I will never forget the huge smile on my brother's face. We pointed the guns toys at each other and started firing imaginary bullets. This was our first true Christmas with chocolate and real presents and I was wondering what good I had done to deserve such clemency from Santa Claus. My brother and I rushed outside into the snow, firing the gun in all directions, under the wondering eyes of the rest of the family. Vincent was the Indian and I was the cowboy and he rushed to the back of a covered truck parked in the street.

"I got you, "touché" you are dead already!" I shouted. "Sure come and get me, your bullets can't hit me here" he replied. Our world of imagination was all that we had to deal with such a destitute life and with our new toys we made the most of it.

The snow and wind were coming down with force -- but in spite of it all, our cowboys and Indian imaginary world kept us warm. Vincent crawled to the front of the truck and entered the cab through the broken back window. He immediately opened the passenger door, so I could join him inside away from the elements to enjoy the delicious chocolates.

All was fine until we started to fight for the chocolates, since he had more bars than me and I wanted my share. Realize of course that we were often starving and chocolate is a treat we rarely enjoyed. We were like wild animals, driven by the instinct of preservation responding violently to the constant cries of an empty stomach. While fighting my brother on the floor of the truck my elbow accidentally hit the stick shift bringing it to the neutral position and the car began going backward. The truck was parked in an elevated area and nothing could stop it from gravity. Suddenly I felt a bump produced by the back wheels hitting the curb but I was more concerned with the chocolate. Then, I saw his face turning pale and he began to scream as loud as he could.

"Stop, Stop, damn Louis we are moving." While on top of him he saw the walls of the houses and trees passing by, and he realized the vehicle was in motion. I stood up immediately, realized the situation, opened my door and jumped outside.

"Damn, get out Vincent, now, come on, hurry," I screamed. I tried to hold on and stop the huge truck in motion but in no way could my tiny body do it. The menacing door was pushing me in the same direction as the truck and I was afraid of being sucked under it and the lethal wheels. "Vincent, open your door, Open your door now," I screamed again and again.

He tried hard, but it was jammed and could not escape fast enough. I ran after the runaway vehicle and re-entered the moving truck. I grasped my brother by his shoulder and pulled him as hard as I could, towards me. Finally I got my brother out of the truck but the door smacked us very hard and we flew a couple of feet in the air then landed on our behinds. Because of the nasty weather no one was either driving or walking the small street that day. Horrified, we watched the truck crashing some parked cars, crippling some trees and then finally, with a big bang it came to rest against the wall of a building.

Marks left in 1961 on the Wall by the Bed of the Truck

A La Citadelle Adventure

Once, my stepfather Daniel took me fishing and while we were riding the almighty Rhone River waters, I saw a small overture located on the North side of the fortress. This old stronghold was built on the 14th to the 18th centuries and used by the Germans because of its logistic location at the entrance of the small city. Many young militia from " La Resistance" were kept captive and suffered atrocities at the hands of the SS in the fortress. The small jail like window is located about fifty feet high above the grassy area at the right side of the picture in the back and cannot be seen from this angle.

Fortress

I always wanted to know what was inside this enormous structure and   told my gang about the treasury we may find inside. I had no idea really of what I would uncover inside the walls of the fortress, but I knew it was going to be dangerous. After a few questions to my Grandpa; he told me horrible stories of POW detained there. After their liberation, the city sealed all the entrances with brick walls in 1945 soon after the end of WW2.

The preparations were made with the clan and I picked the upcoming Sunday, for the expedition. Armed with long ropes, hooks, flashlights, knives and slings, I guided the gang under the opening. In the picture the area appears clean and easy to reach, but during those days an amount of dirt, bushes, trees and rocks had fallen from the citadel walls, making the spot very hard to reach. I convinced the kids that the "treasures" would be very valuable and we could sell some of the rare war items for a few Francs (Euro did not exist in 1964). We made our way closer to the impressive walls by cutting a passageway through the thick undergrowth and trees. Disturbed bees made us run off a couple of times, but I was more worried about cutting ourselves on the deposited junk. I already had a few tetanus shots from previous mishaps and I did not want to get another cut that could make my parents suspicious of my clandestine activities.

We took turns throwing the metal hook attached to the rope as high as possible, hoping to catch one of the bars in the small overture. A few times the piece of metal flew back to earth, just missing eyes and heads simply by miracle. After many trials, finally the hook clasped itself on the iron bar and all the kids were screaming with joy. Well as the leader of the clan I had to climb first and take all the risks. I tested the rope and hook by pulling violently a few times, then reassured I climbed all the way up. The notorious Mistral wind never stops blowing there and made my ascension of the wall even more perilous.

Finally, I made it to the top, but the iron bars were barely wide enough for me to go through. The plan was for me to enter the fortress first and lead the group inside to collect the goods. However, we had only one rope, thus the only way for me to get to the bottom of the old fortress was to use the same rope inside, then proceed to go down.

Hanging by the window with the sun in my eyes, I could not see anything inside the fortress. I screamed against the wind, "Hey guys, its real dark down there, I can't see anything down there, attach the flashlight to the end of the rope" I added. Sadly enough, the only flashlight we brought did not work and no one had enough money to afford a new battery. "OK guys, I am going down, wait for me I'll be right back" I yelled again.

Dealing with the dark was my deepest fears, but no one knew about it and I was not about to turn away now. I have been afraid of the darkness since my first UFO abductions, but little did I know that I was going to be in the sinister citadel for many hours to come. I began my death-defying descent holding to dear life and the rope as hard as I could. It was very dark, cold and damp but my valiant adventurous spirit took over. I reached the end of the rope and still no ground under my feet. At this point I thought the floor could not be that far under my feet and simply let go.

What I did not realize is that; because of the amassed junk the outside level was higher than the inside and after what seemed to be an eternity falling in total darkness, I crash-landed on a pile of dirt. I must have free fallen for nearly ten feet or more and got lucky not to break a single bone in my body. It took me a while for my eyes to adapt to the darkness of my sinister environment. I could only see the light from the opening above and heard the lamenting wind periodically gasping through it

"Oh my God, here we go again I thought, what am I gonna do now? I can't see or even reach the rope now. I am really stuck down here," I thought. I battled my vivid imagination and panic, at the same time knowing that the boys outside knew I was here and the worst that could really happen is that the fire brigade or the police would soon or later come and rescue me. That is if some imaginary evil spirits or hidden demons did not eat me alive, first.

"Damn" I thought; "my tiny red butt will ache for at least a week if my stepfather found out about this new escapade". I could not stay here doing nothing and none of my friends outside could hear my desperate screams. I crawled, cautiously sensing my environment and it felt like a *"Deja Vue"* when I was looking for the deadly traps in the middle of the night only a few weeks ago. I could not make sense to what I was touching and after a while the thin light coming from the opening above, helped me to discern my surroundings.

As time passed, my eyes got used to the shady site and to my horror I realized I had landed on a huge of pile of worn army clothing, gas masks, ration tins, ammunitions, sharp bayonets, rusted rifles and loads of dry bones. I grasped immediately why the city cemented all access to the Citadel and how much serious clean up this place really needed. I wanted treasures and I certainly found it.

I was in pitch darkness and reluctant to move on, I grasped a piece of steel and threw it as far as I could, waiting for resonance. When the metal hit the ground, the immense, church-like deep acoustic echo frightened coming back at me. I thought I was in an extensive confined dome like space and I felt trapped. I had to talk myself down again to avoid panicking and began to look for a way out of this mess. I walked slowly all along the rugged walls, stumbling on rats and disturbing huge bats. I cut my face and hands a few times on sharp metallic objects that were lodged in the wall and tucked on the floor. Sweat of fears downpour my face when I thought of stepping by accident on a mine and die, in this gigantic catacomb.

I was desperately looking for any source of light and the only luminosity was coming from the small opening above and soon it completely disappeared and I found myself scared to death in total darkness. My fears of the dark and its creepy imaginary monsters nearly got the best of me but I had to proceed forward regardless. I walked long corridors, listening to any noise or any sign that could help me out of the sinister catacombs. I could only hear some far away squeals coming from pugnacious rats, flying bats and drops of water crashing on the floor. "The perfect home for any resident vampires" I thought.

Against all odds, I kept walking in the dark and felt cold water in my shoes. I thought of directing myself in the dark in the same manner as the bats and I kept screaming and listening to the echo, but this time a frightened owl passively answered my call. I knew the bird of prey could not be too far from any overture and I kept walking in that direction. Finally, after hours in the darkness of the fortress, I could discern some badly anticipated light and the feeling of hope was simply incredible. My confidence came right back and sprinted towards it. I felt like I cheated death and managed to avoid all the evil spirits stuck forever in the walls of the ancient stronghold. Once more, it took me a while for my strained eyes to adapt to the daily light and I recognized the high columns and walls of a church. I found out years later, that the monks built a church in the fortress.

All the Way up to Freedom

I paused for a while, wondering how to get out and the only way out was up. Once again, my agile daring young body did the job. I hiked my way all the way up, holding to statues of angels, kissing their stony faces and thanking them for their protection. Swiftly lifting my body by grasping cracks, I finally made it all the way safely to the top. I felt exhilarated with the nasty ordeal behind me. I was right inside the forbidden ramparts of the Citadelle, where no one had stood for many years.

I jumped the wall and walked towards the back of the "Citadelle" and towards the river just above the opening where they should be, patiently waiting for me. Here they were sitting down innocent as I was, laughing and wondering when I would reappear from the Citadel's belly. They were very surprised to see me above the little overture on top of the ramparts. I screamed, "Hey guys I am here, all is great join me on the top right away. I have great things to tell you". They immediately grasped their belongings and a few minutes later, we were all sitting on the wall.

"Whoa, it took you a long time Louis, tell us what happened to you down there?" Michel said. I explained exactly what to expect inside the fortress and gave each one of them a bullet that I had collected from the pile of ammunitions that I had landed on hours earlier. We came back a few days later, but well prepared this time and with working flashlights, bags and longer ropes. As planned, we made our way in and out of the overture, without incident. We found all sorts of valuable things and I ordered everyone not to touch any grenades or anything suspicious that could explode in our face. We painfully lifted the treasure back to civilization and all was fine until we sold bullets and bayonets to our schoolmates. Soon the teachers found out who was behind it all and one afternoon the police came home.

Well Mrs. Turi, the gendarme said, "Louis is in trouble again and we must find out where he found those bayonets and bullets, who knows he may bring back a bazooka or a machine gun at school, next". My mother was upset with me but would never be physical with me, so I told them the truth, and as anticipated, my stepfather seriously smashed my juvenile butt again. A few days later, the city ordered a full clean up of the Citadelle and now, millions of people come from all over the world to visit this safe historical place. Little do they know that I am the first one to "explore" the Citadel" and without my intervention, those brick walls may have kept hidden, the mystery and history of this acclaimed fortress.

Alone in total darkness inside the bowel of the fort, I felt the pain and drama of the many doomed POW spirits during WWI and WW2 and the Dark Ages of long gone centuries, inside the Citadelle walls. But most of all, I sensed the deep and sad breath of the Dark Ages departed souls and the sad memories of disappeared Centuries. I know I walked with all of them in the dark. I felt the awful experiences suffered by all of them and acknowledged the essence of life and death and I am glad I did what I did, for life is precious and so are the experiences.

Vincent's Death Wish

Introducing Laws

My painful upbringing also involves the accidental death of my brother Vincent.

He was only two years younger than me and we were very close indeed. His demise resulted in a great deal of pain for the entire family and added serious trauma to my already melodramatic young life. I was about 18-years-old, and I was doing my three days orientation in order to join the French Navy at Toulon, a harbor city located in the south of France.

The following chapter undoubtedly led me to fully recognize that telepathy is not the product of imagination, but indeed really exists. I was also much too young to give credence to any form of "psychic" phenomenon and its after many of those extrasensory experiences that I fully acknowledged its value. Vincent died accidentally crossing a street at night; a drunk driver killed him at the tender age of 16-years-old. Our day life was a constant struggle especially with my stepfather trying hard to launch his own construction business. My older brother Jo was already married with a child and was working in the city of Marcoule, at the steel factory. Thus unlike us, being the older of all the boys, he was spared much of a very harsh time Vincent and I had to deal with. We were "hired" and working like slaves with both my stepfather and my departed Uncle, Andrew. My stepfather contracted a job assignment with the French PTT (Post-Telegraph-Telephone) in the "Gorge De L' Ardeche", a summer camp location. Daniel took the challenge to build a huge concrete storage section for the vacationers. The area is the pictorial-equivalent of the Grand Canyon in the United States because of its picturesque natural beauty, the Wild River and natural wilderness.

Most of the day was spent feeding a never satisfied vociferous concrete mixer, under the blazing sun. Vincent and I were responsible for preparing and providing a constant flow of cement and bricks, to both Daniel and my Uncle Andrew. Our relatives would skillfully use the admixture to build what seemed to be an endless brick wall. The hardest part of the job for us was to throw thousands of shovels of sand, water; cement and gravel inside the noisy starving round steel mouth.

Being older and stronger than Vincent, I was responsible for the burdensome task of passing out the heavy bricks by hand to my Uncle and my stepfather. No leather gloves were available and soon the first layer of skin was wasted on the jagged bricks, wheelbarrow steel and shovels wood handles. Often exasperated, we both had to work with bloody hands and cracked fingers. After a few weeks of inhumane duty, the pain in our hands slowly decreased, then disappeared. Nature took over and slowly our hands and fingers were desensitized by growing tougher leather-like skin.

The blistering sun did not help either, but after shading a few films of burned skin both Vincent and I had the most beautiful tan anyone could ever dream of. The intense physical exercises gave us a sharp muscle line and a robust body that all the young girls around could not help but notice. This excruciating work gave us a Herculean appetite and the most enjoyable part of the day was lunchtime. We did not have the luxury to take a shower at work or home, thus the time spent swimming in the cool water was very relaxing and badly needed to clean away the sweat, dust and cement from our blistered skin.

Years later, the constant shoveling motion resulted in a seriously twisted pelvis and a terrible pain on my right hip joint. Back in 2005, I was advised by doctors to undergo surgery to "fix" the problem and eliminate the awful hip pain. Incredible as it may sound, using Nostradamus Cabalistic Natural Healing, I repaired myself in spite of many Doctor's prognostics. The most difficult part of the day was the twenty miles trip back home through the mountainous Ardeche region. Both my Uncle and my stepfather were sitting in the front of the small 1955, 203 Peugeot flatbed truck. There was no enough room for us in front of the small vehicle and we had to travel with the trash, tools, bricks and cement in the back of the truck. Every single bump on the warped road was painfully felt.

The trips were especially hard during the winter as the freezing mixture of wind and frozen rain came down on us as we gained altitude. We could only hide under a rough tarp-like material used to protect cement bags from the downpour. It was pure hell for us, but we did not have any other choice and we had an obligation to work for the family and complaining was not even an option. Our young bodies and juvenile spirits helped us through this daily pounding. After a few months of this harsh treatment Vincent' young spirit began to deteriorate. I will never forget the deplorable phrase my brother kept repeating night after night on the way back home. Steadily and for many months, Vincent proclaimed the same awful depressive sentence over and over again. Those few words are carved into my memory and will remain there until I join him in death.

"Louis" he used to say, "Un jour de moins a vivre" In English, this means, "Louis, this is one less day to live!" In the beginning, I did not give much attention to his depression, hoping for a change in his wounded spirit and gloomy attitude. His negative outlook on life was not exactly surprising, in view of the fact that we were going through the hell that we endured each day.

I just laughed and pretended not to hear him. I kept resisting his depressive thoughts each day, but I became worried about his state of mind. I purposely talked about our future and emphasized the many great days ahead of us without positive results. The same distasteful phrase kept coming out of his mouth until it seriously got on my nerves. Then one evening on the way back home, I finally snapped. "Hey, stop that Vincent! What the hell's going on with you, bro? Why do you have to carry on, saying this garbage every night?" I was hoping that my surprising violent reaction would work.

"I don't know" he said, "I can't help it." He replied nervously. "What if I smack this filth right back into your throat?" I thought threatening him would make him stop. In spite of my desperate requests, he kept crying and repeating the dreadful sentence on the way back home. The only thing I could do was to hide my own tears from him by projecting the tough big brother image. Back home the situation was also deplorable with our stepfather's impatience and aggressive Aries' personality; but we had to go on. A few months later, I was drafted for sixteen months by the NAVY and called to do the orientation classes in the city of Toulon. It was suppertime on this gloomy November day, and I was enjoying a noisy and smoke-filled dinner with the unruly recruits. We were innocent, happy and young, and dirty jokes were thrown all around the disorderly tables. Suddenly, I felt a sharp poke from the center of my solar plexus and I felt like an overpowering rush of inexplicable heartbreaking feelings hitting me hard. It felt like some weird unseen psychic forces assailed me and I could not understand what was happening to me.

The entire table quieted down looking at my distorted face. I felt like complete despair and an inner panic attack was consuming me alive and I could not either move or speak. I could barely hold on to my tears and managed to walk in direction to the bathroom. Once in the lavatory, the desperate feeling took over me and I could not stop crying. I tried to rationalize and calm myself down, without success and thought "This is not me at all-- what's happening to me?" I felt like as if the entire world had crashed on me. There was nothing that I could do and more and more riotous tears poured out of my distorted eyes. I felt terrible and scared with this crashing emotional situation. I decided to lock myself in one of the bathrooms and hide away from everyone for a while. I was hoping for this dreadful experience to end but the mournful feeling kept worsening. For a minute, I really thought I was going insane then I heard the Commandant calling my name through the facility's loud speakers system. "Soldier Turi, this is an emergency please report to my office immediately." the voice said. I collected myself the best way I could and undoubtedly felt that I was going to experience one of the most dramatic moments in my life.

As I walked in this office, the Commandant said, "Son, you've got to be strong, your brother Jo needs to talk to you." The tone of his voice was authoritative, but I was also able to detect a mixture of sadness and compassion. I knew something was dreadfully wrong, well before my older brother Jo decided to place the disturbing telephone call. The Commandant was silent, looking at me gravely and I could see the flicking light and grasped the telephone from the Commandant's hand and before Jo could say any word I said to him.

"I know Jo, something is very wrong!" With a sobbing voice he said, "Hi Louis, "Vincent had an accident, a drunk driver killed him, you must come back home tonight." Even tough I was prepared by my subconscious for the awful news, my entire world felt apart. I dropped the telephone on the floor. And a wild torrent of what ever tears were left in me kept running down my face as the helpless Commandant tried to comfort me. I could also feel that he was trying really hard to keep his own tears in control. He softly said, "Be strong son, you need to be strong." The man was a tough career soldier who endured quite a lot in his life. Regardless of his toughness, I could easily depict a real strong compassion for his fellow human beings. At this point, he knew exactly what I needed; some sympathy and this means so much when you are under such stress. I put the receiver in front of my mouth and asked Jo; "When did it happen?"

Collecting himself, Jo waited a second then answered. "A couple of hours ago" he added, "The entire family is here and we are all waiting for you, you must come home." He then added, "Your Commandant said that you are on a special leave and we are all waiting for you." "OK" I said, "I am on my way." He then hung up, but not before bursting in tears. This dramatic rainy November day, Vincent was sent to collect a forgotten tool and he was to bring it back to Jo's apartment, where he was doing some improvement work with my stepfather. Sad enough the weather was really bad, the visibility poor, and a perfect setting for any vehicular disaster to happen. And it did, when a drunk driver killed him instantly. Years later when I studied the subconscious, I realized distance does not mean much to the subconscious. I was the recipient of a colossal amount of depressive thoughts coming from the many people mourning my departed brother on his deathbed. Such a massive flux of concentrated depressive "thought energy" generated by them all hit me like a wild train over two hundreds and fifty miles away. The thought is omnipresent and as there is no time in space, I spiritually felt the drama. I "picked up" the collective distress signal sent to me as a "thought block" and simply responded to it emotionally. Vincent was gone and the thought of never seeing him alive again was incessantly tormenting me.

I took the three hours train ride home and I arrived quite late. The entire house was still packed with grieving family members, numerous neighbors, and many close friends. Mom was not to be seen upon my arrival, she was in shock and under strong sedatives and I saw my stepfather crying for the first time. I am sure, many of you reading this material that have experienced the loss of a loved one, can only identify with the stress of a seriously broken heart. After such a dreadful experience, my belief in God disappeared and was replaced by pain and anger. Why would God bless some people with beauty, health, fortune and yet takes young lives and give to others hell and drama? Why the so pure, so loving, so just and powerful creator would differentiate and favor a few of us I thought.

He was working with my stepfather in my brother's new apartment (regulated by the Moon). Vincent went to collect a missing tool and as he crossed the road was killed by a drunk driver. That fatal night the Moon was waning (negative) and cruising through the dramatic sign of Scorpio (death).

The Law of Negativity

* Little did I know about the mighty creative forces of the subconscious and the implacable Universal Laws. In my brother's case, the " **Law of Negativity**" inarguably affirms its dangerous potential and deadly outcome.

Using my own departed brother Vincent example, I will now attempt to explain more about this merciless law and its interaction with others subtle Universal regulations. Note that any of my students will not only easily assimilate the following, but also gather even more wisdom in the process. But for those of you who do not yet possess Cosmic Consciousness, it may be challenging. This will defy your mental process in some ways, but I will use very simple sentences to both teach and guide you accurately in the inner working of the Universal Mind. Vincent was born with his natal Moon (home/family) in the sign of Scorpio (Death/drama). This lunar position predisposes the soul for serious dramatic experiences during the upbringing and in this case fatality. Vincent was also born with his Dragon's Tail (negative) in the sign of Leo (life/children) and combined with a Moon in Scorpio (death/drama) he was prone (by the Universal order) to lose his life at a very young age.

Vincent's constant negative thoughts and recurrent mind set (obsessive) sentence "Un Jour De Moins A vivre" or one less day to live fueled the "Law Of Attraction" manifesto to his own early demise. Thus in order to really "control" the "Law Of Attraction" and because all formula works coherently and in harmony, one must master ALL Universal rules regimenting the procedure of the Universal Mind interacting with our own personal UCI (Unique Celestial Identity).

This may get complicated for those who by birth (skeptics/scientists/atheists) inherited a stern UCI or a weak Mercury (reasoning) location in their natal chart. And unless one willingly takes on the challenge to raise his/her own vibrations through education to bypass the celestial affliction, some fears (Religious souls and/or the fear of the ridicule) not much chance is offered to the soul for mental exploration and the building of Cosmic Consciousness. The sad reality is that 99% of the population of this world is not exactly related to Einstein and will not even honor the word science itself, by doing the badly needed spiritual investigation. An endless amount of entertainments and/or sports will consume the lazy mind to oblivion, religion or false hope by means of blind faith to "The Law Of Attraction.

Remember that the part of God in each one of us is much stronger than the stars, but without a full understanding of ones UCI and its inner interaction with "The Law Of Attraction" there is no chance to apply the will and avoid tragedy.

The same applies to those aiming for a specific wish, and unless the aspiration is supported by the Universal Mind complexity, not much chance for its realization is offered to the soul. I encountered quite a lot of frustrations from many people including gullible friends, because of my findings pertaining to the "secret" but my aim is to educate you in all aspects of a multitude of Universal Laws.   Of course, some people think because I have a "God given gift" I should give it away for free. Universal Laws are priceless and there is nothing wrong in getting remunerated for the pain and suffering I went through all those years to learn them. The loss of my brother through the negative manifestation of the Law of Attraction was particularly dramatic for me.   Unlike certain religious groups, I am not imposing a fat percentage of your earnings for the rest of your life to teach you the word of a "prophet" but instead ask you to pay me for the countless hours I spent crystallizing my thoughts and wisdom in a book form for you. Think of it as any product or anything valuable you would purchase at your local store. I firmly believe that Vincent's negative thoughts "un jour de moins a vivre" definitely played an important part for his demise, as his subconscious set up the fatal outcome. The sad reality is that my brother Vincent subconsciously wrote the script, and then set it all out to experience it.

Broken Heart

Two days later some close friends and I were carrying the coffin into the church towards the large crucifix. The same uneasy feeling I had years ago in the same very church returned as soon as my eyes saw the mutilated body of Christ on the cross. Much of the village was present and I could feel the intense and sorrowful feelings generated by all the people gathering in the church. A constant flow of tears and gasps echoed throughout the church, as the priests' prayers guided Vincent's soul to a higher dimension.

The short trip from the church to the cemetery was pure hell; this was going to be his long lasting resting-place. Mom was born in November and like all Scorpios (the sign of fatality) she gave great attention to the affairs of death .She wanted all of her children, parents and grandparents to be buried together. She even invested on a larger white church like building in the village cemetery and requested all departed members of the family to be moved to that one location, where we will one day ultimately join each other in spirit for eternity.

It was just terrible for every one of us, to see the coffin being lowered six feet under the ground. More tears and dramatic cries from my desperate mother made it quite difficult for many to stay to the end of the burial ceremony. Then, they all left but I stayed behind. I spent several hours on my knees, crying, lamenting and talking to my departed brother. As always, The Mistral wind was cutting right through me and the rain slashed my face. I was cold, crying and desperately trying hard to deal with my loss. Then I made him a promise, one that I will keep until my own end. I promised Vincent that I would make the most out of my own existence and live two lives in one.

I told him that I would not be afraid of facing death that I would travel the world and see all its marvels. I promised him to feel for two, to experience love, pain, success even hate for the two of us. I felt then that God cheated him and reaped his young life away, and I wanted to do something about it. Upon my own death, I wanted to share all the exciting experiences of my own rich life with him. This self-appointment attitude greatly helped me to face the drama I was going through and gave me the reason I needed to stay alive.

I was anxious and hungry for any and all experiences that were ahead of me and I was ready to defy the devil face to face and try the impossible. Living and feeling for both of us became my mission, and if I was to die in the process so be it, I would just join him faster, I thought. If I were going to die today, Vincent would have plenty of his shares of my own incredible and exciting life. I became the wildest desperado on earth; taking chances were no one would dare. I was willing to risk and enjoy it all without any limits in thought, shape or form and as of today, I am still living to the fullest. Sadly, many of my close friends who shared my upbringing were also victims of drama and met with an early death.

I recall Madame Nieto, our neighbor; like my Mother, her personal struggle to deal with the loss of her first son was just inconceivable painful. She did not know then, that her own fears through "The Law Of Attraction" would materialize and she lost two more children. Stimulating the creative forces of her subconscious negatively, engendered by a constant flux of useless thoughts brought back more drama than any human being can endure. Rene, Madame Nieto' son was a good friend of mine, and he and I spent quite a lot of time racing our mopeds in the narrow streets of the small village. Many times Rene's mother voiced her fear of an accident that could harm us.

"Come on you kids" she used to yell, "Drive slowly in those small streets, everyone is complaining about the noise and your speed." As youngsters we never listened to anyone. She even tried to stop by any means. She used to say, "Unless you listen to me and drive slow in the streets, you won't get any more of my pies! She was shucking her head and would say almost anything to us, trying to prevent an accident. She added. "Louis, you've lost a brother already, you should be more careful. Jesus, think of your mother and how much she would suffer if anything bad happens to you! I think I would die if I was to lose another one of my children." She added. Her comment hit home but I was unconsciously nurturing a death wish to join my departed brother. We both would laugh at her and sped away, but not without stealing a piece of her succulent pie left to cool down on the side of the window.

Rene was from a good family and loved by all; unlike me he was a very happy child in a good functioning family. For his birthday his dad got him a expensive and powerful black bike. He was quite proud to own such a mighty machine and he used to say, "Hey guys, who wants to race me?" There was no point for me to take on his challenge with my old moped. I wanted a motorbike good enough to race him and "coincidentally" my subconscious guided me to a farm were my dream materialized. Finding the motorcycle was quite a chance given to me by "The Law Of Attraction" and combined with my natal Dragon's Head placed in the sign of Aries (Germany/fire/danger/mechanics) the ratio of materialization improved drastically.

I worked hard to bring the motorcycle to a working condition. I also knew that, if anything was to break I could never find any of the missing parts and this would mean the end of my racing career with the local kids. The bike belonged to a German soldier who had to flee for his life back to Germany in 1944. The farmer was quite happy to get rid of the old motorbike in need of more room in his garage. I worked for him in "The Vignes" doing all sorts of odd jobs to pay if off and finally brought the old machine home. Rene's new racing monster was too much for my elderly motorbike and he joined a club of wealthy kids who had similar bikes.

Nothing is made to last in life, and our friendships suffered and finally faded away. I was determined to get more power from my bike and I improvised to increase the compression on the cylinder's head, but the ripened carburetor was at its maximum input. I was always trying stupid ways to get more velocity from anything on wheels. My natal Dragon's Head in Aries ruled by Mars (speed/danger/machinery/Germany/fire) was to blame and its about thirty five years later when I built enough cosmic consciousness, that I understood why I did what I did and the way I did it. Finally the spark plug treads not designed to take so much pressure, shot up in the air, hit the gas tank, and missed my face by only a few inches. The spark plug must have traveled a few hundred feet per second in the air and then took a long plunge back to earth. I was sadly watching the doomed bike ending up in an enormous ball of fire. That was the end of it and my short racing career.

In one of his most passive drives through the village, Rene met with his dreadful fate. While taking a sharp turn, a truck driver accidentally ran him over and killed him instantly. I experienced a "déjà vu": Alain, Rene's younger brother who helped me to carry my own brother's coffin just a few months earlier, I was now experiencing the same dreadful feelings. I now helped him to carry the coffin of his departed brother. I could feel what Alain was going through, a true nightmare for all of us, an exact repetition, another drama and the loss of another young precious life. Little did I know then that a few months later I was to carry Alain's casket in the same church too.

I turned my attention to him. "Are you OK bro?" I asked, in a whisper.

"I...uh" His voice faded, and I noticed tears were running down his face. "I miss my brother so much, what am I going to do without him," he added.

"It's going to be okay," I said, putting my arm around him. I did not really know what to say to him, trying hard to hold on to my own tears. But I felt that I had to say something. It's difficult to come up with some words of comfort at a time like this.

"Alain" I said, "I know it's very hard for you to go through this, but it could have been me or you, instead of your older brother. This is life, its tough and now Rene is with Vincent. Life goes on for us," I added. Alain was two years younger than me and a good friend and the same age as my younger brother Yves. Madame Nieto condition was very sad; she was experiencing the same despair as my mother. Did Madame Nieto's powerful thoughts and anticipated fears produce her own son's death a few months after my own brother's passing?

---

* Remember the subconscious does not differentiate and will not separate fears from wishes. Chances are that like Vincent, Rene was born with an afflicted UCI to experience such a drastic death. A rising, a Moon, or an afflicted Dragon will work with The "Law of Negativity" and bring about disaster. I really believe that one of the most important secrets is to uncover your celestial identity and arm yourself with true wisdom; you will avoid any negative manifestation.

Life Goes On

Losing so many people in such a short time made me aware of how precious life really is. I wanted to fulfill my "mission" and live my life to the maximum for Vincent. Life at home with my stepfather became unbearable with the never ending fights between him and my mother. As a child I used to say to them: "Hey guys, is there any way for you to talk instead of screaming all day long? I had enough of your yelling, I wish I could stop hearing you two, why don't you behave like adults and stop fighting?" There is always a time of adaptation between two young people and today's statistics are not exactly encouraging for anyone in a relationship knowing that there is an 85% chance of failure. I was myself to be a victim a few years later with my first wife Marilyse. After a few years of this nasty situation, one day I woke up crying and in serious pain. I noticed a smelly yellowish color on my pillow and brought it to my mother. She was very concerned and took me immediately to the local doctor. During those days, village doctors were not exactly smart and using an ear-flushing syringe he simply forced water in both my ear canals. He was hoping to clear what he thought to be a blockage created by collected wax. The infection behind the eardrums was quite advanced and both were perforated. Doing so made the situation much worse and regardless of my horrendous screams produced by the pain, he never diagnosed me with advanced otitis.

Mom brought me back home trying hard to stop me from crying and put me to bed. A few days later the nasty treatment brought more pain, more putrefying discharge, and speed up the horrific infection. Any noise would become unbearable and I could still hear my parents fighting downstairs. I wished so hard for peace and quietness. My loud screams at night finally led me to the hospital emergency room where the doctor injected my little butt with thousands unities of penicillin. Regardless of the daily injections a week later my immune system did not show any sign of beating the infectious organism eating my ears away. The worrisome doctor gave my mother a very scary prognostic…

"Louis" he said, " does not respond at all to the antibiotics and the infection will progress into his brain and he will die" My mother was frantic not knowing that she was a part of my problem. For years I was wishing for silence and my subconscious, which cannot differentiate anything about a wish, will most certainly in time release its miraculous power to bring about my specific request. Of course in this case "The Law Of Attraction" attracted not only the infectious organism but also the wrong doctor "ET voila". Another manifestation of this powerful law has been clearly explained to you. My situation got much worse and against the doctor's recommendation my mother brought me back home. Wishing for my health back, she followed her formidable intuition and brought me directly to Grandma's house; by doing so, she saved my life.

Guess what? Grandma never screamed or raised her voice with the children and the very next day I felt much better already. By "miracle" the infection stopped and the healing process started immediately. I was not making the "wish" to stop a noise that was not there any longer. Grandma had chicken; rabbits, goats and I wanted to hear them in the early morning hours. I was making a very different and constructive wish and again the incredible natural healing forces of my subconscious did the rest. This is why it is so important for parents to be cautious around their children and avoid disasters through the manifestation of both the subconscious and the law of attraction's inarguable conjuncture.

> * Daniel was born April 3rd, 1940 under the zodiacal sign of Aries (violent) with the Tail of The Dragon (harmful) also in Aries (aggressive/impatient). This sign is ruled by the red (color of blood) planet Mars (The Lord Of War) and predisposes an extreme temper, virility, and a young soul doomed to make many errors. Daniel's moon (home affairs) is located in the sign of Aquarius (eccentric) bringing air (Aquarius is an air sign) to the impatient Aries fire sign. To make the situation worse he was born in the Chinese year of the Fire Dragon equivalent to a turbo charged Aries and this cocktail made him totally unique. He was young, innocent, and right in your face with not a single drop of social skills or "savoir faire". As all Aries, his lesson was to find himself and learn self-discipline. My stepfather is now 67 years old and much of the foul Aries fire has dissipated in his supremely active life.

My Wife and Son

As soon as I felt better I was requested to go back to work and help my stepfather, but after a terrible argument I found myself in the street. I wanted away from my village and all the dreadful memories anyway, I took a bag full of clothes and I hitch hiked down to the French Riviera where misery, I thought, would be better in the sun. The weather was nice and warm this July day and the truck driver dropped me in Saint Raphael, a gorgeous city in the French Riviera. I walked for a while towards the beach and finally made it to the beautiful seaside. I felt free and ready to take on the world and wondered how beautiful it would be for me to sleep on the warm sand at night. The beach was loaded with people and action was everywhere. I sat near the water and my grouchy stomach reminded me when and where I would eat that evening. Then coming out of the sea was the most beautiful girl I have ever seen and she sat just a few feet away from me. Little did I know than that this girl was going to be my wife and would bear my child.

I could not stop looking at her immaculate beauty and went straight for her. I am not exactly the shy type, blame it on my Aries Dragon's Head, and soon we felt like if we knew each other forever. I lost myself in her magnetic piercing blue eyes (a dead give away of a dramatic moon in Scorpio!) and felt like an angel in her presence. We spoke for hours and while explaining my deplorable situation she begged me to go back home with her. She told me her father would be able to help me to find a job and that I should not stay outside all night long. Being very independent by nature I did not want to infringe or create trouble with her parents and politely refused, but I asked her if I could see her again the next day. She insisted telling me it would be all right for me to go home with her but I promised that I would if she first talks to her parents.

I was really hoping to see her the next day not only because she was absolutely gorgeous but also because she could save me a lot of trouble and help me to start my new life. I could not help myself and French kissed her passionately right there on the beach. She responded to me with the same passion begging me come back at the same time at the same place the next day.

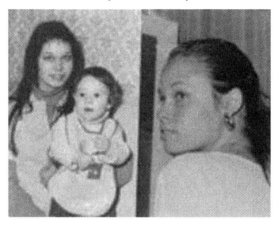

Marilyse and my son Remy

The Law of Hope

* In this case the "**Law of Hope**" worked its magic with me mostly because I was seriously afraid about being homeless. Powerful emotions always stimulate and accelerate any development involving this particular law and the amount of thoughts fuelled by fear produced fast results. This proves that the "Law of Attraction" can be stimulated in one's favor with negativity or staggering fear. You have heard of such cases as a 125-pound mother lifting a 1,500 pound car with one arm to reach for her toddler who accidentally rolled under it. The extreme fear (or extreme love for her child) infused a tremendous amount of supremely powerful emotion which was needed to "unshackle" the colossal energy used to produce the "miracle".

I watched her walk away until she disappeared behind a building across the street. As I walked away I felt like if I was flying. My heart was pounding, my mind was on fire and my feet did not touch the ground, for the first time in my life I was experiencing love. I was looking for a remote area not too far away from our meeting place, exhausted and starving, but very happy; I fell asleep on the sand. Sadly enough for me, I found the hard way that it is against the law to sleep on the beach in that city. At about midnight, the patrolling police woke me up and dragged me to the local jail. Damn I thought I experienced such highs and lows in such a short time and my first experience in jail was terrifying. The police asked me many questions wanting to know why I was homeless and where my parents were. I was only 16- years old but regardless of my young age, the rigorous law had to be enforced and respected.

At about 8.00 AM they finally let me go advising me to stay clear of the beaches or being jailed again for a full 24 hours. I cold not wait to see Marilyse again hoping for some food and shelter. I walked the city streets for many hours patiently waiting for my savior. Finally it was time for us to meet again and I was desperately hoping to see her for many good reasons. I made my way to the beach location and here she was anxiously waiting for me. I could not believe my luck when she asked me to go back with her right away and meet her mother. I grasped her hand and let her guide me to her parents' home. Her mother had a beautiful caring heart (Pisces) and she indeed was to be for many years to come the most loving and thoughtful soul I could ever hope for. Her father gave me a job right away helping him delivering wine to many hotels and restaurants all over the city and I became a part of the family. Finally Marilyse got pregnant and we got married before the birth of my son Remy. Unfortunately we were both much too young and a year later we were separated.

Marilyse's moon (emotions/home/family life) in Scorpio (drama/death) as imposed by the universe played a serious part to the break-up. I was working as hard as I could while she was taking care of our child but her extreme beauty made it practically impossible for any man to behave decently with her and one day she simply had an affair with our young married neighbor. I was devastated and my entire world felt apart. Note also that Marilyse was born with a Dragon's Trail (inauspicious) in the sign of Cancer (home/family) and depicts serious drama in all affairs involving the family nucleus. Marilyse was the daughter of a prostitute and her great stepmother and stepfather could not handle her supremely emotional nature and deadly sarcasm. She finally asked me to live the "domicile Conjugal" so the French government would entirely take care of her and my son.

There is nothing I could say or do to change her mind and I was much too proud to cry a river of tears in front of her. I did not know how to react, I felt cheated, guilty, and totally lost in my despair. My mother in law was appalled and begged her so many times to think of our child, without results. She was very stubborn and I told her when I left that she was as beautiful outside as she was ugly inside and that was the only way I could express my anger to her. I was scared to death to be separated from my baby son but she promised me unlimited visitations and she meant it, but she did not know that her next possessive partner would not allow me near her or my son. I was caught in a terrible situation and ripped apart inside. One side of me wanted to stay and fight for my son and the other side gave up, as I knew she would never love me the way she did when we first met. I searched frantically in my mind to find a decent solution for all of us but I knew I was going to lose this battle. I was wild and also I knew if anything would happen to her or my son because of her new partner, I would get into serious trouble. Over the years Marilyse married five times and gave birth to 4 girls after my son. It wasn't until many years later that I realized Marilyse was born with a moon (children) in Scorpio (death) and a Dragon's Tail (negative) in Cancer (family). My own son Remy was born with a Dragon's Tail (nefarious) in Leo (children/ love) and suffered the many changes tremendously as a child. The last time I saw Marilyse I told her, "I wish I was thousands of miles away from you right now and I am so sorry for my son and I". She replied, "Hurry, take your suitcase and leave now!" I have never seen her since then.

I kissed my son for the last time and with tears running down my face I left our small apartment. I went to her parents' residence next door to say goodbye, they were as upset and distressed as I and could only accept their daughter's unwise decision. A few hours later I found myself totally desperate and completely drunk in the local bar thinking about my mother's words. "Louis" she said, "I will not come to your wedding, it's a waste of time, both of you are much too young to get married. This relationship won't last a year!" And she was right!

I slept in my car that night and drove to Saint Tropez the next day hoping to find a job. The summer was in full force and I found a live-in position as a waiter in one of the numerous restaurants right on the beach. I worked really hard trying to heal a massive broken heart and forget about my baby son I was forced to leave behind. Walking all day long bear foot on the burning sand to serve a never-ending amount of thirty clients was quite painful on my calves. But I enjoyed the diversity of absolutely gorgeous young women tanning on the beach. I wished so hard to find a pretty girl that would take care of my wounded heart and if at all possible, one who was financially secure. As always, under such stress, my intense emotions turned my thoughts into a laser beam and "The Law of Attraction" brought my wish in a very unusual way.

Moving Away

One of my regular clients was a gorgeous girl from Switzerland and I had set my eyes on her. It was totally forbidden by the management to "hit" on any girls while working, but I decided to take a chance on her. While ordering a regular cocktail I asked her name and if she wanted to visit the area with me. "Do you know I could get you fired for asking me out on the job?" she said. "Of course I know, but you are so irresistible and worth anything that could happen to me, even losing my job." I replied. "You are quite gutsy and I like it," she added smiling. "Well there is a lovely old castle not too far from here and I am sure you would love to see it close Gina," I added. I waited for another positive sign to continue luring her into my world. And it came when she asked me for my name. I proceeded immediately by saying, "Would you meet me after work around 9.00 PM at the 'Orangutan', Gina?" I asked.

"We'll see, maybe," she answered with a striking smile. For a minute I was able to forget all the drama I was going through, I was inspired by the chase and she came at the right time and at the right place I thought. She must have liked my dare devil attitude and that was a good start I wondered. It was because of her noticeable beauty and being a regular that everyone in the restaurant knew about Gina. I was very excited and back in the kitchen I announced to the guys my plan to take her out. Bets were going between myself and all the other servers to see if I was going to "score" her that evening and win the grand prize.

I could not wait for my workday to end and finally after a shower and a set of fresh clothes, I went to the local bar. Everyone was there and loud laughs were thrown at me like flying bullets. 9:35 PM and still no sign of Gina... All of a sudden I heard the sound of a powerful car and a door slamming. I did not want to turn my head and look stupid as all the guys were still laughing and joking at me. I really thought that girl liked me; damn what are the chances for her to come and meet me I thought? Then I heard the sound of high heals coming towards me, I did not want to be disappointed or laughed at and kept my nose (and my ego) safe in my beer. For some reason everything seemed to be stopped, not single noise in the bar, like if everyone were looking at something unusual or extraordinary. Then to my astonishment, there she was, standing next to me. She was dressed all in black, (my favorite color) and I never saw her wearing any make up before. I nearly fell on my butt when I heard this gorgeous girl saying, "Hey Louis, are you going to buy me a drink or what?"

"You bet Hun, but not here, lets go somewhere else." I added.

I knew the owner of the restaurant may show up at any moment now and I wanted to keep my only source of income. As we both walked away my feet did not touch the ground and I felt like pointing my finger as high towards the suckers that doubted my masculinity and "savoir faire" with women. Even tough I was married for a year I did not allow myself to believe I was much too "rusted" to pick up a pretty girl easily.

To my surprise she threw the key of her bran new red convertible Porsche asking me to drive. I was exhilarated because driving a Porsche was always a dream of mine. She asked me to go take her to a high-class hotel restaurant equivalent to the Hilton or Hyatt, just around the corner. I was seriously worried because in no way could I afford to pay for the luxurious life style she was used to. She felt my uneasiness and said "Don't worry Louis, this is where I stay, and I'll put the bill on my room." "Thank you Gina. It's going to feel real good to be served for a change." I added smiling. I was relieved and only my ego was hurt. We had a fantastic romantic candle light diner and the most exquisite French wine and food I had for a very long time. We spoke for hours into the night and found out that she was on holiday and on her way to visit Rome in Italy, she decided to stop in Saint Tropez for a week. " Hey, what about this castle Louis, are you going to take me there? She said all excited. " Hell yea Baby, you bet, let's go now" I replied. The castle in question was only 10 minutes walk away and I thought the fresh air would do us real good after a bottle of wine and a couple of shots. I wanted to kiss her so bad but I wanted to keep that imploring sensual feeling alive a little longer. A few minutes later we arrived at the gates and a menacing sign reading (beware of dog) spoiled the moment. I was much too drunk to think clearly and in spite of her warnings I decided to take a chance.

"Let's go back," she said worrying," The dog will bite us if we pass this gate she added. "Come on Baby, do you see any dog here?" I answered. "This sign is there just to scare people away, its safe, let's go in." I said. She reluctantly followed me inside the private property and kept advising me to turn back. I took her hand and kept walking and talking about the gorgeous view we would enjoy once up there. Then all of a sudden I heard the barking of a dog and saw him in the darkness rushing in our direction. The animal was huge and ferocious and like any German Shepherd, very dangerous in their territory. Damn I thought, now I am in serious trouble but in no way will I let this dog hurt Gina. I screamed, "Gina don't move, don't run, stay there!" I instinctively placed myself right in front of her between the animal and I. If anyone will get hurt it is me I thought, because I put us in that stupid situation. The adrenaline shot all over my body and I was waiting for the dog to launch and totally ready to battle with him. Luckily for me he stopped right in his track wondering why I would not run away like anyone else would. Doing so saved my butt from serious injuries, blame it on my instinct or audacity or stupidity but it worked.

The dog was sitting right in front of me growling loudly and his intention was clear - not a step forward or pay the dolorous price… I was staring at him and gently said "Its OK boy, I am sorry, we will leave right now, I am sorry this is your home and I we mean no harm to your family." Using the same tone of voice I moved backwards watching the mighty dog, saying to my frozen new friend. "OK Hun, What ever you do, don't run, don't be afraid, I've got it all under control!" Then to my own astonishment I heard her "passing her water". She was in such a state of shock she simply lost total control of her bodily functions.

Damn, I wanted to impress her but not that way I thought. My priority was to turn back and get out of the private property as soon as possible and without any harm to any of us. I gentry grabbed her hand and we both walked away. I kept talking to her trying to cover the warning growls of our hazardous "escort".

The dog followed our footsteps all the way back to the gates and sat right there to make sure we would get his message and exit his territory which we happily did. As soon as we were safe she screamed her head off and released both her feelings and frustration at me.

"You son of a bitch, she said you nearly got us killed, I can't believe we made it out without a scratch." she kept venting adding, "I have never been so scared in my entire life and never seen someone so courageous, you are really crazy" she added.

I was apologetic but I also knew that she admired my bravery protecting her and I thought I might still have a chance with her. "I've had enough emotion for one night, let's go to my hotel right now!" she added.

She was much too upset to drive and I knew it, then I asked her. " Hun, so I blew it, did I? I have lost you and my job too? Damn, I am so sorry!" I kept saying.

"What are you talking about?" she said, "You are coming with me and I am taking you with me to Italy, after all this is the memorable holiday I ever had and god knows what's next with you" she added laughingly. It was my turn to be shocked; I guess Scorpio girls do like, drama, brushes with danger, and bold guys I thought. I spent a memorable first night with this superbly attractive girl making passionate love to her.

The next day, after collecting my belongings in my small room, I walked proudly in the restaurant saying goodbye to all "my friends" and the stupefied owners. We spent the next couple of weeks in total romance and when I needed it most she helped me starting a new section of my life. I still desperately missed my son and a few weeks later when she asked me to move to Switzerland with her I explained that I could not yet get away from my son. Being an emotional sensitive woman she understood me, she also told me she would wait for me for as long as I needed. But as life's plan unfolded, this gorgeous lady and I were not to remain together.

* In this case through "The Law of Celestial Attraction", my prayers were entirely and swiftly answered. I wanted love, I needed to forget my deplorable emotional situation and I wanted a wealthy girl. But why did "The Law of Attraction" worked so fast for me? First Gina was a Scorpio and the seat of attraction between human being is in the fifth house. The twelve specific areas of the human experience reside in those houses and respective laws. The fifth house is the area of love, romance, creativity and children. Thus a water sign such as Scorpio will attract its element or another water sign such as Pisces (me) or Cancer. If you are a fire sign such as Leo, Aries or Sagittarius you will attract this element and the same apply for all earth signs such as Virgo, Taurus or Capricorn. Be aware that the attraction can also be coming from your seven house of marriage or being karmic in nature The seat of Attraction could also be hidden and operates from your rising, your Dragon's Head and Tail or even your hidden Dragon. Your subconscious can also bring your astrological partner so you can learn "The Law Of Opposites" and all the strengths or weaknesses of this particular sign or a spouse. Science and common unaware people would classify this attraction to a form of "chemistry" but there are so many other interacting laws in action. Combined with the creative forces of your subconscious "miracles can and do happen" and education is the only way to build solid cosmic consciousness and make a good use of any of those laws speedily. Please realize that this book is not designed to teach you the complexity of the universal structure, but to make you aware of a multitude of crucial universal laws interacting with the law of attraction. Only a full course in Astropsychology will bring solid cosmic consciousness.

—

The Table of Celestial Attraction

This Law is astrologically based. Aries attracts Leo, while Leo attracts Sagittarius, and a Sagittarius will attract Aries, etc.

The Law of Celestial Attraction
5th House Attraction:
House of Love and Romance-Count five from April (include April) or;
April (Aries) attracts August (Leo)
May (Taurus) attracts September (Virgo)
June (Gemini) attracts October (Libra)
July (Cancer) attracts November (Scorpio)
August (Leo) attracts December (Sagittarius)
September (Virgo) attracts January (Capricorn)
October (Libra) attracts February (Aquarius)
November (Scorpio) attracts March (Pisces)
December (Sagittarius) attracts April (Aries)
January (Capricorn) attracts May (Taurus)
February (Aquarius) attracts June (Gemini)
March (Pisces) attracts July (Cancer)
Et Voila! How "The Law Of Attraction" really works.
7th House Attraction:
House of Partners and Contracts-Count five from April (include April) or;
April (Aries) attracts October (Libra)
May (Taurus) attracts November (Scorpio)
June (Gemini) attracts December (Sagittarius)
July (Cancer) attracts January (Capricorn)
August (Leo) attracts February (Aquarius)
September (Virgo) attracts March (Pisces)
October (Libra) attracts April (Aries)
November (Scorpio) attracts May (Taurus)
December (Sagittarius) attracts June (Gemini)
January (Capricorn) attracts July (Cancer)
February (Aquarius) attracts August (Leo)
March (Pisces) attracts September (Virgo)

A Scorpio Lesson

The time spent traveling with Gina was phenomenal, but I was about to learn more about the explosive temper of Scorpio. Back in Switzerland, she introduced me to her very wealthy family and much of my time was spent playing her grand piano and taking more pleasure from a very luscious life. Gina's mansion like home was perched on top of a mountain and we had full view of the "Leman" lake. But after three months of facing the high snowy Alp Mountains, I felt like flying above them and going back home to a warmer climate. The thought of hugging my son was a perpetual wish and he often came in my dreams. I honestly approached Gina and told her I could not stay any longer with her and that I decided to move back home. A big mistake, indeed...

Her beautiful face turned red and distorted by her powerful emotions. "I knew it, I was waiting for that day!" she said angrily, "and what about me, my feelings for you? You nearly had me killed, you were homeless, I helped you, I trusted you and now you wanna leave me?" she raged. "You son a bitch, if you think you can hurt me and get away with it, you better think twice!" she screamed. I never saw her behave that way, cursing me like no one ever did before. Then to my surprise, she reached for the heaviest pan she could grab in the kitchen and launched in my direction while shouting obscenities. I literally ran for my life trying to avoid every flying kitchen utensil that was thrown at me.

She kept running after me in the snow, until I was able to put a safe distance from her. Damn, I thought, I would rather face another mad dog, than to try reasoning with that crazy woman. I did not have time to get any of my belongings, not even my wallet, and I wisely decided to hitchhike back home, than to face her one more time. I had my first experience with the depth and the passion included in the dramatic life of a Scorpio and speaking by experiences, this is indeed the best way to learn the strengths and weaknesses of all astrological signs.

Contrary to what modern astrology teaches, Scorpio (death/rebirth) has no problem with letting go of anyone or anything, but it is the Universal Law, regulating the seventh house (marriage/partners) located in the possessive sign of Taurus (ownership) that provokes this "you are mine" attitude. My book 'And God Created The Stars" will shed some valuable light onto the twelve other specific departments of all signs depicting one's behavior in all aspects of life.

The Law of Celestial Opposites

7th House Polarities:
7th House - How one Presents Oneself to the World

Aries (April) presents itself to the world as a Libra (October)

Taurus (May) presents itself to the world as a Scorpio (November)

Gemini (June) presents itself to the world as a Sagittarius (December)

Cancer (July) presents itself to the world as a Capricorn (January)

Leo (August) presents itself to the world as an Aquarius (February)

Virgo (September) presents itself to the world as a Pisces (March)

Libra (October) presents itself to the world as an Aries (April)

Scorpio (November) presents itself to the world as a Taurus (May)

Sagittarius (December) presents itself to the world as a Gemini (June)

Capricorn (January) presents itself to the world as a Cancer (July)

Aquarius (February) presents itself to the world as a Leo (August)

Pisces (March) presents itself to the world as a Virgo (September)

A Death Wish Manifests

Both the summer and my relationship with Gina ended and I anticipated seeing my son, friends, and family. My first thoughts were for my son, but unhappily, Marilyse had moved away without letting anyone, not even her mother, know where she was. I was in despair and realized she was probably in a new relationship and wanted to stay clear from me. There was nothing that I could do but to sympathize with a sad mother in law. I tried for a few days to locate her and my son, without any success. I then decided to go back to Pont Saint Esprit and reconnect with my loved ones. My mother was very happy to see me back home, but I decided to stay with a friend away from my turbulent stepfather. I found myself a job in construction and after many hours operating a fifty tons bulldozer, I joined a local band. I always wanted to be a musician and "The Law Of Attraction" once more worked for me, when I read the advertisement on the local paper.

Since I was a child, my guitar was always my best friend and I wrote many songs to release my broken heart and with time on my side, I learned to play. This guitar was my father's only legacy and I cherished it so much, but I had purposely left it behind with Marilyse, so that she could sell it and use the money for my son. My stepfather is a phenomenal harmonica player and while he was away, I "borrowed" it and learned to play. Later on in life, against all odds, at the age of 26-years old, while residing in the UK, I mastered piano playing and graduated from the Royal School Of Music with high distinction marks, in front of four hundred other competitive students.

Note that I was born with a Dragon's Head in Aries (luck in all matters involving fire, danger, machinery, construction) and I was lucky enough to be trained by the government as a heavy equipment operator and after six moths at the PFA (Professional Formation Accelerated) I also became a highly qualified "ASME section nine" welder. Aries also rules Germany and many years later, I was picked between hundreds of applicants and sent there to work in a nuclear (Aquarius) cooling system station. The same applied for music, my Dragon's Tail in Libra is ruled by Venus (the Goddess of love and the art) and depicts my natural musical ability.

A few days passed and I saw my old friend Jacques. He and I were friends for many years. I knew him as a lucky, happy kind of guy. We both spent great times having fun with all that life offers teenagers and young girls were an important part of our existence. None of us took the vulnerable hearts of those young darlings seriously and many of the "prey" suffered serious heartaches. Then came the day when Jacques got caught in the game of love. Jacques and I had a strong relationship and we spent quite a lot of time together trying to make up for the lost time away from each other, but since he met the girl of his dreams, he began to spend less and less time with the guys. One day, as I was parking my car, at the "La Bourse" cafe, I saw him inside. The small cafe was the "Rendezvous point" for all of us to talk about everything from cars, bikes, sports, and music and of course girls and to hang out with the boys.

I happily walked to his table; sat down and ordered a pastis (we French are crazy about this aperitif!). "Hey Jacques, you've been with the same girl for a while now, what's going on man?" I asked.
He looked embarrassed for a moment, and then he answered, "Hi Louis, it's a long time no see man, yeah, I'm still with her but we've got problems". He paused for a while, sipping on his beer and then added "She's pregnant; I don't know what the hell to do!"

 "You're joking aren't you? Man you're only 18, don't make the same mistake I did, she is too young, she won't stay." I added. "She's gonna break your heart man and take your baby away, there is plenty of girls out there, come on!" I was unleashing my own fears and frustration on him, but I learned later in life, that in the fight between emotion and rationale, emotion usually wins.

He looked up at me and I could see his powerful emotion building up in his eyes. Just a bit late, I realized my mistake and my honest comments brought the worst out in him. I also noticed a few empty beer bottles on the table indicating that

Jacques had also a few drinks before I sat with him.

"No!" he yelled. The problem is that this relationship is not happening the way I wanted! Do you understand? It's not happening?" I love that girl man; if I can't be with her, I'd rather die!"

He then composed himself, tossed a few Francs on the table and to my surprise, simply walked out on me. Jacques never behaved this way with me before; I was in a state of shock. To my disappointment, I realized a side of him I had never dealt with before. He was in some ways like me, surprisingly choleric, bullheaded even destructive when faced with opposition. I felt guilty for my lack of "savoir faire" but Jacques never gave me a chance to either apologize or provide some support. At distance, other friends were watching from the corner of their eyes, they promptly took my side and blamed his reaction was because of the beer.

Later on, I called Jacques, but he never returned any of my calls. I then realized how I felt when Marilyse "dropped" me. I also realized the depth of his trouble, hoping for a solution that I could never be able to offer him. A few weeks later, here he was at the same place, at the same table, and drinking the same beers. This time I kept a safe distance between his destructive temper and myself. Then to my surprise, he called my name and asked me to sit next to him.

"Please Louis, forgive me," he said, "We are good friends, I really need you to help me man." Knowing that I would never be able to help me, reluctantly I sat myself in front of him, trying to avoid his stinking smoky and drinking breath.

"So what's up, buddy?" I said. He tossed his head back in mock exasperation and took another zip from the beer bottle. I noticed his dirty hair and felt sorry for his exhausted, drunken face.

"I don't come here as much, I stay home all the time, crying for her return." he said. How can only a few weeks make such a significant difference in one's life, I thought. Maybe my escapade with Gina in Italy had saved my sorry butt from more trouble than I thought.

"Well, I know man, been there done that, life's a bitch you know!" I answered.

"So, what about you Louis, life treats you good?" He asked.

"It surely does, buddy, I am having fun with the girls and with my music" I said.

"Are you into music?" he surprisingly said.

"I've always been into music, you know that!" I said wondering.

"The only thing I remember about you and music is when you were learning your dad's mouth organ on the way to school," he said jokingly. This remark brought back sweet memories from our close childhood. We both went right back to the cheerful friendship's lost feeling and some of our most memorable adventures. I felt terrible, but I also knew from the bottom of my gut that Jacques was not going to be alive for very long.

"Tell me Jacques," I asked, "What happened to you the last time we met at 'La bourse'?"

"I knew you were going to ask me about that" he said. There was a short silence, then he answered. "Well, I had to deal with a lot of stress, I apologize Louis." He kept going on, "I thought I had a problem then with her pregnancy, nothing compares to what has went wrong since then."

"So Jacques" I courageously said, "what's really going on with you?"

For a moment he collected his confused thoughts then blankly said, "I had it Louis, I want to die, I can't be without her and my kid. She left me for someone else and I can't be in this world without her" he said. I quickly realized that his world had crashed with the loss of his wife and his child and my premonition about his death, sacred the hell out of me. Like so many of us, he was a victim of love and indeed totally emotionally destroyed inside. A long and painful challenge was ahead of him and I knew, right then I had something to do and I had to do it fast. His surrender to alcohol was opening the door to depressions; a serious signal that time was running out. By now, big tears were running down his face, I felt helpless and so bad for my old friend. He gave me an intriguing look and again, reasserted.

"I want to die, you know me well Louis," he continued, "I mean business, I've had enough."

I felt powerless, no matter how much I tried to take him out of his deep depressing mood. The last couple of months had brought him serious stress, continuous depressions and his drinking got totally out of hand. The destructive thought process would finally get the best of him within the next few days. He left the cafe in a state of despair, refusing any help, whatsoever. I had never felt so powerless and dumfounded in my entire life, but I had to get on with my own existence. For the next few days I had to try hard to forget his desperate world and I began to nurture an unhealthy fear for the safety of his life.

Only a week later to my horrifying surprise, I heard that Jacques had been killed in an auto accident. That dramatic night, while taking a sharp turn, the right back tire blew up, and then the car went out of control, then hit a wall and overturned, killing him instantly. The driver was a good friend of Jacques and persuaded him to go with him to a birthday party. The conductor and three young girls traveling in the back seat of the car miraculously escaped serious injury. Incidentally, apart from Jacques, all the occupants were ejected more than twenty feet from the overturned automobile. Both the driver and Jacques did not wear their seat belts. The driver suffered only a broken arm while a direct blow to the head had killed Jacques instantly.

Later on, another troubled close friend working with the emergency care unit in the ambulance told me that the three young women were hysterical. On the way to the local hospital, the girls who involved in the drama, kept breaking down saying; "Jacques wanted to die, everywhere we went, he was saying to everyone that he wanted to die, he couldn't live without his wife and children!" Per his wish, he died, good-bye Jacques, may God bless your soul!

The Law of Verbal Affirmation

*This illustrates the **Law of Verbal Affirmation**. Jacques' constant negative affirmation became death wish directed to his indifferent subconscious. The terrible innocent and unintentional "mental participation" entangling all of us results in "The Law Of Attraction." At its worst manifestation it accelerated his death. Like my innocent friends, I am also a direct participant on the "making" of his fatality since that very moment I began to nurture a strong fear for his life. Jacques was born in October with the Dragon's Tail (negative) in Libra (on himself). Libra rules marriages; contracts, commitments and the cosmic "Law of Opposites." Combined with "The Law of Negativity" this brought him the wrong partner and his ultimately his demise. "For every action either physical or spiritual there will be a reaction". The memorandum is unconditional and has disclosed this sad experience.

A few weeks later, I was to experience the danger of being at the mercy of another driver's inexperience and would think to myself that I must be a very lucky man, having lived to tell about it.

I was performing with my band in another village just a few miles away from my town, and my old car was much too unreliable to take the short trip. A few friends following the band and I got the ride from Eric. I played and sang all night long, until finally the last resilient drunks headed home. I packed the van hoping to catch a ride with the rest of the band, but no room for two other players and me. We started walking, hoping to catch a lone driver on the way back home. It was freezing cold and the rain was already pounding us, we were young, innocent, and tough and no rain or distance would stop us from walking.

That's me second to the right, around 1968.

More Negative Fear

A car came in our direction and we simply turned around and walked towards it right in the middle of the road. Imagine that, we could have been killed right there on the spot, had the driver been totally impaired, but we were so innocent and never thought of anything other than to catch the drive. Luckily for us, it was Eric driving back home with two other friends. As he rolled down his window, I smelled a strong alcohol odor on his breath and his screams of joy and jokes made it obvious that he was well past his ability to operate a car. I was exhausted and I wanted to go home as soon as possible and the city was just three miles away. What could happen to us in such a short distance, I thought?

We hastily jumped in the car and sat right in between Eric and Michael, while Henry and Gerard jumped in the back with Paul. The old 403 Peugeot dragged herself with this precious cargo of six young lives, all in the drunken hands of Eric. Then Eric shouted, "Hey guys let's run over some rabbits *"a la Barandole."* This wooded mountainous area is about twenty miles North of the city and loaded with wild life. Whoops I thought, here comes trouble, as Eric turned the car around, not without hitting a telephone post. This "accident" was an omen for the more serious things to come, but at this age, I did not know the importance of giving attention to any little "things" or that my subconscious that was trying hard to communicate with me. We made it to the location by pure miracle; the tortuous road made each sharp bend a death trap. A few times I screamed, "Come on Eric man, slow down buddy, you're gonna kill us!" But Eric was out of his mind, drunk as a skunk and he never listened or heeded to any of my pleas for him to slow down.

"Hey, relax pussy, I know how to drive!" he answered, excited by the ripping sound of the tires grasping the road. I also knew, that it was only a matter of time before we hit something and then, all of a sudden; he lost control of the car and driving full force, we hit the thick wall of a concrete bridge. The weight and speed of the car crashed into the wall and we went through it, plunging down thirty feet into the river. Falling felt like an eternity. It was total darkness and everything was moving slowly. I heard the sound of cracking branches, then a big splash, and next realized that I was under water. The car and occupants was propelled onto the tree tops and this lucky break cushioned the fall onto the sandy bank of the river. The front end of the car was under water and the back was on the shore. No one wore seatbelts and this in fact saved our lives, as nothing entangled us under the water. I immediately helped my friends gasping for air. I saw flames breaking the darkness from the broken back window. I assessed the dangerous situation immediately and I did not want to die in fire or water. The car was upside down but I managed to get past the seats and crawled towards the back of the car. Henry was crying and that was a good sign I thought, but both Gerard and Paul were unconscious.

I literally ran over their bodies and made it out of the car, then immediately took my leather jacket and fought the flames. The gas tank had cracked on impact and stopping the burning fuel was my priority. The thick smoke was also getting inside of the car and I was terrified, thinking of the possibility of an explosion. After a few minutes, I managed to stop the flames and I began pulling my friends to safety. Henry was the first one out and suffered a broken clavicle and could not help me in my rescue efforts. I ordered him to go by the bridge wall and sit there; I was under the tree canopy and could barely see my environment. For some miraculous reason, one break light was still on and I am sure the outcome would have been very different without it. The adrenaline pumped hard in my body and gave me the strength needed to help them out of trouble. I wanted Eric and Michael out first, for fear of the car sliding into the river's cold water.

I then focused my attention towards Gerard and Paul and both were still unconscious. I knew they had serious damage to their neck and head, but I had to move them and doing so might paralyze or even kill them. Keeping a cool head in such a dramatic situation is very difficult and I could not get any help from anyone, because I was the only one who escaped with minor injuries. I took all the precautions in the world and dragged them out of the car and tried to resuscitate them, but they were deeply comatose. I knew I had to find help really fast, if my friends were to survive the unfortunate ordeal.

I turned around and said, "OK guys, I am going to look for help! I had no freaking clue of where we were at and its dark everywhere in the woods, so I don't know when I will be back, but I will do my best!" I added. I carefully walked along the bridge, trying to find a way to go back to the road above, but the underbrush was much too dense. I decided to climb up the mossy wall of the bridge and after a few falls, I finally made it to the top. I had no sense of direction and started to jog in the darkness, but after five minutes or so of running, I fell on the ground, trying hard to catch my breath. Damn I thought, I am not running that fast, why am I out of breath already? I blamed it on the shock that I had and after catching my breath, I thought of resolving my problem, by walking normally.

While walking, I was throwing up and felt something hot and tasty coming out of my mouth. Little did I know, that it was my own blood coming out of my lungs, but I could not see the bloody red in the dark, that was left on my hand each time I wiped my mouth clean. I kept tumbling and walking for hours in the darkest night ever, but the thought of my injured friends awaiting me, launched a new wave of badly needed adrenaline in my system and I kept moving. I finally heard the far away barking of a dog and this meant that a farm was not too far away. I certainly did not want to face a mad dog again, but I could only remember what to do from my previous perilous experience. Finally, I saw the shadow of a farm roof in the moonless night and jumped upon a tree, knowing the loud barking of the dog would bring the farmer, sooner or later. Armed with a powerful flashlight and a menacing shotgun, he shouted, " Hey, what the hell are you doing here in my tree?"

"Please, please, Monsieur", gasping for air, I screamed to the top of what was left of my lungs, "don't shoot, we had an accident in the forest, my friends are seriously injured and I need your help".

His face was horrified, when the flashlight uncovered my bloody clothing. "Oh my God!" He blurted out, "Come down boy, hurry! Let's call *"les pompiers et les gendarmes"* now!

I was terribly thirsty and his gentle wife gave me some water telling me, "Its all right now, the ambulance is on its way and they are keeping an eye for the broken bridge, where your friends will be rescued soon." I was finally allowing myself to relax and wondered about my own injuries. We ended up in the emergency room and luckily for all us, there were no fatalities. My friends shared broken clavicles, broken necks, broken arms and legs, and concussions. Thankfully, we were back to health a few weeks later. In my case, when the car crashed, I was squeezed between Eric and Michael and the compression was so severe, that it blew up a few veins in my lungs. The entire commotion could have led me to bleed to death or worse yet, to suffocate and drown in my own blood. Once more, I escaped with my life and pondered why I would attract this experience into my life? "The Law of Attraction" works from many levels. That night Eric "stole" his dad's car. Early in the evening, his concerned parents had generated a tremendous amount of negative thoughts. They called a few other people to vent their frustration. Meanwhile, Gerard, Paul and my own fearful disposition had added even more power, bringing the dramatic results to life. Add a serious dose of alcohol, and "The Law of Attraction" did the rest. The most important ingredient is Eric's own fear of a possible accident and that would make stealing the car known to his parents. Fear increases the emotion that stimulates "The Law of Attraction".

Only a few weeks later, I attracted *"a deja vue"* in a similar situation. Following this dramatic incident, I nurtured a fear of car accidents and I understand now, how important it is to "cleanse" oneself against any dormant phobia. That night I was singing and playing at "The Leader" discotheque with the band in another local town. Once more, my unreliable car was left at home and Alain gave me the ride I needed. The night went on and so did Alain with his liquor. I was much too busy performing, and then packing up gear with the band, to keep an eye on my drunken friend. Everyone had left the building and by the time I realized Alain was seriously impaired, we were already driving through town, well above the speed limit. NO way 'en encore' I thought. What have I done to attract these people? Our town was barely seven miles away and I knew Alain would not turn back from trying to run over unlucky rabbits. Instead, he drove past the city asking me to join him for a last drink in a club where he is a member. "Thanks bro, but I am exhausted, take me home Alain, I have some whiskey there, too." I said to lure him out of the dangerous situation we were in. Of course he turned me down, laughing saying some drunken girls will make it home with us, if we get there first.

I was terrified and my heart was pounding inside my chest. How unlucky would it be to die this way, knowing that I had escaped the same type of death only a few weeks ago, I wondered. My entire body was awaiting the shock, it's as if I already knew without a doubt, that we were about to crash. The thoughts and fears were so strong that I used all of my will to control myself from panic. I recall the long road was as straight as can be, for about two miles and the night was cold, but clear. The only things in sight were huge *"platanes"* trees planted by the Romans long ago, to provide shade for Cezar's invading army. Then at about 95 miles per hour, Alain began to look for a new radio station when the signal faded as we drove past the old bridge. In doing so, he also involuntarily turned the steering wheel towards a huge line of trees. The imposing tree trunks were flying by my window and I calmly asked him to focus on the road. My warning came too late and suddenly; I instinctively raised my left arm in front of my horrified face. One of those colossal trees was coming right at us, I heard a big explosion, and that was all. The next thing I recall I was standing up in the middle of a large crowd watching the scene of an accident. The rescue vehicles' bright yellow, blue, and red lights were lighting up the night, while firemen were busy cutting off the entangled doors of a car. Inside an unconscious man was waiting to be liberated from his death trap.

The traffic was stopped from both sides of the road and the police were busy keeping the curious away. Then a person looked at me and screamed, 'OH, MY GOD! Louis, you were in the car?'

I stared at him and responded, "Who is Louis and who are you?"

"Jesus!" he screamed, "It's Michael! It's me! Don't you recognize me?"

"Sorry, no. I don't remember anything, what happened here?" I asked.

"Louis, you were in the car with Alain and you came from "The Leader", you were there all night playing with your band!" he explained sadly..

"I don't know what the Leader is and I don't know you!" I insisted. The shock was so severe that I had lost memory of all that transpired before the accident.

Then my horrified friend screamed, "Help, help, Louis is covered with blood, he was in the car!"

At that very moment, I felt a crucifying pain coming from my left arm and the bone of my elbow could be seen through my tattered leather jacket. I was also bleeding profusely from a multitude of cuts on the head and face. My memory and feelings came back at the same time, along with the crucifying pain associated with my injuries. Shortly afterwards, I found myself inside the ambulance with Alain receiving emergency treatment. We spent a couple of weeks in the hospital and I was upset for a while with Alain's unwillingness to stop the car while we were ahead, but I could only forgive him, knowing he had learned a valuable lesson of not to drink and drive. His injuries were severe and took him months of arduous painful rehabilitation. It was the first time in my life, as if I was left as someone unconscious or more like a living zombie, with no identity or any form of memory. I really wanted to find out how and what really happened the night of the accident. I asked my brother Yves to drive me to the scene of the accident. The large scar left by the car on the tree was a sure reminder of the impact and exact location. I have full memory to the very moment we crashed the automobile; I also recall clearly that not a single car was on the road in this remote location.

Thus, quite a long time must have elapsed for the emergency service to arrive and for the police to stop the traffic, due to the wreckage sprayed all over the road.

Then I realized that I was ejected from the car and my elbow got fractured on the windshield when I instinctively protected my head just before the impact. As I walked slowly inspecting the bushy area, I saw a hole the size of my body. I realized, that I had flown through thick undergrowth planted purposely by landowners to cut off the mighty wind mistral. Being ejected and going through the branches had somehow saved me from serious injury as it cushioned my landing in the vineyard. The wall of growth is about ten feet wide and cut my entire body from head to toe. Incidentally, I also managed to land in between the sharp row of sticks used to support the *"vignes"*. Those sticks are set about three to four feet apart and the chances of being impelled are considerable. I realize once more, how lucky I was to miss both the big tree and any of the thousands of sticks in the large vineyard, but I was concerned with the missing time. I wanted to know how I made it to the road and how long I was turned into a zombie. There was no way for me to go right back through the thick bushes to get to the road and stand there alone. I am sure the first person that called for the police would have noticed me there, thus I was not there just yet. Yves and I talked and walked nearly one half mile to the first opening leading to the road situated on the right side of us and less than twenty feet away. This explains the elapsed time to make it back to the scene of the accident. The commotion and the light must have attracted my attention and I simply walked right back.

> * In this case **"The Law of Negativity"** worked swiftly against me because of the intensity of my fear. Indeed, adrenaline boosted those fears and convincingly enhanced the subconscious creative forces. Combined with a waning moon period (hazardous timing) cruising through the sign of Scorpio (death/drama/police) the perfect recipe for another disaster was to be expected. The **"Universal Law of the Moon"** (pg. 254) combined with Scorpio's own law is an intrinsic part of the collective expression of the **"Universal Code."**

Fate has it all

During those days I was working in construction but all I wanted was to be a singer and a musician. My family knew about my passion for music and in one of our hot around the table discussions, my older Scorpio brother Jo who at that time owned a thriving discothèque called *"L'interdit"* (the forbidden) bluntly said to me, "Hey, Lou, if you really want to do serious music, you'll have to do it the right way."

"What do you mean seriously, of course I am serious about it!" I answered annoyed by his comment.

"Well bro for your information, French music means nothing in the recording industry, only English music is commercial. That's all my DJ plays all night long." he added. I felt an intense feeling coming right from my solar plexus and I knew he was right. The chain of events that took place following this acknowledgement is simply phenomenal and depicts how "The Law of Attraction" really works. However, sitting there and hoping for the "miracle" to take place would have taken forever. Instead, I demanded for action and took a chance. The worst thing that anyone can do is to hope for opportunity but do nothing about it and that's not me. Born with a competitive Dragon's Head (enterprise) in the energetic sign of Aries (action) I could only act promptly upon my wishes.

I still missed my son terribly and decided to move back to Saint Raphael in the warmer south of France. I knew I would have no problem finding another job as the holiday season was about to start. Thousands of people from all over the world congregate to "The French Riviera" to enjoy the great food, a multitude of entertainment, and the warm turquoise waters of the Mediterranean Sea. My search for my ex-wife Marylise and my son Remy took me nowhere and I was very depressed about it. I really trusted her to behave as she promised me, but her Mother and I were to be disappointed for many years to come. I had two other very important wishes in my heart; one was to become a musician and the other to start a new life. I wanted to study music with all of my heart and the circumstance that would lead me from France to the Royal School of Music in London was quite extraordinary in nature. My passion for music combined with a constant flow of intense thoughts, activated "The Law of Attraction." The unfolding events were already set in motion and I was on my way to England just a few months later.

The local newspaper was loaded with advertisements and job opportunities. I needed a live-in position and the only way for me to do so was to work as a dishwasher in a holiday camp. The facility was full of English holiday-makers from Britain and neighboring European countries. The job was very boring, but it kept me going all summer long and my days off were used wastefully looking for Marilyse and my son Remy. My workmate Roland and I developed a strong friendship and together we would "hunt" the prettiest English girls. My job was demanding, as the burgeoning summer brought more tourists to the well-known facility. It was forbidden to mix with the pretty British girls, but at the risk of losing our jobs, Roland and I took many chances. I was quite perplexed by the sound of the English idiom. For the first time in my life I lost some of my high self-esteem remembering the English teacher's detrimental words. I wished so hard to be able to communicate in a foreign language and all I could do to be understood, was to make silly gestures. Finally my efforts paid off and I managed to connect with a young lady named Rose. She was as good in French as I was in English, but we had absolutely no problem with the universal French kiss language. I won her heart without speaking a single word of English and I was proud of my accomplishment. My friend Roland also managed to pick up a date and since that day, our common goal was drinking, dancing, swimming, and hunting more English girls.

Roland was a stalwart sex maniac, reflecting his intense "Scorpionic" precarious nature. One night after a few drinks, his aggressive nature took over and he started up a fight against three English guys. I could do nothing but to join him in the brawl. The girl's boyfriend had suggested Roland to stop courting her or pay the price. His "Scorpionic" magnetism was too much for the sensitive woman and she fell for his sensual spell. The next day management found out about his rumble and destructive temper and he was fired on the spot. He was devastated by what he called an injustice and promised that everyone will pay the price. Many years later I learned that revenge sounds like eating a sweet pie to a Scorpio and you better be ready for an "I'll be back" because they will.

---

* For your information, famous actor and Californian Governor Arnold Schwarzenegger was born with a Dragon's Tail in the sign of Scorpio (lust for power). Any time a Scorpio comes into your life be ready for drama and a form of life and death to take place in your near future. Like any true Scorpio, Roland was supremely emotional and totally impractical in the affairs of love. Remember "The Cosmic Law of Attraction" table where all Scorpios (power/ sex/drama) become Pisces (weakness/guilt/impractical) in their fifth house of love and romance.

Before leaving, Roland assured me that he would be back and we both agreed to travel to London to meet the girls. Little did I know about the Scorpio nature, and a few hours later I had completely forgotten about our deal. Sure enough a few weeks later, to my amazement and right on payday, he was waiting for me by the office with a big smile on his face. He was watching my reaction with his piercing dark eyes and asked me, "Hey Louis, are you ready? We're going to London buddy, you promised me; let's go get the tickets man." A large army bag was holding all his possessions. I had no one waiting for me; I had nowhere and no one to go to and just a few bucks in my pocket.

I made the decision right then, a resolution that changed my entire life and molded my destiny. I had a head full of dreams and I needed to learn English if I ever wanted to be a successful songwriter, I thought. I said to him, "Whoa! Man, you're full of surprises, am glad to see you all right; let's go for a drink first, I am really thirsty."

Happily Roland added, "Great, I know I can trust you, so I got your ticket. You can repay me anytime." I admired his planning gut and after ingesting a cool beer and waiting for the cab that took us to the train station, we both left the very evening for London. Later on in life, I find out that when you deal with a Scorpio, whatever you say or do will follow you for the rest of your life.

I never really left my natal France soil and the idea of living in another country appealed to me. I felt really good about my decision to venture away from home and another new experience, the ferry boat. The voyage across the English Channel with Roland transformed my entire life and opened the path to my remarkable destiny. Roland was a very important step thrown at me by "The Law of Attraction" so I could fulfill my mission to the world years later. Looking back at all the people that came into my life over the years, they all have acted as stepping-stones. That person performed for good or for worse in your life because you needed that vital lesson. This human being did not come to you by accident because there is no accidents per say. Your subconscious knows so much better than you could ever imagine and without this soul's interaction, you are simply stalling.

Some people will do great harm to you while others will love you unselfishly and all is set up by your subconscious to advance you. Thus, if you really want something or someone and you cannot get it, guess what? The power above knows better and you should not battle yourself mentally; instead, completely trust it. Regardless of positive or negative outcomes, each soul is a fateful progressive player that you subconsciously asked for until you learn something or raise your personal vibrations. The creative force of your subconscious always has a plan, and even if you can't conceive it just yet, the power above granted you, that individual. All is designed at the end to reach your deepest and most powerful wishes. Incidentally, some of your own desires are so buried in your subconscious that you do not even know what is best for you. In any case the Universal power and "The Law of Attraction are always at work and ready to answer you. This is why it is so very important for you to acknowledge that your future is nothing else than the reincarnation of your thoughts.

Roland's head was full of dreams and kept talking about "his" girl and how much he missed and loved her. He really anticipated the moment where he would hug that young girl again. "What do you think she'll say when she sees me again, Louis?" he asked.

"Hell, what do I know, maybe she'll kick your ass back home!" I said jokingly.

His face turned red and he gave me one of those Scorpio looks that goes right through the soul. He sat up straight in his chair and shouted. "Hey Lou, you know I feel for that girl, man, and I'll do whatever it takes to make her like me too!" Roland was like a sleeping volcano, very intense and I knew better than to play with his overwhelming emotions.

I thought for myself "whatever" and said, "You will see when you get there, but be cool if she's not interested anymore!" His face went red again and rejected my comment, but at times, I can't help but to be honest.

It was September 1972 and I barely accepted the fact that I was on my way to the UK. The air was still warm when we left the beautiful beaches of the French Riviera and the next day I had my first taste of the infamous cold and rainy English weather. A thick cover of clouds began to build as the ship sailed through the English Channel. I saw my country's coastline quickly fading away and I felt just a little worried about what was yet to come in London. The watery English Channel is an active treacherous, windy inhospitable drizzly place. Standing inside the warm erratic ship, the possibility to build an underwater tunnel speedway crossed my mind and became a reality many years later. The marvelous engineering achievement by both the French and the British workers is a good illustration of what countries working together can do. Over the fifteen years spent in England, I experienced many crossings of the English Channel (La Manche).

In the winter time the cold sea is often tumultuous and some seasick passengers were having the time of their life; it was quite a show to watch many faces turning green as they emptied their stomachs. I spent most of the time at the bar gulping beers and killing time talking with drunken pretty girls. Yes indeed, the English love to drink and I was only 22, happy, and full of life when I arrived in England. Back then I had no idea that I was to reside in this country for so many long years. I have incredible memories of my crazy life in England; I experienced my first true love and total despair, panic attacks, depressions, and met some incredible people. I also had the greatest high when I finally graduated from The Royal School of Music in 1976. My subconscious planned it all for me and each person played a crucial part in the building of my own destiny and life's mission. All along I was gaining experience on the different Laws of Life, and sometime later I would understand their workings in depth.

Part 2

England

Welcome United Kingdom

The sea was placid that September evening and the trip was great, I never ventured so far from home and the excitement of new adventures was growing after each nautical mile. Skillfully, the Captain accosted the huge ship in the harbor and we followed the crowd all the way to the nearby train station. We were getting closer to the largest city in the UK and Roland and I were ecstatic. Upon our arrival at the train station in London, the harsh reality hit me right on the face. We left France unprepared for the English weather, wearing only light summer clothing and the temperature had dropped drastically. The cold rain was poring relentlessly outside and I knew Victoria station was going to be our home for a while.

Victoria Station Inside

Thousands of people were rushing in and out of the noisy trains like crazy ants walking in all directions at the same time. Roland was lost and quite exasperated by the constant action all around him. Being in a foreign country surrounded by lots of people you cannot communicate with is very distressing The thought and words of my old teacher haunted me, but like a bad dream I canceled it out of my mind right away. Experiencing a foreign country in such a way is not exactly recommended for the weak-minded soul, I thought. I tasted some of the weirdest food and drinks accustomed to the British population alone. The British are indeed superior to many nations in producing staggering music, but indeed awful with food. At this point Roland and I realized the mess we were in and I could only milk my last reserve of faith. We were lost and I said to Roland.

Victoria Station Exterior

"Hey Roland, let's go to this bar out there and drink something hot." It was freezing cold that night and he gladly agreed to the suggestion. We fought our way to the counter through a long line of people and learned our first lesson. Unlike the French, English people are very disciplined and as in the US one must patiently wait for his turn to get served. Cold, wet, and starving we kept trying to skip to the front of the line, but were told off a few times by angry customers. We quickly learned the proper manner and I thought how much France needed this type of decency. For the first time in my life, I tasted the famous English hot tea and greasy continental breakfast. The food was simply terrible, but we were so ravenous and cold that anything hot would do for now. Roland had more difficulty than I to ingest the foreign food and regurgitated it all outside, soon afterwards. "Merde, man, this crap is terrible! How can the British eat eggs and oily sausages so early in the morning? I miss my hot croissants and my real strong black coffee, man!" he added. He was quite upset about the food experience, but this was only the beginning of a series of crisis that neither of us could ever have imagined. At least on the ferry we had a choice between French or English cuisine, but right here in the heart of London, in a small coffee shop in Victoria Station, no such luck. We both rapidly realized why the world recognized our reputation for good life, good wine, and good food.

We spent our first day walking aimlessly all over the station and our first sleepless night talking to each other. I waited for the morning with impatience, wondering how I would get out of this mess. At the crack of dawn, I decided to explore the part of the city we landed on. Roland was looking real tired and said. "Are we in hell or what Louis?"

"This is England, Roland, isn't that where you wanted to go?" I asked sarcastically. "We are here now, so we should make the most of it!" I added. I had only a few English pounds left in my pocket and I knew I could only survive with my last coins for only a couple of days. I knew I had to do something soon to get out of this clutter and I was not going to give up that easily. "Time for some walking man, are you coming or what?" I asked. But Roland seemed to be paralyzed and asked me if he could wait for me at the coffee shop. "OK" I said, "but don't go anywhere, we can't lose each other now." I shook my head cynically and wondered if Roland had the guts that it takes to deal with this situation. I also felt that he could become more of a drag than assistance to me, and time proved me right again.

Outside Victoria Station in London

For the first time I ventured out of the safe, noisy, and smoky Victoria station and got another cultural shock. I was staring at all those weird black London taxis wondering how they could coexist safely in such numbers. Smog certificates were not enforced those days in the UK and the automobiles were spitting thick fuel fumes all over. My eyes and my throat were so badly irritated that I could not stop coughing. The dark painting and weird shape of the taxis resembled big and ugly cockroaches dashing all about, but I really got to like the spacious inside many years later, when I took my first trip through London with my musicians. We drove to a recording studio with my British band and produced my first successful single.

England's Double Decker Buses

I was also particularly amazed, when I was able to afford my first ride on the notorious double-decked red English buses. Action was everywhere in the large city, the sun was missing and was not to be seen for a long time. I pondered for a moment if and how long I could stay in this English weather; away from the sea, the great food, and the sunny French Riviera. I took myself out of this mirage and because of my deplorable situation; going back home was out of the question. I resigned myself to the inhospitable, dirty, and noisy train station as the only available option. This situation was getting desperate for Roland, unlike me, he was raised by his very loving and caring grandmother and never had to undergo any serious treatment. I was used to the street life and sleeping on a hard and cold steel bench with an empty stomach. The few English coins left in my pocket were spent wisely on coffee and biscuits, while to my amazement he kept spending his very last pennies at the train station on French newspapers, checking for sport scores.

We were in a grim situation and I felt Roland's lack of concern and dependability on my valiant spirit. I wanted him to be more responsible for himself and help me to find a solution. After all, we were together in that deal and he should make as much effort as I did to find a solution, I thought. "Hey Roland are you looking for a job in France? We're here in London and in deep trouble man!" I said sarcastically.

"So, what the hell do you want me to do about it?" he said in his rich Marseille accent.

"Well, you could start by stop wasting your money on newspapers!" I added.

"I see." Roland said, reading my expression.

I wanted to save his feelings, but I knew that I had to be forceful with him. "You're throwing your money away, man! Checking football results won't feed you, that's stupid!" I replied.

Roland stepped towards me and grinned broadly. "It's my money and I'll do what I want with it." This immature attitude brought the worst out of me. I insisted, asking him to be more "practical" with the spending. Then I was literally blown away with frustration, something I should not have done with a temperamental Scorpio's dangerous nature. Roland was first surprised at my reaction but then calmly said, "I've got to find out what's going on at home, man! You known France versus England is a big football game!"

Then I really lost it and shouted, "Damn it, Roland! What the hell are you doing, man! Who gives a damn about the freaking football game in France! You can see this on TV, right here! Meantime, we are in deep doo-doo, miles away from home and here you are screwing around, wondering about a stupid game! I can't deal with that!" I gave him a good load of nasty attitude and threatened him by saying, "You better wake up or you're going to be dealing with your own ass real soon, Roland!"

He argued for a while, then words quickly changed into menacing gestures. The infamous Scorpionic sarcasm took over and he bluntly said. "It's your entire fault if we are in that ---mess! You could have said 'no' and we would not be here today!" What a lame excuse I thought, we were depressed and exhausted and no one could control the outcome of this deplorable situation.

The tension and frustration escalated to a dangerous level in our explosive quarrel. The loud screams began to attract the attention of curious people waiting for the violent show to start. The last thing I needed was to attract the police and end up in jail for disturbing the peace and I had to find a way to end our aggressive show. I worked hard on my own wild temper and at this point I knew I had to regain control over my emotions or risk injury or worse the police. One thing for sure, that in any other situation, I would never back away from a fight and we were very close to a disaster that evening.

"I guess I'd better leave now, Roland. I have better things to do than to smash your face in. Do what ever the hell you've got to do! You're on your own, buddy!" I shouted. I miraculously managed to control my Martian aggressive nature, avoiding what would have been a nasty bloody fight with Roland and I decided to split right away from him.

Search for Survival

Was Roland's purpose in my life done already? Did my subconscious bring him just for the purpose of leading me to London? So many questions were in my mind and it wasn't until many years later, that I finally understood and saw the picture as a whole. I knew I had to do something and I had to do it fast, to avoid getting deeper into the danger of homelessness. I once again faced the long busy streets outside of Victoria station, wondering what direction to take. As usual the weather was rough and windy and the never-ending English rain kept poring down on me. I had no money left; I was cold, wet, starving, and totally desperate. I did not have any warm clothing, not even a jacket or an umbrella to protect me against the weather and I was already on my way to catch a bad cold. I gathered what was left of my wet spirited self and made it a full time job to resolve my situation as best as I could. The wild city's night crowd became my regular acquaintances for many weeks and offered me with all sorts of nasty endeavors, but I knew inside that I could never do drugs to forget all my troubles or become a crook, even in my most desperate needs.

I walked aimlessly against the constant flow of people in the crowded street of London for days. I felt like a ship without a harbor, lost at sea, hoping for a miracle. Now and then the rich and warm smell of fish and chips grabbed my touchy nostrils and sent a desperate note to my starving belly. I could not help but think of my mom at home and all the security and delicacies of my *"douce France"*. I got myself back together and forced positive thoughts into my depressed mind. I was facing a real dilemma since I did not know anyone, but mostly because I couldn't speak a single word of English. I had to work harder to clean my mind of the degrading words used by the English teacher years earlier. I had to survive and find a way to communicate my needs to my foreign environment. I had only two choices left I thought: ask for a job or beg for money in the street and that was the last thing I was going to do. Incidentally many of the London business owners and employees were foreigners from India and Iran.

In all honesty, I must have pronounced this phrase a few thousands times before succeeding in my plea for a job. *"Excuser moi Monsieur, avez vous du travail pour moi, n'importe quoi s'il vous plait?"* I was simply asking, "Excuse me, Sir. Do you have a job for me? Any job please". As anticipated, most of the people I dealt with could barely speak English and communicated between each other in their native language.

Thus my desperate pleas did not take me anywhere, regardless of embellishing my speech with hand gestures and frantic facial *"communiqué"*. In spite of the many monkey faces I could come up with or my body language, no one offered me a job, simply because none of them could understand my request. Some of those people may have thought I was a lost clown looking for his vanished circus, I am sure.

After numerous hours of unsuccessful trials, exhausted and disheartened I walked miles back to Victoria station, through the cold and misty streets of London. I was exceedingly starved and I tried to ease myself by going shopping with the few pennies collected from the streets. I entered what seemed to be a tiny Indian food store and began to look for something I could afford to eat. I was longing for hot soup or a large juicy steak or anything warm and solid, but I could only afford a small inexpensive can. I bought it and went right back to the soaking wet street. I was ravenous and very tired and sat on a covered stairway to eat my meager dinner. At this point, I wanted to relieve the painful urgency from my empty stomach. I had to eat and I wanted to eat now. I took my pocketknife, wondering how to open the tiny can safely. My hands were wet and in my hasty attempt to open the tin the sharp blade went right inside the palm of my hand. I screamed in pain and threw violently everything right in the middle of the busy street. I saw a rushing taxi run over my diner, while putting pressure on my open wound to stop the blood. My empty stomach quickly forced me to reconsider my action and I promptly collected my knife and what was left of my splashed meal.

With so much pain and frustration and no one to turn to, I never felt so down and insecure in my life. I tried very hard to renew my self-esteem, but my time-tested steel will came to its limit that night. I began to cry heavily feeling lonesome in a cold and cruel alien world. Exhausted, I finally reached the warmer smoky train station. It was about 5.30 AM and the London working class was rushing from all parts of the city to their daily tasks. At least all of those people had a job, a warm home and food, and a loving family to go to, I thought. My empty stomach needed urgent attention, while the cold rain made my wounded hand less sensitive. Like a wild animal, I retired myself to a quiet area of the station and carefully opened the small can without incident. A mixture of blood and cold chunky food made my tummy sick. The content was brownish and tasted really disgusting. Perhaps it would taste better warm, I thought, but the nearest kitchen I knew was at home one thousand miles away. I felt nauseated and forced myself not to regurgitate the sickening chow. I reached for my French-English pocket dictionary bought on the ferry and learned the meaning of the words "dog food". My face went green and for second, I did not know if I should cry or laugh my head off. I could not do anything else than to hysterically giggle myself insane.

The Real Victoria Station I knew

Today's Victoria Station

I've learnt my two first English words, all this without my teacher's help, but this is definitely not the easiest way to learn a foreign language, I thought. Still starving to death and exhausted, in spite of all the noise and activity around me, I fell soundly asleep on a hard long steel bench. The crude smell of a huge locomotive's diesel fumes shook me out of my dreams. People were still running in all directions, just as I saw them before closing my eyes hours earlier. For a while, I hung around the train station, wondering what part of town I should walk to. I had to find a job and made my way up to Piccadilly Circus. I kept wishing for a warm meal and a clean bed and that's all I wanted with all my heart. Walking past many busy restaurant windows, I was longing for breakfast. My watering mouth could only remember the taste of hot eggs, bread, and sausages. I felt like going inside any of those places, to ask the waiter for any discarded food. I felt it would be safer, as I was already battling serious abdominal pain, due to food poisoning collected from Victoria Station's trashcans. The idea of asking for food to survive brought back painful memories from my impoverished childhood.

I cruised the streets aimlessly for hours, then made my way down the "tub". I saw a dirty, long bearded hippie playing his guitar. In my native language I asked him if I could play his guitar and to my surprise he understood me and agreed. While playing he tried hard to tell me something of importance, but I could not catch the meaning. I was singing loudly and soon enough some good-hearted people gave me a few pennies. I was smiling and happy and willing to share the money with the beggar. I was excited with the anticipation of eating something hot soon. The money was pouring into the basket, but the drifter was making nervous hand and facial gestures, pointing out the exit sign. "Go! He said, Go and hurry, go!"

I did not understand his warnings and I realized that something was seriously wrong. He grasped his guitar from my hands and ran away as fast as he could and disappeared in the crowd. What a weirdo, I thought, he did not even pick up his money basket and I was glad about it. Then my trouble started, when three menacing and filthy scumbags appeared from nowhere. They shouted a bunch of what sounded like obscenities in my direction. I had no idea of what was going on, until one of them sneaked behind me and smacked me violently on the back of my head. I quickly realized that I was in a bad part of the underground and once again, well before I could deal with stars, I saw a lot of them that evening. Like a bunch of perilous hyenas, they kicked me while I was on the ground. I was still wondering what the hell I did to upset those three beggars, as I tried hard to protect my head from an avalanche of kicks. Then finally the adrenaline pumped in my veins and I jumped right back on my feet and fought as hard as I could.

Born in the year of the Steel Tiger, combined with my aggressive Aries Dragon's Head and a swift Moon in Gemini must be the reason why I suddenly bounced back and fought for my life. They were quite surprised at my agility and my belligerent spirit. Kicking left and right, smacking, biting, and growling like a wild animal, I managed to get myself against the wall. My skull and nose were bleeding heavily and my left eye was partially closed. I finally grabbed my knife from my pocket, pointing the sharp blade in their direction. They knew I was ready to defend myself to death and would not hesitate to use my knife. They kept shouting obscenities and I could only respond to them in French and they finally realized I was not trying to take over their territory and just walked away. This experience was quite terrifying, but I am a survivor and fighting has always been a part of my life. It was only months later, when I was able to understand English a little more that I realized what had really transpired that night. I was in gang territory and like a bunch of wild beasts they did not want a lost French singer to take money away from their turf. I learned the hard way that Victoria Station had it's own gang-like organization of beggars and had wisely determined to avoid those dangerous areas.

Luckily for me, I managed to keep the money saved in my pocket and after cleaning my wounds in one of the many bathrooms in the underground; I walked back to my own head quarter in Victoria Station and finally enjoyed a well-deserved English breakfast. My left-blackened eye was very painful and completely shut and all the bruises I suffered did not prevent me to look for my salvation. I once more took on the crowded wet street of London in anticipation for better days. I experienced much of the same rejection and then finally, luck smiled at me. I was in front of an old English bed and breakfast when I saw an aged lady dumping heavy plastic bags in a trash can. She reminded of my departed grandmother and she was moving slowly and I could not resist helping her.

"*Laissez moi vous aider, Madame*" I said, this means, "Let me help you, Lady." in English. To my surprise, she softly answered me with a "Merci" in perfect French. I was ecstatic, after so many weeks talking to myself, I was finally able to understand someone. I politely asked her if she was French, she said, "No, I am from Switzerland, it's a French speaking country." she answered. I was so happy to be able to finally communicate in my own native tongue. She quickly assumed my deplorable situation by looking at me and catching whiff of the horrible smell I accustomed myself with for so many weeks.

In a perfect French she asked me, "Where is home, what are you doing here?"

"Oh, Madame, *c'est une longue histoire*" (it's a long story) I replied.

She replied, "OK you'll explain later, right now we have to get off the street, it's raining too hard. Come with me, my bed and breakfast is right there." A huge feeling of relief enveloped me as I walked slowly by her side. When she asked me to come inside her home, tears of joy were running down my face. She reminded me of my mother's caring nature and her concern for my welfare was overwhelming.

I can't believe this, I thought, I walked her street twice a day and everyday for weeks now and her business was located just outside of Victoria Station. She gave me a towel and said, "OK young man, the bathroom is upstairs you need to take a shower right now. Go ahead, you will feel nice and warm." she added. "I'll cook you some food and get you in some fresh clothes when you come down." She said softly. I felt like a million dollars taking a simple shower. It's amazing how we can take normal things, such as washing, for granted. I let the warm water wash away my pain and suffering for a long time and thanked god for my old lady savior. I was disgusted by the amount of dirt rinsing away from my hair and my body and made sure to utterly clean off her bathroom when I was done.

I felt like a new man walking down the stairs and she noticed my radiant face. She gave me a hot cup of tea and asked me many questions. After more cups of tea, bread, biscuits, eggs, jam, orange juice, and fruits, I was still talking about my adventures and how I became homeless in the United

Kingdom. The old Lady was seriously concerned about my family asking me to call my mother. "She must be going crazy without any news from you." she said. I explained that my mother did not have a telephone and that there was no way for me to reach anyone, anywhere. She was petrified and in no way was she going to let me go into the cold and dangerous streets again.

She said, "Look Louis, my husband passed away a month ago, and I need help to run my business. If you are interested, you could stay here and help me. In a few weeks from now you could save enough money to go back home, so what do you say?"

"Merci Madame Merci Beaucoup, J'apprecie votre grande generosity" I said emotionally.

I could not believe my luck; the crazy chain of events that transpired for so long, finally ended and a new opportunity was offered to me. My subconscious had no other way to bring about the break, but the job was finally done. I realize now that my subconscious worked as hard as I did, to lead me to the only person that could offer me the help I so desperately needed. First, I had to find someone that could both speak French and had a position to offer me salvation. I attracted the nasty events that took place in the underground, because of my fear of becoming homeless and my subconscious made sure that I would never "connect" with this deplorable element. I was chased away and against all odds, finally attracted the old lady. In this particular case, the law of attraction worked both in a negative and positive way for me.

"Thank, you Madame, thank you." I said. Thank you was the second set of English words I learned to say and I really meant to say thank you! I could hear the rain and the wind pouring outside by the windows, I kissed the old lady good night, tenderly, like I would kiss my Mom. After many weeks of pure hell, I finally enjoyed my first dinner and my first night in bed, with soft clean white sheets and swiftly went straight to Neptune's sweet world of dreams. My French accent and charm worked miracles for me and the staff adopted me instantly and I became a part of the family. Running this type of business was quite a challenge for the old lady, especially after her husband's death. She was a very hard working person and her words of wisdom helped me to deal with my new life. For the time being, I was somehow secure, but I could not help thinking of my countryman Roland. I was wondering in what condition he was or what had happened to him.

I proudly received my first paycheck of 25 English pounds. This was a lot of money for me then and enough to take a very short ride in a double deck red bus to Victoria station in search of Roland. I was terribly worried, hoping to see him walking around smoking with his head down as he often used to do. Constant waves of rushing people kept coming at me, but Roland was nowhere to be seen. I visited all areas of Victoria Station where I knew he could be. Then from distance, I saw him standing begging for money to an indifferent English crowd.

The pitiful sight of his horrible state that he exposed to the world shocked me. I walked towards him wondering about his reaction. The appalling fate I was so scared of and fought so hard to avoid was now a "current affair" for Roland. He was homeless and helpless; he had lost all hope and was reduced to beg for survival. His hopeless gaze expressed the exhausting experience he was enduring. Roland learned the hard way, the real meaning of survival in a foreign country. I approached him and said "Hey man, how are you?" His eyes turned like flashing headlights and he answered piteously.

"Oh my God, Louis, please help me! Don't leave me here; don't leave me this way, man! Please! I can't take it any more." I could smell putrefaction up-and-coming from his dirty clothing.

"Hey Roland" I said, "I am not going to leave you here, buddy." The glare of his eyes intensified with hope for food. "Let's go, man. I came to get you."

"Thank God" he said, harassing me with tons of pertinent questions. We walked to the nearest bar restaurant where he stuffed himself with every item of food he could ingest or drink.

I did not know what to say to the old lady, but I had to do something for my friend. Without my help, Roland would never survive this experience gracefully. This was a difficult dilemma, I did not want to jeopardize my own security nor leave my pal in his terrible situation. I knew and trusted the old Lady to take care of Roland too, but I also knew Roland's laziness and misplaced aggressive character. I wisely decided to keep Roland away and helped him to buy some time to take care of his self. I set up a strategy for him to sneak in at night through my window and quietly eat and sleep in my bedroom. Like I did, he really enjoyed a badly needed shower and rested like a king for many hours in my room. As expected, Roland was not yet ready to either work or assume any responsibility and fully enjoyed all the benefits.

He spent his days watching TV at Victoria Station's café shop, chain-smoking cigarettes that I paid for. Then late at night when everyone was asleep, he would quietly sneak back in my room to eat and rest. My day's work was exhausting; I was running all over serving clients, cooking, cleaning, etc. In spite of my requests not to smoke in my bedroom or watch sports on television all night long, Roland remained oblivious. The situation got worse, when one of the watchful residents caught him stuffing himself with a freshly made cheesecake in the kitchen. When the resident waitress asked him who he was he smartly answered, "Oh, I am Louis' friend and he asked me to get him some cheesecake." This lie saved him for the remainder of the night.

I asked him what the person who saw him looked like and the very next morning I spoke to her. She told me she wanted a drink and heard noise downstairs and saw Roland in the kitchen. I begged her not to talk to the owner because he was a good friend of mine. We got lucky this time I thought, but I knew it was only a matter of time before Roland would mess things up. I kept reminding him to look for a job anywhere, but as usual he didn't do anything to change his secured situation. Finally he felt too comfortable "at home" and in one of his nocturnal excursions to the kitchen, the sleepless old lady caught him.

As expected, she extended her good nature thinking of him as a very hard and responsible worker, she was indeed badly mistaken. She gave him room and board and took him under her protective angel like wings of love. As expected a few days later disaster struck. The old lady's register was short of cash. I knew Roland would do absolutely anything, even stealing to get money and I had to do something real fast. "Roland" I said, I can't believe you did this man."

"What?" he says vehemently, "do you really believe I took the money?"

"Yes, I know you did, no one here would do that, I know all the staff very well."

His face was red with anger and his eyes lit up with fire, he was caught and he also knew that I knew he did it. I gave him a chance and said "Look, just empty your pockets man, if you don't have the money, I will give you the benefit of the doubt'". He did, but two bran new packs of cigarettes gave him away. "Roland, you bastard." I said, "Yesterday you asked me for money to buy your smokes, where did you get the cash?" I added. In no way would I let him get away with this and I saw red. Then like a mad dog he jumped on me and we both rolled on the floor strangling each other. The noise attracted the old lady and other members of the staff.

"Stop this, right now!" she shouted. "This is deplorable, I am so upset with both of you boys," she added.

She knew inside of her heart that Roland was guilty and I was horrified by his deplorable act. I was determined to find the truth and get her money back. She was a true loving lady and I was simply trying to protect her against this abusive vampire. Finally the tension dissipated, but I had enough of Roland's abuses and from that day on avoided him in every possible ways. Luckily for all of us, after weeks of relentless research, he finally found the young girl he came for and swiftly moved in with her. What karma for those souls I thought, Roland is the worst type of man any weak woman can attract. He left the building without saying either thank you or good-bye to anyone and that was the end of our dramatic relationship. Scorpio can be the stingy, cruel, inconsiderate, jealous, abusive, and disrespectful lizard or the magnificent great Eagle or the ultimate Phoenix of the zodiac. On a negative note, this sign rules other people possessions, sex, corporate endeavors, the police, Mafia, crooks, criminals, serial killers and death itself. Souls born in November, such as Anna Nicole Smith and her dramatic fate speaks volume about Scorpio aims. I blame it all on the desperate situation we were in then and his young age. And that is how I have learned astrology hands-on experience.

Saying Goodbye

Three months passed and my new life in England was getting a bit more interesting. In spite of the old lady's requests for me to move back home to France I decided to stay in the UK. A beautiful waitress named Jennie became my first real English girlfriend and she patiently taught me more English words. Much of my time was spent working, watching television, and making love to my beautiful newfound girlfriend. After six months or so my English improved, but I could not yet communicate as I would in my native tongue. I keep thinking how easy it would be for me to work in a French environment. I was subconsciously wishing to improve my situation, stimulating the creative forces of my subconscious and soon enough the law of attraction set the next stage for action.

I felt a strong urge to spend some time at Victoria station my next day off. I also wanted to make sure Roland did not end up there again. I promised myself to help him financially only, but refrain from any form of relationships. Been there, done that, and I could not bear to see him homeless again. I was walking along the long line of telephone booths when finally I heard someone speaking in French. It had been quite a long time since I could understand or converse with someone without stressing and I waited patiently for the man to finish his conversation. "Hi" I said, "I hope you'll forgive my intrusion, but do you know of any French restaurants in the area?"

He smiled amused and replied, "I am visiting some friends in London, but I am actually from Eastbourne. You're lucky" he continued, 'I am a manager at the Grand Hotel there and we are in great need for French waiters, here is my card, give me a call on Monday, I'll give you a job".

I must have meant serious business with my subconscious to attract the link so fast and I was thinking, hell I should have met this guy the first day in arrived in London. He would have saved me tons of trouble I thought, but in no way would I have changed anything. All those experiences were needed to build my character and my will and made me a stronger and wiser man. The only thing I had in mind was to sing in English. Since that moment, a baffling plan was set in motion by my subconscious to reach my wish. I was ecstatic by the offer, but felt sad about leaving both my girlfriend and the old lady behind. What will I tell them when time comes to leave and will they be able to understand me? I realized soon enough that life is a constant process of changes, but I could not get rid of a growing shadow of guilt enveloping me.

I had no doubt about the legitimate offer made by the French man and a quick call to his office the next day reaffirmed our agreement. We spoke for a while getting directions to the hotel and other precious information. I knew my time in London was over at least for now and I had to break the news to the only people I knew and cherished. I wondered for a while how to do so without hurting their feelings, but there was no way around it. The old lady was holding her tears, but she also knew in her heart that I was honest, dedicated, and intelligent. Before leaving her, she whispered in my ear. "Louis, you are a hard worker, just follow your dreams. One day you will be on top of the world and all your dreams will come true. Take care Louis and kiss your mom for me. If you need me you know where to find me," she added. The old lady finally shed a few tears from her wise blue eyes and after many hugs and kisses, I moved away as swiftly as I came into her life.

My little girl friend was devastated and cried heavily, but I promised her to keep in touch with her. I never did, she called me a few times trying to rekindle my feelings for her, but I was wild and young and she probably experienced her first painful heartbreak with me. She, like Roland, and the old lady, disappeared in the wind of my tumultuous life as dictated by the ultimate order of things above, in the stars.

The Job Wish

I enjoyed the train ride and the greenery of the English countryside on my way south to Eastbourne, Sussex. The rain kept pouring outside and the old noisy locomotive was squeaking and spitting smoke climbing the steep hillsides. A couple of hours later, the short trip from London to Eastbourne was over. I grasped my belongings packed in two small bags and walked in direction of the beaches and the distinguished Lansdowne Grand Hotel. An hour or so later, I was standing by the door of the manager's office ready to take on another section of my adventurous life. The young French man was happy to see me and said. "You made it, all right Louis, sit here and fill up the paper work for me". With his help, I managed the task of reading and writing English and I was hired as a basement cleaner.

Lansdowne Hotel

I was not exactly happy with this dull position, but I couldn't speak English just yet and there was not much he could do for me. He felt my discontent and said, "When you'll be able to speak English, a few months from now, I'll give you a job as a waiter, but for now, you'll make a few pounds get free food and board." I was aware of my own limitation and put my ego in my pocket and accepted the position with courage. We toured the heavily trafficked labyrinths of the old structure as he gave me direction and his expectations from my duty. You don't have to be a brain surgeon to perform this stupid job, I thought, but let him enjoy his well-earned managerial superiority. The tortuous dark and smelly cement floors of the basement were made of rough bricks and had many cracks and holes in it. We were walking and he was mentioning safety measures in case of fire when his shoe got stuck in a fissure. I knew this gloomy underground position would challenge my will against depression, endorsing the life of a grimy rat. He guided me to the staff bedroom area, also located in the rotten basement.

"Here is your room Louis," he said, "You're responsible for the only key and you should make a duplicate in case you lose it." My room felt like a jail or a pit hole with no windows, plastered with appalling yellowish-brown wallpaper. The stinky reddish-brown carpet had been deteriorating for years. A meager light bulb gave me enough glow to see that huge cockroaches took residency long before me. The manager left me there pondering my fate. The bed was big enough for a large dog and I sat in total desperation on a flea-infested mattress and began to cry. I was thinking of the old lady's beautiful bedroom with white clean linen and I had also a serious apprehension about the food I would have to ingest to survive here. All of a sudden it sounded like a bunch of mad horses were running outside my door. Hell, what's going on I thought, reaching for the door handle. I was looking at dozens of young unruly French waiters running back to their quarters from their first service in the large restaurant upstairs.

A snobby and wealthy crowd of about three hundreds businessmen regularly came to this auspicious five stars hotel for conferences. The elegant Grand Hotel ballrooms were packed everyday with an army of French waiters and the consuming congregation. Numerous Head servers and Maitre D' Hotel orchestrated the impressive lunch and dinner services. I was very happy to hear those familiar French voices and started a conversation with a guy smoking a cigarette. "Hi there, I'm Louis, I am new here," I said.

The kid glanced back at me and said with a heavy accent. "Hi, I am Massimo, I am Italian but I have been working here for two years, now I can understand and speak both English and French" he said. Such a young fellow able to speak three languages impressed me greatly. Those few words marked the beginning of a solid friendship, loaded with exciting experiences that would last nearly five years. Massimo was young and joyful in his twenties and like all sensitive Pisces, very concerned with others. He and I were inseparable and he spent hours trying hard to help me master English. I felt lucky with him, mostly because he could speak both languages and help me in the translation.

I harassed him for months and with him my English improved dramatically. He was my guide in this Strange New World and a very trusted friend. A few weeks later following my complaints to the manager, he became my roommate in a larger and cleaner bedroom. We took the same days off and cruised downtown, drinking, fighting, and accumulating a score of beautiful English girlfriends. Right by behind the Grand Hotel, a well-known college brought more and more pretty young ladies to our attention. The meeting place was "The Saloon bar" and an extension of the Grand Hotel, just opposite of the college's main entrance. What a treat for a bunch of experimenting kids! We were so young, so innocent, and so vulnerable and like many of us, the girls experienced their first love with a myriad of young and handsome juvenile French and Italian kids. All the activity attracted also the local English guys and after a few pints of Lager, fights over the girls broke out regularly. As always, Massimo and I were often involved fighting with other hot-blooded French and Italian kids. Over the years of working there, a few black eyes and bumps were inflicted and received, while more respect and tolerance was received from both sides.

Two years later, my English was much improved, especially from the time spent picking up girls. The French man who gave me my first job met love and moved to Liverpool. The new manager became a good friend of mine and benefited largely hanging around Massimo and I with a surplus of gorgeous girls. I was really fed up with my boring routine and asked him for a favor and as expected, he offered me with a position of responsibility in the food department. Over the years, I also realized that being popular with the prettiest ladies in town often offers good opportunities. My self-esteem reached a high level when I became in charge of the newly hired staff. I had to learn how to intelligently and creatively operate around a bunch of young egos and earn their respect to ensure a job well done. Life was great; money, security, and girls everywhere. Massimo and I were in paradise. We were known as inseparable and Massimo became the brother I had lost years earlier.

We were on the job for many years and well respected by all. Improving our job situation brought also a new cleaner and bigger "flat" outside of the hotel, for both of us. This extension of the hotel was designed to reward devotion and years of services with a higher standard of living. The hotel owners wanted to stimulate the management to maintain a better service and cleverly masterminded this privileged selection. I did not have to mix with the working staff anymore but kept hanging around them after work at the Saloon bar. I certainly appreciated a more refined cuisine and never touched the horrid food served to the staff ever again. Working in the steamy and hot food staff's department was better than cleaning the floors, but I wanted more; I wanted to see the pretty girls and work in one of the numerous bars of the Grand Hotel.

My subconscious power kicked in again and in an incredible way, judging by what the law of attraction brought me the following weeks. Many times I said to Massimo "Hey buddy, have you wondered how it would be to just give orders and work in one of the bars in a suit, everyday?"

Massimo could only agree with me and added. "Hell, Louis, get a grasp on reality, the only way to become in charge in any of the bars here is to be born English." The management offered highly paid Supervision positions and training to the locals as a first choice. After all, we were foreigners and living in their country. This type of attitude exists in all parts of the world and may be softened in the US, nowadays. But in 1975, the many laws may not have been existing or enforced in the UK. English are known to be a population reluctant to any form of change and refused to participate with the new European community Euro money exchange. Where else can you find a country with Kings and Queens in Europe? Only the British, their hierarchy is very old and established and its people are very proud of its Royal past and legacy. This is unlike France. We did not hesitate to cut off the abusive heads of King Louis the XV and his wife Marie Antoinette and created freedom for the people with "La Republique".

"Well Massimo, there is something we can do, I am sure!" I said confidently.

With a grimace on his face, Massimo answered sarcastically. "Yea Lou, why don't you ask Jesus for a miracle? You know we are going to hell, with all the damage we did to the girls here!" he said jokingly. Years later I came to realize that the forces of evil are as powerful as the force of good or simply stated, the Devil is as powerful as God, for without each other, there would be no life possible. Regardless of the channels used, prayers are nothing more than words turning into thoughts and thoughts are things made of powerful energy. With emotions fueled by fears or passion, your thoughts become laser-like and will go through the thickest brick wall and reach people in time and space.

This is why I always teach my students that: "**The future is nothing more than the reincarnation of your thoughts**". Intensity is the essence that is needed by your subconscious to establish a chain reaction that will bring your wishes. The idea is to mean business because the concentration of thoughts produced by the need stimulate even more power that will invigorate the miraculous transforming process. One night while my staff was busy cleaning up the aftermath of a busy dinner, I decided to hide away, drink a cup of coffee, and puff on a cigarette. My need to escape to a quiet area was unusual, but I faithfully followed my hint. I walked upstairs and entered one of the large numerous empty meeting rooms. In fear of being caught in that prohibited section of the hotel, I did not turn the lights on. Here I was alone in the dark, smoking, lost in my thoughts, sitting at a long table. The entire place was completely empty, but I could hear an eerie sound lost in time and space by the thousands of loud people who dined and worked in that area over the years. Then I heard someone walking behind the door; I kept quiet and waited for the steps to fade away. Instead, to my surprise the mysterious person entered the large room and turned all the lights on. I was petrified to be caught smoking in a non-smoking area of the hotel. I thought, oh, no! I've lost my job! Cold sweat began to roll down my spine.

"Who are you, what are you doing here?" the well-dressed gentleman said calmly. I immediately recognized Mr. Welsh, the General Manager of the hotel. I am in serious trouble, I thought. He must have heard me walking past his office a couple of doors away or smelled the cigarette smoke emanating from the door.

My mind was racing for any plausible reason why I should be here but I had none, just the truth! Gathering my self I nervously answered in broken English. "I am sorry Mr. Welsh, but I have been quite depressed lately and I needed to get away from it all. I thought this place would be quite right for me to do so."

He immediately recognized my accent and switched from English to perfect French. "Well" he said, "I know it must be quite difficult at times to deal with life, away from home. Are you missing your family?" He asked.

"Yes I do Sir and November is always hard for me" I said. "Why November?" he replied.

"Well I have lost my brother Vincent in November Sir, he was only sixteen and I feel bad, I should be home with my family." As I was talking to him I realized that my depressive thoughts were generated from the deep wound suffered with the loss of Vincent years earlier. I did not know then that the connection and reaction of my loss was still fresh and powerful. It allowed a resilient subconscious mental connection with my relatives and friends left behind.

"I have seen you around a few times" he added, "How long have you been working at the Grand?" he inquired.

"About three years Sir" I whispered politely. He paused for a while, wondering about the ashes falling on the red carpet from my burning cigarette. "I am so sorry Sir, let me get rid of this." I said. I nervously glanced around looking for an astray that could not be there. Apologizing again I trashed the cigarette into my empty coffee cup.

Then the Director said, "What's your name and what can I do to help you?"

This was the last question in the world I thought he would ask me. I answered "Louis, Sir." Here I am caught smoking cigarette in a forbidden area of the hotel with Mr. Welsh the most important person of the hotel, asking me if he could help, I thought; Am I lucky or what? I was amazed, trying to contain my thoughts in my baffled mind. I seized the opportunity and said, "Well Mr. Welsh I would love to go home to see my family more often but I do not make enough money. If I could work in one of the bars, I would make more money. I think my English is also good enough for me to do so." I added.

"All right." he said, "Get yourself together and let me see what I can do for you, you may go now." I was totally amazed by the outcome of the entire deal and most of all; the beneficial meeting with Mr. Welsh and warmly thanked the great man. I couldn't wait to feed my friend Massimo with all the juicy details, I also knew he would have some problem believing in the "miracle" that just took place.

Later on in life, I abandoned the nasty habit of smoking and later realized that Mr. Welsh never smoked hence his acute sense of smell, which picked up the cigarette smoke I emitted, giving my hiding spot away. Later on I also found out that Mr. Welsh, a soft and understanding Pisces, (like Massimo and I) was a very powerful man in his own locality. I saw him many times in the middle of the city streets promoting good causes and performing voluntary work. Massimo was speechless, as I recalled my encounter with the "boss" and the real possibility to get a position in one of the bars in the hotel. "Louis" he said bewildered, "You really are something, man" and added, "will you help me to work there too?" he asked.

"But of course, Bro. You can be sure of that. Let me get there first, then count on me, buddy." I said. This was a great excuse to celebrate the incredible day's events at the Saloon bar drinking pints of lager with some of the prettiest college girls. The very next day a telephone call came through the food department that I was in charge of. The American bar manager called me to set up a meeting within the hour. Mr. Welsh had kept his promise and later on, with a heart full of hopes I made my way up to the notorious American bar's Manager office.

"Hi, you're Louis" he said.

"Yes Sir" I replied happily.

"A special order came from the general Manager office this morning to train you to work as a barman. Do you want this position?" He added.

"You bet I do, and you will be very happy with me, Sir." I added. He was smiling and grasped a pencil and made me sign my name on the bar's schedule.

"OK boy", he said in a warm Italian accent. "Read this carefully, you start tomorrow, be on time." I knew that I would get along with this man, as he acted so much like my best friend, Massimo. I was in paradise and the news of Louis getting a serious promotion traveled fast through the large hotel. Some good friends of mine were very happy for me, while others English trainees hated both my guts and my luck. At this point in my life, I had no idea of how the inner creative forces of my subconscious could alter my destiny so fast.

---

* Was it because of my refusal for failure or my fixed attitude that brought me all this fortune? My deep-seated mind for success combined with inborn enthusiasm may have helped too. Many years later I became a learned Clinical Hypnotherapist and a refined Astropsychologist and I realized so much more about the interaction between **"The Universal Code"** (like attracts like) and **"The Law of Hope."** This puzzle was finally understood. I believe the combination of all of the above is the true recipe needed to reach the creative forces of one's subconscious in time and space. The astrological **Universal Laws** worked miracles in my favor and the cosmic mixture of my Aries (leadership) Dragon's Head (luck) and a Waxing Moon (**Universal Law of the Moon**) or great timing (right time at the right place) undeniably worked in my favor.

I could not ask for more. I had finally reached a position of value and earned even more money and respect from everyone. I broke all the rules and managed a position of power in a foreign country. A deep breath of relief came over my soul, as I recalled the long months of depression, the severe first few weeks in London, and the long months spent cleaning the infinite corridors of the large hotel basement. I made it all the way up, I thought and incredibly my subconscious had so much more in store for me. I enjoyed my well-earned position, but life is a process of constant change and I wanted better and better.

To do so, I had to squeeze my environment to the extreme. My boss was really nice and very helpful, but I was only a trainee and doomed to work behind this bar under his supervision. I mentioned to Massimo, my new upgraded wish to be a real manager in the hotel. He said mockingly to me, "Anything can happen with you, Louis; I have learnt to trust in your luck and maybe the devil will grant this one too soon!" Massimo was right! With my creative subconscious at work, it all began to take place in the same miraculous way.

The Saloon Bar Wish

A few weeks later, Massimo and I heard of another wild "party" at the famous Saloon bar. This little bar was indeed the most popular place in the hotel, due to the constant flow of girls and prodigious night activities. Even the auspicious American bar could not match the Saloon notoriety. My ultimate secret wish was to become the ruler of this joyous harem, I really meant business and my subconscious heard me loud and clear. The parties always attracted many girls and with it, sure trouble with the local Brits. They used to call us "froggies" because we eat frog legs and snails as a delicacy to the palate of cultured gourmet. The amphibians and snails are carefully raised and fed specifically for that purpose. Many times I thought how much people are missing in the name of their culinary ignorance. We have a worldwide reputation for exquisite cuisine and I would rather eat those dry frogs' legs in the morning than a daily dose of harmful greasy bacon, eggs, and sausages. No wonder why France, contrary to the UK and the US has the lowest number of heart attacks in the world!

The news of another party at the saloon bar brought flocks of people ready to enjoy the music, the numerous choices of beers and especially the abundance of pretty girls. An armada of French, English, Italian, Scottish, Turkish, Irish people from both sexes were dancing and laughing in a very smoky environment. Massimo and I were sitting in the most private corner in a large booth, surrounded as usual, by a bunch of longing girls. It was a matter of time before a fight would broke out between two drunken kids over a girl. Then trouble struck when a seriously intoxicated Irishmen refused to pay for his beer. I never saw this person in the bar before and he appeared wild and certainly very dangerous. He swore loudly at the bar manager, pointing a large knife in his direction. He then jumped over the bar, trying to stab him in the chest. The young man's face was distorted and he was fleeing for his life.

The terrified girls sitting at the bar screamed and in the blink of an eye moved away from the crazy man and his menacing blade. Massimo's unconscious grip on my forearm clearly indicated his battle between emotions and the real danger we all faced. Like many of the people there, he never dealt with any weapons such as knifes or guns before. He screamed watchfully. "Whoa, this bloke is nuts! What do we do man?"

"Leave it to me, let me take care of this guy my way!" I said. The night was advanced and I had a few drinks myself and my usual common sense was gone and replaced by a tiger like instinct. Born in that particular tiger year may also be the reason why I react like a wild animal in particular perilous situations. In normal circumstances, I would never put myself in such a dangerous situation, but something triggered the old animalistic street instinct in me. In front of an amazed crowd, I slowly walked towards the mad man.

His pupils were enlarged and indicated that he had also ingested powerful narcotics. He was taken aback and did not expect to be challenged by anyone in the bar. I was boiling with adrenaline and my preservation instinct was at its peak. I worked hard to control myself and presented a calm and secure face. "Hey man, quit this." I said, "You don't need a knife to fight, are you scared of a kid?" The tension was so thick in the bar that you could have cut it with the mad man's knife. The music stopped, everyone was looking at us, and it felt like a duel to the death, like in a movie. The only problem was that it was a real situation; me facing a mad drunken maniac, armed with a sharp knife and ready to use it. I was staring at him into his deep black and reddish eyes. I knew I had to keep my gaze steady and watch all his moves. Luckily for me, the large amount of alcohol and narcotics he consumed worked for me and I knew it. Many of the people witnessing the unfolding drama thought of me suicidal or totally insane.

Then a terrifying moment of my life was to unfold in front of a large audience. With the speed of a striking snake the man's blade ended up stationary, less than an inch in from my solar plexus. A cold sweat went all over my body and I thought; this is it…will this lunatic plunge that knife in me? Everything around me seemed to be happening in slow motion, it felt like an eternity and heard the people's breath. What do I do now, I thought again? I instinctively knew to keep cool and my control over a deadly situation paid off. In a very slowly daring tone of voice, I said to the Irish man. "Get that knife away from me, for if you don't you will be very sorry mate." In no way should I show fear or insecurity at this point and I had to challenge the man to the extreme.

Previous experience with weapons told me that if he was to use his knife, he would already have done so and I would be bleeding to death, fighting for my life. Thank God my assessment was correct (don't try this at home!). I had to make him talk and gear his mind on something else than what was happening and give him also a valuable excuse to save his ego and I said firmly. "What's your problem man? By now the cops are on the way here, you should get the hell out of here man or you're going to jail" I added.

"Who the hell do you think you are mate, you're dead," he said with a very strong Scottish accent. I knew right then it was time for me to act or die. Talking to me was the error he made and indicated little sense left in his disturbed mind. Like lightening, I grasped the man's hand, but his huge size and strength made it impossible for me to remove the knife. The deadly fight had started and I knew better not to let that hand go free, regardless of the exchange of kicks and punches inflicted on each other. Massimo saw the opportunity and quickly came to my rescue.

I was on top of the crazy man's large body, punching his face and I felt his stinking beer breath each time he gasped for air. Massimo finally hit him as hard as he could behind the head with a beer bottle, miraculously missing me. A few minutes later, the police arrived and took the drunk away. The flamboyant party was canceled and everyone went back home. To my horror, the next day I was called to Mr. Well's office to explain what happened the night before in the bar. I really thought this time that I was out for good. In no way could the General Manager accept rough fights on the premises and soon Massimo and I would be out of work. I felt terrible because I had worked so hard to get a form of security and I had planned to attend the Royal School of Music to learn piano in the near future. All my dreams were shattered and Mr. Welsh will never forgive me, I thought. I hated the wild side of myself, and all the trouble it had brought my life. Massimo gave me all the comfort he could, while nurturing a bad cut he received on his own head during the rumble.

The meeting took place with other Managers sitting around an old conference table in his luxurious office with a fantastic view of the English Channel. It felt like I was in a courtroom as I began explaining myself away. To my surprise, he politely stopped my talking and pronounced my first name and said. "Louis I want to thank you so much, for saving my nephew's life! Without your intervention he could have been dead today and I wanted to personally thank you". Nothing could prepare me for what I was hearing and the gratifying shock I was experiencing. I was speechless and kept listening to the man. Then a bigger surprise came my way when he announced. "Louis I need people like you down there, courageous and willing to enforce discipline. Would you like to be the Saloon bar manager?" he added, smiling. I was ecstatic; no words could begin to describe the joy I was experiencing. The most difficult thing for me to do, as I recall, was to keep my own powerful and high-spirited emotions in control. I wanted to jump and scream my head off, but I kept as cool as I could during the circumstances. I gladly accepted the highest position and all its great benefits, as I was aiming for it, for so long. I shook Mr. Welsh's hand and thankfully retired myself.

I thought I was flying, my feet did not touch the ground and I could not wait to break the fantastic news to Massimo. I revealed to my dear friend what took place in the privacy of the Director's office. I will never forget his enlightened young face and his surprise. Not a single word came out of his mouth; he simply stared at me totally baffled, continuously shaking his head like a mad horse laughing his head off. Again, I made a request that seemed to be impossible to reach, but it was more of a demand than a simple request and in time all my wishes became a reality. I came from France to England, totally destitute in 1974; I was young, but smart enough to work and will with a dream in my heart. I suffered interminable weeks of drastic challenges in Victoria station and found myself in 1976 proudly managing the Grant Hotel Saloon bar in Eastbourne, Sussex England. In two years I raised myself from the drizzly London streets to the highest accomplishments that an uneducated wandering "vagabond" could reach. I blamed it all on my usual luck and my will to succeed, but what I did not know then was the multitude of implacable **Universal Laws** at work. I now see all my valuable experiences in retrospect, because of the cosmic consciousness I developed over the years and all this is my gift to you, the reader.

The Sports Car Wish

The first time I saw a Triumph motorcar, my heart melted and since that day I had wished for it. Can the subconscious bring a car to someone? You bet it can and indeed so much more. I dreamed to own one of those beautiful red sports "Spitfire" Triumphs. During those days, my bar manager wages could barely take care of my tuition expenses at the Royal School of Music and my living expenses. Each time I saw one of those great pieces of engineering, I couldn't help but to visualize myself at the wheel driving around town with a beautiful girlfriend sitting next to me. The sheer amount of thought to own such a car was very intense. I did not give my subconscious any length of time or unnecessary worries about my financial situation. I only gave him direct suggestions and a clear image of my dream. I simply wanted the great car and meant it. I also thought myself as a very lucky guy, knowing nothing on the creative forces of my subconscious. Then again just like magic, a few weeks later, it all unfolded right in front of my amazed eyes.

I was about to close my night work, hurrying the last customers to drink up, following the "last order" while anticipating the 10 PM closing time. I was busy ordering the staff around and as usual, retired in the back room doing the till and taking care of the bar inventory. Less than 15 minutes later all was quiet and the bar entrance was safely locked, the large "Guinness beer" sign outside was still on. I could hear the screaming wind outside and I was about to turn some of the remaining the lights off. I had to bravely face the deteriorating weather all the way to my small "flat" a couple of blocks away. I heard a loud resounding noise coming from the front door and thought the gusty wind finally got the large electric sign outside. I was about to open the thick wood door to investigate the forceful noise, but I heard someone calling for help right behind it. "Someone's here please, open the door I need help," the voice shouted.

"What's going on?" I replied. I knew someone was in trouble but I had to be careful.

"I crashed my car! I am hurt! I'm bleeding! Please, help me! Open the door!" He said. I immediately opened the door and brought the bleeding guy right in. I asked him to sit on the booth to relax. He was in shocked, cold, wet, and kept complaining about his awful fate.

"Hey, what happened to you, buddy?" I asked.

"Don't know, I lost control of my car, the road is so wet, I think I fell asleep." He said. His breath had a strong smell of alcohol and I quickly realized he was seriously inebriated and totally impaired to drive a car. He sat there for a while, sobbing and talking about his dramatic break up with his girlfriend. I couldn't help but feel sorry for the guy. I thought of calling the emergency service, but with so much alcohol in his system, God knows what trouble he could get himself into. I asked him a few questions while carefully examined his facial wounds; they were superficial and not at all life threatening.

He begged me not to call the police and to let him recuperate in the bar for a while. By the time I came back with a hot cup of coffee, he was deeply asleep. I went outside to check on the damage inflicted to his car and the building. Luckily for him, the security guard on duty that night was also a friend of mine and I stopped him just in time from calling the police on his portable emergency radio. "Hey Mark, don't do it, the guy is drunk, but he is fine, trust me, he doesn't need any more trouble" I said. Mark and I had a long and strong friendship and we trusted each other well. To my horror, a beautiful convertible red Spitfire Triumph was pitifully jammed against the wall of the bar. I was really sorry for both the driver and the car of my dreams. Steam was coming from the idling engine, so I immediately turned it off. Mark was a big guy and with his help, we pushed the car and parked it in the street.

I removed the keys from the ignition and brought them back to the sleepy owner. Mark followed me inside the bar and glanced at the guy and said, "What's next, what are you going to do with him Louis?" Mark was huge and caring, but as vigilant as a dog.

"I'll take care of him," I said. "Just give us a ride to my flat, will you?"

"Sure mate" he kindly replied. He could barely walk and I did not fancy carrying him through the raining street. "All right, let me give you a hand and let's go now before anyone else shows up, we don't need no witnesses." Mark prudently said. We helped the man into the front seat of the security truck and drove away.

The next day my drunken guest woke up with a huge headache and could barely recall the previous night. I thought the cold wet weather would help and suggested a warm breakfast just a short walk away. After a couple of hours talking, I learned all about his private life. He was an attorney at law and I realized how lucky he was not to be in jail, using his own expertise to save his precious license. He excused himself to a nearby public telephone and spoke a few minutes to his worried mother. We then walked back to the scene of the accident to evaluate the car's severe damage. He was quite devastated looking at the smashed front end of his expensive sport car. The radiator was still leaking a mix of water and oil and snapped belts could be seen under the car. "What I am going to do?" he said desperately. "Well the only thing you can do is to have it towed to a garage" I replied.

"I ain't got the money to do that," he said, sadly.

I was expecting the guy to have some money saved in the bank to own such a pretty car, but surprisingly enough, he did not. He added exasperated "Bloody Hell! I can't even afford the fare train home to London, I drank it all last night." "Damn" he added annoyed, "I even asked my Mother for money, but she can't help me either. Life really stinks, man!" He was very upset and could barely hold onto his emotions.

I could not resist asking him a serious question, "Michael, how the hell did you manage to own such an expansive car?"

He felt uneasy for a second and answered, "Well my girlfriend helped me to purchase it a few months ago." I immediately suspected the real reason for his trouble and my suspicion was clarified when he added. "She paid cash for the car and I still own her a few hundred pounds, but lately I could not pay her back.

Last time I spoke to her she was really mad at me and told me not to see her again," he added sadly. "She now works here in Eastbourne and I caught her with her new boyfriend last night. When I confronted them, she told me she was done with me. I tried to get over this and I drank all night and nearly killed myself for her." I could feel both his sadness and uneasiness, but I admired his honesty. It all began to make sense to me and then I asked him "Mike, does she still own the car?" He gathered his thoughts for a second and said, "Of course not, the car is entirely paid for and it is mine, it was a present for my birthday. All the DMV papers and insurance are in my name," he added convincingly.

Then he went back to complaining about being completely broke and how he would make it back home to London. "I wish I could help you my friend but I can't do much for your car, I am not rich either mate, the only thing I can do is to pay your way to London." I said. "Damn, you would do that for me," Then, he unexpectedly turned around and said. "Hey Louis, you're a really nice fellow, you really are mate; you've saved me so much trouble, so far" he grabbed his wallet and said "here is the title of my car and the rest of the papers you need are in the glove compartment, I give it all to you! Here are ignition keys, catch!" He added. I was completely speechless and stunned, swiftly catching the flying keys in mid air.

"Are you sure you wanna do that, man? Do you really mean it?" I thankfully said.

"What else can I do? I am locked in a bad situation here and this car can't be in the street forever" he answered.

I was astounded and felt overwhelmed with emotions I could never express. I wanted to jump and scream: Oh my god! I just realized my biggest wish ever, but I did not want to rejoice just yet. I wanted to generate quick cash for this fellow and remembered Mark's own wish. For months he begged to give me good money for my expansive state of the art stereo. Following an expeditious telephone call, Mark rushed to my flat with two hundred pounds and walked away with his dream. I gave all the money I received to Michael and he left behind both a broken heart and a broken car. I knew the car was in bad shape but with time and money I would have no problem to put it back to it's original shape and finally drive it around.

With Massimo and Mark's help, we pushed the car behind my flat to the small parking lot and estimated the reparation. Much of the damage was only superficial and a week or so later the car was repaired. The Spitfire front-end was repainted in its bright red original color, a similar second hand radiator was purchased from the local junk yard for next to nothing, and the broken belts were replaced. The oil leak was coming from a snapped rubber hose and was easily replaced. The vital seed was planted just a few months earlier in my subconscious and the law of attraction did the rest. Here I was, proudly driving my red Spitfire Triumph around town and many pretty girls enjoyed the ride. I felt guilty for a while, hoping for a call from Michael that never came, I had no way of reaching him either. I drove this dream car of mine until the day I left England and sold it for great price.

Looking back on this example, you can only accept that "magic" really exists. A magnet will not attract a piece of wood; my wish to own and drive a particular sports car somehow came true. The miraculous chain of events that took place, were with real actors and everyone cooperated fully in their "fated" parts. There was only a unique way for me to own such an expensive car and one specific person to provide the "wish". Certainly a sad situation for Michael but did our thoughts, somewhere, somehow merge and bring about the encounter? Am I responsible for Michael's misfortune? Were my thoughts in time and space stronger than his? Did I actually attract Michael and his car into my own life? Were Michael's thoughts reaching mine and becoming the contributor of my own wish?

The Law of Visualization

* Did Michael subconsciously make himself available and vulnerable to someone else's stronger wish? Did he nurture a form of death wish, following his breakup? The drinking did not help him either, but Michael could have crashed his car anywhere between Eastbourne and London on his way back home. But why the accident took place so close to me? Did an inner force that he could not control drive him? Was I actually seeing into my own future when I saw myself in that car? There are so many unanswered questions, but I can assure you that **"The Law Of Visualization"** worked splendidly for me and to my natal UCI, Dragon's Head (luck) located in the sign of Aries (red/sport/speed/danger) added another complementary colorful element to the mysterious equation. The planet Mars (ruler of Aries) is reddish and this planet is also called in Greek Mythology the Lord of war. Thus red is the color of blood and points out another form of magnetism. Incidentally, red is my favorite color and I own a red convertible Corvette and a red 4X4 Dodge utility truck. Not to forget Dodge emblem is the head of the Ram.

Think for a minute about the possibilities involving man's inner thought process, his complex UCI and the responsibility involving the liberation and channeling of the mighty subconscious creative forces. The fact is clear and simple, there is no awareness or judgment in this phenomenon, no good God, no bad Devil, it just is and all is that and that is all. Unknown to many people, the Universal Mind and the Supraconcious connects us all.

———•———

Miracles Do Happen

I was born in a small village and my family was very poor, but thoughts of wealth and power were never an obsession with me. Meanwhile, the rich environment of the luxurious Grand Hotel and its wealthy guests made me wonder about a prosperous life. I was poor, but for some reason I felt very rich and very special inside. I also knew my limitations and I could only dream of experiencing true wealth and true power. The intensity of my desire for riches has always steered the law of attraction and a beautiful girl named Jane Heaton entered the bar. I could not take my eyes away from her, she was absolutely gorgeous, elegantly dressed, and without warning love hit me right in the face. Our passionate relationship lasted about a year. Our love and obsession with each other ruled our young lives. She was a new student and like all the other girls, she enjoyed the atmosphere of the Saloon Bar. She became my world and I did not anticipate her moving back home after graduation to Homskirk, one of the wealthier states in the UK. Her wealthy father was a regular guest in the prestigious Grand Hotel and attended numerous business conferences for his successful Heaton transportation company.

I felt honored when Jane introduced me to her family and I tried very hard to behave in a proper manner in all circumstances. For the first time in my life, I sat in a brand new Jaguar and was driven by her father to shop for a suit in a high class "couturier". Jane's father was so influential that he managed to get me in as a guest with his family upstairs in the main ballroom, the most luxurious dining room in the hotel. Only VIP can afford such treatment and I could not help but to think of my incredible progression from the sullied, moist, and dark basements which I was hired to clean only a couple of years earlier. Can you for a second, imagine the faces of the "Maitre De Table" conducting the service and all my waiter friends serving me? Everyone knew me well and all must have thought I was from another planet to be able to realize such things. Even Mr. Welsh, the General Director was in shock, when he came personally to shake hands with Jane's dad. Damn, I thought to myself, am I dreaming, or what? Only a few days ago I thought of tasting wealth and here I was living it. To my amazement the powerful man spent more time in my bar, than upstairs in the luxurious American bar with his business partners. He really liked me and we became good friends and as all Leos (king of the family) he was investigating a potential son in law.

The true essence of your faith for success is the main factor that will steer the subconscious power in motion and the law of attraction will bring the actors of your own movie. Combined with solid cosmic consciousness, there is no end to what your subconscious can accomplish. The day came and Jane graduated and left Eastbourne to join her family and she invited me for her twenty first-birthday party, just two weeks away. Like her father, Jane was a true Leo and her thick long wavy hair really looked like a lion's mane. The **Law of 7th House Attraction** worked miraculously for us and made it difficult to be apart for long. I was born in February and Jane was born in August and the seventh house rules the contracts and marriage area. Just before she moved away, Jane said to me, "Louis I want you to see how I live, you will enjoy it". She also flipped through some pictures of her horses and her father's luxurious yacht and said. "Here look, this is my captain, my dad is sending us to an exotic island near Spain for my birthday".

 I was in paradise wondering how people can live such a luxurious life, but I had a weird feeling of losing Jane if I did not move closer to her. A long distance relationship was out of question and I decided to gamble it all and against Massimo's advice and gave my two weeks notice. She was so happy and took my gesture as proof of my true love and commitment. The few days away from her were just terrible, but Jane and I spent long periods of time talking on the phone everyday. I also promised her that I would get a tattoo of an eagle with her name above the wings. It's amazing how silly adolescents really are, when they are in love and I made plans to travel to Hastings to do so. A few days later I was sitting in the tattoo parlor and the refined artist finished the mighty eagle, but did not have enough time to engrave Jane's name. I was to take the long journey to Liverpool then Homskirk the very next day. During those days I had no real idea of the significance of my subconscious inner *"communiqué"* and the omen was a direct indication of the things to come between us in the near future.

Massimo was happy for me but he was going through serious problem with his ex and his son. His high spirit was sinking deeply into depressions. I was quite worried about him and I felt bad to go away when he needed me the most.

"Come on Bro, get a grip on yourself," I said amicably "I know how you feel I've been there and I made it man, you've got to be strong man" I added. I could smell the nauseating smell of cannabis in his breath when he replied.

"I am scared Louis, I not sure if I can do it Louis." For the first time I saw Massimo crying heavy tears of despair and there is nothing I could do to stop his internal emotional hellish battle. I tried hard to ignore his feelings and said.

"Massimo I have to go man, I am sorry but I swear I'll keep in touch with you, you are like my brother and you know that." I affirmed. I hugged my best friend ever for the last time and did not know about it.

I took the lengthy train ride to Liverpool then a taxi to her house in Homskirk. I was wondering what to expect and I was to find out soon enough. It took quite a while to drive from the huge entrance gates to the huge castle like property. Upon my arrival, Jane greeted me warmly and gave me a tour of her large residence. I was fascinated by all the beauty and wealth I saw all around me and I could not understand how people could possess so much. She led me to her stables, put a saddle on a couple of vibrant stallions and we rode for hours on the vast property. Luckily for me, in my childhood I learned how to ride horses by "borrowing" the unbroken animals from one of my friend's parent's farm. We never used saddles because his family could not afford any. I fell off the untamed horses many times and bear the scars for the rest of my life. For her birthday Jane received another costly stallion and a brand new Jaguar. She proudly brought me to her bedroom to see all the presents brought by hundreds of guests. Her room was filled from top to bottom with very expensive flower arrangements and an incalculable amount of well-packed boxes.

"I told you Louis, you would be amazed by my living standards," she said proudly. So many wealthy boys gave me those presents and I can wait to open them," she added happily. I realized that I had serious competition and in no way I could match any of those wealthy kids I thought. Many of those teens were like Jane, from well-off families attending wealthy private institutions and never suffered or worked a day in their blessed lives. The only good thing I had going for me is that I was from France and many of those young snobs tried to impress Jane by talking to me in a poor broken French. I felt inferior and misplaced in the prosperous energy and excused myself in the extravagant backyard. Jane felt my uneasiness and promptly joined me confirming her love and devotion for me.

Her servant called us back to her room, wondering what to do with the constant flow of presents. Receiving so many gifts appeared normal to Jane and she had absolutely no appreciation or thankfulness showing on her pretty face. This type of treatment would have me screaming of joy, because I am from a very poor family who could never afford toys for any of my birthdays. The meager money coming to the family was from the *"allocation familiale"* or the social security and could only be spent on food. The best present I ever had was a cheap toy gun for Christmas and some cookies made by Grandma.

She was coldly ordering the servants to her immediate needs and she would get quite upset if they responded too slowly. When I suggested for more compassion, she said innocently, "But they are servants, Louis. This is why there are here, to serve me!" I did not know about the stars those days and got my first glimpse of the Leo ego, but it was her birthday and I had to keep quiet. I was in a true wealthy environment where her influential family name, money, and power ruled it all. I also realized that the loads of high-priced flower arrangements, sent by a myriad of longing wealthy lovers for her birthday, were to impress her and her family. Jane was very beautiful and the daughter of a very wealthy influential man and indeed seen by the courting crowd as "the grand prize".

I was only a young man then, but I could easily perceive the damnation produced by money and power and its impact on people. I do not lack social skills, but I cannot put on a fake face with anyone for long, and my rough upbringing and honest comments were too much for some of the snobby guests. Incidentally, the worst was to take place during the weekend on the dance floor. Jane's father spent a large amount of money to accommodate and impress all his wealthy guests for her birthday. Her father hired a company to assemble a covered exhibition area for the special event. Inside the large roofed pavilion stood numerous tables, chairs, and bars that were set and ready for the visitors. A well-known band and a disc jockey were hired to perform for the guests. The birthday night celebration started with a constant wave of new people pouring in with more precious presents for my lucky girlfriend.

She was the star of the show and as her French boyfriend I got quite a lot of attention myself. I could also feel some animosity coming from some of the wealthy young men. I was asked to go on stage, where her proud father introduced me to the envious crowd. Back in Eastbourne I used to sing songs for Jane and promised her I would perform for her special day. Jane was standing next to me holding a guitar and to my surprise he announced that I was going to sing a song I made for his daughter. I began to sing a song I wrote for Jane in French and the audience admired both my gut and my talent. She was looking at me, immersed in love and pride, and then finally when I struck the last chord, she approached and kissed me in front of all the applauding guests. We did not know yet the difficulties of our huge differences in upbringing. Ego and wealth were the serious obstacles that would bring an abrupt end to our relationship.

When I arrived in Jane's home I did not have the "right" attire and her proud Leo father took me shopping to a sumptuous clothing store in Homskirk. He knew exactly what the English aristocracy wanted to see in me and bought me a very expensive black tuxedo. I esteemed his gesture, but I also felt out of place and I understood wanting me to look proper for his guests and for his daughter's birthday. We had no idea of the shock we were about to experience a few hours later with his two daughters. A lesson of true shame was about to unfold right in front of hundred of snobby guests. It is part of the family custom for the father and daughter to open the ball under the watchful admiring eyes of all the guests. I was on the side of the dance floor patiently waiting and enjoying watching them dancing. I was told earlier to wait for Jane's signal and join her on the dance floor once the parental dance was over. Jane' younger sister Carol was standing next to me patiently waiting for the song to end.

Then all hell broke loose when she unexpectedly grabbed my hand and literally dragged me on the dance floor. Through the secrets laws of Astro-Psychology, I teach my students that any Leo becomes a powerful emotional, jealous and vindictive Scorpio on their fourth house. This area rules all affairs involving home and family members. Again, during those days I did not have much knowledge of the stars, but many years later I fully comprehended what had transpired that dramatic night. Jane saw her sister and I moving towards the dance floor hand in hand. I quickly realized in only the few days spent near her, Carol's feelings became a little misplaced. Then in front of all the dismayed stuck-up guests, Jane disrespectfully and violently pushed her dad away and started running towards us. Oh no, I thought, this is it; this is the end of all my efforts to become friends with her dad.

She used the same emotional spoiled brat manner used on the servants and she screamed. "You are not going to take Louis away from me, he is mine, find your own boyfriend" she added forcefully. I was speechless and appalled at her behavior hoping for a quick end to this foolish scenery.

Carol ended up sitting on her tiny butt on the dance floor; " You freaking bitch" she screamed, "I hate you!" Ashamed, she launched herself back on her feet and flew away through the door. Carol and her devastated Dad were not to be seen for the remainder of the night. I kept dancing with Jane, who did not seem to care a bit of the serious damage she inflicted on her relatives. I knew we were history, but I kept my control to save unnecessary trouble. I never forgot anyone's date of birth and Jane was born in 1959. Many years later on when investigating her character through the Astro-Psychology, I realized that Jane was born with a self-centered, masculine Dragon's Tail in the child like and aggressive sign of Aries. Since then, I learned many celestial laws that made me aware that "dismissing" Jane was more of liberation, than a loss.

Jane was busy parading herself with a myriad of longing lovers, while I was at the bar stuffing myself with drinks, projecting a cool face while dealing with powerful emotions. What could I or should I say to her dad and Carol? I thought. What excuse would I or could I possibly come up with, to make up for Jane's harebrained behavior? While pondering the issue away from everyone, another surprise came my way. A young girl walked towards me and asked me. "Are you Louis?"

"Yes. What do you need?" I said.

"Well, Carol asked me to tell you to join her by the pool, she's there right now, waiting for you" she said. After all the commotion she suffered, I thought maybe Carol needed some comfort from me and like a ghost I vigilantly disappeared from the noisy tent.

Jane was much too busy being a Leo and did not notice my "escape". I found my way to the pool area and stood silent in the darkness for a while. The August night was warm and humid and I could hear an owl from a short distance. I took this as an omen for secrecy and walked towards the pool bar longing for another drink. Then, out of a dark corner Carol called my name. 'Louis, Louis" she whispered, "I am here". She walked towards me and before I could realize what happened to me, she gave me one of the most passionate French kisses I ever tasted in my life. She had bottled up her deep feelings for me for days and I surely enjoyed her passionate nature.

"Hey girl, do you want me dead or what? I am here for Jane's birthday and if your dad finds out after what went on tonight out there, I am as good as dead" I managed to say. By now, I am sure her father wanted me deceased or gone or both I thought and I had a feeling that all of my English competitors would happily give him a hand to get rid of my magnetic French butt.

We talked for a while in the large property avoiding others and I managed to put some sense into her young passionate heart and mind. Carol liked me a lot, but she also wanted to take her revenge on her sister. At this point I was playing a dangerous game and after many passionate kisses, we both separately joined the party. The week exhausted itself and it was time for me to announce to Jane my decision to stop seeing each other. I was also concerned with my musical study at the music school and my drive to succeed helped me to make the decision to go back to Eastbourne. I waited the very last minute and when she mentioned her dad's yacht and Spain, I broke the news. She was perplexed and never really understood my decision or me.

"But why?" she kept saying, "I thought you really loved me?" Heavy tears came out of her striking blue eyes.

"Jane, you have so many people right here that really love you, you know you will find someone to go with, I really have to go now." I added. She turned back and fled into the house. She came out a few minutes later with her mother, Carol, and her dad. In no way could her proud father ever really like me, I thought, and competing for his daughter's love or respect was out of the question. He and I knew it and after a warm handshake, he and his wife walked away. Carol never said a word and when I hugged her good bye, I knew she still had deep feelings for me. I made it easy for everyone I thought and my street-like energy did not match the wealth and power of such an eminent family. I cared a lot for Jane, but I also knew her ego and aggressive nature would become a source of conflict in the long run. She dropped quite a few tears all the way to the train station and watched me disappearing in a cloud of smoke and I never seen or heard of her since.

What happened there? Did Jane, Carol and her father have to learn about ego? Did my subconscious inferiority complex bring Carol ᴠᴜ ᵎ vital part for the breakup between us all? I surely learned that money and power does not mean happiness but indeed breeds egocentric people. A section of my interesting life was closing, while another was opening.

Law of Intervention

* This illustrates the **Law of Intervention.** There are times in our lives that seemingly negative things happen to pull us away from what we want. Looking back we can see that we have been spared from a worse fate. It is best to surrender and realize there is a higher purpose regardless if we can see it at the time.

Dead and Born Again

The long journey back to Eastbourne allowed me to collect thoughts, wondering if I should go back to my old job at the Grand Hotel. What would I say to my friends about Jane and her dad? Would they laugh at me? What about work, would they give me my job back? So many questions entered my mind and the only place I could go, was to my best friend Massimo's flat. Massimo did not have a telephone and I took a chance hoping to see him at home. Massimo was himself going through serious difficulties, trying to reconnect with his old girlfriend and his baby. I felt bad, because I was dating her before he got her pregnant and he fell madly in love with her. She was young and wild and I knew she would never be marriage material for many years to come. He caught her many times with different people and each time suffered tremendous emotional pain. He was in some way in the same position as me, when I first married Marilyse and I knew exactly how he felt without his son. Massimo was from a Latino background, where family and children are part of manhood. But this young girl was self centered, independent and careless. When I knocked his door late at night and I was horrified by the smell and mess accumulated in his flat. I felt something was very wrong with him when he did not recognize me. He had a far away gaze and his breath smelled like a mixture of cannabis and alcohol.

"Hey Massimo, how are you doing" I said, "It's me Louis, are you OK bro," I asked.

He never answered me, instead he screamed. "Who are you, where is my baby, did you bring him with you?" I did not know what to say or what to do, realizing my worst fear came true. Massimo was a sweet emotional Pisces and this sign is prone to any and all forms of addiction. The constant emotional drain was too much for him and he fell deep into Neptune's irreversible quick sands. This episode brought back my own dreadful memoirs of the relentless battle I fought for so long to defeat anguish and madness. His stare was empty and his pupils enlarged, he was at the early stage of schizophrenia. As I entered his cluttered apartment cautiously and he stopped me by a mirror and asked me, "Is my head bigger than yours? You know I can fly, I am going back home to Italy with my son, soon." he added.

At that very moment, I knew he lost the battle and I lost my dear friend. Looking at his helpless face, I could not hold my tears any longer and simply walked away. I knew Massimo was out of reach and no one would ever be able to help him. I did not want to be the one to take him to the hospital and watch him turning into a medicated zombie. I hated myself for connecting with him again and the awful sight he left me with. I wanted to remember my precious time with Massimo as my handsome, beautiful and healthy companion. I walked past the building office and told the guardian to help someone in apartment number 25. I walked endlessly in the cold rainy night, totally disheartened and never saw Massimo again.

It took me weeks to adapt to my new life without the love of Jane and Massimo precious friendship and I missed them terribly. Coming from a super wealthy lifestyle to a normal life and losing my best friend to madness, took a serious toll on me and I worked really hard to fight my own depression. My shattered heart needed serious healing, but I could only promise myself to work harder, to move on and rebuild a better life for myself.

I found a job at a local Greek restaurant and there I met with an attractive exotic Filipino girl, she later became my sweetheart. She and her sister were trainee nurses and worked long hours at Saint Mary's Hospital. Her sister was under the supervision of a medical intern named Marc and after a while, they became lovers. She introduced me to Marc and we became real good friends. I told Marc about my desperate situation and he offered me a live-in position in the hospital. My part time job was to take care of the nightly hospital switchboard operations.

I was in my second year as a student at the Royal School of Music and my primary job at the "Rumblebelly" restaurant was taking its toll on me. Mike was the owner and we also became good friends. Money was scarce those days and I could not even afford a moped and Saint Mary's Hospital was nearly a forty-five minute walk from downtown Eastbourne.

I recall that memorable winter night, the weather as usual was awful outside and I felt somehow lucky to work in the warm tiny kitchen area. My duties consisted of helping the chef make salads and cleaning everything that came back from the restaurant. The cheap hamburgers and French fries attracted a lot of hungry people in the late hours, when all local bars closed down. The weekends were very busy and exhausting. I was rushing to prepare food and clean the endless chain of pots, plates, and utensils coming from the busy restaurant. The old dishwasher was much too small to handle large loads and I found myself washing much of the dishware by hand. Action was everywhere and in his hastiness, one of the waiters dropped his load in the sink and a broken glass deeply sliced my hand. I screamed in pain and removed the sharp edged glass fragment lodged in my left palm. The liquid soap added a stinging feeling, while blood was gushing everywhere. The chef was much too busy to notice my blood-spattered hand and in no way could I afford to stop working.

I ran downstairs in the basement and enveloped my hand from the wrist up, into a plastic bag used to pack up sandwiches and tied it up with a thick rubber band. I made my way up to the kitchen and went back to work as if nothing ever happened, but boy was I glad it was my left hand that had gotten hurt. With all the action around me, my heart pumped more blood through my dilated veins and much of it escaped from the profound gash, into the bag and the soapy water. I did not want the chef or any of the waiters to see any blood and kept the water tap open. This brainless idea caused me to pass out right in the middle of the kitchen floor, but when you are young, you really think you are invincible.

All around me began to fade away; first the excruciating pain, then the noise, then I felt like being sucked into a black hole, and I was gone. A few moments later, I felt some cold water on my face and I was brought back to the physical world. My wound was serious and called for a few stitches and everyone around me was very concerned. "Let's take him to the hospital right away" a worried waitress said, but I regained enough consciousness to stop anyone from calling for the emergency service. "No, no." I said, "I have a doctor friend at St. Mary Hospital and he will fix my hand when I get there later".

Nick, the restaurant owner came down to the kitchen to assess the damage and then helped me to his apartment upstairs. With the help of a caring waitress, he cleaned the deep gash with alcohol. The procedure was painful and my injured hand was finally enveloped with a proper sanitary dressing. I had another hour left on my shift but Nick gave me the rest of the night off. 'Take care of yourself Louis, go to the hospital then go home and get some rest" he said. I was far from worrying about my injury, instead the thought of not being able to work or practice my Mozart piano piece, petrified me. The entire world crashed on me, knowing that the Graduation Day was only a few months away. My other job at the hospital was less demanding and regardless of my painful wound, I decided to face the elements and took the forty minutes walk to the hospital. I was also hoping for my doctor friend Marc to be at work and stitch my hand back together.

ℒaw of 𝒪bstacles

* Here the **Law of Obstacles** was at work. Obstacles are placed in our way only to make us stronger. Without fear there could be no courage. Without difficulties there could be nothing to challange our Life is an obstacle course and when we make it across the difficulty we are the stronger for it. Though they seem unpleasant, they are the weights that we lift to develop character. If only we could remember that when they appear, and wonder what the lesson is instead of cursing them.

Mother Mary Miracle

The cold rain, freezing coastal wind, and the shooting pain made the walk unbearable. I was young, blessed with a will of steel, and trained to deal with misery with courage. I was hot and sweaty when I left the badly ventilated restaurant and the chilly night was not going to stop me. I was already battling a persistent cold, but I had no other option than to take care of myself. After what seemed an eternity, I finally arrived at St. Mary's Hospital, totally exhausted and in serious pain.

I swiftly gulped a boiling cup of coffee and punched my time card in the indifferent machine. I hated this clock, because it marked a time where my life did not belong to me anymore, but to the long and boring night in front of me. Answering the few calls during my night shift was not exactly physically demanding, apart from the regular walks along the smelly wards for security purposes. All of the patients were terminally ill and painfully waiting for their demise. Sadly enough, Marc was off duty that night. Even though my injury was serious, I did not want to bring him back to the hospital just for me. I hated the entire world around me and I had to call on my supreme spirit to deal with my aching hand and the long night ahead of me.

Night duty Filipino nurses were busy taking care of the sleepless elderly patients. Some of those strong-willed girls had to work very long hours or like me, two jobs to survive. Some of these girls killed time by smoking in the empty corridors, while others took naps in the office. I was aware of all the rules, but I never enforced or reported the girls. Nothing I would say or do would help or hurt the dying patients one bit. This particular hospital was the last stop where the elderly did not have to wait too long for the trip back to God.

For hours I used to play on the church's old organ giving a form of entertainment to the dying. I knew they would miss my melodies for a few weeks to come. An old piano was also a proximity to the ward and my music was the only beautiful thing they had left. I was happy to bring them a sense of relief between the excruciating bed sore cleaning sessions. Before my injury, I painfully recalled an old man asking me for a glass of water and a song. I gave him the water and played an old song on the piano for him. When I returned he was dead; his glass of water was left unfinished on the table and his soul flew away, lifted by the sound of my music. I knew him well and I cried silently for a while, but I was happy to be the person to grant his last wish on earth.

Seated in front of my dead telephone board, I was harassed by a wave of depressive thoughts. I felt dizzy for a while and my running nose was making it difficult for me to breathe. To make the situation worse, I had a pounding headache, and my hand was killing me. I had caught a serious cold and I was at one of the lowest moments in my life feeling very lonely, missing Jane and my family. I could not even turn to my best friend Massimo; he had gone back to Italy just a few weeks ago. I was alone and desperate and I decided to try forgetting my misery by reading a brochure on the hospital history.

Before becoming Saint Mary's Hospital, many centuries ago the small mission was operated by monks and nuns. The story goes that a nun named Mary began to perform healing miracles and many people came from all over the country to see her. When she died, her body was buried in the small chapel, in what is now the hospital. Many nurses and patients have reported seeing her at night, walking the long corridors. Many terminally ill patients proclaimed talking to her and all believed that she was to lead them to the Light of God. I was very young and I was ignorant of any spiritual manifestation and most certainly had no idea that I was going to deal with "Mother Mary" directly in two very different situations. I felt that maybe a prayer would help me out of my gloomy attitude and began to talk to her.

"Dear, St. Mary" I asked "is it worth me staying here in the UK? Is it worth it for me to suffer so much, away from home and my dear family? Will I succeed in my musical tests? Am I wasting my time in the UK? Please, St. Mary, give me a simple sign anything at all will do please," I begged her.

Looking carefully around me I waited patiently for an indicator to take place but nothing happened and I thought this makes no sense, there is no Mary, no sign, all this is bull and I hated myself to make such a silly request. Little did I know I was going to witness a true miracle that will stay with me until I expire myself from this world. I was lethargic and fighting hard to stay awake and while stretching, I glanced behind me into the trash basket. I saw an old newspaper and a bunch of discarded dead roses lying there. I felt a force inside of me pushing me and I reached for the lifeless flowers. For some unknown reason, I brought them right in front of my face and stared at them.

THEN A TRUE MIRACLE HAPPENED! To my stupefaction, the dead roses slowly began to rise in front of my astounded eyes! I could not believe what I was seeing! I could not speak or move and I felt like a life force traveling through my entire body, my head, my arms, and then all the way through my hands. The flowers slowly began to rise and regained both their full red color and vibrant life. My mouth was wide open and I was in total awe. I was looking at the most beautiful bouquet of roses ever, emanating life as if death itself never extended to them. Apart from my UFO encounter as a child, I had never experienced the supernatural like this before and my faith in St. Mary and her powerful messages helped me to get through one of the worst times in my life.

Anyone reading my book can either doubt my integrity or question my sanity, but I can only assure you this miracle took place as such. Many years later, I finally understood the paranormal "manifesto" and the energy field involved. Following this amazing occurrence, my hand healed rapidly and I knew no one would ever buy my story. I prudently decided to keep my miraculous experience with "Mary" for myself and shared the miracle with close friends only. Finally the day came for my Musicianship examination and I was ready. The Audrey Wickens School of Music in Eastbourne was full of anticipating students and proud parents. I was outside smoking and charming the pretty girls, while valuable instructions were given to the virtuous students inside the building. After a while, my name was called and I walked back straight to the maestro's Grand piano and sat there motionless.

The room was packed and silent while the critical judges were waiting for me to start playing my piece. Standing next to me was a tall skinny man, who carefully placed a few sheets of music in front of me. After a while, murmurs floated in the thick atmosphere, wondering why I did not yet start playing. I did not move a finger and the man next to me whispered in my ear, "What are you waiting for Louis, are you stage frozen?"

"No, I am not; I am waiting for you to go! I can't play with someone standing next to me," I answered. The Grand piano had a hidden microphone that picked up all my words, loud and clear and the man finally left. Part of the instructions that I missed while I was outside was this person's job to turn the many pages of the "Praeludium One" piece of music composed by Mozart. I was wondering about the dexterity and speed of my fingers, but as soon as he left, I began to play. The many months of practice paid off and once I finished playing, to my surprise, I received a standing ovation. I was proud of a job well done and left the stage in a hurry.

My mom was missing me too much and I had to go back home regardless of the outcome with Nick. I managed to do so, by finding temporary replacement for my monotonous duties. I had planned to go home right after my examination and I was very late to catch the train to New Heaven and cross over the English Channel to France. Many hours later, I recognized the familiar mountains of the South of France. The weather was still warm as I exited the train in the city of Orange in Provence. My mother took the drive from my little village and after hugging her; I took over the driving back home. We spoke about the latest news about the family and my most recent crazy adventure. After a good dinner and a few glasses of wine late into the night, I went to bed enjoying the safety and love of the place we all call home. I could only stay for two weeks because of my job and an important recording project started with my English musician friends.

Law of Release

* The inexplicable revival of the roses demonstrates the **"Law of Release."** When we are at our wits end, desperate and have nowhere to go, it is possible to release the worry and tension and let the higher powers of our own subconscious take over. This may result in true miracles. The prayer I made to St. Mary was a prayer to my own subconscious. The moments while occupied in prayer, I was not engaged in disappointment or worry but rather appealing to the higher part of myself to show me a sign. This gave my subconscious a chance to show itself in the miracle of the roses

---

My Second UFO Experience

I took the Ferry trip through the English Channel so many times and I always anticipated the people I was going to meet on the ship. I could never escape the thought of when Roland and I took the trip to England for the first time and all the dramatic experiences left behind. I could not help to think about him and where or what he would be doing right now.

My life has always been rich and my adventures are the spice of my existence, just because I always had a healthy thirst for more. Back in the old house, the memories of my encounters with extraterrestrials left me with an unfinished taste in my mouth, I subconsciously wished for more. I was anticipating quality family time, but certainly not another painful encounter that would commemorate this trip home forever. I must emphasize once more to the reader, this material is not fiction and this close encounter of the third kind really took place.

The next day at about 2:00 PM, my older sister Noelle and Mom's agitated discussion woke me. At the time, my sister was a children's coach and worked for an organization deep in the mountainous region of "La Provence". She missed her bus ride and was very upset. "I am going to get fired from work, if I don't make it in time," she said to mom, sobbing. My step dad had long gone to work and none of my brothers were around to drive her to the site, which was about 70 miles away from home.

"Don't worry, honey. Louis is here and he will take you there," mother said calmly.

Driving there meant spending more time with my sister and we happily took the road with mom's recommendation to drive safely and to wear our seat belts. In 1976, the use of a map or owning a cell phone was a foreign thing to anyone. I entirely relied on the road signs and some stops along the way to ask for directions. The South of France's intricate road system was a true nightmare. The tiny tortuous roads often lead to a few crisscrosses where the signs were either gone with the wind or shot down by a frustrated hunter.

It was about 3:30 AM and I was totally lost in all sense of the word and my sister Noelle had been asleep for hours. It was dark and each turn brought more danger and the icy road revealed a high altitude. I was fatigued and hoping for any sign of life or direction. I was especially longing for a hot cup of coffee in order to stay awake and drive safely. After what seemed to be an eternity, I saw a dim light from my vintage view. A feeling of hope reaffirmed all my senses and I woke my sister from Neptune's grasp. "Hey Sis, wake up, we've got to stop here," I said gently "and I need a cup of coffee now!" I added trying to wake her up faster. She complained about the cutting cold, as mom's old car did not have a heater.

I parked the car safely by the road just a few feet from the front door of the little café. I did not see any parked cars there and thought how lucky we were to find an open restaurant in the middle of the night. Walking past the door, I asked Noelle what she wanted to drink. "A coke" she said, half awake. I was surprised by her choice; I was expecting her to ask for a warm drink, especially when she complained of the bitter cold earlier.

I gently asked my sister to sit by the fireplace and wait for me. An eerie feeling came all over me when I noticed three huge men standing at the bar. They were very impressive, matching, and nearly 7 feet in height. The men were speechless, motionless, and facing the bar's mirror. I felt like I was watched and had no idea of their intentions. I am very protective of any of my family members. "Damn, I am in serious trouble if these guys are bad," I thought. But as always I was ready to face death without fear or hesitation, if any of those huge guys were to hurt my little sister.

I carefully approached the bar and politely asked the barman for a coke and a cup of coffee. I was standing just a few inches away one of the very tall men and he seemed even more menacing. I felt like a miniscule ant next to a huge foot, but I willed myself to ignore my fear. I brought the coke to my sister and went back to the bar and collected my cup of coffee. "Those guys must be loggers to be so muscular and probably work in the area," I thought. Then the nightmare started when the one closest engaged me in conversation.

He looked straight into my eyes and said, "Do you wanna play cards with me? You'll be friends with cards for the rest of your life. You don't know that just yet," He added. The stranger's size and his probing, magnetic gaze terrified me. His remark did not make any sense and brought more fright to my entire body. I politely and submissively refused, telling him I was tired and stopped here only for a short time to get directions. He ignored my response and ordered, "Come on, pick a card, do it now!" holding a full deck fanned in front of me in his enormous hands. At this point I was really scared and the last thing I wanted to do was to upset him and thought I had better comply with his demand.

I picked a card in the deck and as soon as I saw it he immediately told me what it was. "Very nice, this is great," I said again respectfully.

"Pick another one," he ordered again. I did not really know how to behave with him but my gut told me to comply and play safe with the weird stranger. He did the card trick on me a few times and each time I respectfully congratulated him. "Take another card Louis," he said ironically, but this time I was in shock because I had never told him my name. I was just frightened and anxious.

After a while I managed to said to him, "Whoa, this is a great game, I really like it."

He replied, "No, Louis this is not just a game!" By now I was totally bewildered and scared to death and realized rendering my will to him. He did his "trick" a few times and I wondered, how can he do this to me? How can he tell me without a doubt what the card was without even looking at it? I felt like he was bringing a mental challenge to me and I did respond accordingly, something I should never have done. He turned the Nine of Diamonds but in my mind I thought of telling him it was the Queen of Spades instead of the Nine of Diamonds.

Oh my God, what have I done, I thought, when he instantly and furiously replied, "Louis you will not change the Nine of Diamonds to the Queen of Spades". Just imagine yourself in my shoes when he said that, and you may remotely feel like I did. I was in a state of shock, wondering how in the world he could actually be able to read my mind so accurately. What was his purpose and what the hell was going on here, I thought. But this episode was nothing compared to what was to follow. His penetrating gaze overwhelmed me and I felt like a screwdriver was forcefully inserted through my mind. It felt like a laser going in from my left temple and exiting through the right side of my head!

I was totally helpless and could only keep my balance by holding myself to the counter. I applied all the will I had left to evade his controlling gaze and I barely made it to the bathroom just a few feet away. The door was open; I reached for the tap and splashed my face with freezing water trying hard to uphold my consciousness. I suffered a massive migraine and I felt like my eyes were about to pop out of my head. What was happening to me? I felt so invaded and so vulnerable, but why me, I thought. Then my sister Noelle came to my terrified mind, she was alone in the room with those frightening individuals and I needed to go back into the room. I could barely contain the growing pain inside my head.

I felt as if a heavy chain connected me with the gigantic man and that I was communicating telepathically with him. Using all of the will I had left, I began talking back to him. As experienced many times before, under a life or death situation, I felt the wild tiger in me was unleashing his ferocious self and my fears volatilized. "What the hell are you doing to me, who the hell are you and what's going on here?" I said loudly. "I am going out now and going to face you Mister and you better talk to me," I screamed. I immediately walked out of the bathroom and to my astonishment the three huge guys were nowhere to be seen, they had simply left the building. But why and how could they leave so fast; I was in the bathroom for such a short time, I thought.

I was relieved to see Noelle was still asleep and she had missed the entire ordeal. I was baffled and held my pounding head. I asked the barman, "Who were those people and where are they?"

"I don't know" he said, "They probably drove here like you did!" He added. I knew that no cars were outside when we arrived. This fact alone was not surprising at all as it was the middle of the night. Collecting all my courage, I ran outside looking for them but I found only a quiet and cold night. I was listening for any noise, but all I heard was the wind cuddling the tips of the tall pine trees in the moonless night. I walked back in the bar, woke Noelle up, and said let's get the hell out of here and we rapidly left the area. My sister was totally oblivious to what just happened to me there and fell right back to sleep.

I will never know what happened that night in that little café lost in the high mountains, but what is even more astonishing is that; I do not recall driving my sister anywhere after the encounter. If I did, she or I would remember asking for directions, or the destination and the goodbyes, etc. I only recall driving off the property in the middle of the night and the rest is a total blank. Instead, what I clearly recall is when it hit 9:00 AM the next day. My memory returned when

I was entering the boundaries of my village. A pounding headache that I battled for more than three consecutive weeks followed the tragic encounter. Indeed, Noelle and I were abducted for countless hours and I believe the restaurant was either a flying saucer made to look like a café or a meeting place, where we both were "hypnotized" and surrendered our will to the space visitors. Was I forced to meet them later or pre-programmed to drive to a secret location to be encoded or analyzed? Did they bring us back to the restaurant once their agenda was fulfilled and simply disappear before Noelle and I woke up? This encounter took place over twenty-six years ago and is still as fresh as yesterday in my mind, but there is also total darkness in the most incredible moments of the encounter.

Rest assured this is neither science fiction nor the product of a vivid imagination; this tragic encounter really took place. Many years later, I finally understood why the space man said to me. "You'll be friends with cards for the rest of your life". I am still unable to play regular card games, such as poker or the famous twenty-one in Las Vegas. How more dim can I be? Well, the only cards that I "play" with are all hands winners and I never lost a single game. This is because I do not "play" with regular cards, but respectfully and wisely handle the mystical Tarot cards to guide and help people.

I still wonder why the "Nordic" tall man got so upset with me when I tried to change the meaning of the cards he picked for me. I can only speculate on the reasons of our meeting, but my feeling about it all is quite clear. The intense pain I experienced was a very painful downloading of a rare lost wisdom found within the twenty-two symbols of the tarot cards, reflecting the twenty-two letters of the Hebrew alphabet. I will never find out the exact secret agenda or what or why I experienced such an encounter. This first "live" acquaintance with ETs was quite intrusive and agonizingly painful, but proved to be nothing less than extraordinary and very valuable for myself, personally. For years, I was left wondering about this miraculous encounter and the mystical purpose that shaped my fate. I was certain that I would meet with the incredible again and the future proved me right.

This experience shocked me badly, but I had to get on with my life and try to erase many disturbing thoughts. A few days later, a telegram from my teacher arrived at mom's house. She urgently asked me to return to the UK to collect my prize. To my delight I had won the Silver Distinction Cup of Higher Achievement and earned my Musicianship. My mother was happy and proud of her son's accomplishment and trumpeted the news to the rest of the family and the local newspaper interviewed me. This was my first ever, famous moment, right in my own little village and I wanted more. Little did I know that many years later, I was going to be featured in the Los Angeles Times and countless newspapers and magazines worldwide would carry my articles and horoscopes.

We celebrated the event and returned to England a few days later. My presence was requested at the Eastbourne City Town Hall where newspapers, the Mayor, and other Royal School of Music authorities would present me with the cup and my diploma. I was very proud, because I was number one in a school of 400 or more musical students. I could barely believe my own achievement, knowing that I never touched a piano before the age of twenty-four years old and graduated with honors in 1986. Against all odds, in two years or so, I mastered piano playing with long hours practicing arpeggio, while the rich kids were getting drunk or smoking pot daily. I mean business in all that I do and accomplished more than some people can do in a lifetime. The power of the subconscious is simply phenomenal, but one must build and maintain enough intensity and drive to reach the anticipated goal. It worked for me and it shall work for you, too.

Beside my Musicianship Award

Music was my First Love

Following my graduation; I concentrated on getting my musical career off the ground and worked even harder to pay for my musicians and the recording studio. I was exhausted but always found the time to write new songs. Losing both Jane to my errors and Massimo to madness was a great stimulant for my creativity. She still haunted my mind and I wanted her back in my life, but I knew her part had been played and was done in my life. I needed to make more money and working two jobs was not enough. What could I do to make more money, when I was working full shift and part time, I wondered? I was in a bad place, but I was not going to give up and thought my friend Marc might be able to help me.

I approached him with my dilemma and he suggested for me to save on my rent by offering me a live-in position at Saint Mary's Hospital. Sadly, I could only have the room if I accepted the most repulsive jobs in the hospital. No one wanted the night post and he urgently needed someone with a "solid stomach" to do so. Indeed, this was the most disgusting job that I have ever done and only later in life was I able to comprehend how "The Law of Attraction" interacted with my UCI and why I did this awful job.

Marc was a medical Doctor in charge of all the hospital functions and for a week or so no one had taken care of the unclaimed dead bodies that were accumulating. The job was terrible, but I did not have to work for Nick in his oven-like tiny kitchen and walk back in the rain to the hospital every night anymore. Marc was short on his mortuary staff and I was ready to take it. The idea of incinerating deceased people was appalling, but I also knew that I had no other options available. I felt that I had to make this sacrifice to further my musical career or waste valuable time looking for a better opportunity that was just not there.

I have learned tremendously from this 'down in the dumps' episode in my life although I did not know then that working for death could only bring it to me faster. It's all about energy and "a magnet will not attract a piece of wood," means a lot more to me today. Work for light and life, children and beauty and this vibrant energy will merge with you. Work for death and drama and be ready to experience it, this is what the worst of the Law of Attraction will undoubtedly bring into your life. I will skip all the nauseating details for some of my sensitive readers, but this degenerating morbid occupation led me to the bottom part of hell. There, I suffered a series of serious depressions, heavy panic attacks, and overpowering suicidal tendencies. It is another true miracle for me to have come out alive from this episode in my life.

I dealt with unseen powerful underworld forces sucking away both my sanity and the very essence of my existence. It started with the room. Marc could not find the key and annoyed said, "Damn, I can not have you near the girls dormitory, this hospital is full or nurses, the only room I have is by the church. A nun named Mother Mary used this remote living quarters. I hope you are not afraid of ghosts," he said jokingly. After wasting precious time searching for a key that was probably long gone, he finally decided to let me kick the door open. The smell coming out of the tiny room was horrid and we were surprised to see the nun's crucifix, humble garments, and shoes in the dusty closet.

Centuries of collected dust fell over me as I moved the long brownish curtains to open the tiny window. The cold fresh air was happily welcomed, "Damn, how long has this room been unoccupied" I asked Marc.

"I can't tell you Louis, but well before you and I were born" he answered. He swiftly went back to work and left me standing in the middle of the tiny room. While trashing the nun's dusty belongings, I felt a cold unwelcoming energy enveloping me. I did not make much of it, not knowing what "her spirit" had in store for me.

I went back to the restaurant and dismissed myself on the spot from three years of an abusive job. Nick tried hard to keep one of his most reliable hard workers and even proposed a significant raise, which I turned down. I went back to my new "home" happily to save myself from interminable walks and bad weather. I thoughtfully cleaned the bedding of its nasty pestilent residence, washed the floor a few times, changed the dissolving curtains, dusted every shelf, and removed all religious pictures. I had a strong urge to keep the old bible that had the nun's small crucifix lodged inside it.

I painted the room bright white and ornamented it with sexy pin-up girls. I slept a few days freezing with the window wide open trying to get rid of the awful odor of the mural and old furniture. All was fine, but the dreadful "job" began to take its toll on my young psyche. I spent more time with my new girlfriend Maria trying to "recharge" my batteries and regenerate with long love and sex sessions. I felt like I was watched yet accepted in Mary's bedroom regardless of the naughty changes that were imposed on the nun's living quarters. Maria's break was around 1:00 AM and as usual, she was "visiting" me. She was a caring girl and never came empty handed. Hot soup, tea and biscuits were always on the meager menu.

Then disaster struck when I was awakened by a knock on my door. Damn, she wants more I of me, she just left me and I was so tired, I thought. "Wait Hun, I'll be right there," I said, unlocking my door. To my surprise, Maria's sister Anita was standing right there. I could smell vodka from her breath, but she had total control of herself. She calmly said, "Louis I am in love with you, I can't stand you being with my sister, I am so much more prettier". I knew Anita liked me, but I did not know to what extent and I was perplexed. "Why don't you like me, what's wrong with me," she added.

"Nothing Hun, indeed you are gorgeous, but…" She never let me finish my sentence and moved for the kill. She kissed me passionately, exactly like Carol did when I visited her sister Jane. "Damn, again. What have I done to have sisters falling in love with me" I thought. During the course of my life, this dilemma plagued me so many times and I could only blame my magnetism on my masculinity or physical beauty. It was only years later that I was able to understand this puzzle coming from my fifth house, the seat of attraction between human beings. Born in February, my fifth house of love and romance is located in the sign of Gemini and this sign rules sibling, twins, and duality and is undeniably why sisters love me. Call it a curse or a gift, but dating a set of beautiful twins or two sisters would make many guys jealous…it is because of such incredible experiences, that I was able to understand and now teach numerous Universal Laws of Attraction.

I really liked Maria a lot, but Anita's passion was really hard to resist, especially when you are an unscrupulous young man craving sexual experiences. "Wait, let me get my bottle of Vodka, let's celebrate," she said, while poring the spirits. Soon, we both were as drunk as skunks and engaged in a passionate love making session. She spent the night with me and carefully returned to her quarters in the early morning hours. I was confused and bit hung over, happy of my new conquest, but "what would I say to Maria, now?" I thought. I did not have to wait very long for a hurricane of emotions and tears to confront me in my bedroom. Maria was a powerful Scorpio and unwilling to let me get away with my weaknesses that easily.

"You son of a bitch, I can't believe you did my sister, you should be ashamed," she screamed. "Don't you have enough with me?" she said angrily. I did not know how to react, trying to avoid a flying shoe. "I hate you," she said, "I wish you death, I don't want to talk to you, ever again" she added crying loudly. She left my room and never returned in a physical form… I had no idea then of the powerful flux of destructive thoughts generated by a Plutonic soul and I was about to find out the hard way. Thoughts are like intense laser beams that will go in time and space through matter and will for good or for worse, reach its target. The deep and passionate nature of a Scorpio liberates unseen dark forces that allied with other dormant phenomenon and all hell broke lose against my spirit.

I awakened perspiring, experiencing both chills and extremely hot temperatures. It was impossible for me to go back to sleep or to even stay in the room. I was experiencing serious psychic attacks that were consuming me alive. Was Mary upset at me using "her" bedroom for adultery? Was Mary's spirit punishing me for my infidelity? Was it Mary's will to get me out of her room or were Maria's vengeful thoughts killing me alive? The attacks always started in the middle of the night, forcing me out of the bedroom. Then when I managed to collect myself and come back to the room, the attacks started again and also intensified.

I was at a loss and could not find a plausible reason for this awful experience. One night the "psychic attack" was so strong, that I found myself running aimlessly in the rain along the sea front, crying for help. Had anyone seen me convulsing and crying endlessly under the pier, I would have certainly landed in a mental institution. I always somehow managed to get back normal and as soon as I passed the hospital gates, the unseen forces immediately possessed me. It was quite incredible that just a few feet and a gate would make such a difference in my behavior. It was like an invisible psychic wall was stopping me from entering the hospital. Each time I reasoned with myself and tried again, I was literally and violently thrown out of the property.

I blamed the nun for my misfortune and begged her for forgiveness. I came to accept that I was "fired" by her spirit and I psychically requested a cease-fire, to pack my possessions and leave the hospital for good. To my stupefaction it worked and I was totally fine, then a doubting thought came in my mind and I was instantly reminded not to mess up or move out with nothing. I packed my stuff and walked for the last time the long corridors to Marc's office. He looked at me and said. "Hey Louis you look like crap, what's the matter with you my friend, are you sick, don't you sleep at night?"

I simply responded, "Marc I have a serious problem and I have to go back home to France".

"What? Just like that, what is it?" he asked surprised. "If you leave now, you are not coming back, you understand, Louis?" he added uncomfortably.

"Yes, I know man, can't tell you anything, you won't understand me, I came to say goodbye". He was baffled and will never know the real reason behind my forced decision.

I left Saint Mary's Hospital safely and never returned. The unhappy vengeful spirits finally left me and I was liberated from the tenacious unbending psychic forces. The revolting job and the guilt constantly drained my batteries, while the pitiless powerful Scorpionic thoughts of Maria and maybe the pious soul of Mary did the rest, I thought. This venomous spiritual soup was liberated unknown to me. Unworldly and nefarious forces poisoned my body, mind, and soul. I was left wondering why Mary's spirit gave me the highest hope and faith in me and the lowest helpless sensation I had ever experienced.

Man's psyche is very complicated and indeed fragile, and I learned that there is only one hair between insanity and a normal state of mind. I won the most complex battle ever imposed on a human being and managed to keep sane and conquer my own world.

"I have a serious assignment to fulfill. I strive to free man's soul from fear and ignorance and enlighten its immortal spirit."
-- Dr. Turi

* Many years later, I understood that "the spirit" of Mary was far from giving life back to the flowers and her "message" strangely resembled a multitude of religious miracles taking place in different parts of the world. The bible says, "Man was made in the image of God" and therefore born with the mighty creative essence of God himself. So we are Gods in training on this dense physical world. The intensity of my emotion was fueled by agony. Concentrated fear triggered my subconscious to release a tremendous influx of life force into my entire body. The desperate need for an answer or a vital "sign" was rewarded and in the process. To my stupefaction, the flowers regenerated to life and my wounds healed rapidly. Also, because of my general unstable and guilty situation (and other important celestial factors) I was utterly vulnerable to Maria's Plutonic (vengeful) thought forces and became an easy target. Many emotionally unstable pious souls are prime targets of Voodoo practitioners or perfect candidates for the "Devil's possession". What I saw that night at Saint Mary's Hospital was positive force energy, channeled by my mighty, powerful subconscious. This phenomenon can also produce poltergeist activity and indeed explains the act of self-mutilation, better known as stigmata. It was because of the intensity of my emotional pledge that I was allowed to access a formidable healing source of power, unknown to both science and religion.

We are what we think. All that we are arises with our thoughts. With our thoughts we make the world.
-- Gautama Siddhartha

My Third UFO Experience

I was still in shock from the psychic attacks, but before taking the long trip back home I had to meet with all my musicians. I told them that I was going to make the money needed to produce my music in France and then shop for a music production company that would make and release the record. The plan was set in motion and my excuse to escape evil forces worked as planned. My latest dramatic experience and draining job took a toll on me and I lost a lot of weight in the process. My mother was happy to see me again after two years away from home, but she could sense something was very wrong with me. I was not the same Louis and I was trying very hard to cover and forget the terrifying incident that I left in England. It took me months to recuperate and finally my high spirit recovered fully.

I worked in the South of France, operating heavy construction machinery, building bridges and highways. My job as a heavy equipment operator and skilled welder, got me quite a lot of money that would be saved to finish my musical project in the UK. All was going just fine in my life and I was happily making great progress. Then the extraordinary took place with my third UFO experience. I was visiting my older brother Jo, enjoying the great food of his refined restaurant and his popular discothèque named *"L'interdit"* or "The Forbidden".

As a child, my older brother Jo had always wanted to be the owner of an old farm that we walked by many times as children. Finally in 1981 his own dream became a reality when he purchased and restored the old structure. The farmhouse was less than fifteen minutes away from the village in a remote wooded area. The nightlife in France starts around 11:00 PM and lasts all night long. We would usually leave the farm around 10:00 PM at night and come back exhausted the morning after. I enjoyed my rich French breakfast at about 9:00 AM and spent the rest of the day sleeping, eating, and riding his horses.

Then on November 11th, 1981 at about 10:15 PM we were to experience one of the most dramatic UFO experiences anyone can ever hope for. We left the farm that night again at about 10:00 PM. It was a cold night, but Jo's brand new Mercedes heater worked well and soon we enjoyed a very comfortable ride to his discothèque just a few miles away. I often thought how much Vincent would have appreciated Jo's sumptuous life. Jo, like me, had to work his way up right from scratch and after so much hell; he was able to finally enjoy his well-deserved luxuries. Vincent had been gone for so many years and I still missed his loud laughs and loving nature. Jo was driving smoothly through the tiny serpentine road, scaring away a multitude of rabbits. A drive of about three miles through endless vineyards separated us from the RN7 main road, and then we had another 30 miles to cover before reaching the discotheque.

The night was quiet and I was wondering about a pretty girl that I met the night before: when from the corner of my eyes I saw what seemed to be some far off flickering lights. We drove further into the night and the lights appeared, coming fast in our direction. Wondering, I asked my brother, "Hey Jo, are people working in the vineyard tonight?" Jo responded sarcastically, "Louis, its November, all the grapes were picked up last September, relax." Jo was born in November and his Scorpio sarcasm was nothing new to me and I never took it personally.

He kept driving, but not without noticing the strange lights above getting much closer. What really grabbed my attention was the circular movement of what seemed to be two powerful beams of light aiming at us. Jo kept driving, denying my requests to stop and check those peculiar lights. All of a sudden, out of nowhere the lights were stationary right above us and for no apparent reason the Mercedes electronic system failed, instantly bringing the car to stop right in the middle of the road. Jo and I looked at each other surprised and wondering, while an immense bright light illuminated the entire area. We both looked up through the windshield but the lights were so intense that we could not discern anything. I thought of a hovering helicopter right above us, but the distinct sound of blades flapping was missing.

There was no noisy engine roaring above us, just a steady quiet humming reverberation. Jo and I were perplexed and I anxiously asked my brother, "Jo what the hell is this? I am going outside to inspect this thing."

"You're crazy, stay in the car you've got no idea of what's up there," he said frantically. I really wanted to investigate whatever stationary object was above us, and I was not thinking about danger. Being the big guy in town, Jo was well respected and feared by all, but on that memorable night his macho personality disappeared. I saw a side of my big brother that I did not expect at all.

I managed to break free from his grip and as if pushed by an unseen force, I moved out of the car. The beam of light was so bright that I could not discern anything above the car. I slowly walked around the car, disregarding Jo's hysterical screams for my safety. After a short while the intense beams steadily dimmed and then went off. It took me a moment for my eyes to adjust from a compelling bright light to semi darkness. I kept looking up and slowly began to distinguish a round shaped outline, with a colorful softer reddish beam coming from its center. I kept squinting, forcing my eyesight to adjust to get a clearer picture of what was there, and then there it was.

The Mercedes froze under the Lights

Less than thirty feet above, I clearly saw a magnificent motionless flying saucer. I pondered for a moment, shaking my head, questioning my senses, and wondering if what I was seeing was real. I was outside of the car and frantically called for Jo to witness the spacecraft with me. I could not stand still and began screaming and banging the top of his car to get his attention. I was breathless and in total shock, "Oh my God, Oh my God, Jo it's a freaking flying saucer, it's real man, this is the real thing, come out Jo, come on, now!" No way was my big brother going to get out, but he saw everything through the windshield and from the safety of the Benz. Time seemed still and I had the rare privilege to see and admire the magnificent spaceship in its entire splendor. No words are yet refined or powerful enough to express the intensity of my feeling and the marvel of such a futuristic machine. I was in total awe!

It felt as if the ET's wanted me to acknowledge the reality of extraterrestrial life. I am also convinced there was intelligence operating the saucer, because when I showed signs of distress, they immediately dimmed and turned off the overwhelming lights. It was only then that I could clearly discern the circular red, yellow, blue, gold, green and white lights under the belly of the saucer. Then in a flash, the powerful beams returned to life, exploding the night into total brightness. As swiftly as it came the flying saucer disappeared into the darkness. In a hurry, Jo successfully restarted the car and said to me. "Louis, this did not happen, you can not say a word to anyone about what we saw tonight." I was still in shock, trying hard to recover from this absolutely unbelievable experience. We drove to our destination, trying hard to appear normal to everyone waiting for us. To our surprise the discotheque was very busy. This made sense to us, because some time was missing and it was as if we were in auto pilot mode and could not react or behave normally. Years later, I fully realized that my brother Jo and I were abducted on that unforgettable night of November 11, 1981 and had experienced missing time.

I never heard or saw a flying saucer before that and I had no idea or reason to accept or believe in the phenomenon. In some ways, I was happy that Jo was a solid witness of this memorable UFO sighting, because he never really trusted anyone or believed in anything before. In his Scorpionic reality, there is no God, no evil, no UFOs, no magic, and no stars. Like the majority of people, Jo was born skeptical and unwilling to accept the incredible. There is no doubt in my mind that my skeptical big brother needed a solemn wake up call and undoubtedly he got it that night. My influential brother had a reputation to maintain and he knew quite a lot of well-known people in town. Talking about a UFO sighting may not be a favorite topic for any of those wealthy snobs. Fearing ridicule, Jo kept this secret from the rest of the family for years. Finally over 20 years later at the Christmas table in front of the whole family, after a few drinks and to my surprise, Jo finally confessed the incredible UFO encounter.

He asked everyone's attention and said, "Well, I don't know how to say this to you guys, but do you remember years ago what Louis was saying about a flying saucer?" Everyone listened carefully. "Well, Louis did not make it up… this really happened on the way to my discotheque that I used to have." He added. "I am sorry Louis, but I had to deny it, because I was afraid to look weird to some of my partners".

Then, my sister Noelle said, "Yeah, something weird happened to us too, in the mountains when Louis drove me to work. I don't know what it was, but I had some creepy dreams after that." she affirmed. It felt pretty good to be supported by my siblings then I asked Jo.

"Hey bro, what made you change your mind about the UFO encounter?"

"Well my son is behaving like you did when you were a child and he is telling me all sorts of things about small people with big eyes. Since that experience together, I have learned to keep an open mind" he responded. I was in shock to learn that my own nephew was going through the same thing. He quickly proposed a toast to the ET's, covering his inner fear by laughing his head off. This was an extreme experience and really hit home. I nurtured unusual thoughts about my very existence and about life in general. I did not know anything about UFO or ET's and here I was, one of the kind touched directly by them. These UFO experiences always left me wondering about their mysterious agenda, but watching a UFO so closely got it's bearing on me. Why me, what do I have they want? Why did I have to go through this, I thought? This was the third time that I had to deal with UFO's and I wondered if an extraterrestrial intelligence was after me. This encounter left a profound impact on me, for months to come. I decided to remain silent and avoid hurtful remarks. Incidentally, many of the people unwilling to accept the facts about UFO's can only be ignorant or jealous. In the vastness of an infinite universe, common sense dictates the real possibility of other life forms. But then again, the majority of people on earth are not even remotely related to Einstein.

Success and Failure

I spent the rest of my vacation pondering this incredible experience and I decided to return to England to finish my project. For many weeks I found it difficult to concentrate on earthy matters. I had enough money saved to survive without working for about three months and spent much of my time writing songs and rehearsing with the band. David was a great songwriter and Marco was a musical genius. Other kids in the band were also gifted musicians. England may not benefit from great weather or fine food, but produces phenomenal music and don't forget the Beatles were from Liverpool. I endured pure hell and finally produced a master tape of my songs, suitable to any record company.

Like me, Marco was blessed with a strong will and being a Scorpio, sarcasm was a problem. I had to adjust to his emotional temper, because I was in need of his talent. David was a Sagittarius and more placid and our creative relationship flourished. We also had a good dose of respect for each other and great intuition. Marco once said, "If you do not make it to fame Louis, then nobody will!" Any comment coming from a Scorpio must be taken seriously.

Finally, I had the songs that I wanted; we all felt very comfortable with it and the anticipation of a hit was very high. A few days later, David found an affordable recording facility in Portsmouth and we all packed the gear into the van and took the rainy British highway to the recording studio. The two songs sounded perfect and after a countless hour of mixing, the master tape was finally ready. It took me many years to accomplish the easier part of a recording, now what do I have to do to get the real deal, I thought? In no way, could I rely on anyone but me to bring this arduous musical work to another level. Marc? Forget it, he was spoiled by an over concerned mother who would never let him out of her sight. David could not be relied on either, as he was newly wed and his priority was for his wife and their new baby. I was free and committed to carry my wish all the way to the top, regardless of what I had to do to make it happen. My legendary will to succeed kicked in again and I was ready to climb the highest mountain.

I tried countless well-known recording companies based in London without success. I had no management and my broken English did not help either. No producers or musical directors took me seriously or even took the time to listen to my precious master tape. There are regulations, contracts and rules to go by in the recording industry and as always I had to learn the hard way. I knew my music was commercial and that my musicians were good in studio or on stage, but I did not have the financial resources to open the door. Just because I did not wear a suit, have management, and could not express myself properly in English, they all turned me down. After months of relentless trial and failure, I changed my method. I kept visualizing the picture of my record in my mind and I could see the people dancing on the sound of my voice. I knew deeply inside that my music was great, David's lyrics fantastic and Marc's arrangements were simply phenomenal. My fervent intuition was telling me to try my natal France. The planned trip to Paris gave me new hope, but I did not know where to start. The yellow pages in any Parisian telephone booth would give me a starting point, I thought. I had faith, I had dreams, and I wanted to make it happen. This type of passionate committed drive can only bring forth the miracles to solidify any wish. I was young, full of hope, and inherited a super will. I simply had to do so and I did it my way. I arrived in Paris in the early afternoon of a rainy Friday autumn day. I avoided the cold and rain by ingesting countless Cappuccinos in bars and restaurants along the "Les Champs Elysees". I walked endlessly through the small streets of Paris until I found an inexpensive motel, where I finally enjoyed real food and got buzzed with some cheap, but delicious wine.

L'Arc de Triomphe　　　**La Tour Eiffel**

After a good night sleep, I checked the motel's telephone book and found Phillips recording Company's address. I had to make my way on foot to the prestigious Phonogram building that's located at "Boulevard de L'hospital". I had never seen the French capital city of Paris before and really enjoyed walking by the Arch of Triumph, the Eiffel Tower, Notre-Dame Cathedral, and the Muse Du Louvre. I kept walking, asking for directions, and the large leather briefcase that carried the heavy magnetic master tapes inside took its toll on my hand and arm. I finally reached my destination and entered the building, when a clerk and the watchful eyes of a big security guard stopped me immediately. "Hey, where do you think you're going, Sir? Do you have an appointment?" he asked in my native tongue.

"Oh, I am sorry Monsieur" I replied "I though I could have a few words with a musical director about my music ".

"It's Saturday." he said nastily "There is nobody in the building and you must make an appointment with one of the employees and comeback on Monday, during regular business hours" he added. I was wet and tired and did not look exactly business ready and he noticed. "This is not a place for vagabonds and I should have you thrown in the street" he added coldly. I was appalled by this person's attitude, reflecting a typical loser, doomed to keep his boring job and frustration forever, I thought. Then, a mass of menacing muscles accompanied me to the large exit sign by the glass doors.

"Gosh, what am I going to do?" I thought "all this money, time and effort, for nothing?" I was very disappointed to suffer the same treatment endured in London, but I was in Paris only for another day and I had to do something. From a distance, I saw people going in and out of the building and noticed moving shadows of bodies in the numerous floors. I am sure, I thought, someone had to be here for me and I had a brilliant idea. I entered a nearby telephone booth and searched for any names of musical directors' listed in the yellow pages. I dialed the front desk and asked for that specific person and got the extension. The telephone was ringing at the other end and my heart was pounding. I had no idea if the person was there or not, I just took a chance. A female voice answered, "Hello, may I help you?" she said. I explained to the lady I was a French musician, but lived and worked in the UK.

"I came all the way from England with a master tape and I need for you to give me your professional judgment of my musical production." I said. When I mentioned England and a master tape, she realized that only a state of the art recording was involved and she took a chance on me. My intensity and the right words did the job and we set to hold the meeting within the hour, on the seventh floor of the building. Just imagine the faces of the stunned clerk and the dangerous bulldog waiting comfortably on the lobby sofa for the Lady to greet me. You've got to love it, when you manage to beat all the odds and show real power to an average employee. My sarcastic smile did more damage than words or brute force. Success breeds self-esteem and each time that you score against any opposition, you get closer to your goal.

She appeared stressed and hastily guided me to the elevator. She did not speak much and seemed annoyed, assuming that dealing with me was a total waste of time. She appeared snobbish and never asked for me to sit down or offered me a cup of coffee. She probably based her judgment on my soaking appearance and my cheap bag and worn-out shoes. She finally said, "I have to go to the audio room to listen to your master tape, don't you have a regular audio tape?" she added unkindly. She left in a hurry, making me feel like she had better things to do with her precious time. I was wondering how she was going to react to my work and how she was going to get rid of me. I rejected those negative thoughts immediately and my heart started pounding uncontrollably. She came back with the biggest smile that I have ever seen on a woman's face. She finally asked me to sit and asked if I wanted a cup of coffee. I knew right then, that I had reached my goal, well before she proposed a recording contract with me. She said, "I am amazed by your music, it is so commercial and you sing so well, I love it. When can you come back to Paris and add some percussion and violins?" She added.

It felt like a wind of pure light was enveloping me. In a fraction of time, I retraced the tremendous effort and pain that I suffered for so many years. I was in a euphoric state of joy, where I had to control my tears and the accompanying feelings of joy exploding inside. I connected with the force that gives life and brings about miracles and at that very precise moment, I was living the feelings of enjoying true accomplishment. I cheerfully thanked the lady and brought the contract back to England for the rest of the band to see. I did not touch the ground all the way back my motel and called the guys waiting for me in England and broke the incredible news. They were hysterical and I could hear screams of joy in the back of the room. I spoke to Marco and told him that his dream of becoming a conductor would soon come true. Two weeks later, we were flown to Paris and Marco was conducting the French Philharmonic Orchestra in Paris. To this day it has been his highest accomplishment and Marco, like David and I, had a dream. I did it my way for all of us.

I was on top of the world and finally I could see in real life people dancing on the sound of my voice. Mission accomplished, I thought, now I want to do it in a big way. Then reality struck when Marco, David, and all other musicians did not trust the French management. Telephone calls were made and separate contract demands fueled a very negative energy and with it the possibility to ruin all of my efforts. Sadly, their suspicions (or creations) became a reality, just a few months later when my brother Yves called me from Switzerland, to congratulate me. "Hey bro, you're the man," he said, "your record is in all shopping centers here! Damn, you're going to be rich soon!" he added laughingly.

"Thanks Yves, but what the hell are you doing in Switzerland," I asked.

"I was sent here by my company, I'll be home next week, and you're coming too, we miss you, Louis!" he said happily. I was happy to know that my record sale had made it out of France and I again gave the good news to David. He was perplexed and asked me to join him immediately with a copy of my contract. Sitting in front of a hot cup of tea, he read the fine lines of my contract. He read it for me "The A-sided record titled 'She is not yours' and the B-sided record 'Lost love' is to sell world wide, but not in France." This way, we could not know our own record sales.

My entire world fell apart and my dream was shattered. David suggested for me to immediately call Phonogram in Paris and ask for some explanations. I did and the Lady told me that a crook had promised to invest some money and then joined in a new contract deal. Incidentally, this person was brought in around the same time, when everyone involved in England generated the feeling of mistrust. Indeed other people's negative thoughts did stimulate "The Law of Attraction" and brought this new element into the equation. Months later, I found out this person was her boyfriend and in the process, she lost it all to him. He was only looking for a quick get rich scheme and was never interested in promoting the band or myself. The signed contract totally protected him and I had no resources to bring any legal action against him.

Law of Focus

* **"The Law Of Focus"** was what I used to accomplish my recording. I had a dream that the world could hear my music and people would dance to it. That dream appeared after many years of hard work, and because I never let go of the ultimate goal. I had to endure grueling jobs and many disappointments along the way, but in the end the work paid off. I had a record made and was heard all through Europe. Even with my success, fate had another goal for me, one I couldn't have imagined back then. And so, focused as I was, life took me in a different direction – but not without first granting me the reward of having a successful recording.

Part 3

America

In the Dark

I was not fired up with music anymore and my creativity suffered enormously. Was it a signal that I had better things to do in my life than cutting records? I pondered over so many reasons why this happened to me. Also my latest UFO close encounter kept coming to mind. My dreams were dreadfully vivid and always involved an interaction with scary aliens. I could not blame my imagination for these visions, because I never read a book or watched a movie involving aliens. I felt deeply that something huge was in store for me, in the near future. Nowadays, I teach omens and dream interpretations, to help others to "perceive" what the future holds. I have learned, that losing or investing in a watch or a pair of glasses, experiencing an accident or investing in a car, are serious omens and you should tighten up your seat belt and be ready for a new ride. Observing a flying saucer so closely is indeed, was a very unusual omen and I was about to fly high and fast to a new world. Once more, my adventurous spirit came to the rescue. I had enough of the wet English weather, I was disgusted by the music industry and I got seriously bored of everything and everyone around me. My only real friend Massimo, was stuck somewhere in a mental institution and I wished to leave it all behind and move to a far away, foreign country.

I escaped my depressive situation by watching American movies. The wild open spaces and dramatic scenery gave me the desperate sense of the freedom I needed. My wish was slowly becoming a reality, while my subconscious creative forces began handling the puzzle in it's own magical way.

My first solid opportunity came a few weeks later at a casual meeting with a guy met at my local bar. His name was Mike; he was from San Diego, California and was visiting a friend in Eastbourne. I recognized his heavy American accent and we struck a lively conversation about France, England, and the US.

Incidentally, a few weeks before, I was looking all over for a bulky silver cross and could not find it. I was about to give up, when one day out of the blue, on my way to the bank I walked past the small jewelry store. To my amazement, I saw the exquisite silver cross of my dreams in the window display. As usual, my subconscious did not forget and brought it to me. I had the money in hand and immediately purchased it. But in my mind, I wanted an eagle engraved on it and meeting Mike was the answer. I also told him that I was a recording artist and had always wanted to go to America. He offered his help and gave me his business card and said, "Just come over, Louis. I have a big house and a small business on

Mission Boulevard, just by the ocean in San Diego. I know some people and I will help you to get started and find a job." I wanted to trust him so much, because I wanted to go away, so badly. "You can stay with me, we will have fun," he added. I felt really good inside and unmistakably recognized the divine force interacting for me. I warmly thanked him for his help and just before living the bar, he tossed a couple of US quarters saying, "Take those coins Louis, they will bring you luck." I was in shock, for the first time in my life I saw the magnificent golden eagle silver coins. I took the two US silver quarters and had them welded onto the front and the back of the thick cross.

The message from my subconscious was quite clear; the eagle symbolizes flying high all the way to the US, while the cross signifies divine protection from above.

My Journey Begins

I wondered where I would find the money for the expensive plane ticket to the US. This was an urgent problem, but somehow I knew deep inside that my subconscious was going to take care of it all in time and in its own way. Also, I was in debt and owed a lot of money to friends and recording facilities. At this pace, it would have taken me years before I'd make it to America. Eastbourne was a small retirement coastal city where the hotel industry dominated all other means. No opportunity was available for me to utilize my Engineering skills, and going back home was out of the question since my situation was so desperate that I could not even afford the trip. I was starving, miserable, sad and unhappy and aimlessly walked the streets. A restaurant owner friend saw me and invited me for a fish and chips lunch. I was her "confident" and we often spoke about her personal problem reinforcing her wounded spirit. She was constantly called to the till by ballooned clients eager to pay their bill. A discarded newspaper was on the nearest table, so I picked it up and began to read the job opportunity section. My curiosity paid off when a German construction company offered astronomical wages for highly skilled welders. Once more, my vigilant subconscious worked for me... The chances for me to buy a newspaper were non-existent, as a single penny meant a lot to me then.

I asked my friend if I could use her telephone and after two minutes of talking, I had the deal in motion. I was asked to fly to Germany as soon as possible and invest in the expensive welding gear. All my expenses were to be reimbursed upon my arrival on the job. I had to find the money to make it happen and I did. I worked steadily for years for Nicky and my paychecks were regularly deposited to the local bank. I thought of asking for a loan and set a meeting with the bank manager. I cautiously explained the opportunity that I was offered and the large amount of money that I was going to make. He politely suggested me to show a form of proof of employment, which he received by fax within the hour, directly from Germany. I was on my way to earning a lot of money and fulfilling my life's dream to move to the United States of America. I took a plane for the first time in my life. I was a bit apprehensive of flying through the English canopy of dirty white clouds. Soon enough, we reached the cruising altitude of thirty-one thousand feet and I was so happy to finally see the blue sky and the sun. I felt the warmth of the sun on my face and realized how much I had missed it. The short flight to Germany brought back the polluted clouds, the rain and the cold. I was anticipating the large amount of money awaiting me, to pay my way to the USA. I had not practiced welding for many years and I was a bit apprehensive because I had to perform a series of sophisticated tests. The German standards are extremely high and the examination required using all of my welding skills to be tested with ultra sound, high air and water pressure, along with radiocarbon for possible leaks.

Under the scrutiny of three inspectors I passed all the tests without a glitch. I thanked my FPA engineering training taken years earlier when back home in France. My contract was only for three months with a possibility for renewal if both parties agreed on new terms. I did not want to get screwed again and I made sure to read all the tiny little lines before signing.

Years later, I realized my Dragon's Tail in Libra (contracts) is ruled by Venus (the arts/music) and the Draconic Law is impartial to anyone's ignorance. Signing a contract on all affairs involving the Dragon's Tail is a sure sign for disaster, especially if the Universal Law of the Moon is not respected. On the other hand, this contract involved my Dragon's Head (luck/protection) in Aries (Fire/ Germany/engineering) and was signed in a Waxing Moon. Both Universal Laws were respected and dictates the smooth operation and the incredible outcome of this period in my life.

My experience in Germany was a reminder of what I was subjected to for those years in England while learning the language, with exception that a good portion of the German population speaks English. Only perfection was expected from my German superintendent and me and other supervisors were extremely tough and unforgiving to a fault. I knew my special welding skills were badly needed and after a few verbal abuses the aggressive tiger in me demanded respect. My "bosses" quickly realized, to exercise their patronizing ego with someone else or deal with the risky consequences. The money was good, but I was young and wild and I worked hard to control my intense emotion and readiness to fight. During the weekend I ventured out in the city, searching for any way to kill the agonizing solitude. Young and full of life, I wanted to find a female companion, especially when the German girls I saw in the streets were astonishingly attractive. I always had a weakness for a thin body, penetrating blue eyes and long blond hair, but I had no problem with good-looking dark-eyed curly brunettes either. Let's blame it on my rotten Gemini dual attitude regulating my fifth house and the seat of attraction, if we may.

I avidly explored the local bars and quickly learned to be cautious with German beer, after throwing up all the way to my hotel. On one of my Saturday night escapades I walked by a discotheque, indeed the best place to find what I was looking for. I struck up a conversation with a tall man smoking a cigarette by the door. "Excuse me, how much is the cover charge here?" I asked.

The man answered my question with another question and his own answer, "Where are you from? Are you from France?"

I was surprised, but Germany is very close to France and he probably visited my country in the past, I thought. "Yes, I am!" I said. Because of the war, I thought the German people hated French, but I was about to find out I was wrong, when his face lit up asking me in a broken French, to join him inside. Great, I thought, someone I can speak with. I followed him on through the busy dance floor to the bar. The busy barman saw us and literally ran in our direction to take his order. They exchanged few words in German and he immediately brought a very expensive bottle of "Dom Perignon" with a bucket of ice.

This brought memories of how the staff would behave with my brother Jo and I in his own nightspot at home. The barman poured the drinks with a big smile and never asked for a bill. "Damn, how more lucky can I be or am I being set up?" I thought. All sorts of crazy thoughts entered my mind, wondering why a stranger would treat me like a king after a few minutes of first meeting me. I knew the French charm worked for ladies, but regardless of my horny nature I was not interested in anything else. I really thought this guy was gay and after me.

His subconscious picked my wandering thoughts and he said, "Oh, by the way, my name is Wolfgang and I am the owner of this place. You are my guest, so enjoy it my friend." He continued, "I love France so much, but I have never been there. I learned French when in school, but I forgot much of it. I don't get to practice my French that often." I felt relieved and almost immediately felt totally at ease. We drank another bottle of sparkling wine and I was happy as can be. I was about to find out why Wolfgang "subconsciously" loved French and how the "Law of Attraction" had worked so well for us.

"Louis, I have to tell you a great story about my grandfather during WW1 in France," He said. I thought to myself, how could someone have anything good to say about war? But I was in for another surprise. His Grandpa, then a very young drafted soldier was sent to war in France. Just past the Swiss border on the French territory, "The Resistance" blew a bridge while he was riding with other young soldiers. Many young Germans were killed in the explosion and derailment following the intense blast. He and other young recruits fled for their lives throughout the French countryside. They separated to increase their chances of survival. After a few nights, his grandfather pushed by hunger found an isolated farm and stuffed himself with eggs he found in the barn. The next day, the farmer's daughter caught him in his sleep. Indeed a strange love story, but the stars and seat of attraction between humans do not care about religion or war and they fell in love. She fed him and kept him safe for many days but her suspicious father caught her with him.

The old farmer must have been a sensitive and spiritual man and understood that war cannot kill the passionate love of two young people, regardless of their nationality. He never reported him to the "resistance" and instead, helped his daughter to save his young life. He spent a good part of the war helping the family by doing odd jobs in exchange for food, love and safety. Then a squad investigating the farm liberated him. The Germans are also human beings and recognized the great chance the family took for one of them and rewarded the farmer with an ample load of sparse provisions. He promised her to comeback after the war if he was lucky enough to escape with his life. A year later, he was seriously wounded but recuperated well. As promised, he came back after the war and married her and two beautiful children came out of the union. Now, I understood why Wolfgang loved the French so much.

We became really good friends and all my spare time was spent with numerous gorgeous ladies in his disco and riding horses on his property which is located on the city outskirts of Kulmbac. Wolfgang was very wealthy and one day he simply asked me to stop working, because he could easily take care of me financially. I was astonished by his request and amicably explained to him that the only way for me to breach my contract and still get paid, was to suffer an accident or a medical emergency. The idea of getting a large lump sum of money from him, and from my company was very appealing to me. My thoughts were constant and my imagination fueled "The Law Of Attraction" to display its destructive force against me. While welding on a large suspended pipe, the sweat on my face moved the protective glass, so that I accidentally suffered a serious "coup d'arc" in my eyes. The powerful beam momentarily blinded me and I fell nearly ten feet to the ground, miraculously avoiding a spinning metal saw.

I was knocked unconscious and brought immediately to the emergency room. I woke up in the ambulance with an intense pain in my eyes, wondering what had happened to me. The emergency crew was asking to move my feet while radioing the hospital. Luckily for me, my spine did not suffer any lasting effects and I was released the very next day. Wolfgang and the girls were by my side, all along and I never went back to work. I was able to cancel my contract and got more money from Wolfgang, my aim was reached and all the money was saved in my bank account. The thought of moving to America haunted me daily, but I was having a great time and I made the most of it for a few more weeks. I did not know much about the subconscious back then, but now I realize that Wolfgang' subconscious attracted me for another reason. He told me, "I've got to fix this gate someday or one of my horses will escape".

"What happened to it?" I asked him.

He replied, "Last year, one of my staff accidentally drove into the gateway with the horse carriage and broke it." I proposed to fix his problem and asked him to stop worrying about it.

"Just rent the gear and a mobile welder and let me take care of it, " I said.

"But what about your eyes, Louis? It's only been three weeks since your accident," He said, uneasily.

"I am fine Wolfgang, I can see very well and I have no pain, don't worry, just get the gear," I said authoritatively. The next day, and in less than two hours I had welded it all back together. I have noticed very often, the subconscious will bring people together to fulfill multiple wishes. Wolfgang's subconscious had magically played its own power through me and my own subconscious brought me all of the money that I needed to pay my debts and start my new life. We were happy, we were delighted and there is no accident for our "connection".

In spite of many requests to stay in Germany, I left Wolfgang and a myriad of beautiful girls behind and like many other souls that shared my existence before, I never saw them again. I was ready to take on another exciting section of my unusual life. I flew back to England, repaid all my creditors and invested in new clothes, bags and shoes. I met for the last time with all my musicians and I could feel a profound sadness in their hearts. We had shared over twelve long years and they all knew the hell I went through to fulfill my wishes alone in a foreign country. I promised to keep in touch, not knowing that I would reenter their lives twenty-one years later. I finally made a very emotional reunion with both David and Marco when I flew to London in 2005 to tape a segment on the life of Nostradamus for the Discovery channel.

Back to my journey to America. The anticipated day finally arrived when the big bird took off from the soaking Heathrow International airport. I could not wait another minute to see the blue sky and the bright sun hiding away in the thick clouds. For many hours, I sat quietly flying west across the vast Atlantic Ocean. A few hours later, the 757 Boeing airplane flew over Iceland, where one of my gorgeous ex-girlfriends named Gudrun might have been indifferently looking up at the white trails left by the airplane. Soon afterwards, I saw the white tips of Greenland as we flew deeper West into the ocean where all sight of land disappeared. I made sure that I had my American friend Mike's business card in my wallet and wondered if and how he would help me upon my arrival in San Diego. My head was full of dreams about California and I was prepared to face anything, with only a few English pounds left in my pocket.

Nearly six months elapsed since I had met Mike in the bar, and I wanted to give a real surprise and did not bother to call him. I could only purchase a two-way return ticket with my provisory tourist visa that I'd gotten from the American Embassy in London. As always, I had no idea of what my intrepid spirit was getting me into, but I had faith and as always was ready for the adventure. The worst that could happen to me was to be forced back to England if things did not go my way, I thought. The airline hostesses treated me like a king and I fell asleep in the warm and quiet cabin of the large airplane. The Captain's voice woke me up from my dream, ordering the flight attendants to prepare the cabin for landing. I put my nose against the tiny window and set my eyes for the first time look at the city of Los Angeles below.

Los Angeles

Mission Boulevard

I had the shock of my life; the city was so vast that even from the air, I could not see its boundaries. I was both excited and worried, wondering about finding my way in such a large city. I took a cab to the Greyhound bus station and enjoyed the huge building I had seen only television. I was about to learn something valuable about traveling in any foreign land. I purchased a ticket to my final destination to San Diego and left my heavy suitcase to the staff in charge to take care of my belongings and trustfully made my way to up to the elevator. I arrived to the appointed floor, where the driver himself was already carefully packing bags into the underbelly of the bus. The bus was stinky and loaded with people; I presented my ticket and sat by the window just behind the driver's seat. It was really hot and I pushed the glass open, to get some fresh air. I noticed a large carriage coming from my right loaded with the remaining of the passengers' luggage. I had a very strong gut feeling and carefully watched the loading process and to my horror, my suitcase was missing. I rushed outside and asked the driver where my huge suitcase was and to check once more for me.

The Wells Fargo Building

"It's in there, it has to be," he said confidently.

"No, its not, I have watched you since I got here and I am sure I made it up to this floor well before my suitcase," I added nervously. Regardless of my many desperate requests, he was behind schedule and refused to "waste time" double-checking on my claim. I was petrified, all that I had was there, this suitcase was my life and contained all my songs, my master tapes, my clothes, even my plane return ticket to London. A very strong feeling engulfed my solar plexus and I wished like I never did before to see my valise. I could not do anything than to stand by the front door sobbing, as the bus began it's way down the busy Los Angeles streets.

I was losing my mind and staring outside, hoping for a miracle. Then, all of a sudden it happened…my huge suitcase was right there, sitting on a trolley by the office door. I screamed at the driver to stop and open the door immediately, and I rushed outside to grab my belongings and brought it back in the bus. This suitcase meant my entire life and was exceptionally heavy, but my subconscious gave me more strength than Arnold Schwarzenegger, when the Tiger in me came out. I was able to calm down and felt so relieved and I took this incident as a great omen. From now on, regardless of what happens to me in this country, I will come out a winner, I thought. I pondered on what happened with my valise for a while and came up with different explanations. When I arrived in the US in 1984, the transport system was not sophisticated or safe, as it is today. Most of the baggage handlers were probably underprivileged themselves and someone read the London return address tag and tried to steal it. Moral of story... do not leave any indication that you are an "alien" visiting a foreign country to avoid this type of stressful experience. Even if your baggage is found the chance of getting it back in your own country is very remote.

At last, the bus was cruising south along the golden California coastline towards the Mexican border. Five hours later, I finally reached the downtown San Diego Greyhound bus station.

Excited, I took another bus to Mission Boulevard anticipating meeting with Mike that very afternoon. I reached my final destination at about 4.00 PM on a warm April day. The unconcerned bus driver quickly discarded me on the sidewalk of a little beach town with my heavy suitcase and a large bag. Here I was: a few thousands miles away from home again, alone in a strange world.

San Diego City

At least my English was good enough for me to converse with people, but a strange feeling enveloped me as I walked along the street. What if Mike was not there I thought? I innocently removed that scary thought and kept walking. I stopped a few times asking for directions and finally the street number on the business card matched a little tee-shirt shop address. I was already imagining - Mike's surprised face, some food and as promised, a safe place to stay. I entered the shop and spoke to an elderly couple.

Bus Stop on Mission Boulevard Near La Jolla California

"Excuse me, may I speak to Mike, please," I said.

They were surprised by my request and the man answered. "There is no one by this name who works here, boy, only my wife and I run the shop."

I was in total denial and could not believe what I was hearing. "Are you sure; am I at the right place? I asked, expressively.

Calmly, the old man adjusted his tiny eyeglass and checked the address on the business card. "Yes, you are at the right place young man, but there is no Mike here, I am sorry" he said.

"But, what about the telephone number here, look, I don't understand," I said panicked.

"Here let me call for you and see who this Mike is," he added. The concerned old lady was looking at me, feeling my pain and disbelief. My last hope to reach Mike was by telephone and my worst fear became a reality. "Here, listen," he said. "This number is longer in service." The number was a non-working number and reality hit me in the face. I kindly thanked the elderly then reluctantly left the shop in total despair. I took my heavy bags and walked under the stinging Sun for what seemed to be a million miles along the sea front. I finally made it to a little coffee shop for a cold drink and to relax my aching arms.

Mission Boulevard In San Diego, California

I was under serious stress, but also enjoyed all the activities that were taking place on the beach around me. People were everywhere talking, laughing, walking, surfing, riding bikes and doing magical stuff on rolling blades. I had never seen so much action before and the myriad of activity kept me from worrying sick about my situation. I realized also, why we call all Americans "big kids" in France. But what really got to me were all the girls wearing bras and the guys running around with long bathing suits! I was experiencing real culture shock because on the golden beaches of the French Riviera, no one wears much clothing. Later I learned that America was built on puritanical principles and going about free and naked on the beach was taboo for this young country. I really enjoyed my first gorgeous California sunset and was brought to the harsh reality of my peculiar circumstance, by my wondering stomach.

Mission Boulevard Sea Front

I only had fifty bucks left in my pocket and enjoyed a cold beer and spent some time looking for the cheapest beach motel. I was exhausted, but my exciting environment and the constant noise outside kept me awake. I decided to take another walk to the busiest bar and get a pack of Marlboros. During those days I had the bad habit of smoking cigarettes and I spent my last change doing so, or so I thought. I began to struggle with the mulish machine that swallowed my change and did not cough out my smokes.

I politely approached someone by the bar and said, "Hi, I was wondering if you could help me with the cigarette machine, I never used these before and I am not sure if I am doing the right thing, there" I said.

"This damn machine is broken, I lost my money, too and I am waiting for the barman to reimburse me," he said." I've got some cigarettes left, do you want one?" he asked me.

"Yes, please" I said politely and even though I had not much money left, I offered him to have a beer with me. For years John and I still laugh at our first meeting in the bar, because he first thought I was gay and was coming on to him. For some karmic reasons we connected almost immediately and after a few beers, he dragged me to the busy discothèque next door.

I was tired and upset with the day's events, but John was the best thing that happened to me so far and I wanted to make the most of it. My French charm worked miracles with a couple of young ladies and John became my "partner in crime" that evening. Little did I know then, that John was a wealthy attorney at law and indeed the first and foremost important friend I could ever need in the US. We ended up, drunk as can be, but my ego prevented me to ask him for money or help. After breakfast my newfound friend dropped me to my motel and offered me his business card. I never saw a business card before and I was very impressed by his powerful new car.

Mission Bay Motel on Mission Boulevard

"Hey, Louis, don't hesitate to call me if you need anything, okay? I will be here for you, man," he said. I warmly thanked him and jumped out of the car promising him to call again, soon. Damn, what a start, I thought. I love America already, and finally I happily succumbed to Neptune's deep dreamy waters. I was awakened the next morning to the noise of heavy traffic along the sea front of Mission Boulevard. I was alone, thousands of miles away from home, with just a few dollars in my pocket. My situation was simply dreadful, but I had been there before and willingly chased away all my depressive thoughts. I trusted my gut feeling that it would be all right, no matter what and my "escapade" with John the night before, was surely a great omen to trust, I thought. As I was getting ready, I noticed the corner of a newspaper that was left under the bed. It read "La Jolla Light" I grasped it and read the job offer section. What I did not know was that in a few years later, a mesmerized spiritual freelance writer from that very paper would investigate my work and share my predictive gift (and my face) with the locals.

Law of Fate

* Here the **Law of Fate** was in motion. This law will decide the direction your life will take. It will bring situations, things, and people into your life to allow Karma to act. Choice seems to disappear and everything falls into place either for good or evil. It is regulated partly by Cosmic order and also the residue of one's own Karma. Did my subconscious know better, by sending John and his legal expertise in my life? I was very concerned about my resident status and because of John, I was able to get my green card and to make things even better. He never charged me a penny. But what other crucial laws interacted with the Law Of Attraction? Note also that John was born in September. The 7th House Law of Attraction (or the law of opposition) regulates both our houses of long lasting partnership and contracts. Incidentally, Venus rules this house and this planet regulates the sign of Libra (the scales) or the judicial system. The Draconic Laws were also involved with my own Dragon's Tail in the sign of Libra and attracted an attorney into my life. These facts also denote that both the Head and the Tail of the Dragon can work for or against its owner. Most importantly, I knew and dearly respected the Universal Law of the Moon and I touched the ground of the United States of America on the first day of a New Moon. Incidentally, I arrived (by accident?) in the US on April 4th 1984 and that is the month of Aries and my natal Dragon's Head. All those ingredients worked together and swiftly "stimulated" the Law of Attraction to perform its miracles in my favor.

The only thing I knew was that I was a daring illegal and I did not have a telephone, a car, a home or a valid US social security number to find a job; but I had faith. I stumbled onto the 'roommate" section and decided to give it a shot. I called the number and a female voice answered. We chatted a while and she gave me directions to her apartment. She told me she lived close by and I did not have enough money for the bus fare, thus I decided to walk. I took her words literally, something I should never have done, as close-by in the US, can easily mean miles away. I walked alongside Mission Boulevard then found the intersection of La Jolla Drive. The heavy bags blistered my hands, but I kept walking under the hot California sun. I stopped many times asking for direction and it took me an eternity to reach my destination, "The Tides" building. I arrived by her doorstep, sweating, thirsty and pooped.

She was quite surprised to see my belongings with me and jokingly said, "Hi, I am Laura, whoa, are you moving in, already?"

The "Tides" building In La Jolla California

I did not know what to tell her and before I could say a word, she added, "Well I am looking for another three or four people, so we can share the rent and afford a big house by the sea front. I think four hundreds dollars each would do" she added. I was petrified; I had only a few dollars left in my pocket and nowhere to go. "Come in, you must be thirty" she said, lovingly. After downing nearly a gallon of water, I began to explain my desolate situation and to my surprise, she happily said to me. "This is great and exactly what Rose needs." She continued explaining that her daughter was learning French and she had difficulties doing so. To my amazement, she happily proposed me a deal I could never turn down. "If you want, you can teach her French after school and in exchange, you can stay on my sofa until you get yourself situated." Once more Lady Luck was watching over me, here I was in a stranger's house and she was offering her badly needed help.

In this case her subconscious lead me, (the only crazy French man in town!) to tuition her daughter for free. She certainly could not afford the coaching, but in this case she got more than what she bargained for, with a real Frenchman. By the same token, my own subconscious directed me to the only sensitive person that would and could help me to transit to a different level. As it is often the case, the Law of Attraction worked its marvel for both of us. Note also, that the Moon was at the beginning of her Waxing period and Laura was born under the altruistic, sensitive and guilty sign of Pisces. In no way will a Pisces refuse to help anyone in serious trouble. The intensity of my request was stimulated by my critical situation and my thoughts were indeed, inordinately powerful. All the right elements were there and so was the outcome.

I felt like as if the world was removed from my shoulders and I was finally able to relax at least for the time being. I gladly accepted my duty, intending to take care of my situation as soon as possible. It felt like I was imposing on them and I wanted to do something about it immediately. My subconscious heard my pledge and had another good surprise in store for me. I was physically exhausted, but emotionally and spiritually loaded with hope. After a good home cooked dinner, I spent my first night talking about my exciting life in France and England and all my dreams in the US. I thanked her warmly and before falling asleep, I assured her that I would look for any job in the village of La Jolla, the next morning.

The next day I awoke to the charming song of a Mockingbird. I was amazed and listened to his complex vocal repertoire and took his composition as a great omen welcoming me to the US. After a hot cup of coffee, I thanked Laura once more and walked in the direction of the village. I really liked the townships personality; lots of luxurious shops lined the well-maintained flowered streets. I could have easily landed in a gang-infested downtown area and would have been in serious trouble, but for some reason (blame it on my lucky rising sign in Sagittarius) my subconscious always took care of me. A myriad of people were walking by the sea front and enjoying all of the numerous activities on the green playground.

I finally had my first real peaceful taste of America and I loved it. As I was walking on Pearl Street, I saw a sign above a restaurant: "French Gourmet" and it felt right to ask for a job. Miraculously, I met with the French owner Michael Malecot and got my first job as a cleaner. I had been in that position before in the UK, only to find myself going right to the top a few months later. A year later I became the General Manager. I developed the wholesale department to four definite sections all over the city and county of San Diego, bringing in about two million dollars a year of bakery product sales.

Michael was also a self-made man and often stimulated me to do better for the business. "Louis, I need bigger accounts and I am sure you can find them" he used to say.
Michael knew how to steer the positive tiger in me and one day I said to him, "Okay, Michael, in order for me to increase the business the way you want me to, you will have to give me full power."

He answered me with faith "Okay, if that is what you need to bring in more accounts, then you are now in charge of all four locations." That was the day he "baptized" me as his new General Manager. Okay, I thought, now I am at the top and I have nearly two hundred or so people to perform for me, so nothing can stop me. I took the time to drive to each location and requested all the French bread to be ready by 5:00 PM upon my request. I started at the La Jolla location, but I soon found myself arguing with Michael. "So what, you told me I had full control over the production and now you stop me?" I asked angrily.

Pearl Street "French Gourmet" In La Jolla California

"Louis, the bakers are complaining," he answered, " their first "fournee" is at 5:00 AM not 5:00 PM and they have never heard of such a request." he added curiously. "What the hell are you up to, Louis? I don't want my bakers to walk away from me with your silly request, at least you could tell me what plan it is that you have in mind." he added nervously.

"Well Michael," I said calmly, "No one offers fresh bread in the evening and I thought that no restaurant would turn down a delivery of hot bread for their consumers." He pondered for a few seconds and finally realized my ingenious idea.

"Damn, that is a freaking good idea, Louis!" he happily said, while picking up the telephone. After a meeting with the boss, my revolutionary idea was accepted and I easily picked up all the local restaurant accounts. My drivers delivered the " baguette croustillante" or French bread, at 5:00 PM, which is now adopted pretty much all over the US. All was going supremely well for me, when Michael offered me more benefits with food, a company car, free gas, a beautiful home with an ocean view, and a decent paycheck. Also, I secretly nurtured a wish to fly and my subconscious led me to one of his four restaurant managers named Patrice. We became inseparable and we took helicopter-flying lessons at the Palomar airport heliport.

My Old House In La Jolla Boulevard

Death Strikes Again

Patrice was a courageous, young and full of life, countryman. His dream was to create his own culinary business in La Jolla and he had it all to succeed. His young wife Olga was also French and nurtured a constant fear of death. She used to say to us. "I hate being up there, I'd rather have my feet on the ground." Both Patrice and I laughed at her and ignored her inner fears, saying nothing is safer than flying. Chances of getting hit by a car are greater than dying in an airplane accident. Sadly, in this case her deep-rooted fears fueled by "The Law of Negativity" worked full speed against her. Months later at our graduation day, Patrice became quite upset because the FAA had imposed a restriction on his flying license. He was color blind and once had scared me to death, when we were flying above San Diego. In the mist of a thin California cloudy marine layer, he could not see the airport from the air. I safely guided him to the runway, where he landed the plane, perfectly.

"Man, you are IFR (Instruments Flight Rules), not VFR (Visual Flight Rules), you'd better stay away from flying at night or in the fog." I strongly suggested to him. He laughed at me to cover his shattered ego and finally realized his hazardous limitation. He called me only a few days later, asking my girlfriend and I to join him on a trip to Las Vegas. "Hey Louis, Olga's parents are visiting from France for her birthday." He said happily "I rented a six seat airplane, will you join us this weekend?" Incidentally, two days earlier, one of my drivers killed himself in an auto accident on highway five, on his way back from a delivery in San Diego. I immediately took this as a personal omen, that the somber death energy was very close to me.

A cold shiver immediately enveloped my entire body and I replied, "Thanks bro, but it's the Waning Moon and I don't usually go anywhere in a Waning Moon."

He laughed his head off, saying, "Louis, you and your stars, this stuff is nonsense. Come on man, the Moon is a dead satellite and does nothing to you." At this point, I knew that I was much too spiritually advanced for him to even remotely connect with any thoughts of heeding my warning.

"Yeah, you may be right Patrice, but I've so much work to do and my only chance to catch up is during the weekend, man," I explained. I knew a rational answer would work better than to waste both of our time with a universal rule that he decided to ignore.

Two days later, my girlfriend Mimi and I were asleep, when a telephone call woke us up in the middle of the night. "Hello, is this Mr. Turi?" the voice said.

"Yes, this is he; who are you?" I asked, apprehensively.

"It's the police, we found your business card in the wreckage of an airplane, there are no survivors and I gather that you knew the victims. We need you to come tomorrow morning to the San Diego police station to identify the bodies." he said. I was dumbfounded and told Mimi the fate of all our friends. She was hysterical and it took me hours to comfort her. This was my first loss of a dear friend in the US and I was to lose many more over the years to come.

An amalgamation of unobserved Universal Laws brought the deadly results and to this day I always insist to never go anywhere after the Full Moon. (See "The Universal Law" near the end of the book). Incidentally, the very same day, Mimi and I were invited to celebrate a girlfriend's birthday in Mexico. I found a silly excuse and turned her down, advising her to be cautious out there. After ingesting some lobster, the four of them were flown back from Tijuana to San Diego's emergency service to be treated for life-threatening food poisoning. The same awful principle applied to Natalie Holloway's situation when she visited Aruba on a Waning Moon. And really this applies to most other people unaware of "The

Universal Law of the Moon". Millions of people from all walks of life, including courageous astronauts have lost their lives in the name of ignorance. My wisdom also saved my good friend Owen and I from the Asia tsunami, when I wisely refused to go to Thailand with him on Christmas day and so he decided not to go too. You know the traffic laws and will stop at a red light. If you are not aware of the Universal laws regimenting over this physical world, you will have to pay a heavy penalty, period! This is why my yearly book, Moon Power, is so precious. For years it has guided thousands of people to safe and productive lives.

This episode was hard for all, but my position and numerous responsibilities helped me to move on. Michael was a very spiritual man and we often talked about metaphysics, but I did not know too much about the "Cosmic Code" or the tarot cards, then. As a Pisces, I always nurtured an interest in metaphysics, but never really studied any subject thoroughly. I had in my possession Mom's old tarot cards and began to use them my own way. The word spread fast that I was into the "mystical" stuff and many co-workers asked me for guidance.

Law of Omens

* We do receive warnings and messages from our higher guidance. This brings **"The Law of Omens"** into play. If we watch carefully and listen to our intuition, we will be steered clear of tragedy and towards our fortunes. Such little things as a book falling off a shelf, finding a coin, or generally just seeing something unusual or out of place, are indications that something is stirring. Just watch and you will begin to understand.

Laura and my Green Card

An amalgamation of unobserved Universal Laws brought the deadly results and to this day I always insist to never go anywhere after the Full Moon. (See "The Universal Law" near the end of the book). Incidentally, the very same day, Mimi and I were invited to celebrate a girlfriend's birthday in Mexico. I found a silly excuse and turned her down, advising her to be cautious out there. After ingesting some lobster, the four of them were flown back from Tijuana to San Diego's emergency service to be treated for life-threatening food poisoning. The same awful principle applied to Natalie Holloway's situation when she visited Aruba on a Waning Moon. And really this applies to most other people unaware of "The Universal Law of the Moon". Millions of people from all walks of life, including courageous astronauts have lost their lives in the name of ignorance. My wisdom also saved my good friend Owen and I from the Asia tsunami, when I wisely refused to go to Thailand with him on Christmas day and so he decided not to go too. You know the traffic laws and will stop at a red light. If you are not aware of the Universal laws regimenting over this physical world, you will have to pay a heavy penalty, period! This is why my yearly book, Moon Power, is so precious. For years it has guided thousands of people to safe and productive lives.

This episode was hard for all, but my position and numerous responsibilities helped me to move on. Michael was a very spiritual man and we often talked about metaphysics, but I did not know too much about the "Cosmic Code" or the tarot cards, then. As a Pisces, I always nurtured an interest in metaphysics, but never really studied any subject thoroughly. I had in my possession Mom's old tarot cards and began to use them my own way. The word spread fast that I was into the "mystical" stuff and many co-workers asked me for guidance.

I was practicing my hobby on the side until one day in 1986 when a man named Sammy (a Libra) came to me for career direction. He had inherited some legacy money and wanted to carefully invest. I consulted my tarot cards and all indications led me to suggest an investment in the food industry. I also emphasized a pizzeria restaurant and Sammy now has hundreds of locations in operation and he is the President and CEO of Sammy's Wood-fired Pizza, with his main office located in La Jolla, California. He was my first paying client and his success boosted my confidence to invest more time and further study of metaphysics. The months passed quickly and I missed my family, but my tourist visa expired and without a green card, I could never comeback to the US. I was doomed to stay in the US until I became a legal alien. I had all that I needed, but no real freedom and an attorney would cost a fortune. My apartment was near Laura's building and one day while visiting her, she said. "Hey, Louis, if you want your green card, you could marry me, you know I'd do anything for you."

"Whoa, really, you would do this for me?"

"Hell, yeah!" smiling, she answered "but it would cost you."

"I don't care Laura, I really want to be a US citizen; I love this country!" I said.

The plan was set for me to legally marry Laura for two years and then get my green card in exchange for financial support for her and daughter Rose. I also had to let go of Michael's apartment and moved into the same building on the floor just above hers. She wanted to "play it safe" by spending more time with me, to learn about my habits, and be ready in case the emigration checked on us living together. I had no idea of the emigration procedures; but in fact they do ask pertinent questions to find out if the marriage is real. I understood Laura's concern and accepted the deal. We got married, I had it all in control and everything went well. I spent time with her and Rose, we were friends and I never emotionally or physically got involved with Laura; it was purely business. She tried a couple of times to get past our deal, but I cautiously and intensely reminded her of our agreement. Two years later, a certified letter sent by an emigration officer had reached her mailbox. I was hysterically happy when Laura and I were given an appointment, to "collect" my green card the very next day at 10:00 AM.

However, I was in disbelief when she announced to me, that she could not and would not go downtown with me. "Oh my god Laura, what are you saying Hun? You can't go with me? But why?" I asked her, wondering.

"Well, I am in probation for abusing the social security, I am a single mother and if they find out that this marriage is illegal, they will send me to jail." she announced. I was petrified and my entire world felt apart, all that I worked for the last two years, was totally wasted. All my time, my efforts, my progress, my dreams, and my life in America, all were gone in the wind. I tried really hard to reason with her, telling her that all would be fine, but it was in vain, as she stubbornly refused to go.

Rose took my side and screamed, "Mom, for god sake, after all he did for us, this is how you thank him? How can you do this to Louis?" she added. I was much too baffled to think clearly and went up to my apartment, hoping for a miracle.

I could not go to work the next day, waiting for my world to fall apart, and at about 1:00 PM Laura received a telephone call from the emigration office. She spoke softly to the agent and wrote down a fax number and after putting the telephone on the receiver, she said. "Louis, they said that you have 24 hours to leave this country or you will be deported. You must fax your plane ticket to the emigration office today and go back to France tomorrow," she added with a guilty face. Rose was crying in silence, as I left her apartment in total despair. I rushed to the local travel agency, bought my return ticket to France and in tears, packed up a valise. A few months earlier Rose had broke her leg in a skiing accident and I had taken care of all her medical expenses. I had also paid for Laura's car, schooling for Rose and made sure that all the bills and food were taken care of. All my dreams were shattered and I was wondering why I had to suffer such a fate, when all I did for two consecutive years was to help Laura and her daughter. I hated myself, wondering loudly "Why had I listened to her? Why didn't I ask for John's help, especially when he proposed it, why didn't I ask Michael to take care of this emigration problem for me?"

The taxi was waiting for me outside and my flight was scheduled for 3:00 PM. I knocked on Laura's door and said "Hey, Laura, before leaving, I wanted to thank you for all you did for me, darling!" I said sarcastically. "By the way, here is the key to my car and my apartment; please sell it and put the money away for Rose." I added.

She never even looked me in the eyes as she responded, "I am sorry Louis, I am sorry." Then, she closed the door. I walked outside to where Rose was waiting for me. She was in tears and I knew for her it was a problem letting go of the only caring father that she had ever known. I hugged her and said, "I promise you Rose, I will be back, I don't know when, but you will see me again, Hun…"

---

* Laura was a caring, but dreamy and impractical Pisces, born with a Pisces Tail. This Draconic Law strongly points to an addictive and deceiving personality. Pisces also rules confinement and jail. Later I found out from Rose that her mother was jailed before I met her. Incidentally, I also suffered the Draconic Law with my own Dragon's Tail (negative) in Libra (marriage) and thus attracted Laura and had naively married her. Note the **"Law of Fear"** pertaining to emigration catching me was also a constant subconscious drag. I did not have the knowledge of the subconscious at that time and could not apply my will to alleviate the negative thoughts from continuously entering my mind. Talking from experience, I am convinced that the Moon was indeed Waning (negative) and probably in the sign of Cancer (ending/beginning) or in Scorpio (dying/wake up call) on the day that I moved back home to France.

Back to the Start

My family was very happy to see me after two years of absence. My brother Yves, offered me to stay in his guesthouse with my faithful Icelandic girlfriend Mimi. I told her I learned a lot from this mishap and we would be back to the US in one year. I took a job as a welder and heavy equipment operator and saved a significant amount of money. I concentrated all of my thoughts and efforts to return to the land of opportunity and planned to arrive from New York, instead of Los Angeles. I was pushed by an unseen force to go right back to the US. I had the money, but I needed to put more time between the emigration and me. Mimi's French visa was about to expire and she decided to go home for a few months and meet me again, in San Diego. We were young and full of life, but destiny decided otherwise and after a long and passionate kiss, she flew away to Iceland and I never saw her again.

Finally the day arrived and once again I very happily took the big 757 Boeing to the United States. My head was full of hopes and dreams and I trusted the New Moon to remove all of the possible trouble awaiting me. I arrived at Kennedy airport. At about 7:00 PM, after picking up my luggage at the baggage claim I walked outside, looking for a taxi. I had no idea where to find a hotel, but I trusted the driver to help me in this uncomplicated dilemma. I waited for a taxi that never arrived; instead a limousine driver approached me and said. "I am sorry, but there are no taxis at this terminal, just limos. Do you need a ride somewhere?"

"Yes, indeed. I am exhausted; can you take me to the nearest hotel please? I have another plane to catch in the morning and I need some rest." I said.

"Okay, no problem," he answered. "I know a nice hotel about ten minutes from here, come in," he said, opening the door.

We spoke about everything and nothing in particular, but his Italian accent was unmistakable and brought back to me the sad memory of my friend Massimo. "So you are Italian, are you? " I said. "Me too, well my mom is French and my dad is from Sicily," I added.

This fact saved me a bundle of money when he surprisingly and patriotically announced. "Well, as an Italian countryman, I will charge you the taxi fare, buddy. Limousine rentals are quite expensive at the airport," he added.

I warmly thanked him and thought, "Whoa, the New Moon is really working for me." I had never sat in a limousine before and the treat was unique and marked the beginning of a long and successful journey ahead. I walked to the guest registration and got myself a room for the night. I took a shower, put on my black suit, and decided to go down to the hotel bar for a drink before going to bed. I sat at the counter and like any decent cowboy, ordered a scotch. I was lost in thought when some giggling took my attention. I turned around and saw two young girls laughing at me. "What the hell, why are those two girls laughing at me? Are they trying to get my attention?" I thought. I am not exactly the shy type and I just walked towards them and sat at their table. "Sorry girls, I know I am not invited, but why are you laughing at me?" I innocently asked.

They were quite surprised at my bravery and barely containing herself, one of the girls said. "Well, you look like Michael Jackson, with your white socks and your black suit."

I was so tired that I had not even noticed my weird attire and after a good laugh, offered them a drink. The next thing I know the three of us were completely drunk and hysterically imitating Michael Jackson on the dance floor. I was wild, daring, young, and handsome and I could feel those girls wanted more of me. It's amazing how alcohol can easily insert sin into one's life and I gladly accepted the girls' invitation to spend the night in their bedroom. Like me, they were catching a plane the next day and wanted to spend some "memorable" time with me. Damn, what a start and what a lucky beggar I am, I thought. The Universal Law of the Moon really works, I mentally added. Of course, I did not yet know about "The Cosmic Law of Attraction" and as imposed by my fifth house in dual Gemini, I blamed it all on the alcohol and my sexy French intonation. The next day, I slept all the way on the domestic flight to San Diego. I was back with revenge and I had a few more days of the Waxing Moon on my side, to make significant progress. I made sure to stay clear from La Jolla, for fear of accidentally meeting with my "wife" Laura, but I wanted to see Rose. I knew this could mean more trouble than good for me and I was not about to jeopardize my new life with another costly mistake.

I took a chance and after a year of absence, called my friend and attorney, John. We happily reunited at the Hyatt by Seaport Village, where I explained my intricate situation. "Louis, I am not an emigration attorney, but I will hook you up with one of my friends." he said, confidently. Great, I thought. John always delivered his promises and we had developed a very strong relationship over the years. After a meeting with his colleague, only a lot of money separated me from becoming a legal alien. Much of my savings went to my new apartment and the expensive deposit. I explained my situation to John and he told me not to worry about money, but I felt bad about him over-extending himself and his resources for me. Regardless of my desperate situation I knew that I needed a lot of money and I trusted my eternal luck. In this case my subconscious and the Draconic Law would take care of me, as it did so many times before and once again, I was right!

The only place I could make this kind of money was at the San Diego Army base by using my welding skills or operating a crane, but without a green card or a social security number, I was stuck. Against all odds, I drove to National City US naval base to observe all the base activity, hoping to find a way in.

Two armed Marines wearing uniforms were stationed there and like vigilant dangerous dogs they stopped everyone, checking badges before granting access to the naval base. Action was everywhere, people flowing in and out with their badges hanging on their chest or placed visibly on the windshield of cars and buses. I knew that I needed the precious badge to pass the main gates and some activity from a little office attracted my attention. The administrative center was located on the left side of the guarded entrance, a few yards away from the base.

Many of them appeared of Asian and Mexican nationality, but many Americans were also waiting in line. Every minute or so a person squeezed out with the precious badge around their neck. They were all in work clothes, ready to take on their daily duty on different parts of the base. I knew it would be easy to blend-in with them, so I parked my car a few blocks away and walked back towards the tiny office. I took the biggest chance ever, and joined a long line of people while listening carefully to what was said and how I should perform. I was scared and as the line got closer to the small door, I thought many times of walking away. I talked myself into confidence knowing the Moon was still Waxing and I could pull it off, if I just behaved like everyone around me.

I finally walked inside, letting a fat Latino man pass me by. In the office interior, I saw a few windows and a short line of people waiting patiently for the words "Next, please". My heart was racing like a mad horse in my chest; knowing that I could be deported or going to jail if caught, but I had to keep going forward. "Next, please" a feminine automated voice said, "Write your name here and your social security on the bottom part of this form," she added. I made up a fake social security number, trembling like a leaf in the wind, but she was much too busy with a mountain of paper work, to pay attention to my hands. "Okay, now move against the wall and stand still for your picture," she said authoritatively "and get your badge on your way out," she said unconcerned. I was smiling at a camera with my back against a dirty white plaster wall. Less than a minute later, someone made me sign another form and gave me a plastic badge with my picture on it. I could not believe my luck and it worked as planned and the daring Tiger in me had made it all possible. I thanked the Waxing Moon and simply walked past the guards and got a job the very same day. I was asked to perform a test less complicated than the German's strict regulations and passed with high marks. I started work on the very following day and made $60.00 an hour performing specific welding tasks.

The same evening, I called John to give him the good news and he said to me. "Louis, you're nuts! If anything went wrong out there, you would be in jail by now, with serious spy charges against you. Man you're crazy, but I admire your guts." He added. Of course, in 1987 Homeland Security did not exist and the emigration laws were not enforced or electronically efficient, as today.

* In this case not only the "**Universal Law**" of the moon was respected in all my moves, but the "**Draconic Law**"(pg. 190) also worked in my favor. Mars (The Lord of War) in Greek mythology rules everything remotely connected with the Army, Navy, and war in general. The "red planet Mars" also rules my natal Aries Dragon's Head (luck/opportunity) and fueled by "The Law of Desire" all my expectations safely took place.

Draconic Law

* *The dragon of the Zodiac whose head and tail-caput and cauda-aquired the status of planets in classical astrology. These points were in fact the two lunar nodes, the places where the moon's path crossed the ecliptic each month. The origin of the Dragon image is unknown. The dial gives the position of the nodes through the year.*
The British library C.7.c.15

The Moon's nodes play a **significant** role in our lives. The past and often trouble originate from the Dragon's Tail (south node). Future opportunities and talents lie in the Dragon's Head (north node).

My Wife Brigitte

I was anxious to start the legal procedures, but I knew it would take at least two years and I was insecure because of Laura's unreliability and I had a record that could make the situation worse. As John mentioned so many times, the ideal way was to get married legally to a born US citizen and I preciously nurtured this thought, hoping to find not only peace of mind, but true love. During my spare time, I used to do readings for people and one day a gorgeous brunette named Brigitte knocked at my door. Little did I know she was going to be my wife and share the next twelve years of my life!

Brigitte and I

Her beauty and calm attitude mesmerized me. She told me she was my neighbor working next door as a caretaker for an old lady. I read her stars and rekindled her wounded heart from a chaotic upbringing and the tragic death of her dad. She left my house very happy and cameback many times bringing all of her friends. Weeks later, I found by one of her friends that she had profound feelings for me. She was also spending her meager paycheck on readings for all her friends and as an excuse to spend more time with me. I waited for her next visit and divulged my

191

sincere love to her. Then one day, she delivered a shock that would once and for all allow me to become a legal alien and better my life. We were talking about my green card and how long and expensive it would be to get it through the normal legal channels, when she passively said, "Well, I could marry you if you want, this way you'll get this green card much faster." Unlike Laura, this "announcement" was real and I trusted Brigitte with all my soul.

Law of Duality

* **"The Law of Duality"** seemed to follow me in every one of my moves, forcing me to experience a periodic "déjà vu" in my endeavors. Years later, I wrote a book on "The Power Of The Dragon" and just I have just uncovered the "Hidden Dragon" within the "Draconic Laws". I have yet to write another book on this hidden, but powerful phenomenon. As stated earlier, my natal Dragon's Head is in the sign of Aries in my third house, which is regulated by dual sign of Gemini; thus endowing me with a dignified hidden Dragon's Head in Gemini, hence, why I am doomed for perpetual duality. The same type of dual energy afflicted O.J. Simpson and explains a few things in his life:

Two people were assassinated.
Two, four, six police cars were after him on the highway.
Two, four, six attorney fought for him
Two judgments took place
Two (or four) children were involved and so forth.

The "Law Of Duality" also plagued both President George Bush and Al Gore when forced to count, recount, and count again and again the votes, making the shamed American political system look like a serious mess in the eyes of the world.

Brigitte knew I needed some time, needed to think about her incredible proposal and I thought of myself being the luckiest man on earth. Brigitte and I modestly married a few days later, in my little one bedroom house in La Jolla and lived together for many beautiful years to come. I was poor during these days and sold my car to afford the wedding rings and a nice present for my wife-to-be. Luckily for us, she received an old 1972 red Dodge Dart as a present from her Grandmother. My subconscious worked over time to bring all my blessings and like me, Brigitte needed love and security. Secretively, Brigitte had a personal wish to marry a very spiritual man and her subconscious brought me in her life.

All was fine and I got Brigitte to work in the office at the French Gourmet, something I should never have done in the super competitive environment. After a couple of arguments with some jealous girls, she revoked her position. These people were happy of her departure, but I felt eminent changes were in store for us. I already knew that life is a constant process of change and with the Dragon's passage in the career and home areas we are all someday forced into those changes. I was using my engineering background on the US naval base in San Diego when I was offered a better position in Pearl Harbor in Hawaii. The process of getting my green card was in motion and I felt safe to do so. I broke the great news to Brigitte. Like me she always wanted to visit Hawaii and she was thrilled by this happy turn of events. We swiftly moved to Hawaii and life was simply wonderful on the island.

Brigitte was born with a Dragon's Head in Taurus and this sign rules the banking industry. The bull is also the "subconsciously" chosen symbol used by Merrill Lynch's thriving financial Corporation to project solidity and stability. Note also that Switzerland, where all the world's wealth and larger financial corporations are based, is a Taurus ruled country.

"Millionaires don't use astrology, billionaires do!"
J.P. Morgan

The Law of Location - Astro-Cartography

During those days I was not aware of a section of my work called Astro-Cartography and I learned the hard way that I had better investigate the stars before relocating. Everything on earth is under the jurisdiction of the heavens. Even geographical areas and those "new" celestial influences will drastically affect your psyche and your fate. Soon after moving to Honolulu my life changed. For what I thought to be unknown reasons, I abandoned myself into drinking heavily and endured deep depression. I had it all; a beautiful, smart loving wife, I was making a good living, I had an incredible house on top of a mountain in the most respected part of Hawaii and enjoyed the most spectacular sunsets anyone could ever dream of. Eventually I could not count on my mental situation to the point where my worried wife had to call Alcoholics Anonymous. I am naturally a happy and highly spirited type of person, but Hawaii enveloped my spirit with both euphoria and depression. When my contract on the US base came to an end, we packed up and moved back to the main land. The very day I walked on California ground, without any efforts or costly investments, I stopped both drinking and smoking!

Law of Location

* Many years later, while investigating the **"Law of Location"** or Astro-Cartography I eventually pinned down a problem that had puzzled me since then. I discovered that I have Neptune's poisoning line right above the Hawaiians Islands and its melancholic impact affected my life in general. In Greek Mythology, Neptune is called "Poseidon" or the Lord of the Seas and this nebulous planet rules all exotic confined places and poisons, whether of the mind or body. Note the similarity between "poison" and the French word for Pisces, "Poisson". Neptune rules myths, religions, churches, synagogues, caves, deities, gurus, drugs, chemicals, alcohol, asylums, hospitals, guilt, deception, depression, and the sign of Pisces. The astrological sign of Pisces (the fish) was subconsciously chosen to represent Christianity, as Jesus fed the world with two fish. No one should relocate without knowing where and what stars are in store for him at the new location. Some people are desperate to find love, better health, or fame; not knowing that they could be just a few hundred miles from a splendid line that would make this dream a reality. You might be, right now, living and striving without any hope of success under a nefarious planet like Saturn (depression), Neptune (drugs), Pluto (death), or Mars (war). From my personal experience and those of friends, family, and clients alike it is easy to see that Astro-Cartography really works. I was Neptune's victim for nearly two years. It's because of my experience with this nebulous planet that I can today expose the "Law of Location" to your benefit. Back home in France and in England, I was under a nefarious Saturn line and the more I worked, the less security or reward I had. When I relocated under my Sun line (fame), blessings showered me in California and Arizona, and since then anything I touch turns into pure gold! Under such a powerful Neptunian energy, the entire Hawaiian Islands and its people are indeed very spiritual and strongly believe in the Holo Mai Pele myth. Neptune rules all religions, all divine beings, and all legends.

My Fourth UFO Experience

At that time we were renting an apartment in Oceanside California and life was treating us well. Brigitte is an extraordinary good-looking girl and wanted to become a model. She entered a contest in a beauty pageant set for the weekend of August 11, 1991 in Anaheim. Brigitte was born in May under the steady and beauty oriented sign of Taurus. She was excited about the opportunity, but a little too reserved to really succeed in this business, I thought. However, like a good husband, I supported her all the way like any man should.

At about 9:00 P.M. I suggested for Brigitte to invest in her "beauty sleep" and by 10:00 P.M. we were lying in bed, she was reading a book and I was already snoozing. I made sure to give her comforting words and hopes and we both fell into Neptune's world of dreams. In the middle of the night, I woke up to the screams of my petrified wife. I immediately thought she was having a nightmare and tried to calm her down. Her face was paroxysmal and her entire body was convulsing. Her beautiful piercing blue eyes turned reddish screaming for help. I really thought she saw the devil that night. Nothing I could do or say to calm her worked and I was a worried sick; in eight years of marriage, I never saw my wife panicking in such way. I had no choice but to cover her mouth with my hand, attempting to silence her terrorized screams in fear of the neighbors calling the police. I dragged her tormented body into the bathroom and splashed cold water on her face while continuously asking her to stop screaming. After a few minutes, she finally was able to regain some control over herself. I glanced at the clock; it was about 4:00 A.M. on Sunday August 11th, 1991. This melodramatic night is still very vivid in my memory and will never fade.

She begged me to take her out for a walk in the warm night in the surrounding area. She warned me that something evil was in the house and she refused to come back in. After thirty minutes, I finally persuaded her that she had a nightmare and nothing would hurt her in our tiny apartment. She was petrified to go back inside, but insisted for me to look all over for those demons. She was carefully following me as I checked under the bed, inside all the closets, and parts of the apartment that I did not even know existed.

I kept talking to her softly, but I could sense her agonizing terror. We went back to bed and I could feel her heart beating fast and loud. She asked me to envelope her in my arms and to not, under any circumstances go anywhere. I was wondering if my stable wife suffered a burgeoning mental disease and what could be done to bring back her sanity. She finally went back to sleep with all the lights on in the apartment. I did not close my eyes for a long time, wondering what Brigitte saw or experienced earlier in the darkness of the bedroom.

The clock woke us at precisely 6:30 AM and my first thought was for my wife. She was still holding me tight and said. "Are they gone?"

"Who, what?" I curiously answered. "What did you see last night? Brigitte" I added, cautiously.

"I don't know Honey, but something was in our bedroom and it scared me to death" she answered.

"Do you really want to go to Anaheim to this beauty pageant Brigitte? You might as well forget it, you look very tired," I said.

"No, let's go" she insisted, I want out of this house and we can always visit Grandma, there," she suggested.

Reluctantly, we took off to the local gas station. At 8:00 AM sharp, I was filling my gas tank and drove to Interstate 5 North, in the direction of Los Angeles. I could not help myself but to cautiously ask Brigitte for more information on what she saw in the apartment, but she could not find any plausible answer to what or why she behaved so erratically the night before.

The morning was nice and sunny and we both enjoyed the driving along the coastline and the Pacific Ocean. We drove past the emigration checkpoint soon after the US base of Camp Pendleton. Shortly past the 405 HWY intersections, I noticed the huge road sign of Jamboree Road.

Last Road Sign we Saw

Interestingly, the road seemed to get wider and wider as I drove through the next underpass. This is the last thing Brigitte and I could remember after penetrating what seemed to be a thick cloud of smoke. "Honey, what are you doing?" she said. "Pick up your speed and drive on your lane, do you want to kill us or what?' she added nervously. I was driving at less than 30 miles per hour on the highway where the speed limit was 55 in those days. The tires thumping on the safety bumps along the edge of the road felt like they woke me up from a dream, and I quickly adjusted my driving to the speed limit. I was wondering why I would drive so slow and blamed it on my sleepless night and I could not help feeling strange and eerie. I was trying hard to make sense to so many weird feelings and did not recognize the landmarks anymore.

Brigitte and I had driven to Los Angeles hundreds of times to visit friends and family and we both knew the way very well. "Where are we, Honey? Are we lost?" I asked her. I could not make sense of my environment and thought that maybe I was driving on a different highway.

"Don't worry darling and keep going, we have a long way to go still. I have not seen any sign for Anaheim or Disneyland, yet." Brigitte answered casually.

I drove another couple of miles looking really hard for any familiar road sign and my frustration got out of hand. I asked Brigitte again for directions and she kept telling me we were still miles from our destination. Then, to my surprise she opened the glove compartment and took the US map and opened it on her lap. I used this map only for very long distance travel from one state to the other. She made no sense to me, why would Brigitte look for Anaheim on the United States map? I thought. We have traveled there hundreds of times and never got lost. It is practically impossible for us to get lost, I thought, still battling an incomprehensible feeling. The weird feeling of disorientation increased and I decided to do something about this unnerving situation. I took the first exit, hoping to find a person or a gas station and once and for all, ask for directions. Brigitte grudgingly agreed and placed the US map back into the glove compartment. "We are so not there, yet. We have a long way to go, honey and we're going to be late," she added, tensely.

"It's okay baby, it won't take me long." I said, while driving off the long Zoo Drive exit.

Zoo Drive Exit

At the Zoo

The ramp lead us to a large and empty parking lot and I carefully parked next to a white Toyota pickup. On the back of the vehicle, three Mexican men were enjoying cold lemonade and warm burritos. "Hey guys, sorry to bother you, but can you tell me where I am?" I shouted, from a short distance. Their facial expressions showed much wonder about a deranged man disturbing their breakfast, but one of them answered in broken English. "Hey Amigo, you're at the Glendale Zoo parking lot, but it won't open for business for another hour."

"Glendale Zoo? How the hell, did we end up in this place?" I thought. "Hey, are you sure I am in LA at the zoo?" I asked again. The three guys were staring at me, wondering about my sanity or if they were in danger by talking to me. I was dumbfounded with absolutely no idea of where I was and most of all, how I got there. "Where is Anaheim?" I asked politely.

"Well you passed it a long time ago, my friend," said the oldest of the three men. "You are well past Los Angeles, on the parking lot of the Glendale Zoo" he reaffirmed to me, annoyed.

I was baffled, I was shocked and I was trying really hard to understand how I could have passed so far from my destination. Nothing made any sense to me and I asked the man again. "Excuse me, what's the time please?"

"It's 9.00 AM amigo, time for breakfast," he said, laughing uncontrollably.

I was speechless and went back to my car to check the clock and to my amazement, he was right! I took a deep breath and realized that we were abducted, but how in the world was I to tell Brigitte that we were nearly two hours past our destination, when we had just left home, less than thirty minutes ago? In her

198

mind, I was supposed to drive north until we reached Katella city, where the event took place and here we were, well after Los Angeles with no ideas on how we got here. To my surprise, she was still looking in the US map for directions, trying to make sense of our location. She still had no clue of the elapsed time and our location. I was wondering how to break the news to her without freaking her out again. The world seemed to have stopped on us and the bewildering feeling that we experienced was intolerable. The last thing I wanted to do was to scare Brigitte again, especially after what she went through the night before, I thought. It then dawned on me, that my wife had a premonition (or a UFO visitation?) the night before and this would also explain her extremely erratic behavior during the night.

I calmly sat next to her and gently held her hands and said, "Honey, do you remember what we talked about just before you married me? I asked.

"Nope, I don't recall, Hun. We talked about so many things," she said.

"Well, I told you that if you were to spend your life with me, you will probably have to experience the incredible, do you remember?" I asked her.

"Oh, my God, do you mean your UFO stuff? You know I don't believe in this, come on!" she answered terrified. She was in total denial and refused to acknowledge anything abnormal. I did not challenge her thinking; I needed more time to reinforce her psyche to accept that she and I were abducted.

"Brigitte sweet heart, what time do you have on your watch"

"Its just after 9.00 AM" she replied.

"Okay Brigitte, now do not panic, stay calm baby, okay? We are about two hours or more north of Anaheim on the zoo parking lot in Glendale, just after Los Angeles," I added. She was at a total loss looking at me with her big blue innocent eyes. She did not say a word for a while and began to cry.

"But, how is it possible honey, we just left home? She said.

"I know girl, but don't worry now, you're safe, and it's over."

I asked Brigitte to secure her seatbelt and we drove back to our initial destination. I quietly kept talking to her, trying my best to help her to accept the incredible reality of UFOs. They could pick us up again at any moment if they chose to do so, I thought. But I had to keep Brigitte's mind away from this very real possibility. I certainly did not want her to experience a panic attack right here in the middle of nowhere. As always, the traffic was very dense through the city of Los Angeles and it took us nearly two hours to reach Anaheim. The feeling experienced after any abduction is quite detrimental to the mind, where common sense has no value whatsoever. A sense of invasion to your body, mind and soul, makes you feel so vulnerable. Such a haunting event involves so much more than words can express and only those who have had similar experiences can relate to us.

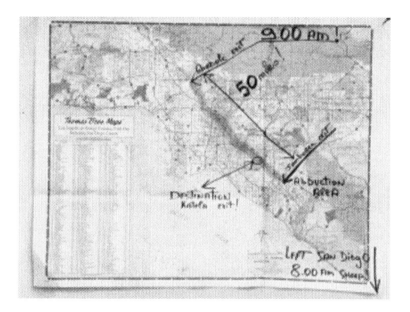

The Exact Area and Distance of Our Missing Time

We were so confused and distressed that I thought it would be wise not to return home just yet and rented a very expensive room at the Hilton. In no way could I convince Brigitte to go back home and as soon as we were in the hotel room she called her good friend Mary in San Diego, begging her to come and pick her up right away. They drove to another friend's home in Phoenix, Arizona. She understandably wanted to distance herself from the extraterrestrials, the apartment, and the experience all together. Regardless of my disapproval, she left me at the hotel the very same night and I could only wish her and Mary a safe trip to the Grand Canyon State. The very next day I drove back home, then again to the Glendale exit, trying to make sense of what happened to us. Logically, I carefully checked the time and the mileage. I came to the conclusion that it was simply impossible to do so in only one hour. This could be done driving at about 100 miles per hour the entire way, providing there was no traffic (or no cops to stop me) in Los Angeles. The next few weeks were spent at home tormenting myself, but I never felt entirely alone. We went through an obvious abduction that memorable

August day and a part of my existence was stolen against my will. The desire to find out more about UFO's and abduction was burning me alive.

I heard of a man named Shawn Atlantis, we set an appointment with him and he came to my home with some recording equipment. Brigitte and I revived the traumatic experience and Shawn taped it all, he also became a very good friend of mine over the years. He knew Brigitte and I hadn't dealt directly with aliens or UFOs before and his compassion and explanations were badly needed. I told Shawn that it was not the first time I dealt with the incredible and he patiently listened to the rest of my incredible experiences. A few days later Shawn mentioned a reputed Doctor in Victorville California who willing to investigate my case using hypnotherapy. I accepted the offer and we drove to her office, I was excited to finally uncover what really happened to us. A famous UFO researcher and film producer was also invited to film the session and promptly installed three cameras in the doctor's office. Brigitte fervently refused to take any part of the regression and demanded to watch everything on the screen set outside the Doctor's room.

I was offered some cold water and asked to lie down on a comfortable sofa. A nice and soft relaxing music was enveloping me and covered all outside noise. The Hypnotherapist's soft voice brought me back to my dramatic childhood, then progressively to the sensational day of August 11, 1991. I felt like slipping into time and space and began to talk. "Brigitte and I were driving on highway 5 North, then I turned the radio off just before the sign of Jamboree road. Brigitte first mentioned the road getting wider as we drove through what seemed to be a thick white cloud. I could not see much and slowed down wondering about the dreamlike feeling enveloping us. I did not feel the road and bumps anymore and Brigitte takes my hand staring at the cloud. We were sucked inside a flying saucer belly and at this juncture we were in what seemed to be a large metallic underground parking area lot. It was a dark cold and silent. Two very large men dressed in silver suits came from the left side of the car. Brigitte was screaming tightly holding on to me." I said.

"Oh my God, what's going to happen to us" she said terrified.

"It's OK Brigitte, I have been there before, and you are safe," I said. I told her we were going to be separated for a while and all would be over soon. One of the tall men (a Nordic) opened the door for me and I followed him towards an opening. The other man took Brigitte to a different area but for some reason I was not worried about my wife. We were like somnambular zombies, the effect induced by a strong pervasive peaceful feeling. The extraterrestrial left me at the entrance, which opened sideways instantly. I entered a bright room and stood in front of a small porthole looking at the distant planet earth. Our world was the size of a basketball or when someone observes a full moon on a clear night sky and certainly indicated a very long distance from home.

View of Mother Earth from the Spaceship

Under the watchful eye of the Doctor, I started to complain about heat and some form of electric light coming from the inside of what seemed to be a decontamination room. The first stage was over and I walked towards another entrance, which immediately slid upward. I entered the flying saucer pilot room and no one is payed attention to me. Teams of dignified robots known as the "Greys" in UFO terminology are handling the ship under the supervision of a few tall human-like creatures positioned in different areas of the saucer. I wanted to see Brigitte and walked towards a large screen. Here she was laying down unconscious with three Grey working on her. I was neither surprise nor upset about her precarious situation. I was powerless, desensitized, and felt as if I knew what was going on and somehow agreed with it. She was lying down on her back on a clear glass table in a position where she appeared delivering a child.

I knew all was going according to a higher order that could not be altered and walked to another door. I was like a semi conscious robot, but with no will of my own, I only knew it was time for me to go there. I entered an immaculate room that could be best described as a bright dentist room where all surgical equipment was replaced with all sorts of electronics. One of the supervisors silently observed my move as I sat on a cold metallic armchair. Then from above a sort of thick electronic helmet device came slowly down from the ceiling of the room and covered my head and eyes.

I was not scared and seemed to have had been there many times before. I felt my entire body turning in to a frozen electrified corpse while a startling field energy was discharged into my brain. The entire experience made me feel like being a God holding all answers to the mystery of life and death. I felt a great surge of peace inside my soul where all the reasons of my being and my fate became clear. I felt like if I had been given a mission and an objective, understanding of the complexity of the universe, and a super drive to make the world aware of it. I was one with God, one with creation, and one with the universe. I was blessed by a downloading of the secrets of the Universal Mind by an extraordinary extraterrestrial intelligence. Due to some dramatic scenes the doctors and the UFO investigators decided not to let me watch or have the tape. Brigitte was speechless and silently crying as I walked out of the room totally soaked. I became soggy when I complained of being hot while in the "decontamination" room. One of the best ways to check if someone is really under hypnosis is to look for any movement during the session and in my case both the first and last frames froze in and identical positions two hours later. But the real shock came days later when Brigitte noticed and showed me an unusual two-inch scar just above her hairline. The cut seems to have been made with a laser beam and not a regular scalpel used in conventional surgery. It became clear that Brigitte did not know she was pregnant and the fetus was taken away. ET's have complicated agendas and the reasons are endless, but I wonder if we will ever find out why people of all ages and race disappear regularly from the face of the earth. I consider us to be the lucky ones because we made it back home. I do not know the entire ramifications involving our abduction, but the incredible changes that took place in our psyches are undeniable.

I Painted My Entire House with UFOs and Strange Art

I filled all the walls of my house with astrological and UFO symbols. Then an immense urge to master Nostradamus' divine astrology and general metaphysics became more of a fanatical obsession that led me to who I am today. I have an inherited an intrinsic wisdom that allows me to "read" people's mind and fate accurately and make inarguable and well documented predictions. Those premonitions are much too numerous to mention here but the 9/11 WTC terrorist attack in New York, the Asia tsunami, the Kobe earthquake, hurricane Andrew, Katrina and all major news were predicted months before they unfolded. I knew I would once more see UFOs in my life and I did!

Yes it's a Flying Saucer

Brigitte and I tried hard to leave that dramatic experience and the memorable apartment behind us and we decided to move to Scottsdale, Arizona. Life took its course and talking about my UFO experiences in my numerous conferences was a way for me to heal, but Brigitte has and probably always will be reluctant to mention a word about it.

Expensive Gun Wish

In this next example I will elaborate a little more on the collective interaction between subconscious forces at work. Being aware of this fact will become a major contribution to help you to assimilate and use this power to your advantage. On a daily basis, we are all subconsciously using psychic influences to stimulate each other to act favorably. Consciously manipulating the celestial will and the subconscious creative forces for selfish ends can work, but you are strongly advised to check your intentions to avoid the inescapable karmic link involving all metaphysical endeavors.

Brigitte and I are against any form of violence especially to animals and we treat our pets with love and respect. We also enjoy shooting our guns in the remote desert area. We do usually choose somewhere between Arizona and California and drive our 4X4 truck on the trail until the highway disappears behind us. Safety is very important when dealing with firearms and I always make sure to face a mountainside or drive down to a washout. Brigitte's first experience with a gun was very interesting. Money was scarce in those days for us and I could only afford cheap guns that jammed frequently.

She picked a small Italian gun from the shop because it was pretty and because Brigitte was also afraid of big guns. We went to a shooting range in Scottsdale to school ourselves with the dangerous firearms, but we felt quite uncomfortable with the constant blast of others people's big guns.

"What's going on, honey?" I said.

"It's too noisy and it smells like gun powder here," she said.

"But what do you expect," I answered laughing. I helped her to focus on the target and she fired the ridiculously small gun for the first time. She looked pretty funny smiling behind her large protective gargoyle glasses and her cowboy hat. Brigitte is a very touchy girl all over and the blast annoyed her sensitive ears. I knew the shooting party was going to be over sooner than anticipated and I had still quite a lot of ammunition left.

"OK darling," I said "let's go." She knew I was annoyed.

"Honey, why don't we try in the desert?" she asked.

"Yes, you're right, why don't we do just that," I replied and we took off into the wild open spaces far enough from the city of Scottsdale and its residents.

The beautiful red colors of the sunset fading on the surrounding mountains left us with a feeling of happiness and tranquility. The air was warm and the silence was now and then broken by the call of a wild bird. I picked a remote and safe spot close to the disappearing trail and stopped the truck. We walked for a while between some tall and impressive saguaro cactuses into a dry wash. Carefully scrutinizing the ground for snakes we enjoyed every minute of the wilderness of the Arizona desert. Brigitte was carrying a bag with a couple of empty bottles of water which were to be used as target practice.

We walked carefully avoiding the menacing spikes of many cactuses while Brigitte stopped periodically collecting colorful rocks avoiding the stinging bites of desert ants doing their thing. Looking to the horizon and high mountains in front of me I wondered of the hardship endured by the first pioneers crossing such a wilderness. Brigitte and I were dehydrating fast and many people made the fatal mistake not to carry water and died of exposure. During the hot months desert temperature can reach up to125 degrees Fahrenheit.

We had plenty water in the truck and were in no danger at all unless the truck decided to die on that very spot. Snake bites and over-exposure are always serious possibilities in Arizona and only shortly before, the local newspaper reported an unfortunate woman who decided to visit her daughter only twenty miles away from town. For some unknown reason she got lost in the desert and ran out of fuel. She attempted the five mile walk to the highway without water and was found dead in the desert the next day. It is necessary to bring a considerable amount of water with you, even if you are a few miles away from civilization. Luckily for us, we soon arrived to a perfect spot; I loaded the firearms and gave Brigitte her ridiculously small gun.

"Honey, I am scared to fire it, would you like to try it first?" she said.

"Babe" I answered, "This is such a small gun, what are you afraid of?"

"I don't know, this thing might hurt me!" she replied anxiously.

"Right, give it to me and watch out." I pressed gently the trigger and fired the little gun in the air. Brigitte was behind me blindfolding her face and covering her ears with her hands.

"Noisy thing" she said, I could not help but to laugh my head off.

She smiled and put her hand on my shoulder and said. "Honey, I feel better now."

I shook my head and replied, "Well, let me try the other gun."

She quickly moved away from me to a safe distance where the blast would not affect her sensitive hearing. "Be careful, Honey" she said "and keep your glasses on." I glanced behind me, to make sure she was okay and then fired the bigger gun a couple of times, missing the target sitting less than ten feet away. The bullet ricocheted off a rock and made a piercing sound that really scared her away. After many attempts to hit the target, I finally enjoyed shooting the target successfully. Brigitte was sitting a short distance away and from the safety of the truck, she was watching me and listening to the radio. After awhile, she felt more comfortable with the detonations and finally took a chance on her own tiny gun. "Okay, I will try mine, now." she said, "My confidence is back!" That sight made the entire trip worthwhile. Here she was, petrified, trembling and holding the small gun with both of her tiny hands, aiming at the target.

"Honey, if you are to have any chance of hitting the bottle, then you must keep your eyes open!" I said giggling. She smiled back and finally after what seemed like an eternity, she fired the gun. She was impressed by her own courage and kept firing it over and over again.

All of a sudden, to my surprise, she asked. "Honey, can I try yours?"

"Are you sure you want to do that?" I said.

"Yeah, let me do it, I know I can do it!" She replied. I loaded the gun and carefully passed it on to her. Without any hesitation whatsoever, she discharged the gun right on the target. I was amazed, not only of her courage and unsuspected reaction, but at her ability to hit the small target so many times. Her confidence with guns went right up and over the many months of practice (with my gun!), her performance and accuracy also improved dramatically. Then one day, at the local gun shop, while buying ammo (and another cheap gun for myself) she kept asking me for a more reliable firearm to use.

As you know a decent gun can easily cost over a thousand dollars and apart from occasional desert target practices, there was no real reason for us to own such an expensive and deadly toy. Nevertheless, Brigitte is a stubborn Taurus and her own powerful subconscious led to a chain of events that would finally bring to us the very expensive gun. Brigitte was missing her family and often complained about the scorching heat, so a few months later we moved back to San Diego, California. Then one day my dear friend Owen and his wife Denny invited us to spend the weekend in their gorgeous home in Los Angeles. I met Owen years ago at one of my numerous conferences in Los Angeles and did a reading for him. I took care of thousands of people in my career as an Astrologer Counselor, but this specific karmic relationship rapidly turned from casual to a genuine friendship. The great couple has two beautiful young girls named Adrienne and Michelle that we both love immensely.

Owen proudly took us for a tour of the immense house he had built himself and we all ended up in the basement. Excited, Owen directed us to a big steel box and said, "I keep this locked all the time. I don't want my girls to get hurt." He nervously tried a few keys and finally unlocked it. At this point Brigitte and I had no idea that the heavy safe container was loaded with some of the most expensive and rare firearms that we have ever seen. Owen is a decorated Vietnam War Vet and carefully went through each and every rifle, gun, and knife, cautiously unpacking them for us to see. Each weapon had a story to tell, including a dangerously sharp rare Japanese Hara Kiri knife and a WW1 bayonet.

Brigitte was carefully handling an unloaded "9 mm" and I was holding a mighty Magnum 44. We were amazed by the quality of so many firearms owned by a single person. Then honestly Brigitte said, "I always wanted to own one of those guns, one day I'll have one." I did not feel very good about that comment, as Owen might feel obligated to give her one of his precious guns.

With his usual big smile, Owen quickly replied, "None of those babies are for sale." packing the armaments away. That was the end of it. The time spent with this family is always rewarding no matter what we all decide to do. A couple of days later after plenty kisses and hugs we drove back home in San Diego.

On the way home, Brigitte commented about some of the guns. "Nice guns, huh Honey?" she said.

"Yeah, but expensive" I replied.

"Yes, but one day we will own one of those, aren't we?" She won't give up, I thought! We made it home safely and returned to our routine and a few days later while watching television, the telephone rang.

"Hey, Louis, how are you doing, buddy?" I immediately recognized Owens' voice. He's got that deep sound that makes it so great to listen to; I always thought he'd be a good candidate to work on the radio with such a voice. Incidentally, Owen was born in June and Gemini rules general communication and indeed the radio industry.

"I'm doing great, what's up?" I said. I could also feel a form of anxiety in his voice, something I was not used to.

"Well, uh, I am going through some changes Louis and …I need your help." He said.

"What kind of changes is it?" I asked.

"Career changes" he said, "I can't take it no more, and I'm really fed up with construction." This did not surprise me a bit, as Owen is a very spiritual man, a form of a philosopher and natural healer and indeed a very intellectual guy. Some transits were affecting his 4th house (home/family matters) and his 10th house (career area) and subjected to important changes. I took the time to explain to him how "The Universal Code" operates or what a typical psychologist would refer to as "middle age crisis".

"Does this also mean a change of career?" he asked nervously.

"Indeed, especially with the Dragon's Tail about to enter your 10th house of career soon," I said. So many people are totally unaware of the "Draconic Laws" and find themselves in serious depressions instead of working diligently with the Universal Will.

"Whoops! Is that why I feel so crabby with all I do, but the problem is that I do not know what direction to take." he said. I could feel the amount of stress he was under and told him.

"Listen Owen, there is too much going on with the stars now, I can't explain that much to you over the phone, so we've got to find a way to connect soon," I said.

"Okay, when?" he impatiently said, like all Gemini (speed) patience is not exactly their virtue. I glanced at my appointment calendar and picked a date that would fit both our busy schedules.

A week or so later, he was behind my door and right on time for his appointment. We sat in my large and commodious sofa and we began talking and sipping on a hot cup of cafe. Soon enough, he began to express his feelings openly as any trusted friend would do in times of serious stress.

"Well, Louis, I am experiencing some serious emotional and financial trouble" he said "and I don't really know what to do anymore." He paused for a few seconds, looking at me and added. Before I could answer him, he added. "I know you will take no money from me as usual, but I really want to be fair with you and I was wondering if you would accept one of my guns for your service. I know Brigitte loves my Heckler," he confidently added.

To my amazement, he quickly opened a thick greenish box that was sitting on the coffee table, showing me the powerful weapon. He leaned toward me, saying, "Look at the box, this babe was made in Germany and its top quality." I was amazed by his generous offer and answered,

"You're crazy or what? You don't have to give us this expensive gun for a reading, especially if you are in trouble, I can't accept that."

He laughed, "Louis, your readings are worth more than what you think, trust me!" he said "Anyway, if that makes it better for you, I am also worried about my two girls and having all those guns in the house."

I looked at his warm eyes for a second, and then asked, "But what about the big safe metal box?"

"Well, they managed to get the key and my wife caught them downstairs, trying to open it. She is really upset with me now and wants me to get rid of all of them." He added, sadly. At this point, I realized Owen was really concerned with the safety of his two little girls.

I felt somehow guilty knowing this gun was worth over 1,600 US dollars. I grabbed the box and began to read the inscriptions loudly. "Mod.4K VP 70 Z - HECKLER & KOCH -GMBH OBERNDOR F/N - 18 Rounds, guaranteed by the manufacturer to never jam". I was speechless and asked again. "Owen, are you sure?" I could not help thinking to myself of how delighted Brigitte would be, when she found out her wish just came true.

He looked at me with a grin, and said. "Yes, I'm sure." I felt uncomfortable with the deal and said.

"Okay Owen, I accept your gun, but from now on you and your family will never pay anything for my services" He laughed loudly and replied, "You've got a deal."

By nature, Owen is a great guy and incredibly generous. The type of friend you can count on and someone that you keep for life. We spent a few hours together in the office, rebuilding my friend's confidence. After consulting with all the stars and the Tarot De Marseille, Owen left my house with a brand new spirit and extra faith, as always, I knew the job was well done.

* Looking back at this situation, Brigitte's friend, Jackie, had a boyfriend who worked as manager in a Scottsdale gun shop. Unlike Brigitte, Jackie had never fired her gun, but she was proud to own a 9mm and often carefully exposed her unloaded toy around. Brigitte wanted to own a powerful 9 mm gun and with "The Law of Attraction" and the right "Universal Code" in action, the miraculous circumstances took place. Time and distance will not diminish the subconscious power, but with a definite thought (in this case a 9mm) the wish is foreordained. Owen's wife, Denny, is a sensitive and protective Cancer; she subconsciously participated and played an important part of her own wish to get rid of the weapons. She must have been quite concerned with the safety of her fast growing girls and the potential danger waiting in the basement. The girls often played downstairs and Denny's fear of an accidental shooting was very real. Many children have accidentally lost their precious lives by playing with firearms. In this example, Denny's protective instinct and fears had energized the set and all the players.

The Law of Negativity in Action

This is an example of how one's fearful attitude can become a wish. The combination of fear and imagination is a potential mixture to stimulate the commanding expression of the subconscious. While extraordinarily powerful, your subconscious is incapable of rationalizing with you and maintaining your worries can easily turn into wishes. In November 1996, I was doing personal readings for my wealthy La Jolla clientele in my suite at the Pointe Hilton in Phoenix, Arizona. There I met with an old client of mine named Mary whose appointment was set for 3:30 P.M. and a few minutes before her scheduled time, she knocked at the door. I was still doing a reading for another client and Brigitte greeted her at the door. They both knew each other well and went in the other room, chatting about life in general. Soon she was sitting in front of me, tears running down her face. She was talking incessantly, I glanced at her astrological chart and spotted a Gemini Moon and politely asked her not to interfere with my channeling in the recorded session. Discipline is a must when doing a reading, especially with natural chatterboxes. Combined with a talkative Gemini Moon, she was born with a very emotional Pisces difficult Dragon's Tail in her 7th house of marriage. Thus, I already knew that she was experiencing serious trouble in her relationships. She presented me with a letter sent by her husband's attorney, requesting a divorce with no chance for reconciliation.

"How can he do that? After so many years of marriage, what I am going to do now?" she asked, devastated. I knew that I had only thirty minutes in front of me to "fix" the problem and my chances in succeeding were minimal if I could not stop her complaining. She was dealing with a karmic situation and Mary was much too emotional to listen or even grasp the situation she was in. I tried hard in her thirty minutes of session to "erase" a situation that took her twenty-five years to build and I knew she badly needed a two hours session, at minimum, to reach her. People under mental stress regenerate their spirit by "releasing" their frustrations and I knew she wouldn't leave my tarot table easily when her time was up. I was already behind in my schedule and Brigitte was concerned for my next client and was getting impatient. As always in such a situation, she saved me from Mary and took the devastated Lady with her in the back room. I worked hard all day, taking care of all my clients and I was anxiously watching the clock in the corner of my eyes. By 8 PM, I was finally done and mentally worn out. I do personal live readings on special occasions today, but at that time I was taking care of twenty people a day for three consecutive days, which was extremely exhausting. The trip was over and we were driving back home.

A few days later the telephone rang, "Hello?"

"Yeah, Dr. Turi, can I help you?"

"Oh, I am so glad to talk to you, this is Mary." Ouch, I thought! Knowing Mary I knew I was on to talk for a while. "Guess what" she said, "the tape you gave me is completely empty"

"Oh, no, I am so sorry" I said. The tone of her voice quickly changed when I told her that I couldn't make another tape for her right away. Mary was born in September, but her Moon in Gemini brought "The Law of Duality" and this Air sign is well known for not only its impatience but having to repeat things twice. (Hence having to redo the tape). "Listen, Mary," I added, "I don't believe in accidents, please call my office tomorrow and find a way to record the conversation from your end, okay?" She was happy for my concern and thanked me warmly. I will always go to a great extent to make sure my client is satisfied, especially in this type of service where word of mouth is your real advertisement. As expected, Mary called the same evening with questions that were previously answered; I also knew that she was so emotionally drained and could not wait to get her reading. I accepted my fate and again politely asked her to do the listening.

"Mary, how many years were you married?" was my first question.

She answered very precisely "It will be 16 years in December, Dr. Turi."

"Okay, and did he give you any reason to leave you behind and move to your summer condo in Florida?"

"No, is there another woman with him?" she anxiously asked me.

"Mary, I am trying to establish the reason why he would behave that way with you"

She asked again, "Is there another woman, Dr. Turi?"

"There is always the possibility of your husband having an affair, Mary."

Sobbing, she added, "Who is she? Is she younger than me?"

"Mary, what's your husband's date of birth?" I asked. I knew to change subject right away, if I had any chance to control her powerful emotions and lead the conversation."

"He was born in July, but I do not have his time of birth."

"Mary, you know I do not practice modern Astrology, but Nostradamus 16th century Divine Astrology; I do not need exact time." (Nostradamus did not use a watch over 500 years ago and could not care less about the rising sign!)

"Sorry, I forgot" she said. My trained brain swiftly worked out her husband's housing system and I realized the negative Dragon's Tail was entering Mary's 7th house of marriage. She was on for a difficult ride, I thought.

"Mary" I said, "your husband is a Cancer and the Dragon's Tail has been on your marriage area for nearly two years now". "Cancer is a very tenacious nurturing sign and he will not let go of the past easily." I said. She confirmed my knowledge, by saying that since her husband left he continued to support her financially. Providing Mary understood her situation and controlled her super emotional behavior, she would have a chance to save her marriage, I thought. I knew I was in for a long and arduous work to help her auto-analyze herself. To make the situation worse, Mary was a Virgo and the nasty Dragon was already moving into her own 7th house of marriage. Because of her husband's own stars, a repetition and a continuation of the past two years of struggle was taking place. I teach my students that it takes approximately two years or so for the Dragon to travel through a sign and a house. With 99% of the population unaware of the "Universal Code" the current statistics point out 87% of all relationships will end up in divorce. It took me a while to pass this crucial information to Mary and it finally made sense to her, especially when her Cancer friend was experiencing the exact same stress with her own husband, through the "Universal Code" order.

"Mary," I said. "You will have to be very strong, as you are about to be tested to the max by the stars. The stars do not really care about you, me, your husband, or anything else for that matter. When the negative Dragon resides in a sign or a specific house, you better be aware of its impact, for if you are not, you will certainly pay an heavy penalty for your ignorance."

"Dr. Turi, please help me, I really love my husband, I can't be without him!" was her answer.

"Listen carefully, Mary." I said. "There is a power in you that can turn things around for you, but you must understand its dynamics, first." I said.

Mary was sobbing again, " I will do anything you say Dr. Turi, just help me, please!" Thirty-five intense minutes later, Mary began to understand "The Law of Negativity" and the daily poisonous dose generated against herself and her husband. "The Draconic Law" was doing the damage in her marriage area and she was unaware of it. I also explained to Mary that Virgo is a sign of neatness, regulating health and flawlessness. Thus, health played an important part of her perfectionist and vegetarian life. A difficult attitude to deal with, knowing that Cancer loves cooking and good food! I had to make sure she could analyze herself correctly and understand her "idiosyncrasy". I told her not to poison herself and her partner with subconscious fears of diseases and perfectionism. I told her that she was not designed like a cow, with huge flat teeth and three stomachs to ruminate grass. She's not a tiger either, designed to tear apart flesh with fangs and claws. Interfering with the normal scheme of things because of Virgo's subconscious desire for purity and perfection is simply a subconscious reaction against an inner fear of death and disease. I also told her that this herbal regime was affecting her sex drive and neutralized the magnetism and the seat of attraction between human beings. Vegetarianism is recommended only if you are in a "cleansing" mode and a good balance with all sorts of food is always recommended.

I also had to explained to Mary that she presented herself to the world as an over-sensitive Pisces. The acidic Neptunian energy overwhelmed her 7th house of marriage and warned her to switch off the toxic process immediately or she'd lose her husband. Mary was slowly building her cosmic consciousness, listening attentively to my counsel. I explained, Pisces is a karmic sign and is indeed, one of the most difficult zodiac sign to master, due to the elusive and deceiving power of Neptune. I teach my students, that wherever Pisces is located in your chart, there is not much grounding or practicability and rationalism is usually missing. I began to ask Mary precise questions directly related to her regular communication with her husband. "Mary," I asked "do you complain often to your husband?"

"Well, um, I believe so, but he doesn't listen to me." She answered.

"So, you do repeat yourself often, don't you?" I said.

"Constantly. I have to! He doesn't know how I feel!" she added.

Carefully, I asked Mary, "Does he answer you?"

"No, he drives me mad! I can't get his attention, I asked him many times if he had an affair" she said "and he never answered me". Her powerful hypersensitive Pisces attitude spilled again, a large flow of uncontrolled thoughts and there was nothing I could do to stop her talking and sobbing. She kept going on and complaining about him, doing to me now, the same thing that she was doing to her husband for years. As expected, her over-emotional nature rapidly took over and she began to cry heavily.

I thought, how can she be so blind of her own destructive insecure thoughts and I began to admire her poor husband for his patience. "He doesn't eat right, he's messy, and when I ask him if he loves me, he doesn't answer," she continued complaining on and on and on! The deceiving power of Neptune in her natal 7th house of "destructive marital behavior" was in full force and I wanted her to do so and catch her in the act. Making her aware of "The Law of Negativity" was very important to her success and me, I thought. I knew now, Mary was ready for her wake up call and I softly began to make her aware of the impact that she had on me.

"Mary," I said, "For a minute or so, please, please, listen carefully to what I have to tell you, I am so happy I am not married to you!"

"What?" she said, spontaneously.

"If I was your husband, I would run away from you too, you are a nightmare to be around!" I continued saying how lucky I was to be married to Brigitte and how she never behaved that way. I had no way to spare her and she was hurting, but I finally got her attention!

"Dr. Turi, you should be compassionate and not criticizing me. You are the only one that can really understand me and I am quite surprised by your remarks". She kept going on, saying "and my psychologist told me that my father's drinking problem is the reason why I behave this way" she added.

"Stop, stop right now Mary and listen to me," I ordered. I had wanted to create a reaction, which I obviously did, but I did not want to start a fight, speaking to her with a more compassionate voice. My goal was to keep her on the edge, without loosing her rational thoughts or hanging up on me. The idea was for me to help Mary to help herself auto analyze her worst behavior. She was haunted by uncontrollable feelings and an over emotional attitude and that was the reason for her trouble. Unlike her many previous psychologists, I did not want to end up not resolving her self-inflicted problem. "Mary, telling you what you want to hear or furthering your destructive thought process, won't work here." I continued to explain, "You must understand the impact produced by your insecurity and your harmful verbal attitude directed at your husband" I insisted. Finally, after a few minutes of "sensible" conversation, she began to realize more about the damage inflicted to her partner and why her sensitive Cancer husband left her behind.

"Dr. Turi," she said. "I do appreciate your directness and honesty; I had no idea that I was actually responsible for him leaving me." Her comment jolted me. Finally, I thought.

"Well, that's your new challenge, Mary. You must purify your thought process and replace it with love, happiness, joy, trust and faith in you and God." I explained to Mary that her will was much stronger than her disrupting natal stars (UCI) and with some behavioral work she could modify her inner solicitation for troubles. Doing so, she would be able to gain control over her husbands' decision to leave her and tackle the problem she put herself in.

"You really gave me some somber insight, Dr. Turi. Now I really have something to think about and I am glad I called you back," she said.

"Yes," I answered, "I do not believe in accidents and the messed up taping happened for a specific reason. Please, Mary" I added "understand that like attracts like and if you work for death, crime, and deception then you will attract it to you. You are a magnet and a magnet will not attract a piece of wood, be happy and increase your vibrations." I suggested.

"What do you mean?" she asked.

I kept myself in check and answered. "There are numerous Universal Laws acting up in your life that you are not aware of and ignorance is evil." I also realized how she really was uneducated about the subconscious power and metaphysics in general. "How could it be possible for people live in harmony or reach their goals, while lacking such vital wisdom?" I asked her. "I mean that, if you are in a positive environment then you will think and behave positive, and if you think and behave positively, you can only attract positivism." I added. I knew that I had her full attention and I also knew I was finally making progress. I kept explaining that light, love, health and happiness were the vital ingredients needed to breed a positive thought process. My next question to her was, "Where do you work now, Mary?"

"Well, I am still working at the hospital for the terminally ill patients." she answered. While asking, I thought how Virgo does rules health in general, but this type of confirmation is how I learned to be precise in reading the characteristics and fate of all signs of the zodiac.
"Do you work at night?"

"Yes." she said.

"Are you happy there?" I asked her.

"Well, my schedule does not allow me and my husband to spend much time together." I repeated my question.

"Mary, are you happy there?"

"No, but I need to work!" she said. She was again, becoming irritable and I quickly toned down.

"I understand," I said. Her inborn insecure nature and the depressing hospital environment she was in "intellectually" asked for trouble. Facing the world as a Pisces, she attracted a job involving hospitals, asylum, jails, churches, and all confined and deceptive areas ruled by Neptune.

Mary quickly applied her common sense and with an irritable voice, said to me. "Dr. Turi, we need nurses, firemen, police officers, etc.," she said.

"I am fully aware of this," I politely responded "but by looking at your UCI (unique celestial identity) you are much too sensitive to handle such a taxing environment." I also did not fancy explaining all the ramifications of the "Universal Code" or the sound verdict I had made on her and quickly changed the topic. It takes about a week of six hours a day of heavy-duty teachings for any of my students to grasp the dynamics of the Universal Mind. Like so many of those who are "soul searching" Mary regenerated with spiritual food, but I was not going to further her cosmic consciousness over the telephone. I asked another question, "Mary, do you take anti depressants?"

As expected she answered, "Yes, I do."

"What do you take?" before her reply, I said "Prozac?"

"Yes, how do you know, Dr. Turi? You really are a psychic," she added. Sure, I am indeed the most rational man on earth. It's not psychic stuff, but applying true wisdom and common sense, I thought. In Mary's case, her inborn Neptunian energy would not mingle too well with any medical prescriptions and should be avoided like the plague. Ingesting more drugs or "Neptune" can only further the deterioration of her common sense and would bring more chemical unbalance in the brain. Then again, how many traditionally educated doctors know about Neptune's deceiving powers and its impact on a Neptunian patient? Furthermore, how many doctors possess cosmic consciousness and understand "The Universal Code" and a multitude of Universal Laws interacting with the subconscious? This world is so young and this is why I have devoted myself to write this book for mankind's mental health. The side effects of drugs are dangerous and as complex as the patient's problem itself and can only work for a certain time. Common sense, education, and solid mental coaching is what Mary needed, not drugs I thought. "Mary, how long have you been on this product?" I asked.

"Three years now, well, they say it's safe," she added.

"Sure." I answered sarcastically. I did not want to scare her or induce more traumas in her fragile psyche. She caught the sarcastic remark and I could picture her worried face. I quickly reversed, mentioning some research was done with Prozac and the FDA did not find any dangerous agents that could hurt anyone. As if the financial giants of pharmaceutical companies would even care about your mental health, I thought. There is only so much the public can do against the FDA regulations and their smart, but apathetic attorneys. My second and very important step was for me to convince Mary to cautiously quit the addictive products. I asked her to research and read on the merchandise and to notify her physician right away if she ever experienced any of the side affects. I knew by experience that it would be difficult to reestablish Mary to a more lucid life and rational reasoning, since she took the product for many years now. Chances are, that Mary was addicted to the lethargic effect on her mind and body and made it a normal part of her daily routine to do "legal" drugs. I recall how difficult it was for me to quit smoking and like any other drug tobacco is very addictive. Only my supreme will and education helped me out of this bad habit.

I did what I could do for Mary, with concern and commitment to the best of my knowledge. I am fully aware of the subconscious power, but in Mary's case, this supremacy was channeled destructively especially when chemicals were involved. Any use of narcotics, prescriptions, drugs, alcohol, and a myriad of other "Neptunian" products can and will seriously alter your inner thought process. I also knew the depth of Mary's wish to find true help with me and somehow her subconscious (or mine?) screwed up the taping. I also knew that the thirty minutes consultation would never have done the trick. She needed more consideration to relate to the "Universal Code" and acknowledge her subconscious destructive thoughts. I do not believe in "accidents" per say, but in some magical interference induced by a higher force. She warmly thanked me again and I could feel a great relief on her part. Mary regained a form of control and hopes for her husband's return to be happily married ever after - and she did!

A Love Story Solved

The Moon is responsible for many of our destructive emotions, especially when a powerful planet such as dramatic Pluto rules the day. This next example is an explanation of the workings of the subtle {Lunar-Plutonic} energy upon Julie's (a client of mine) love life. 9:30 AM, Monday December 16th, 1996 after gulping a strong cup of coffee, I was right back at my computer channeling divine information for a new book. I hate being disturbed when writing. If I can avoid it I will not answer my phone. It is hard enough to get into that writing mode and I must discipline myself to sit and write. I was right in the middle of an interesting chapter when the telephone rang. I chose not to answer the call, trying hard to stay focused on my chain of thoughts. Someone in Indiana left me with a message saying that he was looking for my predictions on some groups where I did not post any longer. Another call came through; this time I could hear a distressing sound coming from the answer machine in the sitting room. One of my clients must be in trouble, I thought. I felt the urgency and picked it up.

"Good morning, this is Dr. Turi, what can I do for you?" I said.

"Hi! Dr. Turi, this is Julie in Phoenix Arizona, I saw you in your last conference at the Hilton a few weeks ago, thank you for taking my call, I really need to talk to you" she said. Julie happens to be a retired 911 operator and worked for the Phoenix police department for many years. The sound of her voice was moving as she was trying hard to hold onto her powerful emotions. I also knew that I was going to be on that call for a while! "I am so sorry for what happened to me, I made a big mistake with my boyfriend"

"What type of mistake did you make?" I asked her. "Well, we had a fight and he left me" she replied.

"When did this happen?"

"Last week-end," she added "last Saturday". I quickly glanced at the calendar suspended above my computer; the date was December 7th, 1996. I noticed a nasty Pluto window was in action those days and I knew exactly what she had gone through. I was not surprised at all and patiently listened to the saddening details of her fight. I opened my 1996 Moon Power book and realized either she did not read the book or did not understand my work.

My next question was "Julie, did you read your book?" and a weak yes was the answer. Obviously, she did not follow or sufficiently understand the written directions for that fatalistic day. Being aware of the hurtful power of Pluto, especially after the Full Moon, I had specifically made a note of this passage on my own calendar for good reasons. I politely asked her to open the book to the particular page and patiently read the excerpt with her. Julie is an intelligent girl, born with a powerful Dragon's Head in curious Gemini. Incidentally, she spent most of her career as a 911-telephone police operator and Gemini rules telecommunication. The stars never lie and I could not help but wonder how much invaluable information the world and especially the police were missing. My Astro-Psychology students are accustomed with my work and there is nothing more obvious and dramatic than the often-fatal influence of Pluto during his jurisdiction. The deadly Scorpio stinger is an obvious symbolic meaning of how sarcasm, sex or money endeavors can quickly turn into a bloodthirsty fight. Many unaware souls have met with their deaths under his power. The worst elements of our society become destructive upon Pluto's dreadful command. Appalling news of all sorts from serial killers to suicide, takes place under his terrifying power and many underdogs will continue to pay the ultimate price.

To illustrate the cosmic interaction with Pluto, here is one of many examples from my yearly Moon Power 2002 Universal Predictions: "Washington, D.C.- area has been on edge ever since a sniper struck on October 2, 2002 the first in a wave of fatal attacks that have occurred with stunning regularity in the subsequent weeks. Local, state and federal investigators have launched an extensive effort to find the killer, but the lack of an arrest has compounded the community's anxiety, as going outside has become a potentially life-threatening endeavor".

2002 - MON., TUE., WED., THU., FRI. — OCTOBER 7, 8, 9, 10, 11:

RULERS — Pluto (drama/Death)

Travel and Communication: Regardless of the New Moon, be aware on the road, because with Pluto, absolutely anything nasty can happen to you now.

Events: If you are a police officer or a security guard, beware of Pluto. The crooks will be active and deadly. Passion may take over, as Pluto will lead a bad young spirit to kill innocent people. Furthermore, I also mentioned to her that the same sensational Pluto energy was responsible for the Rodney King beatings in Los

Angeles and in Carlsbad, California during the summer of 1994. In both cases, the police department suffered a lawsuit of millions of dollars in damages, subsequent to the L.A.P.D, Laurence Powell's case and all the other officers involved. The police used abusive force to constrain some very unlucky residents.

Back to Julie's story. By now, Brigitte was discretely making faces trying to get my attention, as I was less than fifteen minutes away from my next appointment and I had not yet gulped down my breakfast. Time was running out and I could not give any more specific direction to Julie's situation with her boyfriend. As always, teaching astrology in my office was out of question as the discussion involving the direct connection with the police and Pluto deadly energy could last forever and I had to bring the interesting discussion to an end. I was hoping for her to react to the information and maybe open a door for me to lecture and educate the academy.

"I am sorry Julie," I said, "but your time is up and you have to go now."

As expected she asked. "So, Dr. Turi, what shall I do with John? Do you have any suggestions?"

"Is John religious or spiritual?" I asked her.

"He was raised religiously but he won't support my research in astrology." she responded. She also told me that John was on a serious quest for his spirit and had changed his religion a few times. Julie was highly spiritual, while John was religious and this difference created stress in communication and ultimately their relationship. Julie was born with "an advanced" Mercury (critical thinking) in Aquarius (astrology) while John inherited Mercury in religious, dreamy Pisces. "The Cosmic Code" had spoken loud and clear to me, but neither Julie or John had any cosmic consciousness and ignorance can only breed animosity. "Well, the best thing to do" I suggested, "is to tap into John's spiritual nature and give him a copy of the page explaining the plutonic energy and send it to him along with a nice letter expressing a mixture of love and apology. Make him realize that, like you, he was under the brawling spell of Pluto."

"Would it work?" she asked.

"I believe so," I said, mostly because I noticed that John Dragon's Tail was in the very sensitive and understanding sign of Pisces. I also knew that this karmic position generates a tremendous amount of guilt and John was probably missing Julie too!

"All right, Dr. Turi," she said, "When should I do this?"

"The Moon is waxing right now, it's like a protective green light, so I wouldn't wait and suggest for you to get on with it right away", I answered. She had hopes to be in control of the situation with her boyfriend! Mostly because Julie spent so many years in the force, I continued speaking about the police and Pluto's interaction in a cop's life. "Do you know Julie, that I sent a certified letter dated July 12, 1991, to Daryl Gate, the Los Angeles ex-Chief of police, predicting the dramatic events with the Rodney King, months in advance." I said.

"You are too much" she said. "Did you also foresee the Los Angeles riots?" she asked.

"Not only the exact dates of the riots, but also the deceiving judgment that was to spark the riots" I concluded, "and all this is well documented in my slide presentation that I hope someday to provide in my lectures to the police force". Julies was now dumbfounded and to my surprise, her powerful Dragon's Head in Gemini did not interfere with me and she kept listening to the rest of the story without any interruption. Brigitte was getting very impatient, especially with her natal Moon in Aries, so I politely ended the conversation with Julie for the second time, asking her to keep me posted and swiftly went outside on the patio, to enjoy my cold breakfast. A few days later, she brought John for a reading, I suspected the fight was the starting point for Julie to get enough spiritual food to pass on to John, so he could regenerate and free his spirit from induced religious guilt. John bought all of my books and took my course by mail. The stressful dilemma became a worthwhile learning experience for both parties.

"Another job well done, Honey!" Brigitte said smiling.

Heather's Office Wish

Back in 1999, I had a great secretary named Heather and she mentioned a few times to me, "Dr. Turi over the years you have spent enough money making copies to own a few expensive copy machines."

"Yes, I know. But in order for me to invest in such a costly piece of equipment I need to make more money, and right now I can't do it!" I replied.

"I understand," she said with compassion. "We also need a bigger file cabinet to organize all this paper work," she said, pointing out a huge pile of mail.

"Well, let's put it out there in the universe and let's see if our subconscious will take care of us." I laughingly answered her.

We did not have to wait too long, before the supremacy unfolded in its usual miraculous ways. The very next day we had a meeting with Bonnie, who was then the President of the Truth Seeker Co. We were to discuss the best way to teach astrology to the masses and produce a workbook for my upcoming infomercial. We arrived at the office about thirty minutes early and no one was present, but we could hear noise coming from the corridor. I saw my good friend "Graphy" running and he shouted, "Come on guys, there is a huge sell-out upstairs; you don't want to miss this one!" The entire staff of the Truth Seeker Co. was there, coming up and down the stairs, carrying all sorts of office business supplies and furniture.

"Whoa!" I said to Heather, "Let's go and look to see if there is anything we can use here!"

"Okay!" she replied. We both went our separate ways to investigate all the goodies on sale. The first thing I noticed was a large white file cabinet. Good, I thought it's the exact same color and material that we already had in Heather's office. I immediately asked for the person in charge. A white, gray haired middle-aged man was busy answering peoples questions and cashing money from happy customers

"Excuse me, Sir, how much for this file cabinet" I yelled.

"Make me an offer he said nonchalantly."

"Twenty bucks!" I shouted from the other side of the room.

"You got it!" he replied. I approached the man and gave him a $20.00 bill. Looking at the "sold" sign on the piece of furniture, I was very happy with the results of my first bid.

Then another guy came to me and asked me. "Did you get this file cabinet?"

"Yeah! I did," I said. I perceived sadness in his eyes and he said.

"Look, what ever you paid for it, I will give you $20.00 more."

"This is a real good offer, Sir," I said politely, "but we need it so much that I must turn you down." He apologized for the intrusion and kept looking around. Heather also came up with some good deals; I trusted her Virgo gift to perceive all details and to pick what was good for us. Thirty minutes or so later, the room slowly became quiet. I was still looking around for something in the pile of junk left behind, but I did not know what just yet. Then, Heather came to me and said.

"Dr. Turi, did you notice the copy machine?"

"Yes, I did, but it's much too big, how do you want me to carry this monster downstairs? My Nissan Pathfinder is not big enough anyway to carry such a large copy machine," I added. I felt her disappointment and said to her "I am sure that this copy machine, even on sale would be quite expensive Heather, forget it and let's go down to our meeting now." She reluctantly turned away from the machine and began walking towards the stairway.

Then for some unknown reason I asked the man in charge. "Excuse me, Sir, how much for the copy machine?" While writing on a yellow pad, he answered.

"Which one?"

"Well, I can only see only one copy machine there" I replied innocently. He smiled and patted my shoulder.

"No," he said, "There are two of them." I was perplexed and wondered how both Heather and I could have missed two copiers. "Okay, let me show them to you" he said and we went right back to the corner of the large room. I could not believe my eyes; the only reason why this machine did not go anywhere is because it was accidentally covered with papers and discarded boxes.

"Sir how much for this copy machine?"

"Well" he said scratching the back of his head, I don't really know and I am not sure if it works. Are you going to be in the building for a while?" he asked me.

"For sure" I said, "I have a meeting downstairs and my meeting will take at least a couple of hours."

"Okay," he said, "Give me your number and I will call you as soon as I find out." I gave him my business card and asked him to leave me a message. I shook his warm hand, and full of hope, I walked away. The progressive meeting took place, clarifying the best course of action for the infomercial astrological workbook.

The telephones kept ringing. Over and over again, I was hoping for a good message that finally arrived. Heather and I rushed upstairs to get the copy machine. Two young ladies were sitting there, talking to each other. "Excuse me," I said, "May I talk to the gentleman in charge of the sales?"

"Are you Dr. Turi?" the younger girl asked me.

"Yes, I am." I answered.

She looked at me smiling and happily said, "The manager had to leave, but he told us about you and we were waiting for you." I could not believe my ears, when she added. "You can have the "sharp copy machine for one hundred bucks!"

I immediately felt suspicious and asked, "Is this machine in good working order?"

"Absolutely, and trust me, you've got the best deal of all, I worked here and we had it serviced last week." she said. I reached for my wallet, gave her the money, grasped the heavy copier, and thanked them for their help as I was leaving the building. As I walked to my car, Heather was totally amazed and very happy at the prospects of being more efficient and organized while saving precious time with the additional office equipment.

> * It is so very important to "notice" those deals coming from the universe, because I can guarantee that you have also experienced such strikes of luck in your life. Unfortunately, many people lack the power of attention and reflection and do not tap more often or faithfully into the creative forces of the subconscious. Subconsciously, Heather powerfully stirred "The Law Of Hope" that played the important part of this lucky strike for all of us. Incidentally the Moon was also waxing (New) and into the sign of Cancer (beginning and endings) adding more prospects to reach one's wishes.

Divorce

Brigitte and I spent nearly 13 years together and we were indeed the "perfect" couple to the eyes of all the people we knew including my family. But the "Universal Code" will always impose changes where those needed transformations make life what it is. After so many years spent together, habits took over and the passion slowly faded. Many times a saddened Brigitte reminded me to spark the romance and bring more excitement to what she perceived as our dull life; but to no avail. I was concentrating on building a new career while exhausting myself everyday in the construction field. After operating a fifty-ton bulldozer for 10 hours, the only need I had was food and sleep. I awoke early and got ready for the next demanding day.

Indeed many husbands do not understand the deep emotional needs their wives require and how important variety is in a relationship. I was about to learn the hard way. She subconsciously began to generate thoughts of changes and new challenges in her life. I recall being asked to do an infomercial in Las Vegas for the "Truth Seeker Corporation" marking the beginning of the end of our relationship.

We met with a gentleman who had all she needed, or at least she thought. He was an astute, sharp Virgo. He worked in television and Brigitte always wanted to be involved in this field. This person had a very important part to play in our lives and he was the "ingredient" needed to stimulate her to make a move she so reluctantly wanted.

He was a magnetic man with a very soft deep voice that instantly mesmerized Brigitte. I saw my wife's face change almost immediately and how radiant her gaze became. I previously asked for his date of birth and to make the situation totally unavoidable he was also born with his Dragon's Tail in the sign of Virgo; right in the fifth house (seat of attraction between human beings) of Brigitte. As a rule earth signs will attract themselves but when the Dragon's Tail is involved, the magnetism seems to explode and the attraction is simply irresistible. Many people fall for that karmic celestial manifesto and fall in love at first sight. Brigitte's behavior changed almost immediately and I knew I was in trouble and my worst fear came true while driving back home from Las Vegas.

"Why are you crying Brigitte?" I asked her concerned.

"Well I don't know really, I feel so sad" she said.

"About what?" I asked trying to prompt her into a conversation. "I think you feel guilty Brigitte" I said, "I know you well Hun and you are battling deep feelings between him and I aren't you?"

"Yes" she said, "but I never felt that way for anyone and I feel terrible about us," she added.

"Well I know I did not really take care of you the way a good husband should but

I promise I will Baby," I answered.

"Oh no" she said, you are a really good hard working, reliable and committed husband, it's nothing to do with you. I just feel weird about today and I am afraid".

"It's Ok Hun, I am sure we will be fine regardless of what the future has in store for us," I added.

I was seriously hoping for the best. I knew this type of karmic "connection" in time would not work in my favor because we had signed a contract and scheduled many more meetings with him. I could only hope for the best and for Brigitte to stand strong in my favor. Little did I know that a serious wake up call was ahead of me that same very evening.

Once we arrived home, I felt she needed to speak to someone else about her troubles. So I decided to go out for a drink and collect my own thoughts about this stressing development. I had a hint to return, so less than thirty-five minutes later I was parking in my driveway wondering if she had resolved her feelings.

Her Mercedes was not in the garage and I became suspicious. The door was open, something that Brigitte would never do because of our Persian cat Cezar. I entered the house and called her name but no answer. I was so disturbed that I even thought she might be downstairs in the bedroom sleeping. I walked down and to my surprise two suitcases, the cat and all her clothing were gone. I had not realized the depth of her connection to this person until I recalled the many hours she spent talking with him the previous days. Meeting him in person and connecting with his energy was the breaking point. Thirteen years spent together, and she left me after less than a week knowing him.

I knew Brigitte well. There was no way she would cheat on me, not with a Scorpio Dragon's Tail (fixed, committed). It would mean she would have to die and be reborn into a new section of her life. When I married Brigitte I told her that her stars supported my demise (or divorce) with her Dragon's Tail (negative) in Scorpio (death) in her seventh house (marriage). Incidentally Brigitte's mother was also born in May and she lost her husband dramatically. Scorpio rules police, drama and death. The cops shot her father over a bad drug deal when she was only a child. The stars have spoken and I knew somehow I was going to die and I did, in my own way.

This was indeed the most difficult interval in my life because I was so used to seeing her next to me. Being up and suddenly alone and forced into celibacy was just terrible. Only two days later I was to do readings at a conference in Santa

Rosa in California and I had to drive for the first time after so many years by myself. I call highway 5 North towards San Francisco, the "Highway of Tears." I cried every single inch of the way, wondering how I would be able to work and survive this dreadful period of my life. Many times looking at my clients I was thinking, "Damn if someone needs help right now it is me, not you". But I threw myself into my work and was able just for a short time to "forget" about my terrible situation.

After each reading, I was hit again by a mad train of sorrow and I could not hold back the tears running down my face. I had to go outside and collect myself to finish my job. I had a made a commitment, people signed the long list and I had to do it regardless of what I was going through. The trip back was even worse as I knew no one was waiting for me home, I was not used to going back to an empty house and I did not know how I would handle myself the next few days. I was desperate and thought of calling my family for the love and attention I so desperately needed but I decided not to tell anyone until I was sure Brigitte was gone for sure. I was in total denial and hoped for a call or from anyone to tell me where she was and if she was all right. But no one told me anything.

I was going crazy walking back and forth in my house and I was incapable of doing any work. I nurtured serious thoughts of killing myself and understood an old friend back home in France that had committed suicide because his wife dropped him for someone else. I was laughing at him back then, asking him to be a man and to take it like a man not knowing what he was going through emotionally. I felt guilty for such a lack of understanding or compassion for a man that was, like me, dying inside.

I made a habit to put all my bottles of alcohol in front of me and get wasted before reaching my loaded gun. While watching television trying to forget my misery, I knew I had to get dead drunk and pass out or I might find enough courage to pull the trigger.

It was horrible and I was literally dying each and every single day. Finally I received my credit card statement and discovered she was in Phoenix with a friend.

I drove to Arizona like a crazy maniac exceeding speeds of 140 MPH and went straight to one of the two girlfriends homes. I knew she could be there but her friend didn't want to see or talk to me. I thanked her and left for the next friend's house but she must have called them in between and when I arrived there all curtains were closed. I was suspicious and walked around the property and saw the Mercedes parked in the back. She must have tried to hide the car before I came but she did not have time to move it to a distant location. I knew now that Brigitte was here and I was very excited to finally be able to communicate with her.

I called both telephone numbers and as anticipated no one picked up, then I decided to go and peep by the window in the back of the house and called Brigitte's friend again. I saw both of them standing by the answering machine and I said. "Come on girls, I can see you from the back window, I know you are here and I am not crazy, I am not going to make a scene, I just want to give Brigitte another credit card and some clothes she left behind and talk to her."

They were very surprised as I was describing what they were wearing to prove my case and they both disappeared in the bedroom. I was happy because I thought after 3 months I would be able to see my wife and communicate with her but I was wrong. All of a sudden two police cars arrived at the house and 4 police officers had their guns pointed at me. I could not believe it; they called the cops on me. I tried to explain my situation to the police officers but they advised me to turn back to San Diego to avoid going to jail.

I took their advice seriously and saddened, drove back home. After one hour or so on the road my cell phone rang. "Hi, its me, I wanted to know that I am not the one who called the cops but it was my crazy friend," Brigitte said. I was ecstatic, after so many weeks I was finally talking to my wife and I tried really hard to convince her to return home and to forget all the mess. But I was nevertheless in denial and Brigitte was still going through some problems of her own with the guy and her situation.

I avoided talking about him. But she told me she was not coming home but instead going to another friend's house, and for me to stop looking for her. She also told me that her friend was nuts and she had enough and made new arrangements to relocate. I tried again and again to make sense to this situation but she hung up on me, begging me to stop trying to bring her back home.

I drove back as depressed as anyone can, hating myself for the missed opportunity to get our life together. I was still in denial and hoped for Brigitte to come home. I arrived exhausted and depressed and collapsed for the remaining of the night.

The next day to my surprise she called me again. "Hun" she screamed, the car is broken, I am stuck on the highway, its 115 degrees outside, I don't know what to do".

"Damn where are you exactly" I asked. " I am just outside of Phoenix, I left my crazy friend's house", she added.

"Are you coming home?' I asked totally surprised.

"No" she said, I am going to LA".

I was confused but I was more concerned with her safety than anything else for the moment.

"OK can you tell me exactly where you are?"

"Well I am in the Goodyear area and I am on the side of the road".

"OK is the car running and the AC working?" I asked.

"Yes she replied and I am inside with the cat and I am OK for now".

"What's going on with the car?' I asked.

"Well when I accelerate it does not go," she answered.

I realized that the accelerator cable was broken and felt relieved and added, "Brigitte, Mercedes cars are very reliable. You should take this as an omen that maybe you should come back home and forget about going wherever you are headed".

She exploded and said, "No I am not going home, its over between us get it once and for all, I am going to Los Angeles and my friend is waiting for me" she added.

I calmed her down and said, "OK Brigitte I will call a tow truck and a taxi to get you. I know exactly where you are, I am also getting you a hotel room OK?"

"Thank you," she said.

I knew you are the only one that could and would help me," she added calmly.

I made a few telephone calls and I was thrilled because I finally knew where Brigitte was and I had been given another chance to bring her back home. I drove back to Phoenix the very next day at the speed of light, I arrived at the hotel where I knew she was and knocked at her door. My heart was pounding and I was sure Brigitte expected me. She opened the door and I was surprised by the way she looked. She must have lost at least ten pounds or more I thought, she was so skinny. I realized then that she was also going through some serious turmoil.

We spoke for a while then she asked me if I had any cash on me and to take her to the airport. I was as depressed as can be but I had to respect her wish and drove her there. Regardless of my desperate requests she did not budge and flew off. Her girlfriend had birds and she could not take the cat with her, thus Cezar went back home with me that night. I felt less miserable to have my pet back, he is still at home with me but Brigitte never came back.

Months later I found out that the guy never fulfilled Brigitte's wish for love and I knew he would never let his wife and 3 kids behind for any woman. I told Brigitte that she was wasting her time all along but the power of the stars in this karmic phase of her life was intended to bring an end to our marriage and start a new section of her life.

Brigitte and I now are the best of friends and we are both highly spiritual forgiving souls. The players played their part and a section of our lives has gone. I still love Brigitte unconditionally for all the good she provided for the thirteen years we spent together. She gave as much love and commitment as I did in that relationship. We both are ready for more experiences because we know that life is a constant process of change that touches every human being on earth.

Part 4

Teachings

The Law of Hope vs the Law of Obsession

Back in 2004 a concerned lady named Michelle called my office and asked "Dr. Turi I have cancer and I am going to die, I am so scared, can you please help me"?

"Of course" I replied, " let's schedule you for tomorrow as this is an emergency treatment," I added. I am well aware of the subconscious mighty forces and as a rule I do not take anything literally until I talk to any of my clients. She came the next day and after introducing herself to me I said, "Do you know there is no death per se? It's only passing through a door and even if you don't know about it, your fear is more painful than the process of dying itself," I added.

She was listening carefully and said, "Well my cancer is not painful yet but I am afraid it will be" she added discouraged. I detected what seemed to be an enormous tumor on her waist area vigilantly covered by her bulky clothing. I asked her all pertinent questions I needed and printed her chart, knowing her UCI would tell me much more than what she could ever tell me about her own self and that is the beauty of practicing Astropsychology. I glanced at her chart and saw her sun located in the health oriented sign of Virgo. "What did your doctor said about your condition Michelle?" I asked.

"Well I did not see any physicians yet I do not want to ingest any drugs or undergo chemotherapy, I feel this is wrong," she answered. As expected, like all Virgos she was a very health conscious sign and incredibly critical about anything under the sun. After the initial reading and Cabalistic cleansing I politely asked her to move to the Healing Room. I asked Michelle to lie down on her back and after a while she fell into a light hypnotic trance, I then asked her a simple question.

The first one was "what is your most important wish Michelle?" Just before answering I cold see her face literally changing, even glowing when she answered.

"My greatest wish is to be pregnant by my boyfriend whom I love so much and carry our baby. My god," she added, "this would be the most beautiful day of my life."

"OK great Michelle, I softly said, "Now tell me what is the most terrible thing that could happen to you? Almost immediately her facial features change from happiness to distortions and tears. I gave her time to release the induced emotion until she answered.

"Well its already happening Dr. Turi, I am living a total nightmare because about three months ago my boyfriend dropped me for another woman and I have been dying inside since then," she added. I immediately realized how her subconscious was taking over her body mind and soul trying hard to reward her wish. I checked the growth with my pendulum and I cautiously lead her out of her hypnotic trance. I helped her to sit up and waited for a while for her blood pressure to sufficiently bring enough oxygen supply to her brain and helped her to walk back to my office. I offered her a cold drink of water and I knew she was ready for the announcement.

"Well Michelle you don't have Cancer, let me clarify what happened to you". I explained to Michelle that her subconscious wanted to grant her wish to become pregnant and began an incredible physical process that would build fat around her waistline. Not being educated on the subconscious forces she thought the growth to be a cancerous tumor.

She was amazed and perplexed and kept saying, "Are you sure Dr. Turi? I don't have Cancer? I won't die?"

"No you wont Hun I confidently said, you may have to go and have this growth removed, but I guarantee you it is not cancerous, my pendulum never lies to me," I added. I counseled her appropriately by taping our conversation and giving her a Hypnotherapy DVD asking her to learn more about her own subconscious creative forces.

The Law of Fear

* As a child I suffered my own subconscious forces answering my wish for silencing my arguing parents, by destroying my hearing. This produced chronic otitis. Your subconscious will not differentiate between "**The Law of Hope**" and "**The Law of Fear**" and the destructive type of results are clearly demonstrated in Michelle's case. In her case, left unchecked her fat-building process in time could easily have turned cancerous. Subconsciously people will attract Cancer or a multitude of other ailments to free themselves from a job, a situation, or a person. If your heredity or UCI supports contracting specific diseases you will swiftly open a can of worms. In this case Michelle was born with a Dragon's Tail in Cancer (abdomen, the womb) and suffered also a manifestation of "The Draconic Law".

Another interesting case with another client of mine, Nicole, took place only a few weeks later. She was wondering why her jaw suddenly locked shut and after the ordeal she called me to shed some light on this mystery. Nicole's case did not require any hypnotic session as I gathered the right answer by talking with her over the telephone. One day Nicole found herself in the emergency room fed intravenously because she could not open her mouth and ingest food naturally. The only good thing about this hospitalization she said was her tremendous weight loss and that was exactly the reason why her subconscious put her there. She had three children and did not have the time or the money to afford an expensive exercise program to reduce her heaviness. In her subconscious mind the only practical and affordable way to get lighter was to stop eating and her subconscious took her thoughts literally by stopping the food entering her mouth.

The Law of Obsession

* **"The Law Of Obsession"** found a way to express itself negatively, but brought about positive results to Nicole. She focused her energy to the point that it manifested in the physical realm. Yet it was not conscious, but rather the obsessive thoughts which brought the results. Left unchecked your subconscious will alter even stop the good working of parts of your body and in Nicole's case her subconscious froze her facial muscles. Her Dragon's Tail was located in Pisces and this self-hypnotizing sign rules hospitals and is a powerful gateway to the subconscious. As always "The Draconic Law" played an important part of this mysterious dilemma.

Mrs. Smith's Wake-Up Call

My career has brought me so many people and some of them need time to appreciate my work. The "Universal Mind" is impartial and regiments everything on earth. Regardless of how much I want to be compassionate with people, telling them what they want to hear may not be for their own best interest. Once a lady came in my office and she was amazed when I told her the type of people and signs she would attract in her life. Of course, she thought of me being a real good psychic when I was only using "The Law of Celestial Attraction". Guessing is not my forte, but true wisdom gained over thirty-five years of arduous work is the real reason behind my uncanny perception. I explained to her that "The Draconic Law" was in effect and brought her a doomed karmic relationship.

She was concerned about her marriage and wondered about the fidelity of her husband. Her husband was a Gemini born with a Dragon's Tail also in this sign, making the situation and prediction of a multitude of marriages and the upcoming break unmistakable. Well, it looks like your husband is "suffering" "The Law Of Duality" and this is why he had been married three times before." I announced. I continued by telling her that the Dragon's location depends on the year of birth. I also explained to the best of my wisdom, that the Dragon is in constant motion and is still cruising for a few more months in her marriage area. I immediately told her that regardless of what the "Universal Code" or the "The Draconic Law" imposed in her life, she still had full power to control the situation, providing that she builds enough cosmic consciousness to wisely avoid the traps. I also mentioned how her subconscious could alter the situation for the better or could even make it worse if she let "The Law Of Fear" take over her life. Her face turned red and she said convincingly, "What about Elizabeth Taylor? She's been married a million times and she was not born the same year than my husband or I," she said, rather annoyed. I understood again, that people would rather be in denial or refuse to grow spiritually by using common sense.

"Yes, I know all about Elizabeth Taylor's UCI, I did her stars for a magazine in the past, " I said. "She was born under the artistic sign of Pisces and her Moon (emotions) is in the deadly sign of Scorpio. I explained to my client that the Moon represents the emotional response to life and in the dramatic sign of Scorpio; she was doomed to "kill" many husbands. I made some sense to her with my explanation, but again, I am such a deep recipient for true celestial wisdom and very often, I feel unable to educate people with information that took thirty-five years of my life to assimilate. I clearly exposed her fate with her husband and unless educated, she had little or no chances to fight the Dragon. I suggested for her to read my five hundred and twenty five pages book entitled "The Power of The Dragon". "Understanding all the Dragons by house and signs will quickly help you to assimilate the power and control of the outcome," I innocently said.

To my disbelief, she said loudly, "You are just trying to sell me one of your books and you never answered my question directly, I wasted my time on visiting you!" She then stood up, grasped her handbag and walked directly to my front door, opened it and slammed it shut as hard as she could, behind her. I was shocked by her reaction, wondering how clearer I could have been. I understood her frustration and unwillingness to hear the possibility of separation. I knew deep inside that the future was going to be, as usual, my only real witness.

A year or so elapsed, then a lady in need of information for a reading called me. "Hello Dr. Turi," she said. "I was referred to you by Mrs. Smith, do you remember her?" she said happily. What people don't know is that I get tons of referral calls everyday and the name of Mrs. Smith, meant absolutely nothing to me.

"No, I am sorry, I am so busy with so many people and I am not exactly good with names." I answered her politely.

"Oh no, Dr. Turi, you must remember her, she is the one who left your office slamming the door and never paid you for your time," she said.

"Gee! Hell, yeah! How can I forget such a person," I said.

"Well, she is the one who referred me to you Dr. Turi and by the way, she also asked me to see if you had saved her reading, because all that you said did happen to her. She feels real bad and she wants to see you again, soon," she added. Mrs. Smith reappeared in my office and after another reading she left me with a fat tip and a lot of excuses for her offensive behavior. She bought all of my books, became a student and has endorsed my work and me for years. She was her own worst enemy and suffered a multitude of Universal Laws that she finally mastered in the appropriate time. I realized that people could only relate to me because of their UCI, education, and experiences. This is why I never took her behavior personally and gave her enough time to grow up spiritually.

*Your subconscious will find any possible way to bring about the answer you are looking for. Your subconscious will bring people and situations that will force you to get to your wish. Often true wisdom can only be reached with pain and suffering while disagreement brings regret and guilt, forcing you to learn a valuable lesson. Most of the time we do not know what we have until we lose it but once the lesson has been learned the option to build a solid relationship with love becomes a real possibility. Your subconscious will give you a myriad of omens that you must learn to decipher and use to your advantage. We are constantly bombarded by other people's thoughts traveling in time and space. Some of those thoughts stimulate you to write, to act, to pick up the phone, to find out it is about to ring with your best friend on the other end.

Timing is Everything

The Law of Synchronicity

* We have covered the idea of space with the Law of Location. The **Law of Synchronicity** is similar to the **Law of Omens** only it specifically involves TIME. It It is the timing of curious events that reveal a message which should not be ignored. Our subconscious minds will produce a series of circumstances that correspond to events that are in play in our lives. We may often think it is only circumstance but if we examine more closely and allow our intuition to follow the clues, we will then discover the exact path to pursue. Refer to the works of Carl Jung for a thorogh study.

Here is a firm example of how I was stirred to write about my UFO experiences in one of my newsletters answering someone else' subconscious request from distance.

Sent: Tuesday, October 15, 2002 8:42 PM
Subject: Re: Hello from Victor/ / / in Texas!

Dear Dr. Turi,

Are you familiar with the saying "if you ask the universe question, the universe will respond"? Well, last night I was thinking about the subject of UFO's. And I asked myself "I wonder if this Dr. Turi guy has ever seen a UFO, or had any experience with them"? I didn't ask the question verbally (only mentally). Then, this morning when I checked my e-mail, you provided a detailed answer to my psychic question with your UFO experiences. To me, that is REALLY AMAZING! Now, you have given me direct proof of your psychic nature. Was that synchronicity in action, or did you read my mind? "If" you read my thoughts from Arizona, I am very impressed with your personal ESP power! Does this mean that I too am on a good level of thought, or does it mean that I have an easy mind to read?

Sincerely,

Victor

Well Victor like all of us is blessed with an unseen powerful antenna and on occasion emits or a receives information but the masses are not yet aware of the subtle processes taking place in the Superconscious in time and space. And this is why you are reading my book, just because you asked for it!

Here is another example from one of my students:

From Craig
Sent: Friday, March 23, 2007 9:25 AM
Subject: Synchronicity

Dr. Turi;

Last night I decided to start reading "I Know All About You" so was lying in bed with it. Also decided to listen to a meditation of yours, so had that in my MP3 player lying on my table next to the bed. So I decide to listen to coast to coast. And just after hitting the on button you came on. It is amazing how it all works. We create what we think about. If people only knew the power they have. Just hold what you want joyously and lovingly and persistently in mind, and the garden will grow and sprout the flowers of your thought.

Craig

"What the Bleep" Do They Know?

In August 2006, some 2,500 astronomers from 75 nations had a conference to "alienate" Pluto from the Celestial family and decided to see it as "dwarf" planet. Note also, that only about 300 showed up to vote, this means that, 2200 other people did not vote and that is a significant number that could easily have turned the balance around. It's really a shame that they proceeded with the vote, knowing that 2200 other persons were missing and that is an injustice in itself. Since when is it that numbers don't mean anything to science, when science is all about numbers? Right from there, common sense dictates the vote is not effective. Imagine if any politician running for office found out that 2200 votes were missing from the ballots? But you see, that is something they will not talk about and it's simply disgusting and even unlawful.

Realize also, that this vote is coming from a bunch of "educated" mental elite who have absolutely NO clue to the spiritual values of the planet Pluto and its vital role in our solar system. I am not surprised of this conclusion, knowing that 99.9% of the entire world's population (especially scientists) do not possess cosmic consciousness. I'd say that the biased minds of those astronomers make them incapable to enter or even conceive of the archetypal realm of consciousness. I wonder how Copernicus and so many other elite astrologers feel about this "decision" made by a bunch of badly informed people. But again, this generation of scientists was born with a Pluto (perception/discernment/depth of the thoughts/metaphysics etc.) into the logical, rational scientifically oriented sign of Virgo. So again, it is not surprising for them to miss the entire forest for the tree and it's literally impossible to auto-analyze themselves and this ridiculous vote.

I doubt any of them knows the fact that Astronomy is a by-product of a much older science called Astrology. During the time of Copernicus, the word astronomer did not exist yet and only astrology was acted upon. Its later that the "born scientists then/ present astronomers" stole the clay tablets of astrologers to accurately and mathematically predict the time of eclipses and so was born Astronomy. Right then, man began to challenge God's Universal laws and created the huge disorderly spiritual chaos mankind is suffering nowadays. I mentioned many times before in my previous newsletters, that NO man could ever alter the laws of the Universe, not even the Pope. So, if the Pope decides to "invite" the gay population and the gypsies (forever persecuted by the Christians) to bring about more money, then the International Astronomical Union (a branch of NASA) who needs publicity and your tax dollar to survive, can do the same. Pluto rules true power, investigation, the FBI/CIA, corporations, supreme wealth, real power, sex, life, and death. Pluto rules the decay and reincarnation principle and will transform a worm in the water into a butterfly, from the Water to Air elements. Pluto rules the Mafia and the underworld. Pluto in Greek mythology is the discarded son of great Jupiter ruling the underworld and hell. Where ever Pluto is located in your chart, death, sex, and supreme power will enter your life.

Now any of my students will have absolutely no problem to recognize this fact, because they spent days with me learning the true meaning, values, and inner manifestation of the most intense planet in our solar system. But NONE of those "learned" scientists took the time to do so and would rather be caught dead than to honor the very word of Science and INVESTIGATE my findings. Well, the born Astronomers as mentioned many times inherited a limited UCI (Unique Celestial Identity) and indeed a very weak Pluto, because of their lack of intuitive power and their reluctance to investigate anything that cannot be seen or touched. It's just their stars, put it that way. Moreover, I can guarantee you that those scientists were born with "pathetic" Mercury (mental power) in an Earth sign (logic, critical thinking) that does not support deep metaphysical research. I am glad I understand astrology because I know they cannot help themselves, they were born that way and it is no more their fault than mine for understanding what I do.

There is huge difference between education and intelligence. Those young souls hide their ignorance behind accredited schools, and produced the International Astronomical Union or IAU (which I call the Idiotic Astronomical Union). The astronomers are like little kids and now and then, one of them will scream "See I discovered another planet!" But, there are billion of them out there…Its like Christopher Columbus discovering America, guess what, the continent was always there! The scientists do not want to appear stupid and they finally realized that there are billions of celestial bodies in the vastness of our universe. So now they are, with the authority of (Imbeciles Astronomical Union!) creating new concepts and new names, new theories, and CRAZE as they go along planets such as Pluto, recognized for centuries by some of the most powerful elites minds of all times.

Pluto is there to stay, simply because Pluto has always been part of our celestial family. Pluto's energy is real and it takes a little more than an astronomer's educated mind to understand its power and purpose in both the personal and universal human affairs. As of right now, Pluto the planet of death and rebirth is in the philosophical, religious sign of Sagittarius and propels the events taking place in the Middle East. Its impact is also affecting and changing (RE-birthing) the higher educational system to a higher level of perception. Thus, as of August 25th, 2006 in Prague in the Czech Republic, Pluto has done his job with science and killed whatever little common sense astronomers had, opening the door for people like me to ask questions and teach you the real meaning of Pluto.

Pluto and the Secret Service

On February 18th and 19th 2004, I was invited to do a television show in Los Angeles. The show was called "More Than Human" and used to air every Thursday night at 10 pm on the Discovery Channel. The Production Company's management arranged transportation and accommodations at the Hilton for all their guests, and paid us for our time and expertise. Unlike many shows that I planned with "The Universal Law of The Moon" I could not control the taping dates. Like 99% of the rest of the world, the producers do not possess cosmic consciousness and any endeavors performed after a Full Moon, can only mean trouble or annoying happenings. The effects of this negative lunation were fully experienced by all of the guests, traveling by air or driving. I was especially amused with Bonnie (the Poker player in the show) and the trouble she went through with her taxi driver losing himself in Los Angeles. I teach my students that there are no accidents in life, really. In my own case at the end of this show, I learned a lot more about my own methodology, the FBI, human nature, and advanced technology used in lie detection by the law enforcement.

Before leaving the studio, I gave my business cards to everyone involved, and told them I would enter their names in my newsletter and give some feedback on the show, to my readers worldwide. I am sure that all of the guests and the other few thousand subscribers did appreciate my findings, my teachings, and my legendary honesty in my writings. In any case, I also gave the option to any of the TV show guests to respond to me directly if needed, by emailing me with their feedback. I will if requested, insert their comments into my next newsletter, so no one thinks of my views and experiences as being unfair or one sided.

Fictitious names have been used to respect the privacy of all the guests;

Andre - Forensic Psychology Consultant and Trainer; teaches Forensic Psychology in Massachusetts. Formerly was a Forensic Psycho-Physiologist with the Central Intelligence Agency (CIA).

Daniel - Former FBI Special Agent, he also is a Consultant for the FBI, and teaches Interviewing Techniques and Nonverbal Behavior at the FBI Academy and several universities and colleges. He also co-authored a book about interviewing techniques.

Jacques - Layered Voice Analysis (LVA) expert (Ex-Police Chief)

Robert - Polygraph expert, Polygraph Examiner

Bonnie - Professional poker player

Yves - (The would-be liar).

Taping a television program is demanding, time consuming, and often stressful for all parties. The studio was packed with guests and staff, all assigned to a multitude of endeavors from the direction of dedicated producers, floor managers, to the crew handling the cameras, etc. The studio is full of regulations, actions and sounds that are nerve-wracking for unacquainted guests. Suddenly, the awaited countdown arrives to have total silence as the taping starts. Any noisy mistake on the floor will immediately become known to everyone on the set and will annoy the dedicated perfectionist producer of the show.

The host of the show (a sweet and pretty Pisces) performed well and as planned, during the entire show. A few minutes earlier, I had a deep spiritual conversation with her and she really enjoyed some of my teachings about Pisces characteristics. I strongly felt her desire to learn more about the divine, but I also detected an inner fear of the unknown that was probably induced through her early religious teachings. She walked all the way down the stairs followed by Andre, a handsome and articulated man. Andre is a Forensic Interviewer, Interrogation and Training Consultant and both the audience and guests, including myself were impressed with his knowledge.

From the very first moment I met Andre, I felt his uneasiness, he was quite perplexed with me altogether and could not really comprehend what or where I was coming from. If you watched one of my shows on TLC, an astronomer had that same "attitude" with me and tried really hard to dismiss me as another kooky "Miss Cleo" type. However, as the show progressed, more comments from the subjects interviewed, confirmed my research as a valuable investigative tool.

I have experienced this type of reaction and its accompanying preposterous behavior many times before. This attitude is stirred by a fear of ridicule and a negative response to the unfamiliar. The hard-core rational scientists, having been victimized by a mainstream traditional educational system, quite often generate obvious reactions such as this.

Astro-Psychology classifies this type of reaction as the "mental snob syndrome" or a mixture of ego fueled by academic superiority. They are only responding to their own limited UCI, not knowing yet, that there is big difference between education and intelligence.

Andre did not know me personally, nor had he ever investigated my work in-depth and his perception and reaction was anticipated. He simply saw me as an oddity and was very perplexed.

* Note for my students; My Tail of the Dragon in Libra is located into Andre's (a Leo) 3rd house of communication (assimilation/critical thinking/learning and teaching) and I was already expecting a serious mental conflict. In no way was Andre capable of entering the archetypal realm of consciousness to stir up any advanced spiritual exchanges. My comments may appear harsh, but it's not directed at Andre or anyone else for that matter. They are only meant to explain a friction between an old soul teaching and a young logical soul. I have profound respect for anyone's academic achievement, including Andre and as a true scientist myself; I do support education in all its forms. I can only hope for Andre to somehow respect the word "science" and investigate the "Cosmic Code" in depth and reach cosmic consciousness. Doing so would eliminate any pre-conceived ideas or doubts involving the therapeutic values Astro-Psychology and its incredible potential in any form of investigation of the human mind. The very fact that Andre is a Libra (regulation/parameter) in his 3rd house (scholarship/coaching) reveals a natural fascination with the law and a solid gift in logical psychology. But like a parrot, he is only assimilating and repeating traditional information, giving no room for an independent genius to breach the incredible. Of course, this fact can be understood and appreciated by my students, only. Without honoring the word science or doing the proper investigation, some people will immediately lump me with Miss Cleo or accuse me of wasting time in impractical pursuits. Again, I neither support nor deny psychic phenomenon. My take on that subject is very clear; a financially oriented daily newspaper horoscope reduces astrology to a punch line and seriously hurts the integrity of my research. Unless they are well documented, able to be explained, accurate, and repetitive, I will not endorse any psychic claims. Incidentally, all my claims and premonitions are well documented and the dated printing process in my books makes them inarguable.

At the initial meeting that morning, I asked Andre's date of birth and he politely answered me. He was born under the constellation of Leo; I immediately felt his reluctance to investigate the topic of Astro-Psychology. I speculated on the possibility of religious poisoning or an over-developed rationale. It could also be like anyone involved in law enforcement; a very strong need for privacy. As a rule, all souls born under the sign of Leo (the sign of France, love, the arts, children, light and life) carry a subconscious fear of the unknown, death and decay. This is why many Leo swallow vitamins by the bucket and exercise daily to stay attractive and healthy. I have encountered this attitude too many times in my unusual expertise with traditionalists/scientists and understand much more than they will ever be capable of knowing. I chose to back off, being aware that I was against a thick wall of stupidity and criticism. I also gave Andre the option to honor the word investigation and offered to email him his own private UCI. As expected, he refused, confirming my own theory on the spot. I wonder why the word investigation is a part of the English language, since it's lacking with some people we see as investigators?

Note also, that this option to investigate for free the true power of Astro-Psychology was offered to all of the other guests, but as expected they all refused and no one took the time to investigate my claims. They also made it very clear to me not to mention their names or profession, not knowing that I do respect people's privacy and would never do such a thing. They all simply suffered a fear of the ridicule, a huge ego and in the process missed a world of valuable information.

You will find a lot of Leos in the justice department or in religious Ministries, as Leo's mental process and interest comes from the 3rd house of communication (learning/teaching/assimilation) located in the sign of Libra (psychology/Astro-Psychology/The law). This gives them natural interests and gifts in affairs ruled by Libra (scale of justice/the law/psychology/Astro-Psychology). I gave Andre another shot at the dinner table,revealing his back and knee problems often encountered with Leos. Andre kept a straight face and did not acknowledge my obvious claim. All that I divulged perplexed him but his ego and traditional education stopped him from making further spiritual progress, yet I could also feel his curiosity. Andre remained patient and a true respectful gentleman all the way to the last day of our meeting. Andre's skepticism is based upon a lack of understanding on the dynamics of my methodology. Taping a show in a Waning Moon is against the Universal Law for anyone trying to make progress. Thus the opportunity to "connect" with the scientists and further Astro-Psychology potential into the law enforcement was wasted. Andre mentioned that any judge could not either rely on, or make sound judgments based upon my methodology. I politely explained to him that UCI can pin point certain Plutonic individuals and terrorists naturally predisposed to carry out criminal acts, thus saving precious time and resources in the investigation. The UCI of the worst elements of our society (cases of many infamous serial killers) is also available in my book "The Power of the Dragon" but again, none of the "investigators" made an attempt to learn more or check my work and findings.

Like all Leos, Andre is a smart human being and with proper training he would, like any of my students born in August, acknowledge and appreciate the true values of Astro-Psychology. I am convinced that "accidents" do not happen and in time, even a proficient teacher like Andre can gain cosmic consciousness outside of conventionally accepted academic disciplines. Many of my Leo students did! The fragile but oversized human ego must be put aside to further a research that can only benefit society at large. I am at a loss when science ignores the very word of investigation because of a suppressed curiosity!

Daniel was blessed with a progressive UCI and spent his life as FBI special agent; He is now retired and we connected immediately. The man's deep gaze and warm heart impressed me. When I asked for his date of birth, he responded immediately showing a natural and healthy curiosity. He was born in May; I explained to him that as a Taurus "The Law of Celestial Opposites" made him face the world on his 7th house as a Scorpio or (the natural FBI agent of the zodiac). Scorpio is ruled by Pluto or "The Lord Of Hades" in Greek mythology and the underworld, this sign rules both the police force and the mafia, representing the perpetual battle between the forces of good and evil. Note also, well before President George Bush mentioned anything about the FBI and CIA, the Tail of the Dragon was in Scorpio and induced serious errors of judgment and forced a complete restructure of the secret service agencies. Nothing, not even the FBI is higher than "The Draconic Law" and "The Cosmic Code". My inarguable prediction is well documented in all of my previous Moon Powers books and crystallized in many of my radio and television appearances.

Daniel is indeed a true investigator and listened attentively to all that I had to say. However, his 7th Scorpionic house deals with the public and in this particular department Daniel became a very private man and his reaction to be left "incognito" was fully anticipated. I also told him that, food, family and real estate endeavors were a part of in his intrinsic consciousness. Daniel's 3rd house of communication/natal thinking process is located in the overly-sensitive and family oriented sign of Cancer, making him very touchy with any affairs involving the family nucleus and how people treat children. My confirmation of his sensitive UCI came through by observing his obvious reaction with the dismaying scenery of Saddam and a child that was broadcasted on national television during these days. I explained to him the true reasons behind my low scores on the show and he was very supportive. He probably also understood why my reaction and facial expressions were as cool as can be when I read my own results on TV, because I was tricked into a false birth date and all the questions were for entertainment purposes only.

Jacques is a retired Police Chief. Incidentally (and to prove the value of UCI) Jacques like Daniel and Robert was also born in May under the solid sign of Taurus and again under the jurisdiction of Pluto (police/FBI/CIA/investigation) controlling the 7th house (facing the world/danger/death/privacy). This UCI connection obviously reveals why Jacques, like other invited guests born in May, spent most of his life in Law Enforcement. Jacques came across as a quiet family man (3rd house in Cancer) and his research and involvement with another researcher (Robert) could bring about serious and progressive results to Law Enforcement, using state of the art technology in lie detection. I had a smashing time with Jacques, Robert and Yves at the local restaurant. After a few margaritas, the discussion went from talking about police matters to funny jokes that brought tears to our eyes. Jacques scored the highest numbers with his electronic equipment and I was amazed by his honest and straight comment, he said in front of everyone, "You've got nothing to prove Dr. Turi, you hit me dead on when you read my stars!"

Robert is a Certified Polygraph Examiner and a blast to be with. He loves to play jokes on people and he is a very funny curious character. Note (and to prove the value of UCI) that Robert incredibly, was also born in May! There is so much more in "The Universal Code" than what science can offer and at least Jacques was able to perceive it.

Bonnie is a Professional Poker Player and projects a form of innocence, a sort of charming little girl that will never really grow up. When I first met her, I noticed her magnetic eyes and her speedy nature. I already knew just by watching her, that she had a strong Mercury in her makeup. I asked her month of birth and she replied "September". The magnetic deep and often pretty blue or green eyes are a sure give away to anyone born in September or under the constellation of Virgo. I had absolutely no problem communicating with Bonnie as she is born a communicator. Bonnie was born with a Dragon's Head (growth/luck) in Gemini (hands/communication) and I explained how her UCI would display in her make up. The Head of the Dragon in Gemini is ruled by Mercury (The Lord of communication in Greek Mythology) talking is something she does great and all the time... I told her a few things about her that cannot be divulged in this book, but by watching her reaction it was a homerun. Her mental process (or the 3rd house of communication) is into the sign of Scorpio (super wealth /other people's money/investigation) made her a natural born investigator and also demanded privacy. Gemini rules duality, incidentally, she had mentioned on the televised show that she was able to "split" into another person, when gaming and dealing with people. Gifted and beautiful, Bonnie is a sure ticket to success in anything she wants to do and displays a very refined mind.

Yves was the guinea pig or "would be liar" and was confined to a chair that was attached to a multitude or wires and electronic devices all over his body. I did not have Yves's date of birth, but Kiki (Episode Producer) gave me that information on stage just before the show started. Then disaster struck...a huge guy from Romania came to my table and said, "Dr. Turi, I heard lots of good things about you from many people on the floor, would you have time to "read" me before the show." At that point we were only a few minutes before the taping and the staff was busy making the last preparations.

I said "Okay, my friend, what's your date of birth?" I entered his stars on my laptop and told him he was in construction before doing this television job. He was amazed and said, "Yes, I was."... I told him a few other accurate things and he left my table totally amazed. This reaction is very normal to me, as any UCI is simply and incredibly obvious. But if so, then what happened to the science of

UCI and my expertise? Why was I so confident, so sure to get the top marks and yet got the lowest score you may ask?

Here are the reasons. First the show took place after the Full Moon and "accidents" will happen and it did in my case. Secondly, after the big guy left my table, I clicked on my saved chart to find out that I did not save Yves stars on my laptop and the only thing I could recall was that he was born in December! But I am sure enough of my wisdom to read anyone, only with the month of birth, like I did with the episode writer and the producers. All was fine in my mind thus, I did not have to stop the show and ask for Yves's correct date of birth again. I was still quite confident because the questions I had submitted would give me justice for sure. Not so…Then came the set of questions… and none were the regular repertoire that I was expecting.

Here are a few samples of the questions I had anticipated asking, as they have an astrological basis:

Are you afraid of flying? Is there any heart disease in your family? Do your like photography? Are you a good writer? Do you speak any languages?

Instead to my horror this is what I read…"Have you ever bought a condom in a foreign land?"

I have thousands of clients worldwide and especially my students would know that my questionnaire is much more refined and I would never ask such a stupid question. Most of all, I did not expect to ask any questions, I already know the answer providing I have the right date of birth. Forgetting to save Yves' data on my computer was a serious omen for me to realize I was about to be tricked into a wrong date of birth and a banal questionnaire. Not only that, but my assistant at the time even warned me before I left to "make sure you get the right birthday."

From that point on, I knew that I would have some serious problems with the entire show and already knew I would fail in proving the value of Astro-Psychology, but no one in or out of the stage was really interested in my advanced findings. I did not belong to that mundane energy and the Waning Moon proved me right again. But I was the only one who perceived this fact and the only one who had cosmic consciousness. I tried to save myself and asked Yves if he ever wanted to learn or speak Japanese. I was immediately told not to ask any questions or change the script on the set. My abilities to perceive the Divine allowed me to make a premonition that came true.

The reason why I asked Yves if he thought of learning Japanese, is because I knew his Mars (desire principle) was located in Aquarius (electronics) in Yves's 3rd house of communication and interest, thus I could not miss, nor could he have lied to me. None, of the anticipated questions were from part of my Astro-

Psychology methodology and without the correct birthday, I felt totally out of balance. Even some of my students noticed the negative timing and pointed out the possibility of unseen trouble doing that show.

After the TV show, Jacques, Robert and I decided to meet at a local restaurant. We all met at the lobby and drove off to a restaurant. To our big surprise (there are NO accidents) Yves was there outside talking on his cell phone. What were the chances to meet him there? Pretty remote, I would say. My subconscious wanted justice and brought the action.

We ordered food and drinks and then I asked again, Yves's date of birth. I explained what happened earlier. I also found out that I had both the year and the day wrong and this explained the disaster that took place earlier. Then, I wanted to show Yves the true value of UCI and asked him, "Do you remember on the show I asked you if you ever wanted to learn or if you spoke Japanese? And I could not get an answer because I was not allowed to ask my questions, but only the producer's questions?" Then, right in front off Jacques and Robert, at the restaurant, Yves began to speak a few words in Japanese and we found out that his wife is also Japanese! How more precise can I be? Everyone was astounded and realized the values of Astro-Psychology and this is what I wanted to emphasize on TV for the entire world to see.

I still wanted to prove my claim on the values of UCI and with both Taurus investigators sitting next to me, I was not going to let that opportunity go by. I told Yves that being a Gemini (the joker/hands/communication/cards/telephone games) he should be on stage as an entertainer. Guess what? No one knew at that point that Yves was a part time stand up comedian, another direct hit for me, I thought. I waited for the right moment then asked, "You do have flat feet, do you Yves? He was blown away and said, "Yes, I do!" The power of UCI is inarguable and goes well beyond anyone's expectations. I knew again, I had read him flawlessly. Both Jacques and Robert heard me, clearly and saw Yves' face changing color, acknowledging the facts. Yves finally said, "Dr. Turi you are really good at what you do". He was really impressed and I finally had proven my case, but sadly enough it was off of the set. I had two of the best human lie detectors (an ex-Police Chief and a Polygraph Examiner) as witnesses. I wrote the plain truth to my best recollection of what transpired that night after the show with Yves. I learned the differences between human lie detectors and me, a human life detector.

I had sent a certified letter to Los Angeles Police Chief Daryl Gates, giving all information on the Rodney King case and what to expect 2 full weeks before the beating! I also wrote to San Diego Police Chief Burgreen clearly denunciating the Scorpionic news, weeks ahead of time. As "predicted" on August 15th, it all came true with the capture of "The Torrey Pines Rapist police officer". But none of the people in charge took the time to either read my mail or took my premonitions seriously and never responded. They made the same error as that of other people in positions of power by lumping me and my research in with some deceptive psychics. In spite of my efforts over the years to save the lives of courageous astronauts and educate NASA scientists on "The Cosmic Code" they did not perceive my warnings.

Too many brave police officers have died and will continue to die because of ignorance; I stand firm, knowing right inside of my soul that Astro-Psychology is priceless and that understanding changes our perception of human nature. My expertise would enormously benefit the Department of Justice and protect all courageous police officers. When will someone in authority take a chance on my capability and save the lives of people and put the criminals in jail. When will they finally be able to anticipate, judge, and perceive the potentially destructive elements of our society, by uncovering and using "The Universal Code" accordingly?

Pluto (the very essence and regulator of the police force) requires that many officers are put at a great risk daily. Recognizing both the deadly timing and the dangerous criminals plaguing our cities is as important as handling advanced technology. All this can be easily assimilated with my software and inserted in the patrol car's computer system. Looking at a driving record allows the officer to connect with multitudes of paper work generating the record (positive or negative) of the offender and most importantly the date of birth and the UCI. The trained police officer could recognize and would use serious caution and this very wisdom will save many lives. Like all citizens, the police must respect the physical laws and stop at red lights or the stop sign in the street. If he does not, he will become a potential danger to the very society he tried so hard to protect. Physical laws are enforced and respected by the police. The same applies from "The Universal Code" and its accompanying unforgiving celestial laws. Those laws are impartial and must be acknowledged and respected by all, including the police.

The police do not respect these laws and aren't even aware of them. Because fear of ridicule keeps the police administration from educating themselves to astropsychology, they simply ignore the very essence of investigation. As yet, they have not taken chances on my unique methodology and expertise. (They will, someday soon!)

Pluto (and the sign of Scorpio) is the ruler of Law enforcement and I have for years been tracking all police events. This database cannot be wasted. I came to the undeniable conclusion that there is a direct relationship with Pluto and the police force. My years of tedious research are available to the department and my teachings are available to the Police. Bringing new knowledge will also bring more security to their dangerous occupation. Too many have died and many others will die in the name of ignorance. It should be a priority for the

Secret Service Department to take a chance and investigate "The Secret Code" to uncover potentially dangerous criminal characters as soon as possible and in any situation. A date of birth depicting a UCI is inherited. Unlike a driver's license or a social security number produced by human systems, the spiritual records (and afflictions) are pre-written and involve very high and unforgiving schemes of celestial regulation. It's a shame for this to go unknown to the police force administrators. I can only hope that all my readers will appreciate my honesty and determination to teach the true meaning of science and investigation. I reaffirm my own Discovery to all, I am not a human lie detector, but for those who know me well; a true "Human Life Detector" and even though I am usually misunderstood by the majority, my ability to handle and recognize each unique UCI allows for me to be tolerant and enhances forgiving to all the people sharing my life's experiences.

One's chance to learn and grow is often offered in a disguised manner that can be discerned and mastered if investigated properly. Reading "Beyond the Secret" would be a good start I think, but no rush, we all have eternity to learn!

The Universal Law of the Moon

There is also another very important law in the Universal Code that must be taken into earnest consideration. I was a very young child when my grandmother told me what she knew about the secret of the Moon. She explained to me how the moon would regiment the farmer's crops, affect the sea, our emotions and to be particularly careful while she is Full. Grandma left this world in 1968 may her soul rest in peace, but ironically it seems to be in the family, to be well ahead of traditional science. It amazes me that this "infantile science" is just beginning to acknowledge the power of the Moon upon man's psyche and her impact on our daily affairs. The wisdom imparted by my grandmother and my own investigative nature since then, was so set in me that I have spent thirty five years documenting our close satellite's celestial whereabouts. I have guided people from all walks of life with my book Moon Power for many years, now and I am still receiving support and great endorsements since the first issue was published in 1987.

Depending on the mystical rhythm of the Moon and her relationship---harmonious or discordant---to the constellation and Houses of the sky over which they rule, she will govern our human activities and give birth to our vices and virtues. The infinite and concealed dance of the Moon through the Zodiac affects us all. You are a "microcosm" or a Child of the Universe and there is reason for you to be. You are a part of this incredible physical and spiritual structure called a "macrocosm." Sir Isaac Newton wrote, "For every action there is an equal and opposite reaction". We are what we think, having become what we thought. This is another smart explanation of "The Law of Attraction" but the Moon plays a vital role in the outcome of all your wishes. Other famous men wrote about the Moon's powers, but they could only give you a hint.

"There is a tide in the affairs of men, which taken at its floods, leads on to fortune; omitted, all the voyage of their life is bound in shallows and in miseries." --Shakespeare, from Julius Caesar, Act IV, Scene iii

For every thought or action, there will be an effect and we could attribute this fact to the law of gravity and another manifestation of numerous "Universal Laws". The law of cause and effect or the yin/yang principle is accepted as the law of karma. As incredible as it may sound, I am convinced the Moon is totally responsible for the world and people's fate. I have been tracking the Universal Law of the Moon since 1987 and thousands of endorsements depict the values found in my book Moon Power. To my faithful clients and students worldwide, there is no doubt of the lunar impact in their lives, but that is because they did pay attention to my warnings over the years.

To me, scientists are like little kids discovering or removing planets (Pluto) while missing the entire forest looking at a tree. Trust me, Pluto is very much alive and kicking and the action of removing Pluto from the family of planets, showed me how many ignorant young souls walk the earth. It's about your tax dollars, ego, politics, religion and fear of ridicule, but no one can eliminate the truth about Pluto and the planet is still there and will always be. Simply realize how little science really knows about Pluto, the Moon, the archetypal realm of consciousness and metaphysics in general. When the moon wanders through the sign of Scorpio or is in aspect to Pluto, much public drama takes place:

* Pluto also rules suicide and on March 11, 2007 during a Waning Moon and a deadly Plutonic window, I received this email.

----- Original Message -----
Sent: Sunday, March 11, 2007 4:51 PM
Subject: RE: YOUR FREE FORECAST until March 19
From: "Joe////
Dr. Turi,
I saw the news on Richard Jeni & got chills thinking about Moon Power for this weekend: "Famous Personalities: The world will lose a famous personality under Pluto's command. He may also decide to do it dramatically (assassination)." Truly amazing people think nothing of the planets in their lives...your teachings & awareness are needed in this 21st century. Keep up the great work...
Regards,
Joe ////d

The Waxing and Waning periods of our closest satellite will produce the daily process of tides. Women are directly affected by the Moon's fluctuations and must endure the physical manifestations (menstruation). Some respond erratically, subconsciously manifesting the word "lunatic." Without opposition such as the Moon's fluctuations, there would be no reaction and thus no life would be possible on both spiritual and physical planes.

The Moon irrefutably commands women's menstrual periods, sharing the same twenty-eight-day time period. Pay attention to the Moon's passage through the belt of the zodiac and then her secrets will be yours. The Moon stays between two to three days in one astrological sign; she will merge with the energies found in each sign and color your emotions and reactions for best or worst depending on your awareness of the cosmic clock. Mastering the twelve specific Moon positions by house and sign will help you understand people's idiosyncrasies. Unknowingly, better scientists created the word "Bi Polar" for wild personality fluctuations, and will prescribe dangerous drugs.

"Our so-called "dead" satellite is very much alive; she is the beating heart of the earth. Vigilantly observing her whereabouts will aid understanding of the psychology of man."
—Dr. Turi

The Universal Law of the Moon

* The changing face of the Moon was revered and used wisely by the ancients. It symbolized the feminine creative principle as the Moon ruled growth, fertility and magic. Your awareness of the Moon's passage through the Zodiac will enable you to uncover energy patterns that regulate the changes and circumstances of your life. The purpose of a good astrologer is to reveal an order or meaning hidden from what often appears to be random or chaotic situations. The Moon's passage through the housing system is one expression of the archetypal structure that we call a cycle and an intrinsic part of the "Universal Code". The moon reflects different energies as she travels through each of the unique signs of the zodiac. Our emotions are likewise affected in her travels. When the moon is new, this is the time for starting (planting) new endeavors. When she is full, this is the time for endings (reaping).

If you can recognize the lunar "energy" you will be able to use "The Universal Law of The Moon" to bring about positive results much faster. Our lives unfold according to a specific cyclic pattern, interacting with the Universal Code memento.

Conventionally educated scientists may never be able to build cosmic consciousness and discover "The Universal Code". The Moon and her Nodes (Dragon's Head and

Tail) will always remain a mystery to the skeptics, hard-core scientists, oblivious atheists, mental snobs or lost religious souls. This illustrates a crowd born with weak or afflicted Mercurys in their charts. That which may be invisible to our senses, nevertheless still exists. That's what makes a real scientist, investigation! Sadly enough, the majority of these souls fear ridicule or abandonment by their peers or churches. The easy answer is "ridicule or against God" instead of taking the time to upgrade their vibration with rigorous mental gymnastics.

Working in relationship to the Divine order is a sure ticket to success and this is why I will always proclaim that the biggest secret ever is uncovering your divinity through your celestial identity. The sad reality is that; many people are much too lazy to undertake a study of "Universal Laws" that would turn them into millionaires and very successful entrepreneurs.

"*He is happy who having learned the scheme of his nativity and knowing his Guardian Angel, becomes liberated from Fate.*"
– Porphyry

The Moon's cycle is derived from the fact that it consists of a beginning, middle and an end. The monthly lunar cycle suggests that it is divided into two halves. During the first half, the movement is outward, as our close satellite travels away from the area of space occupied by the Sun. As this happens, the powerful light of the Sun increases, "Waxing" (positive) on the white face of the Moon. The Full Moon symbolizes the turning point when it reverses motion. The Moon begins to approach the Sun as the reflected light on its surface "Wanes" (negative), until they meet again at the New Moon (new start).

Halfway between the New Moon and the Full Moon, we notice another important division point where light and darkness are equal on the Moon's surface. At the first Waxing Quarter, the light is increasing, while at the last Waning Quarter it is decreasing. These simple astronomical observations can only provide the scientist's mind with knowledge for interpreting the physical lunar cycle's phase. Now if the positive cannot be with the negative, and knowing that it takes "Two to Tango" for anything to be, then the scientist should be able to enter the intuitional domain of my work. There are hidden truths beyond this "lunar manifestation," all based upon critical observations. Later in life when I mastered astrology, I realized that there was so much more than the science of Astronomy available to men.

As a child, I always thought of the Moon to be something more than a dead satellite orbiting the earth. Many times in the darkness of the night, I found myself staring at her, wondering about her hidden power. She is the swiftest of the planets, passing through the 12 signs of the zodiac in about 28 days. I knew that eventually, I was to uncover her subtle ways and find some plausible answers to life events. However, it takes more than our five senses to tap into her subtle manifestations and realize her impact upon our psyches and life in general. Nothing happens randomly in the universe and the eternal returns each month depict a divine order.

Month after month, I patiently watched the Moon becoming New and Full, and learned one of the most important lessons in metaphysics, "The undiluted truth is not to be found inside man's selfish world, but above in the stars." The Moon's gravitational forces are so great, that she is solely responsible for the oceans tides. Curiosity, observation and comparison become the essential elements to promote anyone's cosmic consciousness and perceive the divine. Watching the Moon in all her actions, becoming Full and New, month after month, I began to uncover her powers. By watching my environment, friends and family members, she began to speak about her impact over man's psyche. As the years went by, I became conscious of her impact on our daily affairs. I made notes day after day, week after week and month after month, realizing the heavy consequences of ignoring her passage through the twelve signs of the Zodiac. I also learned that the farmers of the past carefully followed her fluctuations for the betterment of their crops.

I carefully put my observations to the test in my life and the lives of those around me. It did not take long to realize that by respecting the Universal Law, my life became much more productive. Her positive and negative affect on man's emotions, actions and reactions became so obvious to me that I decided to make a full time job telling others and wrote forecasts that became my book "Moon Power." I watched the news in time of a Full Moon and understood why people became destructive, "lunatic," eccentric, moody crabby and psychopathic. I then named it "The Universal Law of the Moon." Since then, as a professional Astro-Psychologist, wherever I am needed I teach the value of this simple and powerful law.

When you first learned to drive a car, you were carefully introduced to the rules of the road. You understood to stop at a red light or follow a road sign, because your life depended on respecting these laws. These learned codes must be respected at all times and anywhere you happen to be in the world, doing so assures your safety. But the fact is that many people do not respect the rules of the road and innocent people die in accidents. Awareness, knowledge and the respect of a myriad of rules are desperately needed to operate safely in this world.

God wrote specific spiritual rules and they are written in the stars. This Universal Code has been lost and ignored by the majority of people on earth. Only a handful of erudite men are aware of the impact produced by the stars and the Moon on earth. This lack of awareness turns into formidable chaos, which produces despair, psychopaths, drug addicts, depression, violence and criminals. The list goes on. Ignoring the physical or spiritual rules will lead to a badly informed population to pay a heavy penalty. I soon began to realize that nothing would exist without its counterpart, and the "Law of Opposition" is much too obvious to be challenged or ignored. I began to wonder if God would exist without the Devil.

One month is made up of two 2-week cycles, one year of two 6-month periods. The lunar cycle start with a two-week period or "Waxing time." About two weeks later the Moon becomes full, she is white and round and for the following two weeks the light is red on "the Waning time." As the Moon ascending the heavens (Waxing) you should plant your seeds for life. Go out, meet new people, socialize, become engaged, get married, buy a new car, go shopping, sign important contracts, travel, visit family members and generally promote all you can during this positive trend. After the Full Moon (and for two weeks) as the Moon descends (Waning), practice positive metaphysical endeavors. You will feel like cleaning and may possibly suffer spiritually, as the Moon is the regulator of your inner emotions. Use your will to fight depression, clean your house, prepare your next move, and write long overdue letters, but don't send them just yet. Observe and listen to all the people around you. Many will suffer the Waning Moon's power and will become negative, moody and lunatic. Watch the news and see for yourself the dramatic differences in these two periods. However, good things can happen during a Waning Moon and could mean that you started something during her Waxing, positive time, and you are now being paid-off.

My book Moon Power Starguide is designed to guide you and points out when and in which sign the New Moon or the Full Moon will mature throughout the entire year. Like me, you can use this knowledge to master the outcome of all your endeavors. Synchronize with "The Universal Law Of The Moon". Sad things can also happen to you when the Moon is supposedly positive. It might only be a tap on your hand, compared to what could have happened during the waning moon. Keep in mind that you have been going through your life not knowing nor using the Universal Law. You are like a car (your life) that seriously needs a tune up and if you don't, somewhere, somehow you will be stopped. Apply your knowledge right away and I guarantee you will see the results within the next few days.

I often use this sample for my students. If you were to travel in China and you could not read, understand or follow the road signs there, chances are that you would end up getting hurt. Those laws, physical or spiritual, even if you are not aware of them, are solid and practical. There is no room for ignorance in this dense physical world. The same applies for the spiritual world and a heavy penalty awaits both ignorant and skeptical souls. Depression is not based on our daily boring routine but how we feel about it. How we feel about things is determined by our Moon's location at birth. Since misery loves company, those suffering commiserate with the ignorance of God's celestial rules by the academic field. Nevertheless, the impact felt upon our fragile psyches is devastating and translates into a myriad of mental problems. Incidentally, our higher subconscious awareness knows better and interprets it into words such as moody, crabby and lunatic (Luna means the Moon, in Latin). The eternal Moon's fluctuations are especially noticeable upon the masses during a Full or New Moon period.

"All great spirits have encountered opposition from mediocre minds; a human being is part of a whole, called by us the 'Universe,' a part limited in time and space. He experiences himself, his thoughts and feelings, as something separated from the rest--a kind of optical delusion of his consciousness. The stars are the elixir of life."
Albert Einstein

Just Say No

On March 2007 I read another disturbing article posted on CNN website, about the danger of sleeping pills. The FDA says those pills may be the cause of "Sleep-driving". How more dumb can such an organization and their scientists be? This is serious people; think twice before taking any sleeping pills. The Food and Drug Administration warned that all sleeping pills, including the best seller Ambien and Lunesta apparently cause dangerous side effects like sleep driving, talking to others with no memory of doing so, some swelling in the face, etc. These types of sleeping aids known as sedative-hypnotic products are dangerous. They know it, but who cares? It makes money and that's where the problem is, because they don't care about your welfare. My suggestion is, if you cannot sleep, chances are that you are not tired enough. I would strongly recommend for you to get up a 5:00 am everyday and run all day long, instead of sitting on your couch watching television. I guarantee you that you will be sleeping tight the next night. Where has science and people's common sense gone? The FDA should not strengthen warnings but order them off the market and for once be responsible and save people from abusive pharmaceutical corporations.

That same day, one of my concerned students sent me this article pertaining to another ridiculous study wasting our precious tax dollars. This is really laughable and portrays not only ignorance, but also an extreme stupidity from an infantile science. Mouse study may explain teens' 'raging hormones'. This might help explain why teenagers act like, well, teenagers and what's so abnormal about it? I am so glad that none of those drugs existed in my days to turn my extremely powerful UCI, blessed by AHAD and ADD, into a zombie. It's this type of research that kills young lives or turns those children into killers. Supposedly, researchers found a hormone in the body that would calm adults and younger children, but increased anxiety in adolescents, while conducting experiments with mice focusing on the hormone THP that demonstrated this paradoxical effect, and described the brain mechanism that explains it.

* Wait, wait right here…what do scientists really know about the brain? For many years they took Einstein's brain out of their freezer and dissected thousands of times, to find out why he was a genius! Your brain is nothing more than a complex computer, reacting to the outside stimulus produced by the Universal Mind. There is no difference between your brain, the one of Einstein or a criminal for that matter, all healthy brains have the same weight, same density, the same chemicals and share the same functions. What's different is the UCI (Unique Celestial Identity) inherited at birth through the "Universal Code". Thus common sense dictates, in order to uncover all answers involving the mind, one must look above in the Universal structure and not down to a dead piece of meat. All those researches are treacherous and meant to sell you dangerous drugs. Its pure bologna!

A professor of physiology and pharmacology at the State University of New York Downstate Medical Center, said. "But it really is a mood swing, where things seem fine and calm, and then the next thing is someone's crying or angry, and I think that's why people have used the term 'raging hormones. So, the beginning of puberty is a time when a lot of emotions and responses to stress are increased. It's nothing new that teenagers go through a difficult time. Hopefully, this research will shed some new light on it" the team reported in an issue of the journal Nature Neuroscience.

* Again, none of those educated scientists knows that the Moon is responsible for (Mood/Moon?) swings! Astro-Psychology teaches that the Moon regulates our emotional response to life, our sins and virtues. Science does not embrace anything spiritual or unconventional, missing the very essence of their research. Furthermore, the inherited Moon sign will influence the child all the way to puberty and this is why some are bullies and others kids are more submissive. A child born with an aggressive Moon in Aries (war) will undoubtedly be much more aggressive, than a child born with a very shy introverted Moon in Pisces. Once the puberty age is reached, the UCI kicks in, preparing the child for his adult life. This "shock" or change of gears produces all sorts of behavioral changes not yet understood by science. A multitude of valuable and safe information pertaining to any child is available through the science of Astro-Psychology. But the unhappy truth is, this type of information is readily available and does not require those manipulative scientific organizations to suck on your tax dollars in order to survive.

The fact is the body is naturally well equipped to deal with any disorder and those drugs increase suicide in all patients. The medication will alter the brain activity, generally serving the body as a natural tranquilizer.

* The sad reality is when the Moon is Waning and parallel to the Dragon's Tail, depressions leading to suicidal tendencies increase dramatically and any drug prescription can only accentuate what science refers to as a "chemicals imbalance" and poison the fragile psyche of any child. There are a multitude of astrological reasons why a child would become prone to suicide and the location of Saturn (The Great Malefic) or Neptune (deception) plays a crucial role, especially if Mars (stimulant) is also part of the equation. All major drug industries provide financial support for scientists and their research and even control the FDA, so their deadly products can be on sale on your local store. Time is overdue to teach Astro-Psychology in our colleges and universities and be accepted as a safe and solid discipline. I can only hope for the day, to be the recipient of a large sum of money by a concerned reader willing to help me to build my Astro-Psychology schools and save the children of tomorrow from abusive and financially oriented corporations.

Common Disorders and Astro-Psychology

Psychosis/Schizophrenia:

This mental disorder usually depicts a reclusive, socially awkward, indisposed character with poor or inappropriate feelings and an inability to perform or function well in our society. The inward world of hallucinations is too much for the subject, who falls victim to these make-believe, destructive and grandiose thought processes. This hallucinatory person, over a period of time, will need assistance and will become dependent on other family members and will require supervision. Neptune (confusion), the planet of deception, plays an important part in all mental disorders, and when badly aspected by Pluto (destruction) or Mercury (mental processes) the person becomes aggressive. Hard aspects to disturbing planets such as Uranus, Pluto, Neptune, or Mars to the Dragon's Tail (past lives) also induce serious mental disorders. In many cases, the amount of past-life residue is much too strong to be controlled by the soul. Paul Jennings Hill (anti-abortion activist/murderer) is an obvious example of having a past life as a woman (Dragon's Tail in Cancer — protective mother), bringing children into this world. All Water signs especially Pisces, are prone to Psychosis/Schizophrenia, especially if drugs are used.

Hysteria:

This mental disorder is characterized by a strong desire for excitement, drama, attention, and constant reassurance. The hysterical personality will do all that he can to attract attention and exaggerate any situation. This type of endeavor is seen within the melodramatic performance of an actor in a televised soap opera or "over acting" on the big screen. A hard aspect to a Dragon's Tail, the Moon (emotions) or/and Mercury (communication) in Leo (love) combined with other nefarious planets such as Neptune (imagination) Pluto (drama) can also induce hysteria. The desire for attention, drama and respect from others is quite strong and manufactures exhibitionists, ready to shock others and gain the desperate attention they crave. All Fire signs are prone to suffer Hysteria.

Dissociate States:

Dissociate states occur when a person is under great stress from external influences such as other people's cruelty and internal conflicts induced by depression. A recurring disturbing harmful situation will produce fears and phobia that could also lead to a dissociate state. The Moon (emotion) in Pisces or Cancer (sensitivity) on the Dragon's Tail (karma) is a major contribution to this disorder. This affliction brings dissociation with others, especially to the close family or an abusive lover. The upbringing is usually very dramatic and the subject learns early in childhood, to cope with traumatic sexual or emotional abuse. If the Dragon's Tail (negative) affects the 4th house (home/family) in the sign of Scorpio (sex) or if there is any hard aspects to the Moon (home) and Pluto, violent death and drama is to be expected.

Hence, they are forced to learn to disconnect from their feelings to avoid further emotional or physical pain. By adulthood, their emotions are locked behind protective walls and can be accessed if needed. A strong Pluto (power) aspect to Mercury (the mind), and the Moon (emotions) gives the subject a powerful will to dissociate (or hypnotize) himself from any destructive situation and avoid pain. The strength of Pluto, aspects to Mercury, Neptune or the Moon give this person a form of subconscious (protection) self-hypnotic trance. In extreme cases, these individuals can experience periods of "missing time," confusion and disorientation. All signs are prone to suffer this disease.

Sociopath Personality:

This disorder commonly called Multiple Personality Disorder or MPD is usually found with people born with a strong negative affliction to Mercury (the mind) and hard aspects to the Dragon's Tail in Gemini and especially Pluto (morbid). They do learn at an early age to lie to avoid trouble and they are also somehow superficial and have problems with established rules and authority. The past-life residue in Gemini (double personality) is not yet eliminated or understood by the subject and is used in the form of manipulation and deceit. Afflicted by negative Mercury (Lord of the Thieves), they appear to be charming and smooth in their dealings, but they can be manipulative and insensitive. In order to stay alive, in previous past lives, the soul mastered the art of stealing and lying to survive.

Many of them were involved in metaphysical work and had to perform their second occupation at night. Their endeavors involved witchcraft, healing with herbs, plants, using the Cabala and Astrology. To avoid serious repercussion from the church authority of their time, they developed a gift of disguise, where lying and adapting fast to any situation, meant saving their precious lives. Many famous serial killers suffer this sickness. All signs are prone to suffer this disease.

Attention Deficit Disorder (A.D.D.)
(Attention -Deficit/Hyperactivity Disorder). A.D.H.D):

This has nothing to do with MPD and should be considered a gift from God. Curious by nature and intellectually challenging, an ADD person is, by nature (and purposely) ill equipped to accept all forms of codification of thought. Thus, avoiding traditional education, an A.D.D. (Einstein/Clinton/Myself) will sidestep the barrier of educational dogma and breach the barrier of what was previously thought of as impossible. Reluctant to obtain education due to a poor memory many of them end up as a "Jack of all trades," unable to focus and crystallize the thought processes. Nevertheless, discipline and basic education should be encouraged to promote the inborn genius quality of the A.D.D. subject and lead a prosperous life. All Air signs are prone to suffer this "disease".

Paranoid Personality:

A strong negative aspect to the Moon (feelings), Mercury (the mind) and the Dragon's Tail (past lives) in Pisces (deception) predisposes the soul for a network of distorted ideas, fears, and uncontrolled imagination. Self-analysis is very difficult, if not impossible, with this individual who has serious trouble accepting his own intensely emotional and destructive imagination. An attraction to chemicals, drugs, and alcohol is also very common and acts as a shield against the harsh reality of the physical world. Lacking objectivity, this individual rejects the reality of his own feelings and directs them toward other people, believing that they are the ones with the offensive intent.

Although very attracted to the intangible, this soul is in a terminal stage of physical incarnation and should not participate in hypnotic regression sessions or psychic séances. Due to his deceiving interstellar conception, this soul is a prime target for possession or invasion by low astral entities. The tremendous amount of dramatic subconscious memories from the past-life residue makes it very difficult to distinguish fiction from reality. All signs are prone to suffer this disease.

To protect society from all of these dangerous neurotics, psychiatry, psychology and neuroscientists can only use powerful drugs to control the expression of fear, rather than erase it completely from the memory bank. The constant use of dangerous chemicals can only further the degradation of the fragile psyche of the individual and produces more chemical imbalance and should only be used on extreme cases with utmost caution. Those afflicted souls have a natural negative reaction to all chemicals, which could induce more stress, confusion and paralysis to the subject.

---

* March 3rd 2007 I received another email from a student this time involving the use of drugs to control obesity. A Doctor uses ADHD drug Adderall, an amphetamine, to treat childhood obesity. The doctor said about 90 percent of his patients on Adderall have lost weight. Of course the critics say the off-label use, while legal, is questionable and too risky and I can only agree. But it's easier to use drugs than to dedicate ones self to exercise and apply the will to eat less fattening foods. The kid is now 17 and reached a normal weight after taking Adderall for more than four years -- from age 11 until about 16. I understand concerned parents, but in time I can guarantee you that this teenager will develop serious psychological problems that may kill him, because all drugs are detrimental to a well-balanced brain. As I always say to my students "The future is my witness" check the news about this case, in the yet to come facts.

Our infantile scientists must breach into the spirit and invest in a very different type of research. Accurately evaluating the subjects UCI will become a major contribution to understand and correct the subtle astrological forces producing the mental sickness of an individual. Accurate diagnosis is winning more than half of the battle and with the help of new and safer drugs, significant progress can be made. Doing so, will bring about a powerful preventive therapeutic mental regeneration, neutralizing the chances for further mental deterioration. Nothing is to be found in the complexity of the brains physical, subatomic structure. The answers that all scientists are so desperately trying to uncover is not within the human mind, but in the Universal Mind. All they need to do is to look above to the stars.

Understanding and using Astro-Psychology and ancient wisdom, will help scientists that are wasting precious time with our precious tax dollars. This capital should be used to revive and further the much older, deeper and more reliable, forfeited star knowledge. Doing so, will re-establish the direct relationship with man's psyche to the Universal Mind and avoid for mankind, the frightening mental deterioration and provide real help to a multitude of mentally ill patients.

"All our science, measured against reality, is primitive and childlike--and yet it is the most precious thing we have." (Albert Einstein)
Super Nova Window Law

A Super Nova Window is also known as a Mercury Retrograde period. Three times a year the tiny planet Mercury (The Messenger of the Gods) appears to go backwards, note also that all planets will go as imposed by the Universal clock, back and forth in their eternal dance around our Sun. However, because all the planets are moving in orbits of different sizes at different rates of speed, there will be periods in the orbit of the earth when they seem to reverse direction for a period of time. Call it an optical illusion because of the angle of the earth in relationship to those planets. More than any other planets, all affairs ruled by Mercury, which is much closer to the earth, will be much more noticeable. My book yearly publication "Moon Power" clearly advises you to be aware of a concentration of negative celestial energies approaching.

During any of the three windows, I strongly recommend my readers to be extremely prudent in driving and to expect chain-reaction accidents. Be prepared for delays, strikes, and nature disasters such as hurricanes, volcanoes, eruptions, tornadoes, etc. The same energy that produced previous volcanic eruptions, the Titanic disaster, and the Northridge California and Kobe Japan earthquakes, is approaching again. Double-check all your appointments and if you can, postpone traveling and flying during this Supernova "Window". Furthermore, communication and electricity will be cut off and a general loss of power is to be expected. Previous Supernova windows produced the New York and many other states' black outs and scientists are still scratching their huge heads, wondering what happened to their computers?

When will they honor the word "science" and investigate the stars? Isn't science's purpose to explore all possibilities? Appliances, computers, telephones, planes, trains, cars, all types of electronic "tools" will be affected by this energy. They will be stopped in one way or another. The people and affairs of the past will make the news and will re-enter your life. Expect trouble with the post office, education, strikes, prisoner escapes, jail riots, newspapers, plane crashes, broadcasting industries, and computer viruses.

Many failed missions, expensive electronic equipment (Mars probe etc.), and our tax dollars have been wasted because of the scientists' lack of knowledge of the stars. As usual NASA, which is not aware of the "Universal Code", will waste our tax money with failed missions, due to bad weather and electronic malfunctions. In the name of ignorance, the Challenger explosion killed seven astronauts when NASA launched the shuttle under a "Supernova Window". Regardless of my desperate attempts to make NASA officials aware of another dangerous Super Nova Windows by posting my predictions on my website, the Columbia was launched and once more upon re-entry killed all of the courageous astronauts.

Marine life such as sharks and whales may also beach themselves, due to Mercury retrograde which affects their natural inborn navigational systems. There is no room for ignorance and those who are not aware of the celestial order, including the NASA space-program management team, will continue to pay a heavy price. In all mankind's affairs, ignorance is true evil. Why any scientists who are against my research do not honor the word science, which is based upon solid investigation, is a solid proof of mental snobbery. Ignoring "The Universal Code" can only bring heavy penalty, all these malevolent predictions do not have to hurt or touch you, as they unfold. Instead, they are printed to prepare you for setbacks and frustrations, thus advising you to be patient and prudent during this trend. Remember what the bible says, "Men have ears, but they do not hear, they have eyes, but they do not see." Only when man raises his cosmic consciousness and asks, shall he then receive God's manifestation through his creation, in the light.... in the stars.

Tragic Souls

In one of my many newsletters, I wrote about the stars of Brittany Spears. Yes, I know she hasn't contributed much to the world, but aren't you a tad bit curious to know why she is in all the news? I cannot go to a store or click on a website, without seeing her recently baldhead everywhere. There are amazing progressive events occurring and sadly, horrible atrocities, yet we somehow are fed more fluff about celebrities. So while we are forced to see Brittany and other celebrity's lives, we might as well learn something from tehm. It's more than too much money, drugs and fame, combined with a lack of common sense and humanitarian ambition can lead to path of disaster. What else can we learn? We can learn the influences that push these people, so we can educate the masses and ourselves on why we feel the way we do. There isn't a better way to control yourself and your fate, than to first 'understand "The Universal Code". The only things that we're 'standing under' are the stars.

Here I will be breaking down the stars of the discharged astronaut, Lisa Nowak, as simply as I can. As most know, Lisa was charged with attempted murder on February 5, 2007. She was involved in what the news has described as "a bizarre space love triangle." Lisa was involved in a secret love affair with Naval Commander, William Oefelein, while still married to her husband Richard, a flight controller in Mission Control for NASA. U.S. Air Force Captain, Colleen Shipman, was also romantically involved with Mr. Oefelein, hence the drama. Obviously, I do not know Ms. Nowak, yet from mere news reports and previous interviews, you can see the stars manifesting as usual. All you have to do is 'google' the name Lisa Nowak and watch a myriad of results appear.

LISA NOWAK
was born with the following planetary placements:

PLANET - SIGN POSITION - (HOUSE)
Sun in Taurus
Moon in Sagittarius
Mercury in Gemini
Mars in Leo
Venus in Aries
Jupiter in Aries
Uranus in Virgo
Neptune in Scorpio
Saturn in Aquarius
Pluto in Virgo
Her Natal Dragon's Head in Cancer
Her Natal Dragon's Tail in Capricorn

Also, to lightly touch on her Progressive Chart:
The Universal Dragon's Head is currently in Pisces
The Universal Dragon's Tail is currently in Virgo

First House (the body, the soul's purpose) is the sign of Taurus (strength, love, stability): Lisa has the Sun (love, children, soul's purpose) in the jealous, possessive, and stubborn sign of Taurus. This makes her love oriented, striving for stability for her love life and her children. She was married for 19 years and has a son and twin daughters. One must also be a very strong and stable individual to become an astronaut. She was also very stubborn and fixed, when stalking the competitor (Colleen Shipman) in the affair of her new found love (William Oefelein). Taurus also rules flowers and gardening, Lisa has stated that she enjoys tending to her garden of African Violets in her home.

Second House (self-esteem, finances, material possessions) is the sign of Gemini (travel, exploration, mind): Lisa has Mercury (communication, travel, duality) in the sign of Gemini (speaking, writing, education), giving her double mercurial energy. Her prestigious educational travels gave her self-esteem a great boost. She received her income through a very Mercurial company, NASA; she traveled through space, ran communication systems, and explored as she expanded her mind. Before NASA, she worked as a Naval Flight Officer, running communications and navigation systems. She also stated in one interview that a few of her hobbies were reading and crossword puzzles, both very Mercurial activities. NASA being a Mercurial entity is the reason why it suffers tremendously every time they launch a shuttle during Mercury retrograde, which I refer to as a Supernova Window. We already lost 2 shuttles filled with brave crewmembers. When will my predictions be heard and used by NASA, as all they have to do is simply change the launch date.

Third House (mind, communication, travel) is the sign of Cancer (home, food, USA): Lisa has the Dragon's Head in this house which makes her strive for domestic things, usually lucky in these areas, and have karmic lessons to be learned here. Her soul wishes to balance home and travel. The Moon rules Cancer, making her mental state fluctuate like the tides of the Moon. Although most Taurus souls are good at keeping their composure, they are very emotionally deep inside. She was very lucky in affairs dealing with the USA, being a heroine until she let the Plutonic energy get the best of her. In a previous interview, she also boasts about having another hobby of gourmet cooking. She has been labeled a dedicated and caring mother and speaks of her family in many of her interviews.

Fourth House (home, family, emotions, childhood) is the sign of Leo (love, children, fame): Here Lisa has Mars (drive, aggression, fights, competitive) in the sign of Leo (love, pride, and fame) in her home area. A former classmate stated she was very competitive and driven. She had the drive for love, a family, and fame and built them all. She had fights with her husband and has been reportedly separated since January 2007. Her pride over her lover made her aggressive and drove her to take her opponent down. In a woman's chart, Mars also regulates what type of love she needs from a man, in the sign of Leo she needed someone loving, good with children, and had some form of fame on their own, someone she could feel proud of. With William being born in April, that makes him a Leo in his 5th house of love & romance. Hence, why she had the Mars fueled drive to pursue him and keep him. William's position is also more recognizably prestigious, than her husband's.

Fifth House (love, fame, pride, creativity, children) is the sign of Virgo (critical, work, health, perfection): Here, Lisa has the planets Uranus (space, electronics, friends) and Pluto (death and rebirth, regeneration, drama, sex). She received her spot on the stage through her inspection and testing of the electronics on the shuttle in space, she fell in love with her friend, and co-worker, and reportedly consoled him after the death of his ex-wife. She received her notoriety through the love, sex, and drama that unfolded through her love triangle. After this whole ordeal, she has died to an extent and will be forced to rebirth. Right now the Universal Dragon's Tail is in the sign of Virgo, negatively affecting this area, hence; all that occurred. She will be forced to rebuild all within this house.

Sixth House (work, health, service to the world) is the sign of Libra (laws, marriage, balance, partnerships): Here you can see Lisa's action of not abiding the law has taken her from her work, destroying her partnership with NASA. Her marriage has been cut since the demands and dramatic ordeal through her work, where she met Oefelein and began the affair. In a previous interview, she spoke about the hard to maintain balance between her married life and work life. The Moon was on the Virgo/Libra axis on February 5, 2007 when charges were made and this whole legal ordeal began.

Seventh House (partnerships, marriage, how one faces the world) is the sign of Scorpio (sex, drama, death, rebirth, power): Here, Lisa has Neptune (deception, guilt, fear, jail). I teach that you are the opposite of your Sun sign, when facing the world (the Law of Celestial Attraction – 7th house polarities). Here, you can see her facing the world as a truly passionate Scorpio, the mad woman who attempted to kill her lover's new lover. There was deception between all the people involved in their affair. I'm sure she felt guilt all along, and also had fears of losing power or control of her lover. A neighbor reported hearing the fighting between Lisa and her husband in November (Scorpio's month). Her partnerships with her husband and NASA are broken. She will be forced to rebirth from this ordeal, as she does every time a partnership is broken. This is why I had figured she was a Taurus, as everything she is known for is of Scorpio/Plutonic energy. She could have very easily been one of those wasted astronauts who lost their lives in the name of ignorance. Maybe being discharged even saved her life in the long run, as the chances of NASA sending yet another shuttle off during a Mercury Retrograde are very high. Maybe her and NASA should own a copy of my Moon Power book and I also strongly recommend for you to get it, if you don't already have my book.

Eighth House (sex, drama, investigation, death, power) is the sign of Sagittarius (publishing, exploring, wide open spaces, wild, freedom) Here, Lisa has the Moon (home, family, emotions) and you can see how this drama affected her home. Lisa's hidden Moon is also in the dramatic sign of Scorpio (the sign that rules the 8th house), bringing even more destructive emotions and drama into her life. She left home behind many times to explore space; she had freedom with her sexual life, and went wild when her power was taken from her. She did extensive investigative work, to find and stalk this woman who threatened her position with her lover. Her drama was published all over the news. Her emotional health is under investigation and it is because of her space travels and the stress at home, that her emotional state is being questioned.

Ninth House (travel, publishing, exploring, learning, teaching) is the sign of Capricorn (government, manipulation, status, career): Here, Lisa has her Natal Dragon's Tail which denotes a strong pull towards these affairs, as well as danger and bad luck with these areas. The focus on her education, travel, and need for freedom and exploring is what broke her family apart. She and her husband split in January (Capricorn month). Being naturally unlucky with the government, her career has fallen after breaking the law. She had to explore the man with more status. She was driven to have a career that allowed her to be free and explore, and she did have that for quite some time, but she abused her position and fell. Once more knowing the location of your Dragon by house and sign could save you lots of trouble, get the book "The Power Of The Dragon" and find out for yourself.

Tenth House (career, public standing, structure) is the sign of Aquarius (outer space, friends, groups, electronics, freedom): Here, she has Saturn (depression, restrictions, karma, manipulation, government) She made a career with the Aquarian energy and the government, cruising through space, working with groups and friends on the electronic equipment. She received restriction in her career after her dramatic ordeal. She received her karma after she had an affair with Oefelein behind her husband's back, when Oefelein did the same to her shortly after. Wherever one has Saturn, they must be cautious and honest, as the karma principle is extremely strong here.

Eleventh House (wishes, friends, groups) is the sign of Pisces (escape, deception, disillusion, subconscious, fear, guilt, religion): Here, Lisa can be impractical with her wishes and friends and also deceived by them. Her friend William deceived her into believing that she was his only love. She also had wishes to murder Colleen and probably believed she could get away with it. It's more than quite possible that her subconscious thoughts of fear and guilt lead her to being caught before she could commit the crime. The current Universal Dragon's Head in Pisces is affecting this house, forcing her to re-evaluate former wishes and friends and make changes where necessary, I'm sure she has lost quite a few friends, as she already had to disassociate herself from the NASA groups. They are also making a point that she hasn't been the same since some of her friends and colleagues died in the space shuttle Colombia's crash.

Twelfth House (how one finds themselves or God, institutions, jail, secret enemies, guilt, fear, illusion, escape) is the sign of Aries (first, leadership, competitive, greedy, fighting) Here, she has the planets of Venus (love, stability, beauty) and Jupiter (expansion, travel, publishing, freedom, luck). She is stated as being a Roman Catholic and would feel guilt from her adultery, hence, why the affair was kept secret for so long, as well as her and her husband's separation. It was her fear of losing her newly conquered lover, that caused her to become aggressive and tried to attack her secret enemy. She may lose her freedom in the process. Her affairs and travel were an escape for her and also a possible disillusionment. Wherever Venus is in a woman's chart, it represents the love she has to offer a man, with Lisa's Venus in Aries, she is strong, competitive, and wins her love through bold accomplishments and pure animalistic advances. Even with her Venus in Aries, you can also see her red flushed face, as Venus rules beauty and aesthetics and Aries rules the head and red. She was bailed from jail and allowed to go home. With the planet of luck in this area, she probably won't be getting a serious sentence such as prison and will probably be sent to an easy psychiatric therapy clinic. There is so much more that could be described about this woman through her stars. "As Above, so Below – all is Divine."

All told, everything happens for a reason. The major lessons in life can be found through the hardships and lowest points, and when you are at the bottom, there's nowhere to go but up. The lessons are created through the Laws of Karma and the Dragon is a key reference to understanding one's lessons. It's obvious from looking at Lisa's natal chart and hearing and reading a few news reports that her lesson of balance is home (Cancer) vs. career (Capricorn). Now that she has abused her position at home and in her career, she has had it all "destroyed," so she may rebuild. While facing the bleak future possibility of losing her freedom and the option to enjoy her children, she will undoubtedly take on a new appreciation of what she has at home. Lisa is a very educated competitive person in all-physical affairs involving space, but indeed not enough with "The Universal Code" and the spiritual essence of the stars. As I have said so many times "ignorance is evil, knowledge is power" and NASA would certainly never make such a drastic psychological mistake again if they were using my Astro-Psychology methodology.

CNN - 02/07/07 - NASA "Are there any 'lessons to be learned?" I'll let you be the judge of that question.

> * Incidentally, I had also a specific prediction for NASA that came to pass in February 2007. The prediction made was "Amazing technological advances and total restructure ahead for NASA." Here are the results because of Lisa Nowak: "Scandal sparks NASA review - NASA reviewing its medical and psychological care services." This Prediction was written on Dec 28, 2006 and was posted on the Coast to Coast Website.

Note also, that my early publication of Moon Power 2007 was written in August 2006 and proclaims the drama that was to unfold on these very days. Just before Anna Nicole Smith's death, I wrote this quatrain on my website that signals the Scorpionic dramatic celestial energy at work on her last days:

NEGATIVE DRAGON WINDOW FOR FEBRUARY *9th

(*) Famous Death/Dramatic News/Police/FBI/CIA/Secrets/Scandals/Terrorism/Finances/Sex/Serial Killers.

DRAGON EYE

Anna Nicole Smith dies

(*) Famous Death - (The Smell Of Death Disaster For Some)
Three men say that they could be Smith baby's Father (Secret To Light Shame Reign)

Terror Secret Villains Plot For God
Evil Dance Killers Rise
Secret To Light Shame Reign
The Smell Of Death Disaster For Some

Written by Dr. Turi 2/3/07

An Autopsy is planned to find out why Anna Nicole Smith died, don't waste our tax dollars again, here you go, save time, save money, it's because of DRUGS!

ANNA NICOLE SMITH
born 11/28/1967

PLANET - SIGN POSITION - (HOUSE)

Soul's Purpose Scorpio (1) SELF - Sex – Magnetism – Power – Magnetic - Death
Sun - Sagittarius (2) MONEY – Luck – Expansion – Foreigners – Publishing
Moon - Libra (12) SUBCONSCIOUS – Partnership – Imagination – Deception
Mercury - Scorpio (1) SELF – Sarcastic – Secretive – Intuitive – Manipulative
Venus - Libra (12) SUBCONCIOUS – Secret Love – Artistic -Deceptive
Mars - Capricorn (3) MIND – Driven - Planning – Dedicated – Lure for power
(Mars in a female chart depicts the best man that would fit her deepest need)
Jupiter - Virgo (11) FRIENDS – Critical – Foreign Friends – Publishing –
Saturn - Aries (6) WORK – Competitive – Impatient – Insecure
Uranus - Virgo (11) WISHES – Television – Internet – Eccentric - Original
Neptune - Scorpio (1) SELF – Addictions – Depressions – Poisoning – STDs –
Pluto - Virgo (11) FRIENDS – Regeneration – Organized – Using Friends

Dragon's Head - Aries (6) SERVICE TO THE WORLD – Born to be #1 – The body – The Mind

Dragon's Tail - Libra (12) SUBCONSCIOUS – Attracting wrong partners – Secret enemies – Dedicated

MOON PHASE: Balsamic - Anna Nicole Smith was born in a Waning (negative)

Moon and among other things points to having a short life. These souls need my book Moon Power and RESPECT for the Moon's fluctuations, to avoid an ill fate.

As I teach my students, born in the constellation of Scorpio predisposes the soul for dramatic experiences and not long ago, she gave birth to a child and her son died a few days later of an overdose. This is part of the true metaphysical "legend" of the Scorpio energy, that when a soul is born, a soul will die!

Born with the Dragon's Head in Aries in her 6th house of work, she was to be number one in her field and Scorpio rules anything and everything that deals with sex, power, other peoples wealth, metaphysics, and witchcraft.

The tail of the Dragon is located in the sign of Libra (marriage) and brought quite a lot of controversy in her relationships. She was to marry her lawyer, Howard Stern (Libra rules the law). Nicole Simpson was also born with the same Dragon axis in Aries (the head) and Libra (marriage) and we all know that her husband O. J. Simpson, literally cut her head off.

My book "The Power of the Dragon" has so much for you pertaining to the Dragon of serial killers, including famous and infamous people. You had better find out where yours is located and run for the Head, to avoid realizing a dramatic fate. As you know, "Knowledge is power, ignorance is evil". One important element in Anna Nicole Smith's chart is the location of her Mars in Capricorn. Mars is the drive principle and depicts how the energy will be channeled to get something or someone. Capricorn rules older people that have reached a position of respect in society, having something concrete to offer, such as money, fame or both. Capricorn is a cold and calculated sign and its ruler, (karmic Saturn) regulation politics, elite snobs, Kings, Presidents, CEOs, CFOs and ALL people that have reached a high level of fame, wealth and power. This sign also rules the skeleton, old age, England, the government, the Illuminati, the Freemasons and all-powerful secret societies.

Incidentally, Hitler was born with his Dragon's Tail in the manipulative sign of Capricorn - more in my book "The Power of the Dragon". Anna's Saturn (career) is strongly and luckily placed in her 6th house (work) on the Dragon Head (luck) in the competitive sign of Aries (the body) - et VOILA!

This was a small sample of what and how to use "The Cosmic Code" that explains a little bit more about "The Scorpionic Law". Of course in her case, the stars were in the right location and "The Law Of Fame" did the rest and brought money, notoriety, wealth and power to Anna Nicole Smith.

With Jupiter (luck) Pluto (power) and Uranus (great timing) on her 11th house of wishes and friends, all the vital ingredients were present for "The Cosmic Laws" to work in her favor. If you think you can reach all your wishes by knowing or mastering only one law, you are in for serious deception.

But how and why did Anna Nicole Smith die?

First and foremost, her Dragon's Tail was in her 12th house and the hidden Dragon kicked in. One of the aspects of the 12th house is the aspect to death. (Sorry, don't want to lose you and I can't teach you all the ramifications of Astro-Psychology, so join me for a course in Hawaii or Sedona and build your own cosmic consciousness). The 12th house regulating the subconscious, guilt, drugs, or doctor's medications, (I am sure Anna Nicole Smith was on medications) undoubtedly creates serious complications even death.

And like her son who died of a mixture of drug complications and antidepressants, Anna Nicole Smith also fell victim to the medical system. But, as in the case of her son, all this deception will be covered up so her attorney and other attorneys involved, like a bunch of stinking hyenas, will work under the table to benefit from her demise and save the good doctors. Then they will give you a plausible, accepted explanation for her death and life goes on.

CHO
born 4/19/2007

The Mind of a Killer:

First let me offer my sincere condolences to the families affected by the Virginia Tech dramatic shooting. May God bless the souls of all the victims that suffered this awful tragedy. On Monday April 16th 2007 a gunman massacred 32 people at Virginia Tech in the deadliest shooting rampage in modern U.S. history. I can only hope for the millions of people involved in the fields of mental health, criminology, psychology, psychiatry, law enforcement, and community leaders to read my work. May they be able to acknowledge "The Universal Code" in action. Furthering one's cosmic consciousness can only sharpen the perception and anticipate the action of a potential killer as to avoid another terrible tragedy.

Erudite men from all ages understood the Universal Clock and dwelt with the Universal Mind accordingly and as Porphyry wrote, "He is happy who having learned the scheme of his nativity and knowing his guardian angel, becomes liberated from Fate." A modern infantile science still challenges the opulent life of illustrious men's spiritual findings who have made history. "Perhaps there is a pattern in the heavens for one who desires to see it, and having seen it, to find one in himself "– Plato. The enemy is an oversized educated ego, a weak UCI, religious poisoning, fear of ridicule or plain mental stupidity. They refuse to conceive what can't be seen, touched or analyzed just yet still may exist. Stubbornness and repudiation for spiritual growth to move forward belongs to donkeys, not to refined minds. I will now attempt to denunciate the UCI and actions of serial killer Cho Seung-Hu and how the "Cosmic Code" stirred this lost soul to perform such an awful act. Cho was born January 18, 1984 in Seoul, South Korea and for an educated Astropsychologist his UCI (Unique Celestial Identity) depict all the ingredients of a psychotic killer.

PLANET - SIGN POSITION - (HOUSE)

Sun – 27 Capricorn 12 (1) – Personality - Head of the goat – Planning – Structure – Engineering – Snobbism – Accomplishments.

Soul's Purpose: The soul wants to make an impact and gather a position of respect in society. Capricorn is a feminine, introverted sign, meticulous and will do all he can (positively or negatively in this case) to climb the ladder of recognition in society. This is a karmic sign chosen subconsciously by the Christians as the head of the devil to represents manipulation, greed, planning, political power and all accomplished people (Presidents/CEO/FCO/Colonels/Snobs/Royalties). This sign rules England, the English hierarchy, classical music, poetry and any and all forms of imposing structures. This is a winter sign regulated by the month of January and there are no fruits on the tree this season. This symbolizes hardship and a long struggle in the subject's life to get recognition and reach a solid position on the top of the mountain. The cold, the wind, the treacherous terrain and the snow represent the imposed challenges.

Moon – 20 Cancer 47 (7) Partnerships, emotional response to life under the jurisdiction of the moon's fluctuations.

Home and family: Cho was a very emotional person facing the world as a feminine, shy water sign. The hidden moon is in Libra which is a sign concerned with justice and harmony. Cho was constantly unbalanced by the pressure and bully's treatments he suffered. Long before he boiled over, Virginia Tech gunman Cho Seung-Hui was picked on, pushed around and laughed at over his shyness and the strange way he talked when he was a schoolboy in the Washington suburbs, former classmates say. Furthermore the South Korean immigrant almost never opened his mouth and would ignore attempts to strike up a conversation. Note also that Cho inherited five water signs (feminine/introvert/shyness) in his chart elements making up for the 42 % of his celestial femininity. Past 50% in the water element would induce homosexuality and a natural attraction to males. Cho was highly aware and respectful of his own family but much too shy to "request" a constant need for nurturing. Note also that Cho was born in a Gibbous Moon Phase (waning/negative) and the moon was also waning and Gibbous on the day of the massacre. The moon plays an important part of his emotional response to life and was responsible for his depression. Uneducated Psychologists or Psychiatrists can only bring more confusion and depression to the soul by prescribing dangerous drugs. In many cases the drugs itself fuels the chemically poisoned mind to act drastically or erratically by inducing suicidal or criminal thoughts to the subject.

Mercury – 03 Capricorn 24 (1) The Mind, the thoughts, Critical thinking, General Communication.

Mental process: Cho's mental aptitudes were constructive, planned and detailed oriented. A drive for academic accomplishments stirred him to study a structured form of art or poetry. Mercury (The Messenger of the Gods in Greek mythology) is located once again in an introverted feminine sign. The negative attention his accent attracted seriously affected his ego. "Once, in English class, the teacher had the students read aloud, and when it was Cho's turn, he just looked down in silence," Davids recalled. Finally, after the teacher threatened him with an F for participation, Cho started to read in a strange, deep voice that sounded "like he had something in his mouth," Davids said. I teach my students that a certain give away of a strong Capricorn is his deep, cavernous sound but the ignorant teacher, like 99% of his professional mates do not possess Cosmic Consciousness and failed in assesses sing Cho's mental capacity. Note also that: famous radio host show "Art Bell" was born with a Dragon's Tail in Capricorn and one can only appreciate his deep "radio voice".

"As soon as he started reading, the whole class started laughing and pointing and saying, `Go back to China,'" Davids said. A solid plan was set in motion then to make sure Cho would get back at his enemies and gain fame in the process. This mercurial position strives for mental accomplishments and recognition, and led Cho to send NBC a video of himself between the first and second attack on campus. In the often-incoherent video, the 23-year-old Cho portrayed himself as persecuted and rants about rich kids. Not understanding "The Universal Code" brought this tragedy where universal ignorance resulted in the death of 32 people. I seriously hope that Astropsychology will be taught and accepted as a solid discipline in ALL our colleges and Universities. Unless Astropsychology becomes an indispensable part of the curriculums do not expect any of your children to be safe in any accredited schools. Let's hope the educated responsible will read my work and acknowledge this fact. With this knowledge, they need to take the appropriate measures to improve the safety and education of all the children of tomorrow. Billions of tax dollars have been wrongly invested in fruitless research and dogmatic, dangerous religious teachings. I can only hope to finally attract enough attention and support to build my own Astropsychology schools and eliminate ignorance by creating a crowd of "Teachers of Teachers". Those teachers of light will in turn make an impact to the educational system and bring safety, love and respect to all the children of tomorrow.

Venus – 20 Sagittarius 39 (12) Love principle, inspiration, stimulation.

Love: Sadly for Cho, Venus the "Goddess of Love" rides his Dragon's Tail (negative) and is found in his subconscious 12th house. This position denounces an imaginary girlfriend named "Jelly," who was a supermodel in his deceived mind. I teach my students this position breeds people who are in love with love, deceived in all affairs of the heart, or attract secret love affairs. Note also this house is ruled by Neptune "The Lord of Deception" and ruler of the seas in Greek Mythology. See how the Neptunian deceiving water-energy created Cho's imaginary lover "Jelly". It's all about energy. But how can anyone understand the archetypal realm of consciousness of creative forces in the subconscious accurately, without the considered necessary education? I am a Clinical Hypnotherapist and my new book "Beyond The Secret" has so much to offer to the reader pertaining to the subconscious and its interaction with "The Universal Code".

Mars – 03 Scorpio 32 (11) Action, Competitiveness, Aggressivity, Sarcasm.

Drive principle: I also teach my students the location of Mars in the UCI depicts where danger or accidents will enter the subject's life. Mars is called in Greek Mythology "The Lord of War" and translates in this dense physical world as the Army, Navy, ammunition, weaponry, guns etc. Mars (the red planet) depicts also the color of the blood and rules the animal kingdom, natural weaponry (fangs/claws) and how they treat themselves in the wild. Mars in a man's chart represent his masculinity and how he will perform with the opposite sex. Mars in a female chart represent the type of man she is subconsciously looking for. Note also while I am at it that; famous writer John Gray "Men are from Mars, Women from Venus" is a student and a client of mine. In Cho's chart, this dangerous planet is negatively located in the 11th house. This area rules groups, (classmates) friends and wishes. Cho's twisted, violence-filled writings and menacing, uncommunicative demeanor had disturbed professors and students so much that he was removed from one English class and was repeatedly urged to get counseling. With women Cho became a Scorpio and wherever this sign is located, sex, death, control, and the police will enter your life. Two roommates from a previous year told CNN in an interview that Cho "stalked" three different women and that one of them was so "freaked out by his behavior" that she called the police on him. Scorpio is ruled by the planet Pluto (death/drama/the police/sex) and it is the most fixed sign of the zodiac. Combined with Mars (action/weapons/war/blood) the recipe is set for disaster. One troubling play Cho wrote called, "Richard McBeef," was about a 13-year-old who accuses his stepfather of trying to molest him. The teenage character in the play smiles as he throws darts at his stepfather's picture, saying, "I hate him. Must kill Dick. Dick must die. You don't think I can kill you?" Cho's roommates said they didn't think they could have done anything differently to reach out to Cho and change what had happened and that is a false statement in my world.

"Never ever take the Plutonic intonation and affliction lightly because this essence of this energy is REVENGE and the subject will follow through any and all planned actions. Again I can only hope the world to swiftly understand the depth and importance of my message, and for someone in position to help me in my mission to raise this world's cosmic consciousness. My books "And God Created the Stars" or "The Power of the Dragon" have so much to offer society and could literally save so many lives. "Ignorance is evil, knowledge is power." My students relate this axiom to me after graduation once they become proficient Astropsychologists. Pamela Blake a dedicated psychiatrist at Memorial Hermann NW Hospital in Houston, calls Cho's writing chilling, scary and disturbing. She should investigate my work and make good use of it by assessing correctly Cho's UCI.

Jupiter – 29 Sagittarius 41 (12) Higher education, colleges, Universities, religions, foreigners.

The codification of thoughts: Once more Cho was born with Jupiter on his Dragon's Tail (negative manifestation). Jupiter is called ion Greek Mythology 'The Great Benefic". Jupiter's placement in the chart depicts protection and academic aptitudes, connection with foreigners, and life on foreign ground, higher education, success and growth. Because this planet is located on the Dragon's Tail most of Jupiter's enormous power will be geared the wrong way. In Cho's case the Jupiterian energy repels foreigners and all foreign ground. It has a malicious dynamic affect in colleges, universities, teachers and students at large. Jupiter happens to be the largest celestial body in our solar system and so can reward the soul for his "academic" accomplishments in a HUGE way, and in foreign lands. This simply translates to the incredible negative shocking news broadcast worldwide. Incidentally Jupiter rules also religious books such as the bible, the Koran and depicts why subconsciously Cho used the words "Ismail Ax". Like the young souls born in January such as Mel Gibson (see his movie about Christ), and Casssius Clay turning into Muslim Ali, the Pisces/Neptunian mind is concerned with biblical terms and religions. Capricorn is also prone to chemical addictions as seen with the famous radio host Rush Limbaugh's dilemma. There is no doubt in my mind that Cho's religious celestial inclinations played an important part of his meaningful research for his complicated life to justify his dreadful act and eliminate tremendous guilt.

Saturn – 15 Scorpio 13 (11) Career, public standing, structure, accomplishments.

Fear Principle: Saturn is called in Greek Mythology "The Great Malefic", its placement in the 11th house of friends and wishes in Scorpio (Secrets) made him a silent power-freak denouncing his fear of losing control and the (?) name he chose to be called. Saturn's location represents also the career drive and in the sign of Scorpio (death/drama) the stars have spoken their undiluted truth once more. Saturn is a karmic cold planet and always induces limitation and secretiveness making Cho antisocial and a loner.

Uranus –12 Sagittarius 02 (12) Shocking, ingenious, weird, electronics. Sudden release of energy: Uranus is called in Greek Mythology "The Lord of the Sky" and rules all that is unconventional and futuristic. It rules NASA, UFOs, technology, television, new Age matters, video games etc. Cho was again born with this eccentric planet on his Dragon's Tail (negative manifestation) and part of the five planets or a very negative stellium. Jupiter (expansion/foreign lands/ Universities) rules the sign of Sagittarius and with Uranus indeed depicts the sudden release of nefarious energy (explosions) of the fired guns against the students in the Campus of Virginia Tech. Uranus is also located in the secretive, deceiving subconscious 12th house and like a time bomb: exploded, shocking everyone.

Here is a memo of my quatrain posted on my website (http://www.drturi.com/) and my premonition during those days, note also that I gave this window on Coast-To-Coast radio. http://www.coasttocoastam.com/shows/2007/03/22. html

"*The intuitive mind is a sacred gift and the rational mind is a faithful servant. We have created a society that honors the servant and has forgotten the gift.*"
--Albert Einstein

For those of you who purchased 2007 Moon Power simply open it to page 186. Here is another sample of my book, make sure to check my regular quatrains on my site.

Environment: On a sad note, keep in mind that Uranus rules explosions, earthquakes and volcanoes. He may also decide to throw a tornado or produce violent explosions. Let's hope he won't. RESULTS:

An explosion rockets the Iraqi Parliament in Baghdad.

My quatrain for the exact day was – (Terror Future Power Challenged).

Killer Tornadoes spotted in Texas Louisiana, Arkansas.

My quatrain for the exact day was (Surprise Power To Kill)

Wildfire brings destruction to Beverly Hills.

My quatrain for the exact day was ((Wind, Fire Water Boil)

Guerrero, Mexico April 12 - 6.0 earthquake (Quake)

Northeaster slams East Coast.

My quatrain for the exact day was (Wind, Fire Water Boil)

Thai flash flood sweeps scores over waterfalls kill scores.

My quatrain for the exact day was (Surprise Power To Kill).

Lastly read what Moon Power read and my quatrain about the dramatic news involving the latest massacre at Virginia Tech. Famous Personalities: Much will be done for children during this trend, but the negative tendency could touch some of them. Let's hope I am wrong, I hate to say anything drastic about the children. Sadly enough, Uranus or Pluto couldn't care a bit about my personal feelings and will do whatever pleases them. Events: Under Uranus' surprising incredible news tends to take place.

Gunman 23-year-old senior English major kills 32 people!
My site and quatrain for these days were - (Shocking News - Surprise Power to Kill).
Now take the time to read my quatrain and realize why it is so important to acknowledge and respect the Universal Laws. As mentioned before event if you have your Moon Power copy, make sure to read my quatrain to further understanding of the current celestial energy. CURRENT NEGATIVE DRAGON WINDOW APRIL +12th 2007

(+)Cosmos/Nuke/Weird/Surprises/Explosions/Shocking/Quakes/Volcanoe/
Tornadoes/NASA/Aeronautics.

Mountains Earth Tremble
Wind, Fire Water Boil
Surprise Power To Kill
Terror Future Power Challenged

Written by Dr. Turi 4/7/07DRAGON EYE
Massacre at Virginia Tech (Shocking News - Surprise Power To Kill)

Uranus rules shocking news and Pluto in Sagittarius clearly depict my premonitions of the latest drama that took place at Virginia Tech. Be smart get the book and "anticipate" and be cautious during those windows. "Ignorance is Evil, Knowledge is power" if you do not respect the "Universal Code" be aware of the upcoming heavy penalty! Neptune – 29 Sagittarius 58 (12) Deception, Religion, Imagination, Drugs, the Arts. Martyrdom: The nebulous planet Neptune rules all religions, deities and its martyrs such as Jesus suffering and dying on the cross to save mankind. Incidentally the entire Middle East region and its 3 youngest and deadliest religions are under the jurisdiction of Neptune. Neptune rules also poisoning such as oil and chemicals, confined areas such as churches synagogues, asylums, hospitals, jails, mental institutions, etc. Cho's video show rails against wealth and debauchery, and portrays himself as a defender of the weak and voicing admiration for the 1999 Columbine High School massacre. Neptune's deceiving religious energy adds to the Jupiterian minister-like speech. "You have vandalized my heart, raped my soul and tortured my conscience," said Cho. He also mentioned the name of Jesus speaking directly to the camera. "Your Mercedes wasn't enough, you brats," says Cho, who came to the U.S. in 1992 and whose parents worked at a dry cleaner sin suburban Washington. "Your golden necklaces weren't enough, you snobs. Your trust funds weren't enough. Your vodka and cognac wasn't enough. All your debaucheries weren't enough. Those weren't enough to fulfill your hedonistic needs. You had everything." "You had a hundred billion chances and ways to have avoided today," a snarling Cho says on video. "But you decided to spill my blood. You forced me into a corner and gave me only one option. The decision was yours. Now you have blood on your hands that will never wash off."

Pluto – 02 Scorpio 02 (11) Drama, Terrorism, Death, Sex, Power.
The Death Wish Generation. I wrote intensely about this deadly generation in my book entitled "The Power Of The Dragon". – Pluto then inhabited, from 1983 until 1995, his own daredevil sign of Scorpio. Those very young and wild children have already made dramatic news by executing each other and murdering adults and classmates for any reason. Our society is witnessing "The Dramatic Death Wish Generation" in action. They are strong-willed, unwavering in thought and action, immensely emotional and totally fearless in front of death. Pluto (sex) is making them very active sexually at an early age, and they will also look for a mixture of sex, crime and drugs to survive their harsh young lives. At the tender age of 12 years many of those children have already experienced the use of drugs and sex and some others have committed repellent murders. The passion for self-discovery is extreme and if left without legitimate spiritual food, the worst can only happen to many of these children. They will not react to dogma and common religious teachings, as they "naturally" understand the motivation behind the

manifestation. The miserably failing psychological field won't be of any help in the understanding and motivation behind the upcoming killer generation. Unless the old science of Astrology is reinstated, (Astropsychology) in our colleges and universities, there will be either no understanding or therapeutic healing measures available for these children. A few years from now, once in power, indeed, this unyielding generation has the awful potential to destroy the world with the use of irreversible atomic weapons. God's implacable Universal Rules have been broken and ignored for too long and a serious penalty is awaiting mankind. There is no room for ignorance at any level of consciousness.

All the sympathy in the world for the victims of the school shooting won't stop this ugly problem. The people of the world lament on the American culture that would breed such people and so many awful tragedies. That is NOT the problem or the answer, and it will happen again. The educational, psychological, police and government systems and the church are all loosing the battle. Soon you will soon watch the breaking-down of our young society if nothing is done to help this generation of killers. Scientists from all levels out there are mesmerized and baffled by the awful event that took place on March 25th, 1998 in JONESBORO, Arkansas and April 16th, 2007. Unless those educated "mental snobs" cast aside their fear of the ridicule (fueling their academically oriented ignorance and their mental snootiness) they will not be able to even get closer to fix the problem. If you are one of them, you might have to challenge your precious books, pass the limitations of your rational mind and realize that the higher truths have never been printed by your kind. Time to look above your head; in the Universal Mind and master the Universal Code if you have any hope, whatsoever, to provide serious help to this " Death Wish Generation. "School Shootings? Note the dates please!

Monday April 16th 2007 a gunman massacred 32 people at Virginia Tech in the deadliest shooting rampage in modern U.S. history. April 20, 1999. As many as 25 students and a teacher died in a Colorado's school attack! Mars, the red planet of blood, war, danger and guns, rules the month of April. Hitler was born in April and Germany is an Aries country…

That specific dreadful day was carefully planned by the young killers as it marks Hitler's birthday. Incidentally like Cho, both teens are also part of the "Death Wish Generation" and in this case both kids were born like Hitler with a Dragon's Tail (negative) in Capricorn (politics, planning). It is obvious in my work that those two souls previously died in the name and memory of Hitler and wasted their young lives. Note: Stone, sheriff of Jefferson County, said he believed the two suspects died of self-inflicted wounds in an apparent "suicide mission."

Dragon's Head –13 Gemini 38 (6) Duality, Dual Personality. Cho's Dragon's Head is located in the dual sign of Gemini; Mercury or "The Lord Of The Thieves" in Greek Mythology rules this sign. This Dragon supports any and all forms of printed information and rules all broadcasting industry making the soul famous through the media. O.J. Simpson and POW Jessica Lynch share the same Dragon and all made international news for good or for worse. This Dragon rules transportation, radio, writing, and always imposed a duality in the affairs of the subject. O.J. Simpson killed 2 people, had many police cars following him, he had 2 judgments 2 or 4 attorneys (Gemini Head) to save his tail, 2 people died etc. "Wilder recalled high school teachers trying to get Cho to participate, but "he would only shrug his shoulders or he'd give like two-word responses, and I think it just got to the point where teachers just gave up because they realized he wasn't going to come out of the shell he was in, so they just kind of passed him over for the most part as time went on." In Cho's case his writings and videos were dual and 32 victims denounces the dual number imposed by the hidden scheme of things at the end, further reinforcing my theory. Had Cho dealt with any of my students or an educated Astropsychologist, the wall of ignorance would have been broken and the regeneration principle would have healed Cho's intellectual UCI affliction. This entire process would have saved the lives of all the victims and eliminate the pull of the Dragon's Tail.

Dragon's Tail – 13 Sagittarius 38 (12) Education, the codification of Thoughts, Universities, Colleges, Books, Libraries.

General Education: Let me refresh your memory by pointing out that Pluto (death/drama/terrorism) is still going through the sign of Sagittarius (education/colleges/Universities). Undoubtedly and obviously this depicts the state of this world where religion, philosophy general education is undergoing an overhaul. People like me will point out something other than what science or religion wants you to believe. Never forget that "whatever is accepted by the majority does not make it true" because there is a BIG difference between education and intelligence. As a rule we are all under the jurisdiction of the stars and mostly stuck on the Dragon's Tail nefarious pull. What Cho's Dragon Tail in Sagittarius wanted was to do was to TEACH the world in a big and nasty way, and it all happened as such. Now the question is, will the commanding educational administration put a lid on another lost soul's dramatic cry for help? Will the scholastic system accept its own limitations, wake up and be responsible and allow Astropsychology to finally become a part of the educational curriculum? For now the entire educational system is to blame and soon enough another lost soul will act drastically and kill more innocent students. How many students must die before doing the right thing? But one can only relate to my expertise. Because of Cho' education, experiences and UCI, much work needs to be done with our relationship to the Divine. Science and religion is not the answer to such a dilemma, never been, never will. I can only hope that my new book "Beyond The Secret" will shed new light on the fragile human psyche and that my own cry to help the children of the future is finally heard by a society drowning in its own spiritual ignorance.

"We will not solve the problems of the world from the same level of thinking we were at when we created them." --Albert Einstein
More than anything else, this new century demands new thinking: We must change our

materially based analyses of the world around us to include broader, more multidimensional perspectives." --Albert Einstein

PARIS HILTON

It seems that being rich, pretty and famous does not mean much to the stars if the recipient is uninformed. The stars are impartial. If you do not know or respect the Universal rules, perhaps you will be next to suffer the effects of ignorance. Incidentally 99% of the world's population, both political and religious leaders, (and most famous pretty girls out there) have no cosmic consciousness. They have absolutely NO clue to the star's regimentation over their lives. What's really interesting is that the very same Plutonic stars that forever changed the lives of famous radio host Imus and comedian Michael Richards, also victimized Paris Hilton. I can barely comprehend how innocent she and the rest of the world really are. Because of their ignorance of the "Universal Code," Imus, Michael Richards, Paris Hilton and others, could have avoided tragedy had they my celestial understanding. Much money is wasted on exuberant parties, luxuries or wasted donations to the church. It's not spent on the right people who could help them understand their star patterns, so what good does their money do? Emotional distress, shame, guilt, mental and physical health is much more important than the incredible wealth these persons have. None of those famous people have crossed my path. Call it karma, but I must remind you that the human will is more powerful than the stars. How can one apply the will when there is no foundation or wisdom to tap, you may ask? There are SO MANY prominent people reading my newsletters and perhaps someday, some will choose to "connect" with me to avoid misfortune. But if they don't, its because they are not yet ready for the truth I wish to offer.

It saddens me that only a handful of highly spiritual people possess this vital wisdom (they are my students). It could mend this torn world and not stop political and religious leaders such as the President Bush, the Pope or even the Dali Llama to be real and honest. All said, I do respect those great men and their accomplishments. To me they are like little kids playing with matches but not really capable of handling those cursed positions and responsibilities. By hearing any of them on television I can immediately find an old wise soul, or a celebrity forced into a position by the stars. One such as Paris Hilton has to learn the hard way. I may sound egocentric but in fifty years or so from today (when I will be 6 feet under) the world will finally understand me and realize I was speaking the truth. Being born in Provence, France (like the great Prophet Nostradamus), I share the same fate and will be heard in time. I have another major book to write (it will be the last of my series) in my desperate attempt to reach the world. However I am confident that the children of the future will make good use of my predictions and heeding.

PLANET - SIGN POSITION - (HOUSE)

Sun 28Aqu57 (1) Soul's Purpose – Freedom – Eccentricity – Friends – Original – Shocking – Independent

Moon 14Leo08 (7) Emotional response to life – Famous partners – Wealthy Family background - Non-domestic -Artistic

Mercury 28Aqu27 (1) Personally – Dual – Speedy – Communicative – Futuristic – Original – Smart – Internet – New Age oriented

Venus 16Aqu50 (1) Personality – Magnetic – independent – Universal Love – Friends (I was born with the same Venus position)

Mars 08Pis31 (2) Possession – Stirred to use drugs, pot, alcohol, loves water, the spirit, acting, photography, jail, hospitals.

Jupiter 09Lib30 (9) Higher learning – Lucky with foreigners and foreign lands, philosophical love of animals, marriage with a foreigner

Saturn 09Lib01 (9) Higher learning – Good student, fear of never finding true love, Karma with justice (Libra rules the law)

Uranus 00Sag00 (11) Friends and groups – Eccentric –unusual – shocking weird – negative friends and groups

Neptune 24Sag28 (11) Friends and groups – Deception – drugs – alcohol – deception – jail – mental institution – Rehabilitation

Pluto 24Lib12 (9) Higher learning – Plutonic powerful friends – Regeneration – Sex – Manipulation – Legality –Power.

Dragon's Head 09Leo59 (7) Luck-protection – growth - Public life – France – Italy (princess Diana had the same Dragon's Head

Dragon's Tail 09Aqu59 (1) Self – Weird – eccentric – Unruly – Independent – aggressive – learn the hard way –Violent death flying.

Fixed 6 50 % Paris Hilton has 50% planets in fixed sign and this makes her very stubborn about everything.

SIGN ELEMENTS:

Air 7 58 % Paris Hilton has 58% planets in air sign. Get bored easily, impatient, speedy, communicative ADD.

IN CRITICAL DEGREES: (Mansions of the Moon):

MOON PHASE: Gibbous - Paris Hilton was born in a waning (negative) moon phase and depicts a short life if she doesn't learn to respect the "Universal Code" while she has the chance. "The crocodile Hunter" (Steve Irwin) was born with the same dragon and died, shocking the world when he was stung by a sting ray while doing a television program. You may read my prediction of his death at http://www.drturi.com/news/1157428706.html - (The Stars and Fate of Steve Irwin).

Serial killer Cho Seung-Hu a 23-year-old senior English major that killed 32 people at the Virginia Tech was also born during a gibbous Moon phase. Paris Hilton's Hidden Dragon Tail is in the sign of Aries. This is a very masculine self-centered war-like sign that rules aggression, impatience, and denounces why she has to learn the hard way to respect the laws of men. As with all of those born in February she is still experiencing the year nasty Dragon's Tail in her 8th house of death. Paris is undergoing serious deep psychological changes and seeks refuge in drugs and alcohol. Sadly, the fortune she could spend on an educated psychologist or a well-known Beverly Hills psychiatrist would do her cosmic education no good. None of those professionals possess Cosmic Consciousness; they could only worsen her situation by subscribing dangerous anti-depressants. Ingesting medical prescriptions can only further suicidal thoughts and poison Paris' body mind and soul.

The next two years ahead of Mrs. Paris Hilton (2007-2009) will be crucial and I can only hope she will sail through unharmed. But my predictions are real, and August 2007/2008 and February 2008 are the dates of significant happenings in her life. Let's hope its all positive for her sake and if my newsletter reach her before then, the worst of her fate can be avoided. The future has and will always be my only witness.

The Passing of a Great Friend

The same sad fate also happened to Dave, a good friend of mine born in late October under the sign of Scorpio. Like thousands of unaware people trusting their doctors with dangerous medical prescriptions, he also suddenly lost his life. I had a vivid and very prophetic dream and again my subconscious was preparing me for a terrible shock that took place days later on July 7th, 2005. In my dream, I was back home in France; my long gone ex mother-in-law was telling me that my son was dead. I was horrified and woke up perspiring and upset, but happy to realize it was "only a dream." Incidentally, I always associated David with my son Remy, because both were born the same year and with a dragon's Tail (negative) in Leo (love/romance/children).

Dave called me from Las Vegas and told me he was finally going to take his beautiful daughter Jenny on a road trip to Sedona, Phoenix, and then to visit me. I saw his daughter growing up and because her father was such a spiritual man, she was well initiated and loved the stars. He deeply loved her and many times told me "Louis, if it was not for her, I would have been gone a long time ago." and I knew she was the main reason for his holding on to life. Born with a Leo Dragon's Tail, Dave went through many devasting relationships and for a while he abused both drugs and alcohol, seeking refuse in Neptune's world. Like Jacques, David always said to me. "Louis, we've known each other for so many years and I know I will not live long. I always have that fear that I will die young, because of drugs."

I helped him through on many occasions to fight his suicidal thoughts, by breathing hope and supporting words into his beautiful heart. He took the time to write me a piece of poetry on the zodiac and told me, "Louis, this is for you, man. This is the only way I know how to show you how much I love you and how much you mean to me." he said.

In his memory, I shall always keep his artwork in my office, until I join him. Dave was always promoting my work and me. Countless people, called me from Las Vegas looking for relief. We had a very strong and deep connection that lasted over twenty years and I was totally devastated and had no one to talk about it with, so I decided to write about our friendship in one of my many newsletters and let my feelings go. His brother's wife called me and told me that Dave died in his sleep and they did not know why, he was only 34 years old. I was speechless and trying hard to make sense to the appalling news. "David thought very highly of you" she said "and I am calling all his close friends." She felt how deeply wounded I was and politely excused herself from the telephone.

I was in shock, trying hard to hold back from rushing tears and went to my piano as I always do when I need to collect myself. I played the music he was listening to just a few days ago, while standing with his daughter next to me, right here in my house in Phoenix. When Dave visited me he was so happy, so high, and so much in love with a lady. He was so hopeful to finally find love and have someone sharing his life. I could see in his eyes how much he really cared for her. He constantly talked about this person during his stay and knowing his tail in Leo (love/children) and deep emotional and sometimes-destructive nature (Sun in Scorpio) I simply prepared him for any possible setbacks. "Dave, use your head man, not your heart, give yourself a chance to find out if she really cares for you, it's easy to be in denial when you are in love." He laughed and told me "Louis, she is all I want and I will not be able to live without her."

The day before he died Dave checked into a substance abuse clinic in Vegas, and I found out by calling his brother, that Dave had been on anti-depressants for many months. I always taught my students if you were born in October under the sign of Libra, your six house of health is Pisces, making all Libras very vulnerable to any and all chemicals including drugs, alcohol, and doctor prescriptions. We spent a couple of great days catching up and I taught him more about the working of the Universal Mind. He was so full of hopes and had so many dreams to fulfill. Just before driving back, he told me something that will always be engraved in my memory for as long as I live.

"Louis," he said. "You had yesterday, you're blessed, you may have tomorrow because it is a promissory note, but you have cash in hand now, just make the most of it my friend." Those were his last words before hugging me…and that was the last time that I saw him alive.

Following my show on Coast-to-Coast, I have been asked to finish my book "You Are God" (now this book, 'Beyond the Secret'). Some movie producers in Hollywood have volunteered to turn it into a movie. I have been writing non-stop for many hours each day while still taking care of business. I was exhausted and very sad then, but I have faith in my powers and my will to use my own life's experiences to prove to all of you, that we are gods in training in this dense physical world.

"Beyond the Secret" is the story of my life, loaded with very dramatic experiences since childhood. It has been very hard for me to go back to those emotional days and re-visit my life and all the people who have left this world already. Many of you will never believe what I went through as a child and this why some movie producers want to make a movie out of it. I shed quite a few tears while writing this book, wondering how I made it so far, especially with so much drama and pain since my childhood. Now, one of my best friends joined them all in the afterworld.

The Moon was in Leo and right on his Dragon's Tail when he died on July 7th, 2005, reaffirming my lifetime work on the "Dragon Windows" and how important it is to know about it. Well, I do not have to wait for the autopsy; I already knew what happened to Dave. The day the Moon entered Leo (the heart) on his Dragon's Tail (negative), combined with the medical prescriptions he ingested, his heart simply stopped, while asleep. Dave was a victim of the system, but also of "The law of Negativity". He was considered as a family member and indeed one of my best students, I miss him terribly.

With dedication and a good teacher, anyone can become an efficient Astro-Psychologist and build enough cosmic consciousness to do reliable work in predictive astrology. The following dated quatrain is a perfect example of the dramatic chain of events that shocked Florida residents and killed many innocent people. The celestial energies are unmistakable for a trained Astro-Psychologist and this profound acquired wisdom allowed me to unarguably predict the 911 terrorists attack in New York, the Asia tsunami, the Kobe earthquake, the Washington sniper dilemma, and every single major news development. My website is like a future version of CNN and with time, mankind will learn to decipher the cosmic forces at work in order to save precious lives.

> * All year, like the great Prophet Nostradamus, I write quatrains that unmistakably will estimate the future. Here is another sample pertaining to natural disasters. As mentioned numerous times on many of my radio and television programs, I do not predict anything! We all know that nature and the weather have a specific pattern; we all know that history tends to repeat itself and I know how to read the hieroglyphs of the universe. I speak the language of the Gods and unlike science, I have the natural ability to perceive the realm of super consciousness and it's transcending applications taking place on this dense physical world.

NEGATIVE DRAGON WINDOW FOR FEBRUARY *1st 2007

(*) Beginning/Ending of Important Portion of Life/Forced Relocation/ Destructive Weather.

Children Mothers Cry Home No More
Face Fear Nature Rules
Earth Water Fire Wind Scream
Changes Imposed Pray For Souls

Written by Dr. Turi 1/21/07

DRAGON EYE
AS PREDICTED ON COAST TO COAST!

02/02/07 - Florida storms kill at least 14
02/02/07 - Floods displace 200,000 in Jakarta kill 29

Man is superior to the stars if he lives in the power of superior wisdom. Such a person being the master over heaven and earth, by means of his will, is a magus, and magic is not sorcery, but supreme wisdom. ~ Paracelsus

The Law of Magnetism

The Law of Magnetism

* The "**Law of Magnetism**" relates to your center of attraction. It is possible to enhance your Animal Magnetism and this will will help you attract what you desire. A healthy body, mind and spirit will allow the energy to flow, and you will draw like people to yourself. Believe you are worth what it is you want to attract and take care of yourself. Belief alone is not enough - you must also act. The following are tips to improve your health and raise your magnetism.

First stop ingesting drugs and aim for homeopathic healing. Before I begin I must state that no one is to go off his medication and must consult his doctor, before undergoing any kind of change. The following information is meant to supplement health and bring more magnetism to you, not as a substitute. The constant battle between people's common sense and doctors' ignorance of natural cures is still raging. Back in 2005 the FDA announced the nasty sides effects of the arthritis painkiller Celebrex (and all other drugs on the market without any exception, I may add!). * Also, Vioxx has just been removed and Aleve is in question. How many times have you heard this type of news? But who cares? After all, you pay good money for it and your outrageous pricey insurance will cover the deadly cocktail. Someone has to maintain the DRUGLORDS' (the pharmaceutical companies) outlandish lifestyles, never mind if it impoverishes your family's resources. You are just a commodity and what really gets me, is that some are naive to be test candidates for their bodies, minds, and spirits. There are those who respond to deceptive radio and television advertisements for better lifestyle free from pain, if they "try" the lethal product under the doctor's "all knowing" supervision.

The scientific community is well aware of the serious damage any new drug can and will inflict on the human "guinea pigs." You will never, ever see any of those scientists testing their own drugs! Someone like Marie Curie was a real scientist with genuine integrity. She injected herself with some vaccines she made and of course, died in the process. The well-established, wealthy pharmaceutical corporations cleverly hide their self-seeking financial motivations behind the words science and research. New names are formulated daily to classify the new deadly medicines, and even new "dis-eases" are cleverly created, so the medicines can be sold as valuable healing products to the uneducated, trusting masses. The statistics are real and don't lie. Licensed medical surgeons and doctors will kill over 1 million people each year in hospitals all over the US due to medical mistakes, wrong diagnosis involving blood transfusions, toxic drugs, and surgical errors. That adds up to more losses in human lives than all the combined wars this great country ever suffered. With such a nasty cocktail in your blood stream, do not expect to bring more magnetism to you.

I really see the medical field failing miserably in some areas, as there are more deaths by cancer and heart attacks nowadays, then a decade ago. Over one million US citizens have and will die of those plagues each year. Your doctors will make you believe they can fix your disease or poison it out of your body with drugs or surgery. More must be known, so that we stay healthy and do not contract these diseases in the first place. In reality, you are far from healing yourself, but receiving only a quick and financially exorbitant fix. In 2004 the FDA advised doctors to consider "alternative therapy" to Celebrex. The same warning came for Naproxen after federal researchers found an increased number of heart attacks and strokes among users. Incredibly, an independent study on Vioxx found the drug doubled the incidence of heart attacks and strokes among patients taking it to prevent colon polyps that cause cancer. If your system is loaded with fat, drugs, pot, alcohol and doctor prescriptions, you are on your way to your tomb. More FDA advice came on a daily basis, issuing warnings about a multitude of side effects produced by new drugs. This is totally ridiculous and very dangerous to your health. There are so many stocks investments in the pharmaceutical industry that would hurt the pockets of those CEOs who don't really care about you and your health, but your money. Pfizer Inc. said it had no plans to pull the popular painkiller Celebrex off the market, despite data showing that patients using the drug in a long-term cancer study, had more than double the risk of a heart attack. Does this comment say something about true abuse, power, greed and money?

All drugs are lethal to your body; Celebrex was approved by the Food and Drug Administration in 1998 for arthritis pain, and has been prescribed to thirty million Americans and is the world's most widely prescribed arthritis drug. I can guarantee you that out of those million people, a great portion will suffer and die from the side effects of Celebrex. In the long run, the drug will be worse than the arthritis itself and will shorten your lives. If you suffer arthritis pain, simply perform the hot and cold therapy in your shower for a few minutes each day and see the results after a while. If you ever come to any of my lectures I will teach you all sorts of Cabalistic natural healing that will save you a lot of money and enjoy a better life, altogether. If you suffer back, neck, or joint problems, I will show you how to benefit from this rare wisdom. There won't be any side effects, because I do not prescribe dangerous drugs. I will help you to build more magnetism, recognize and tap on your own subconscious healing forces, and educate you with natural exercises and a natural diet. All doctors in all hospitals use the same book of diagnosis and prognosis. You do not need to be educated in medicinal terminology, to name drugs and diseases. It is cerebral jargon designed to make you look inferior, because you can't read or pronounce the words correctly. Simplicity doesn't work too well with those overly educated nerds born with great memories, but not much straightforward common sense. You have been conditioned to accept and suffer a cold every winter season and it becomes an epidemic of enormous proportion. Before cleansing my own filters and boosting my immune system, I used to catch colds every year.

I knew by listening to my intuition that somewhere, somehow, I was not doing the right thing and I was determined to find out. I put all my efforts to freeing myself from all my bad habits and "re-birth" myself, into a wiser educated person. I used to be one of those miserable patients, coughing, sneezing, with hot and cold fevers victimized by influenza. I used to sit in the doctor's office with others feeling terrible, hoping for antibiotics to bring me back to a normal life. When I learned that the cold virus couldn't be eradicated from my system with antibiotics, I made the choice to stop wasting my time and my money. This is where I decided to make a difference by making radical changes in my diet and my attitude that would provide me with a stronger immune system. A magnet will not attract a piece of wood, if you want to become healthier and more magnetic you must understand and use "**The Law of Magnetism**". Start by cleansing your entire body of all its poisonous junk. If you keep ingesting antidepressants, drugs, alcohol, or cigarette smoke in your body, the only thing you will attract is death.

· Americans get 1 billion colds and flu annually and those numbers are growing drastically.
· 40,000 Americans die every year because of the flu with no end in sight.
· 200,000 more are hospitalized each year because of the flu and more each year.
· Three out of five Americans get the flu every year and nothing will change those numbers.

The numbers are undisputable and influenza kills more than breast or prostate Cancer. Just a few years ago, a vaccine shortage panicked America, because 48 million doses were contaminated and declared unsafe and finally banned. What a good way to insert fears and make you run to get those shots. The FDA, like the church Inc. are adept in stimulating fear to tap on the human survival instinct, to get deeper into your pocket. As proof mounts against the flu vaccine toxicity, I never got inoculated because those companies are aware of the danger and the worthlessness of their products and sell them to the public, anyway. The fact is that throughout history, no influenza virus blend has ever repeated itself, and no virus is the same each year or will ever be the same. These viruses shift and mutate into completely different organisms each time. The reality is that pharmaceutical corporations are making billions of dollars manufacturing the products. Over the years, hospitalizations and deaths from influenza have increased 100% and it's obvious that the flu shot did not, does not, and will never work.

What are the ingredients making up the flu shots?

· Carbolic Acid (poison) Ethylene Glycol (anti-freeze)
· Carbolic Acid (poison)
· Formaldehyde (causes Cancer)
· Aluminum (associated with Alzheimer's disease)
· Mercury (destroys immune cells)

Do you really want to bring more magnetism to you? The answer is simple:

· Don't poison yourself with chemicals
· Change your attitude, and trust the vision of a new you
· Stop bad habits immediately and stop doing what kills you
· Don't eat anything lifeless and stay with nature
· Be active and bring more circulation and elimination in your system

Do progressive mental gymnastics, as knowledge is power and mastering all the Universal Laws will work for you. Use common sense - Put a rose seed in the ground and in a few months that small seed will produce a beautiful flower, full of life. Plant vegetables or fruits and collect and eat organic food, for a better health. Now, put a hot dog or a burger in the ground and don't expect much life to come out of it in the future.

Animal fat consumption, in time will plug your arteries and induce heart attack. Many people fool themselves, thinking they are eating healthy when eating boiled vegetables. During the war the population was advised to drink only boiled water to kill all bacteria. Any time you bring water to a boil, you kill germs and also destroy all healing properties found in vegetables. Instead, clean all your vegetables thoroughly, by adding some vinegar to the water, then rinse them and put them in your pot and never bring the water to boil. Steaming is also an effective and healthy way to cook vegetables. You may also cook them without any water at all. Simply, put them in your pan covered, on the lowest heat possible and let them cook slowly for as long as it takes. The natural moisture in the vegetable will be drawn out to steam them. Simply, stop doing what kills you and build a better healthy lifestyle and free yourself from any diseases, naturally. Bring yourself to purity, to health and accede tons of magnetism. Fast service, fast expectation or watching a movie will not help you, stop being in denial and work intelligently by gathering the right information. Don't stuff yourself with French fries and

McDonalds, because the only thing you will attract fast is a terminal disease.

Getting Rid of Colds:

Try this, the next time you feel like you are getting a cold and if you do it right, you will be spared. Cook your favorite soup and dice a full glove of garlic and an entire onion (preferably organic). I know your breath will stink for a while, but who cares, you don't want to be in public anyway. If you are in a relationship, ask your partner to ingest a slice of bread covered with butter and garlic, too. This way he/she will not smell the garlic in your breath and you will be able to French kiss without problems. You will also offer the real option to save your partner from influenza. You will probably hate me during the night as a burning sensation in your throat may keep you awake. The garlic and onion's vapor acts as natural antibiotics and will "burn away" the virus in your lungs and esophagus. Repeat this magical disgusting, but healing concoction as needed.

For Smokers:

Again you may be in denial, but don't expect to passionately kiss your fancy, if he or she doesn't smoke. No one will willingly kiss an ashtray or anyone with bad breath. Your weakness is your downfall and if you want to be attractive, then you must apply your will.

· How long can you stay without food?
· How long can you stay without water?
· How long can you stay without air?

Your lungs are the most important organs in your body, why would you ruin them? You cannot order another set, if they fail to function properly by butchering them with cigarettes. Your lungs transport oxygen to your heart, which is distributed to all vital parts of your body. Now, if I ask you why you smoke, you may say, "I like it or it makes me feel more relaxed". The fact is that you are in denial and hooked to harmful chemicals that will induce cancer and kill you, if you keep smoking. Meanwhile, if you listen to that little voice inside you (and it never lies to you) it would say, "I really should stop smoking, because I know it will kill me." Well, I was also a smoker and my little voice used to say, "Hey moron, when will you stop smoking…do it right now, you are killing yourself. Don't lie to yourself and listen to yourself because you know (*the little voice) I am right". So for your own sake, if you smoke, listen to reason right now, stop and make the changes that will keep you alive for many more years. In my case, the most successful method to stop smoking is to quit 'cold turkey', you will stay clean and never start again. If you have tried and failed, keep trying again, it took me several tries, but eventually you will free yourself from nicotine addiction.

Besides maintaining a healthy immune system, how can you avoid colds and the flu? Well, believe it or not, the most effective means is to wash your hands frequently, especially before eating and don't touch your face. The germs are spread through touch (unless you receive a direct cough from someone). When you put gas in your car or to the grocery store wipe all handles; carry wipes in your car, so that you can clean your hands after being in a public place. They did an experiment in a public school with young children. They were taught to wash their hands for a full minute, at several intervals during the day. This reduced the rate of colds and flu by half with this group of children.

Your attitude will also play a very important part of staying healthy. Constant depressions insecurity, fears or guilt poison your body, mind and soul and neutralize your immune system. You may also be the recipient of psychic influences generated by vengeful people or victimized by low entities from the astral plane. A few hours session in my Cabalistic Healing Room will take care of you, but my techniques and disciplines cannot be fully explained in this book. I can guarantee this rare methodology will take care of you, much better than any drugs or prescriptions made by your mental health professionals.

If you want to bring more magnetism to you, stay natural, use homeopathic medicine, and you will enjoy a healthier and longer life. Your overly educated doctors have lost the very essence of the art of healing naturally and won't spend much time in their busy office connecting with you from the heart. Your doctor has no time to spare with a packed waiting room with sick people trusting his medicinal education. Doctors are committed to help people, but are reluctant to investigate preventative natural medicines. Drug companies offer them with tons of free samples to pass out to their patients and note the symptoms with a secret financial deal from the drug company. Accept the fact, this is a business deal and like organized religion, aimed to tap into your resources.

You have been made in the image of God and created as a God, you have also inherited healing powers and you need to recognize this blessing. You were born to unleash and own this power of creation, attraction and healing naturally. This is why your future is nothing more than the reincarnation of your thoughts. You have a choice use your will, ascend towards wisdom, and bring health and magnetism to your life. Feel the power, enjoy total health, true happiness, success, security, and love and free yourself from the forces of evil. You will get more magnetism and build a stronger immune system as you regularly practice the:

Natural 'Blood Transfusion':

Juice & Blend the following Items:
· Beetroot
· Celery
· Apples
· Carrots
· Oranges

Add a spoon of unsulphured molasses; I can guarantee you that not only you will look much younger and healthier, but also your magnetism will increase drastically, if you stay the course. This natural cheap recipe will upgrade both your physical and spiritual vibrations. I am extremely popular, very magnetic, and I use every Universal Law accordingly. This formula increases the Seat of Attraction between human beings, while losing unwanted pounds. In time without expensive and dangerous surgery, your stomach will shrink in size, while your appetite will distinctly decrease. All my friends are telling me how great, healthy, and younger I look, thus I am a full example and result of my own teachings. It is a proven fact that a positive attitude boosts both your immune and lymphatic systems and brings a surge of unquestionable energy in your being. Your brain generates neurons that directly affect the atomic structure of your entire being. Doctors are not bad people per say, some of my students who are surgeons have accomplished physical miracles with their patients and they are mostly logical, rational traditionally educated humans. I am a doctor of doctors; a teacher of teachers and my inner wisdom is not restricted to the physical realm of consciousness.

This straight-thinking logical scientific attitude gave rise to traditional disciplines and brought about today's health margins and serious limitations, by revoking the power of the divine. Over the years, man's "scholarly" ego took over by challenging natural laws dictated by nature, and blurred doctors' common sense. Your physician undoubtedly gives you his best, but "his best" may not be in your greatest interest and that's where you and your doctor differ. By educating you on your habit, your options for more magnetism, I will make a powerful difference in understanding and using "The Law Of Magnetism" to the maximum.

Healing With The Subconscious:

Back in 1998 during one of my numerous conferences I was walking through the lobby of the prestigious Hilton hotel in Los Angeles. Then all of a sudden I felt a crucifying pain coming from my right hip and simply fell on the floor. Many worried people came to my rescue but I begged them not to touch me and after a few minutes the emergency crew were surrounding me. They asked me a few questions from medical prescriptions to heart problem wondering what my problem was. Just a few months earlier I experienced the same dilemma while riding my bicycle with my wife Brigitte along the La Jolla sea front. I also told them that the pain had subsided and I was able to walk back home. I was expecting the same and against their recommendation I refused to be taken to the emergency room. I was right but the few motionless minutes spent on my back seemed like an eternity. I asked for some painkiller to ease the remaining pain without success refusing to give me anything that could "jeopardize" their actions. I knew I was going to be able to walk very slowly again and politely asked them to help me to sit on the nearby sofa waiting for Brigitte to "rescue" me. I was offered some water and after a while stud up and walked on my own.

The pain was very intense, but manageable and we were allowed to go our way. Brigitte was worried sick and begged me to seek medical attention as soon as we back home or the very next day. I called my local doctor and made an appointment, he was perplexed and he suggested me to take X-rays and come back with the radiology results. I also explained to him as a child I spent countless hours shoveling, helping my stepfather to launch his construction business. I mentioned also that many years as a heavy equipment operator may have contributed and made my situation much worse. My instinct was telling me that my fragile pelvis took a serious hit and the many years operating machineries was the only reason for my deteriorating hip situation and accompanying pain. I came back a few days later looking at my twisted pelvis demonstrating arthritis in my right hip. The radiographic exam concluded a mild early arthritis, but I knew the diagnostic was much more serious and indeed wrong. I challenged the doctor with my usual common sense explaining that my symptoms were much worse than the radiographic findings, but he responded not being able to assess my symptoms more accurately without a MRI. He prescribed me with Voltaren to ease the pain, but I never ingested the medication. Before leaving his office we also discussed the indication for a hip replacement surgical procedure. Not only I could not afford the expensive procedures, but also I knew I could "fix" myself my own way, and I did!

I went to bed that night begging my subconscious to give me the right course of action. I literally went inside my own hip spiritually and saw an invading army of skeletons riding black horses. I decided to become the leader of a powerful army of angels riding white horses and begin a mental fight to stop the deterioration of my right hip. I kept submitting constructive and healing thoughts, visualizing a healthy bone and cartilage and to my surprise slowly but surely, the pain subsided.

I tested myself for flexibility by putting my chin against my chest and slowly began bending forward with both my hands on my legs, just above my knees.

I could barely bend past my knees and my back pain was intolerable. I was as pliable as an old tree and I knew if I cold bring back elasticity and extend my back muscles I would somehow "release" some of the stress in my pelvis and my hips. My subconscious was giving me full speed information and I faithfully acted upon it. The pain was unendurable, but I thought of regaining elasticity with those exercises under a nearly boiling hot water shower. The roasting pain felt on my entire back made it easier for me not to focus on my right hip and the "trick" worked its magic. I would do absolutely anything to get rid of my pain and heal my body and I knew I was on the right track. I did some hydrotherapy and turned the water from boiling hot to freezing cold and again the shock helped to take away the pain (and my mind) from my right hip. I kept practicing the homeopathic avenue for months at the time and inch by inch regained full elasticity in my back and lost all pain. I now can bend my entire body without effort and touch both the tip of my toes, something that was totally out of question only a few months earlier. Doing so was the right thing that brought my pelvis and my hips in good working condition without ingesting harmful prescription or undergoing surgery. Look into your subconscious, ask for help and take it's suggestions and you will be surprised by the results.

---

* What I really did was to strongly subjugate my subconscious to guide me into certain actions that would ultimately bring my health back. With the right food and the right action, there is nothing your body cannot fix on its own. All diseases are preventable and any damage to the body can be repaired with your subconscious, you only have to mean business when demanding for answers and apply your will all along. Many people have spent fortunes to better themselves and even though in certain cases medical procedures seems to be the only way, there are exceptions, I am one of them.

As you all know, I am also a Clinical Hypnotherapist and over the years I realize how little is known of both the Subconscious' and the Supraconcious' huge productive forces. When I arrived in the US, back in 1984, I was totally destitute with no friends, no social security, literally homeless, and only $50 left in my pocket. Yet, today I enjoy the true American dream; I achieved worldwide fame, I own my own publishing company, and I am also included in "Whose Who" in America. I have been on all major radio and television programs, I enjoy very famous friends, I drive a red convertible Corvette, sail my boat, enjoy my two Dobermans (Draco & Tessa), and both of my Cats (Cesar and Blacko). I am also, financially and spiritually secure and this is just the beginning. More fantastic opportunities are coming everyday and many of my friends call me, The Luckiest Man on Earth.

Friends

Gary Bussey and I in my Corvette

In my Boat

With Dr. Leir and Jordan Maxwell

With Host of Coast to Coast Am, George Noorey

With Actor, Peter Fonda

From left to right: Jim Karol, Miko Brando , Gary Busey,
Bryant McGill, Jon Lovitz and myself

William McNamara, Actor

Dean Haglund, Actor from X-Files

Scott, the 'Human Calculator'

Tom Danheiser (Coast to Coast), Dr. Leir and I in Vegas

My Doberman, Draco

'Famous Host' Pat MacMahon at KTAR in Phoenix

I enjoy tremendous popularity wherever I go and the most beautiful girls in the world flock around me. I own beautiful animals but what makes me who I am and why? For those students, clients, and close friends that know me well, my motto has always been. "Your future is nothing more than the reincarnation of your thoughts." Remember that ignorance is evil while knowledge is power. Unfortunately, everyday I receive tons of emails, faxes; letters, telephone calls from all over the world and a good chunk of those messages are from desperate people. Many of these souls are suffering depression following dramatic experiences and some at the brink of suicide. Losing a loved one, a pet, a job, your health, hope, security, a large amount of money, or suffering rejection are a serious matters that can start slow but brutal mental and physical decay. Most of the time and unknown to the victim, the Dragon's Tail will enforce the terrible experience for specific karmic purpose and/or for your own growing process but nevertheless, the deep psychological changes are extremely painful.

You may wonder how would I know how you really feel inside? Well guess what, I come from hell myself, I have been there and this allows me to be compassionate to your suffering. I was in the street at the age of 12 with no one to look after me, since my father had died a year earlier. With eight other brothers and sisters, Mom could never take care of such a large family on her own, especially after WW2, when food was scarce.

What is it that I did not experience; tell me?

* Death?
* Trauma?
* Starvation?
* Cold?
* Insecurity?
* Loneliness?
* Despair?
* Destitution?
* Sickness?
* Guilt?

Just name it, been there, done that! And its because I have walked in your shoes that I can help you. That is if you are willing to help yourself, because NO ONE but ME, helped me to become who I am today. Trust me, I do appreciate all the luxury and all the blessings life offers me today, just because I came from hell. Four times I have even experienced the incredible with ETs and their crafts that any skeptical mind could never comprehend. But again, a magnet will never attract a piece of wood and those low vibrating souls could NEVER exert a pull on such encounters. Am I a chosen one? Not at all or if I am, I don't know it yet.

The Rest of the Secret

This little test I developed is based on your inner ability to manifest your own reality, where the objective is to establish emotional, financial and spiritual stability in your life or even attract the incredible. First clean up your environment by doing a thorough "Cabalistic Candle Ritual Cleansing" as to get rid of all negative energy inside and outside of yourself.

Everything around you is made of vibrations, they can be regenerative or harmful, thus be aware of the type of influences you bring home through your television set. Do you feel angry after watching any programs? Do you know what kind of energy is cloaked in your house or apartment? Did someone get sick for a long period of time or die there? Do you have a weird feeling in any of the rooms or the basement? Do you or your children sleep well in this house? Are you happy living there? Are your dreams nightmarish or happy? Did any of your pets get lost or die in this house? Is your home stressful with lots of yelling and screaming? If this is the case, you better clean this house thoughtfully and as soon as possible. Make a habit of listening to peaceful soft music. Like the sound of scraping nails, rock, rap, or pop music will scratch your etheric body and muddle your state of mind. Gang-bangers and skinheads feed on that upsetting Martian energy and lose all sense of control of the body, mind, and soul. Sadly like the drug industry, the music industry doesn't know and doesn't care about the impact left on your teen's psyche, as long as the "music" sells. During my days, music was harmonious and singers were singing, not talking fast like crazy parrots. The worst energy of a "low life" criminal generation abusing sex and drugs, musically represents its major influence sucking the youngest members of the US society. This nefarious beat and appalling lyrics feed a "Pluto in Scorpio" or the "Death Wish Generation" Children. The results are terrifying with a raging number of kids using drugs, becoming criminals or committing suicide. But this is capitalist America where children are the growing victims of an unconcerned consuming society controlled by wealthy corporations. It is not surprising for this younger victimized generation to feel an urgent need to "escape" this polluted world. Changing the "vibrations" through education and returning to a pure art form without evil influence would bring back sanity and hopes to the children of tomorrow. I am wondering if it is too late for those children and can only hope for my message to reach those who can be "saved" by urging them to start the healing process. Armies are trained to kill, marched at the sound and beat of Mars; children need angelic, peaceful and loving sounds, but many of them can only subconsciously associate to the dreadful energy as a form of rebellion against their own mental decay and future extermination.

Invest in beautiful living plants and rearrange your home with light pleasant colors and Feng Shui your environment by getting rid of anything dead. Play soft music at all times and make sure to have all bulbs and electronic equipment, including all your clocks in the house and car in good working order. Remember, a clean and organized environment is a clear representation of a sharp and positive state of mind. If you cannot keep a plant alive for long, your energy may be low or negative and you must do all you can to correct the problem by removing the sucking energy. Use your intuition to find who or what it is and remove it. These are your first steps to establish the atmosphere of serenity needed to work on your own soul. A messy or stressful environment must be cleared before starting any spiritual work. In other words, don't try meditating in the middle of a busy smoky highway, you have to find the time and place where you can be at peace. Once this first step is established, you will naturally be inspired and ready to deal with the spiritual world.

Like vampires, dark spirits strive to take residence in your mind and steal your soul and your body. Evil can only survive in your home, if you feed it and wicked spirits are always starving. The only way evil can survive is by constantly nurturing all your fears, sins, and guilt and soon this nefarious soup will shut down your immune system and open the door to a multitude of diseases. Before any spiritual endeavors, you must clean both the physical and spiritual world with a powerful cabalistic candle ritual. This cleansing must be performed after the New Moon for more intensity. Is it witchcraft? Yes it is, but there is more danger in your perception of the word itself, than in the witch in you. There are bad witches who strive to control the forces of nature and the "Universal Cosmic Code" to hurt and control others for selfish ends and they are good white witches that practice the craft to heal and help others. A witch is perceived in France, as a wise Lady with great mystical powers and noble talents, but USA a country built upon puritanical principles and a politically oriented church repressing any form of spiritual growth, has cursed the true meaning of the craft for centuries. Do not worry about going to hell by practicing "witchcraft" because you already are in hell, this is a harsh learning ground, where your pain and misery are the results of your fears and ignorance.

About the FDA

Incidentally one of my major predictions for March 2007 took place. It involved the FDA and the damage inflicted to a drugged nation. Note also those predictions were printed in both my 2005 and 2006 Moon Power books.

Prediction # 18 (2007) - Dramatic news involving pharmaceutical corporations in March and September 2007

Prediction # 8 (2006) - Full restructure of the pharmaceutical companies, legal battles due to bad medications.

I strongly recommend all my readers to visit my website www.drturi.com. From there scroll down to this banner entitled " SOS To The World" and take the time to read what I wrote years ago about drugs and Neptune "The Lord Of Deception." Doing so may safe your life.

Sadly, using any type of drugs can only invite lower entities from the astral plane, which leads to "possessions" and heavy bad luck. Phobias induced by fear will also keep growing and interact with your subconscious and will adversely affect your physical and spiritual atomic structure. This means you could suffer a lack of enthusiasm, deep depression, insecurity, lack of self-esteem, and the feeling of being trapped in a body with no energy and with no drive. These "entities" endlessly suck your life force away and subdue your creative forces and hurt your body, mind and soul making your life misery. Not knowing about metaphysics or the subconscious' inner forces interacting with your UCI, your psychologist or psychiatrist can only rely on drugs to "fix" your problems. The reality is that this unawareness of the world of metaphysics will ultimately make your situation worse, turn you into a zombie, or even a killer as presented in "SOS To The World".

What are your options?

Get a Full Life reading and understand your divinity. Doing so will bring light to your purpose on this dense physical plain and bring you many answers. Work with the Universal Laws or pay the price of ignorance. If you are suffering psychic poisoning or feel you are under the influence of a nefarious spirit, your only option is to undergo a Full Cabalistic Healing. Fill up the form, and then call me at (602) 265-7667 for your appointment. By using powerful crystals, Indian rituals, and Nostradamus' rare Cabalistic Healing methodology, I will clean your body mind and soul after three or four hours of work.

Cabalistic Healing

A Revival of Nostradamus' Healing Techniques

CABALISTIC CANDLE RITUAL

Cleansing one's environment, body, mind and soul, is a must for true peace and happiness. You may use and enjoy the Cabalistic Candle Ritual and send it to those you care about. Instructions for cleansing your physical and spiritual selves: The Cabalistic Candle Ritual is designed to clear negative energy and should be performed after a dramatic experience such as the loss of a loved one, a lover, a pet, or any difficult mental or spiritual situation you find yourself going through. You may also use the Cabalistic Healing Ritual to remove negative thoughts incrusted in your apartment/home walls that could harm you by initiating a depressive mental process. Someone may have died in the house or suffered drastically and the thoughts could still be very much alive. This negative energy MUST be removed, if you want to feel good or sleep peacefully. The Cabalistic Candles Ritual is for removing basic negative energy only. Most severe cases of depressions, bad luck, bad health, possession by evil spirits, and negative entities can only be cured with a three to four hours Cabalistic Healing session in my healing room in Phoenix. The released negative energy is replaced by a dense umbilical cord of light connecting you directly from this dense world to the archetypal realm of consciousness with your guardian angel or a departed loved one. The transitions taking place with the Cabalistic Candle Ritual allows the departed soul to connect with you, as your personal guardian angel on this dense physical world where guilt, sadness, and pain are replaced with forgiveness, acceptance, love and peace of mind.

Purchase a white, green, and blue candle during the New Moon period (Waxing Moon) and always perform this ritual for the very first time during a New Moon trend. For best results, choose the first day of the New Moon or when the Moon rides your natal Dragon's Head. Before anything is started, grab a full hand of powdered salt with the left hand and turn clock wise, dropping the salt in a circle around the entire area where the ritual will be performed. The salt quartzes act like diamonds, reflecting light and all energies from the outside world. Do the candle ritual inside the circle of protection only. This ritual has tremendous power and will clean the inside and outside of your house. Arrange the candles in a triangle. At the tip of the triangle (farthest away from you) place the white candle. The green will be to your left and the blue to your right. The green and blue candles form the base of the pyramid. You will stand and operate behind it. A small bit of incense is placed in the center--any type of incense will do.

If you do not have a protective figure in your possession, you may buy a Guardian Angel (after the New Moon only) and place it in front of the white candle. You may also use the picture of someone you cherish that has gone on to the other side and place it in front of the Guardian Angel. Chances are this person is your protector. First light the incense, then the white candle, the green candle, and lastly, the blue candle. One inch of incense is more than enough to last for the duration of the ritual. The prayer or meditation is made for the length of time the incense is burning. The candles themselves (Fire) the mix of the colors and the smoke from the incense create a vacuum funnel right into the Supraconcious in time and space and reach the entity's protective spirit. This spirit will grant any of your wishes and will protect you in any situation. Pray intensely and use your power of visualization. When the incense is burnt, the ritual is over and you can extinguish the candles. You may repeat this ritual anytime you choose thereafter, before or after a New Moon. Very often, following the Cabalistic Candles Ritual, the intuition or the dreams becomes clearer and should be used as guidance. The ritual should be performed under the protection of a Guardian Angel that will bring luck, good news and protection to the soul from any low astral plane enti- ties. If you cannot sleep well, if you are distressed or often depressed, chances are you could be "invaded/infected" and this ritual becomes a must, for your mental and physical health.

The Law of Focus

Consciously think about a specific wish, just for a few minutes per day. Do not confuse your subconscious by becoming a "Jack of all Trades" in your mind. Re- view your intention and remember your subconscious doesn't know what's right or wrong and focus your creative conscious energy on the positive outcome, only. Don't pray, hope, ask, or ever doubt. DEMAND your wish to be granted and if you do mean business, in time your desires will manifest. The goal is to keep our thoughts consciously focused on manifesting what you want, while minimizing divergent thoughts (such as "I am foolish to believe in this" or "it won't work", etc.).

- The power of focusing, combined with your imagination must be developed.
- Focus your thoughts on the goal of attracting all your wishes and wealth, in a

way that serves others, too.
- There is nothing you cannot be or do, have faith.
- There's nothing to lose other than investing some of your time each day, holding the intention.
- There is a Supraconscious effect to this test and you can only succeed if you mean business.
- The subconscious effect is very real and you must believe this fact.
- Remember to follow your intentions with action because body, mind and spirit must all be one.

Thoughts are electric in nature and they are very magnetic. In time and space your thoughts become a laser beam. Passing through the thickest concrete walls, reaching and attracting the people that can help you build your future and bring you love. To reinforce your faith, you may have to educate yourself on how the Universal Code shaped your twelfth house, which rules your subconscious.

If you have been "practicing" depression for many years and find yourself unhappy, unhealthy, unsuccessful, unloved, scared with no self-esteem, or constantly depressed; do not expect to fix your problem in five minutes. If you want to fly (free yourself) as high as the astronauts, you will have to invest some time learning to pilot the shuttle (your life) and learn all aeronautical rules (your connection with the Universal Mind and your subconscious). There is an old saying, "Give what you need." Or – practice that which you want to achieve.

There is no magic wand, deities, or religion that will help you. Only YOU can help yourself because whether you accept it or not, you have been made in the Image of God. You must acknowledge your Divinity and the reality that you are a God in training, learning to direct your thoughts on this dense physical world.

- Will you challenge yourself?
- Will you cast aside your fears?
- Will you raise your own vibration?
- Will you aim for your Godly powers?
- Will you accept the new challenges?
- Will you take a chance on the new you?
- Will you re-evaluate your philosophy?
- Will you get off the pit of religious poisoning?
- Will you take a chance on your new way of thinking?

If you do so, then a new light and a new life will be yours, because mastering the Divine is the key. You have been taught since you are a child to respect the laws of men and all his books, (science and religions), now I will teach you many Universal laws written in light through God's Universal Code. "And God created the earth and heaven and signs" for interpretation, so that you can live a safe and more productive life. You are not going to hell; I already told you, hell is here on earth, in your own fears, ignorance, and the darkness of despair. God did not and will not punish me by healing you, educating you, and helping you; just the opposite may I add. Trust me to shed some light in your existence and be ready to invest in your future, because you have the right and the power to do so. In all practicality, the worst thing you can do for yourself is to expect to bring all those marvelous changes in your life and change nothing about you or your education. That is an unquestionable failure and you are getting stuck in the pit of illusion and deception, hoping for Allah or Jesus (or Elvis) or a sixty minute positively turbo charged movie production to do it for you.

I have a problem with stupidity and I will not compromise in exposing the facts, because I am true to myself and to you.

* Do you really want a better life?
* Do you really want love?
* Do you really want money?
* Do you really want happiness?
* Do you really want success?
* Do you really want security?
* Do you really want fulfillment
* Do you really want a better health?
* Do you really want a new you?

If your attitude stinks, your life will too and you must die to who you are...

* With all your limitations
* With all your fears
* With all your ignorance
* With all your depressions
* With all your bad thoughts

...and be born again; updated, upgraded, and advanced from an old obsolete computer to a powerful brand new technology. Your subconscious marvelous creative force is the essence of your ingenious mind and its limitless imagination. Do you want to enjoy a better life, like I do and be blessed with it all? Here is the deal!

* Build your cosmic consciousness
* Understand and use your subconscious creative forces
* Don't sleep through life (you'll have plenty time to do so, when you die)

* Challenge yourself with education
* Take chances and make decisions
* Have faith and most of all listen to your intuition
* Use your subconscious at your own advantage.

These words of advice are clear and simple explain it all.

* Watch your thoughts; they become your words.
* Watch your words; they become your actions.
* Watch your actions; they become your habits.
* Watch your habits; they become your character.
* Watch your character for it will become your destiny.

How to deal with Rejection

With the statistics pointing out to more than 50% of relationships ending in failure, many will have to experience one of the most difficult emotional states dealing with invalidation of who we are. Rejection may come from many sources and some of those causes can be somewhat ridiculous for some, but seem terrible for others. Incidentally, the most common reason for rejection is a feeling of inadequacy and a fear of failure from your partner. Regardless of the reason your significant other is dropping you is still devastating to the ego. The list is endless, but let me mention a few reasons why you could be dropped.

* A lack of communication
* A lack of chemistry
* A lack of mental support
* A lack of sexual activity
* A lack of understanding
* A lack of good health
* A lack of spirituality

One must remember, that you can only perceive someone's view through your own senses, your own stars (UCI or Unique Celestial Identity) and most of all your education and experiences. Often, friends and family members may not agree with your love choice. Here are more reasons for them to do so.

* Ethnicity
* Age
* Status
* Education
* Wealth
* Past

Note, that your loved ones or close friends really believe what they preach and what they perceive as being good or bad for you. Most of the time, they are only seeing their own world and subconsciously projecting their own inner fears onto you. This is especially the case if the people are older and think they know better than you. Often a hidden jealousy can also support the fear of never finding love and "if I can't or may not find love, then why should you before me?" In some cases, fear and insecurity steers the behavior of a sibling for not supporting your relationship and risk a form of humiliation. For instance, "I am older than you are, thus I should marry before you," or insecurity such as "I can't let you spend too much time with your lover, he can't have you that much." The phobic reason for motivating someone to go a specific way is usually well hidden in his or her own subconscious. Your "benefactor" is totally unaware of the behind the scenes stimulus, but will be legitimately concerned for your welfare. In most of the cases, under the constant pressure and need to please others, the new "Psyche" predominates and leads to the decision-making. Just remember that because you have been dropped, doesn't mean your partner is having a good time doing so. The question is that he/she now has to deal with GUILT, especially if you did not do anything wrong to them and behaved intelligently and lovingly all along the duration of your relationship.

Often one of the partners may choose to lie to avoid hurting the person's feelings directly. A forced separation or meeting/dealing with a nice new person brings a myriad of new feelings and puts the weak relationship in jeopardy. I know for sure any woman is set naturally to love and respect her lover almost immediately and only under specific circumstances would a woman decide to break up her relationships. Be sure that many questions arise to the mind of your lover before making the decision to let you go. Very often sleepless nights, confusion, tears, and a good dose of guilt are present. It feels like being caught in a sandwich, wondering who has to be hurt. What's your priority, you may ask yourself? Well, shall I make all those people that care so much for me happy? If I do so, they wont harass me anymore, as I have to live with them. And what about my lover now? How do I tell him/her that it's over? He/she never did anything wrong, but logically speaking, I must do the right thing. It's simply a nightmare for both parties and regardless of the reasons it's going to hurt both of you severely. In my crazy life, I have been on both sides of the scale and each time the profound wounds took months to heal. Because humans are machines of habits, the longer you stay in a relationship, the harder it is to break.

I firmly believe women should be treated with love and respect no matter what and I absolutely disapprove of any form of chauvinistic brutal attitude, regardless of the motivation. I know from experience that there is only a fine red line with any woman and once a man crosses this line, there is absolutely no return for the abuser. In the name of love or security, a woman can take a tremendous amount of abuse and stay in a harmful relationship for a very long period of time. Only when she has exhausted all her options will she finally free herself from the damaging relationship. This is a valuable argument and "dropping" her partner is a must.

However the situation changes if you are the good guy and feel victimized, or think of it as a deplorable injustice done to you. Once you collect yourself from the shock, a myriad of emotions and thoughts will have to be dealt with. If you are a bad person, simply "cry about it" and learn your lesson to treat your lover properly, and you simply deserve what happened to you. Grow up, behave decently, stop drinking or doing drugs, realize your mistakes, be responsible, work harder, and understand that people are not toys, but living feeling respectable souls. Some bullies wont take NO for an answer and will make some unlucky people's lives miserable with threats or long messages begging for forgiveness. In some extreme cases the police will be the only option to stop the nightmare.

If you think you are a "victim" then lets start the healing process.

*You will be in denial for a while and refuse all the facts.
* You will wonder why you have been dropped and your ego will be badly smashed.
*You will have many mixed emotions and in some cases become very resentful.
*You will "review" the movie many times, wondering what went wrong.
*You will hate all the people you may think are responsible for the break up.
*You will probably cry heavily and feel very sad and at times, totally empty.

In some cases, you will need spiritual help to regenerate your wounded spirit, but in no case addict yourself to antidepressants. (Read "SOS to the world" and realize the power of Neptune from my home page).

What to do and NOT to do:

Realize that your future is the reincarnation of your thoughts, thus the faster you change your thought process, the easier for the healing process to take place. Like a bad cigarette smoking habit that kills you, remove the mental poison from your body, mind, and spirit as soon as possible. If he or she makes a request for you not to call, simply do not. Respect their demands and be a better, stronger person. He or she will soon realize your emotional depth and how much you mean business in all you do, including your love. Keep in mind that it might be easier to win the lottery than to find genuine love. In the constant search for love, the people that have hurt you will ALWAYS remember they were once truly loved and this will be in itself, a forever reminder of the good thing they had thrown away. Avoid revisiting places where you went, as your subconscious will trigger painful memory by associations. Let me explain, if the person drives a specific car, you will immediately associate the car with the person. Your heartbreak will feel wretched, so don't put yourself in a situation where you could do damage to your psyche. Avoid listening to sad soft music, change rhythms. He or she asked you to move on, so do so. Like you, they are also having a hard time; don't think you are the only one with feelings.

Avoid drinking at all costs and avoid complaining to others. However, find a way to "relieve" yourself and regenerate. Get busy, go out, and meet new friends, for they will bring about your wishes and you can be sure of that. You are dying and rebirthing into a new person, thus get rid all that could remind you of that person. He/she must become a stranger to your life again. Undo the damage inflicted upon your body, mind, and spirit, as no one will help you really, but you. You are in charge and demand the Universe to bring you someone who will appreciate your priceless love and your gifts. I know it's hard to do at the early stages of a break, but your happiness depends on your thoughts and actions. Put all the pictures, presents, letters etc. in a box and then trash or put them away. Never ever ask for the presents you gave him/her and do not take anything away. Doing so gives away your insecurity or inner fear of being manipulated. Now if any of the parties keeps it all, there are still some deep feelings that must be dealt with and time is of the essence.

Do not nurture feelings of insecurity, resentment, and revenge; instead, rebuild your self-esteem. Exercise harder, become more magnetic, educate yourself more, be more competitive, take a chance, go out more, travel, and do all it takes to upgrade to a new, a better you. Any break up has always stimulated me to become much more and much better than I already am. This is why I always surpassed who I was, because I know who I am and what I have to offer and that is the best to that lucky girl. You are priceless and a beautiful human being and this person came into your life for a specific purpose. If you have to recall anything, simply be thankful for all the great times you had. This individual made you feel alive, wanted, and so special in so many ways and guess what? You are. How can you attract a new lover if you hate yourself? How can you ask for happiness if you are not happy, secure, and safe within? A magnet will not attract a piece of wood, you MUST upgrade your vibrations, love yourself more, and bring your vitality and magnetism to a much higher level. The right person for you is around the corner. Remember that life is a process of change and what happened is nothing more than a wish in disguise. He or she could not bring you what you really needed and truly wanted, so the Universal order made that decision for you, so take it, deal with it and be strong.

You may want someone more attractive, more spiritual, older, younger, smarter, wealthier, or simply dedicated to you, but most of all, someone that can recognize and appreciate the real you and your true love. This person did not see that in you or could not appreciate it, so why waste it? This world is loaded with great people, so allow yourself to be available to them now. What you have to offer is priceless and that is you. You are a beautiful, invaluable, unique human being destined to do miracles, enjoy true love, and the respect of all other human beings. You would never hurt anyone and you must only and truly offer your essence, your body, mind, and spirit for that special person only. Guess what, you may also be looking for your true soul mate and for sure she/he was not the one. But be happy because now you are free and can aim for that special person and reward him/her with the deepest, strongest and purest form of love a human being is able to offer another.

Be at peace with yourself, be happy with yourself, and trust your future, mostly because the universe knows better than you do and will always take care of you. Lastly, believe like I do and don't doubt that you can only find much better and in my case, it has proven to be right each time. Regardless of the reason involving a break up in the majority of cases, both partners somehow do suffer both emotionally and financially. If you are in a situation that could produce such an end, a comparison chart will shed light on the strengths and weaknesses involving your relationship. If you are a victim, then order a 90-minute Soul Cleansing tape (I will also give you a free 90-minute hypnotherapy tape) and let me recharge your batteries. If you are looking for true love, here is a poem I wrote for you. Memorize it and let the magical wonder of the Universe bless you with your wish.

I will Love You for Eternity

In the ocean of existence my wounded heart is reaching for your magic.
A tear of shade blinds my aspiration but just for the blink of an eye.
I know soon your loving heart and wise soul to be before me.
There is only but you, one bright star in the vastness of the universe.

Ultimate Wisdom

How can you expect the universe that you live within, to respect you when you do not respect the universes above and below yourself?" Let me explain this clearly to you. This is an old saying by Heraclitus: "As above, so below. All is Divine." As a god, you are responsible for your own universe because you are made from an infinity of worlds interacting with each other. In time and space you stand in your own parallel world learning that you are not alone, but are in a divine "connection" with the infinite. As a microcosm you reverberate at a certain speed and the "illusion" of this dense physical world becomes your only reality. What you don't know is that inside yourself there are canyons, mountains, oceans, cities, and pious souls praying for a better life and as their god, you are responsible for their welfare.

Let's try another approach. If you take the latest technology available to mankind and build the most powerful microscope ever to check on the human subatomic structure, you will see is a replica of our solar system. This is what science and metaphysics ultimately will uncover in time, but as you know, in my own right, I am ahead of them all. This is why it is so important to respect your divinity and build good healthy habits so worlds under you benefit from your consciousness and will. This chain of right behavior will be then passed above you to god himself and grant you health, happiness, and riches. Not many people will be able to assimilate or accept my findings just yet, but indeed it is the essence of the secret of what it means to be human.

Ultimate Wisdom

The **Laws of Ascending and Attunement**: Those two words mean, opening your heart and mind and connecting with your higher self. Adjust to the Universal Code where true peace and order resides and tune yourself to become one with God and recognize yourself as an ingenious God. With all the universal creative forces expenditures at your service, you will increase and refine your vibrations and melt into the divine. You will ascend and become one with the productive forces of your subconscious, where your own limitations are set by the law of karma. Metaphysical and celestial knowledge are the true ingredients that will convey the power to materialize all your wishes from the archetypal realm of consciousness.

Remember: "*Man is superior to the stars, if he lives in the power of superior wisdom. Such a person, being the master over heaven and earth by means of his will is a magus and magic is not sorcery but supreme wisdom.*"
— Paracelsus

The **Laws of Acceptance and Receiving**: Realize and accept that your future is nothing more than the reincarnation of your thoughts. Your wishes will be fulfilled when you accept this fact. The universe will manifest your demand if you clean your thought process of all fear and limitation. Use the Law of Focus and be firm in the realm of your imagination and your subconscious will bring it to you. Accept it mentally, with the fullness of all your being and you will be rewarded in time. You are a God in training on this dense physical manifestation, where all your thoughts will become your reality, if you work diligently. Many "terminal" souls are on earth teaching "younger souls" of their immortal nature and their god-given gift to create at will. In time and space your turn will come once you "retire" back home, to becomes a co-creator with God himself.

The **Laws of Choices and Desires**: A magnet will not attract a piece of wood and like attracts like. You have a choice; make the right choice for yourself. Avoid dwelling on your failures, past, and guilt, thus unconsciously becoming a magnet for pain and suffering. Choose to think positive, it's your choice and upgrade your vibrations by mastering "The Universal Code". Work to better your self, as gathering powerful knowledge brings hope and healthy thoughts. Choose the people with whom you deal, the circumstances you need, the best locations, and the right situations where all your wishes can become a reality. If you deal with potheads, drunks, and morons, your chances of success are very remote. . Without the right choices, you neutralize your desires, because your wishes can materialize if you socialize and deal with worthwhile friends. Generate a list of all you want; take the time to write it down in great detail to reinforce your choosing process. Make your choices and desires known to your subconscious and trust the creative forces that have created your own soul to act in your favor. Have faith in your choices and stimulate your desires at all times. Your road will be safer and you will be guided away from the crooked places and wicked people. Expect the equivalent for what you desire in a spiritual form first and this mental process will turn into your reality through unseen cosmic forces at work.

The **Laws of Having and Owning**: Be aware, accept and tune yourself to your desires. Once you have made a choice and believe, you already have it in your possession. If you really accept something or a person, you have put in motion an invisible law that is what you have accepted, even though in an invisible form. In time, it will come to you in its physical form and you must accept this fact. You have a wish and the Universal forces in action will give you fulfillment of that wish. Accepting and acknowledging a wish will shift energy from need to have. What you want may not be what you really need and once more, the universe knows better. So next time you are rejected from a person or a position, take it as a blessing instead of crucifying yourself and move on.

The **Laws of Visualizing and Hoping:** Train yourself to visualize all your dreams and hope to see them manifesting right in your life. When you use the visualizing powers of your mind, you are tuned and communicating to the Superconscious and the Universal Code. Like an unfolding movie, practice and control all the imagery, see yourself in the movie you created and feel the hope of being there now! Do not subjugate your subconscious with time or limitation and expect all your wishes to become a reality within a decent frame of time. See, feel, and hope yourself doing and having it all; create colors, flowers, bodies of water, people, angels, and sunlight and enjoy your creative world as an accomplished fact. You are creating your world, your reality, with your thoughts, by seeing it all in your mind.

The **Laws of Loving and Caring**: Never let yourself down; find, cherish, and love yourself! You have never, ever done anything wrong to you or the world, because karma does not apply when errors are made unwillingly or unconsciously. You are a child of the Universe and there are reasons for you to be, and a child always messes up, it is expected and pardoned immediately by God. Do not ever indulge your mind with guilty feelings to avoid poisoning your spirit. Visualize a better you and see in your mind's eye all the good you can offer the world. Love energy happens to be the most powerful drive in the universe, as love conquers it all. The more you love something or someone, the clearer the picture will become to your subconscious. True love unites the conscious, the subconscious, and Supraconcious within your own mind and magnificently represents the honorable drive and profound feeling behind your wishes to heal or help others. One night, I left my Corvette unattended

unattended in the parking lot, only to find out after my return that someone
had thrown a cigarette butt on my leather seat and spit on my windshield.
Never in millions of years, will such a person ever own a Corvette, because
his envious subconscious saw it as something he could never have.

The **Laws of Forgiving and Forgetting**: No one is perfect, laugh at
you and others people's weaknesses and be above any form of pettiness. Do
not criticize anyone, not even yourself, and when looking at you or others,
see both the physical and spiritual beauty you are aiming for. Let go and let
the universal laws above do the work and bring all you want in this world.
Surrender yourself to the forces of universal love, where forgiveness will free
your soul and body from any ailments. Surrender to a greater purpose, to a
higher degree of happiness than you could ever realize. Trust the Universal
Code and turn everything over to the Supraconcious in time and space. You
are far from being alone, not realizing yet, the incredible forces at work within
and above you. Do not poison your divine vision and limit your power with
the affairs of your past. You had your past, been there done that, move on. You
have NOW, and with it, the option to build a better tomorrow. Be thankful
to the universe. You are alive, you can feel, love, and be born human and
this is one of the greatest achievements your soul could ever accomplish for
himself. Enjoy being alive now, and make it a full time job to be happy. You are
a marvel of life in its entire splendor! Just realize how lucky you really are!

The **Laws of Speaking and Demanding**: If the future is the reincarnation
of your thoughts, then words are mighty things, be aware of all the terms
that come out of your mouth and the incredible process behind them. Each
one of your words causes a vibration in the universal energy field and you
gave birth to that energy. The law of effect will take place immediately, if you
create a wrong word and this "faux Pas" could be costly. These words vibrate
like you and will immediately return in accordance to fulfill the negative field
you created. Make sure to discipline your spirit at all times and clean up
dirty and nasty words out of your vocabulary. The impact upon others can be
devastative, creating a chain of nefarious energy you can live without. Stay clear
of any form of destructive judgment, as decree stimulates negative action and
reaction of the spirit. Be sure to use your words creatively and progressively
at all times, until it becomes a useful and worthwhile habit. Through your
spoken words, you let your good nature come forth and announce to yourself
and the universe that it is all done. Bringing purity into motion through the
good use of words becomes the groundwork for all your demands.

The **Laws of Common Sense and Reality**: This is a physical world where you must operate on a practical level, while understanding and using unseen mystical forces. Leaving all to the universe and God will not cut it; you have your celestial homework to do. The harsh reality is that this world is hell, this is the harsh unforgiving ground, where a mother will kill her children or a criminal will do serious damage to society. The forces you are so desperately trying to master and use, worked also for religiously poisoned souls and gave birth to the 911 terrorists attack in New York. Your subconscious is in charge of all your bodily functions and will work overtime to stop an infection and guide you from a higher dimension of comprehension. This unseen power has many names and referred as God or as terrorist acts, where the divine principles involved are not understood by men's mental limitations. The Law Of Duality involves all manifestations for Good or Evil and will impact our world; ignorance is true evil, in my book.

The **Laws of Perception and Intuition**: These laws become the vital ingredient to satisfy a thirst for knowledge and discovery to help and guide others. The Kobe earthquake for example, killed over 5000 people on January 1995 and man blames nature, not realizing the natural world and men are all under the jurisdiction of "The Universal Law Of The Moon" and "The Universal Code". God, Universal rules, and the Supraconcious are neutral and will not take sides or rationalize with the unaware uneducated earthy souls. A criminal or a vicious person can be successful; Successful in hurting you and the universe doesn't care, but be sure only the sealed karma will become the ultimate justice. The forces of evil are as powerful as the forces of light and your awareness of all the Universal laws in actions are very real, very solid, and often very painful for the victims. The universe and God will help you, if you "Ask and you shall receive" Supra-knowledge and true wisdom can be yours by mastering God's celestial tools and the working of the subconscious. This is why you have been attracted to my work, to teach you those laws.

The **Laws of Achievement and Action**s: You have the power to make the changes. You need to better your life, every day. Start now and step out into action, you have a position to reach or a dream to accomplish. You must do all that is required, both physically and spiritually and soon the universe will be working through you to perform all that is appointed for you to do. Make a goal to master "The Universal Code", become a beholder of God's universal tools, and utilize them through your actions and drive to serve others. Keep active and your actions will become your memorable achievements.

The **Laws of Gratitude and Thankfulness**: People from all walks of life have invested tremendous amounts of money looking for the true happiness and never found it. They are the unlucky onlookers who refused any opportunity to grow and surrendered to religious poisoning. Their demands were weak and could not attract advanced souls and spiritual exploration. Reading this material is a sure indication of your intense request to tune to a higher vibrational system. Your thirsty soul is reaching for Supra-knowledge and your subconscious brought my advanced teachings into your life. Be in tune with "The Universal Code" and build your cosmic consciousness and be grateful for the opportunity you have received. Your thankfulness is the driving forces to bring you more of this spiritual food. Gratitude releases a dynamic feeling of completeness and exerts a plenteousness influence in your life. Thank the universe and God for all the blessings you already have and become a connecting link to those in need for healing powers and Supra-knowledge.

"*Since the dawn of time, the Creator has shown his truth to the humble, a truth that is hidden from the vain blinded by worldly pleasures, but which is written in the skies, which nightly speaks of the glory of God.*"
—Nostradamus

Affirm Your Position to the Universe:

I'm not immobilized by my fear and I'm ready to make the necessary changes.

I recognize that my physical shell is just temporary and will always respect and honor my body.

I will build cosmic consciousness and master "The Universal Code" to serve others appropriately.

I will fulfill my soul's purpose and make a positive impact on the children of this world.

I will find my divinity and ascend into the stars, while loving and respecting the Creator.

Know Thyself:

I know that the undiluted power that created my soul is the essence of eternity.

I identify my soul to be a genuine part of the eternal spirit of light, love, and life.

I identify with the millions of people who honor and believe in God.

I know my study of the heavens will open a divine door to the undiluted truth.

I know mastering God's Universal Laws will transform my life for the better.

Transformation:
I will eliminate the weakness of my ego and subjugate its power over my self.
I recognize ignorance as the seed of all evil and love as the answer for peace.
I will work to become conscious of my own power to transform and grow.
I will work to bring to fruition the best of my celestial gifts unto others.
I will ascend to the heavens' mystery protected by the angels of light.

Changes:
I will honor my body, mind, and spirit as God intended for me to do.
I accept to raise my perception to all I am supposed to learn in my lifetime.
I ask for a much higher level of awareness and create my own reality.
I demand to change for the betterment of my life and the world around me

Pardoning:
I forget and forgive all the mistakes I made myself, for I am a human being.
I pardon all the young souls in training on this world and accept the lessons for myself.
I excuse ignorance and exonerate guilt from slowing down my own progress.
I will not blame my closest family members or dears friends for my own karma.
I am free from all prejudices and will enrich my own power to succeed.

Demanding:
I ask for guidance and peace of mind within my requests to grow one with the light.
I demand those I love to return the love and respect I unselfishly offer them and others.
I request higher spirits to guide my every move towards my own divine powers.
I apply for a new and more powerful spiritual identity by raising my own values.
I make a claim to reach for true wisdom and fulfill my purpose in this world.

Thanking:
I show gratitude to all the wise Spirits to hear and provide me with healing powers.
I appreciate all the unknown forces at work in all level of consciousness.
I recognize and accept all my experiences knowing all my wishes will be fulfilled.
I am thankful for the blessings of exploring my immortality and supremacy.
I am blessed and enthusiastic in mastering God's universal tools and helping others.

Dedication

- I devote my life and power to ascend towards the light and true wisdom.
- I lavish others with the infinite forces I am allowed to explore to serve others.
- I confirm my wish to get ample supply of healing power and wisdom for the world.
- I dedicate myself to Supra-knowledge for the well being of mankind and myself.
- I go forth with the knowledge and confidence to bring joy, peace and health to the world.

Cleansing the Soul of Enemies Within

The first enemy is Fear: The first enemy in anyone's life is fear, because we are not born with courage, yet neither are we born with fear. Fears breed powerful phobias that are brought on by dramatic experiences or by what someone you trusted has taught you. Some fears are valid and act as the inborn preservation instinct, such as walking alone in a bad part of town at two o'clock in the morning. But if you learn to avoid dangerous situations, you won't need to live in fear any longer. Fears, even the most basic ones, can totally destroy your ambitions and poison your entire life. Fear can destroy fortunes, destroy relationships, and if left unchecked, will destroy our life. Fear is one of the most powerful enemies lurking inside us. Induced religious fears (you're going to go to hell!) suffocate the spirit and happen to be the most common and deadliest of all. Let me tell you about five of the other enemies we face from within. The first enemy is indifference. What a tragic habit smoking really is, in time it will kill you. "Ho-hum, let it slide, I'll just drift along." Here's one problem with drifting: you can't drift your way to the top of the mountain and expect to survive. But you are drifting into Neptune's deceiving quick sands with your bad habits or with religious doctrines. Your spirit is frozen and your excuses are endless, I do not want to appear weird or upset my family, I'd rather drift along attitude is your worst enemy. What the majority of people accept as the truth doesn't mean it is and drifting with them will numb your spirit.

The second enemy is Indecision: Indecision is the thief of opportunity and enterprise. It will steal your chances for a better future or mastering a few Universal laws that could make the difference between success and failure in your life.

The third enemy is Doubt: Sure, there's room for healthy skepticism and you can't believe everything anyone will tells you. But you can't let doubt take over your creativity or drive to succeed. Many people doubt the past, doubt the future, doubt each other, doubt the government, doubt the possibilities, and doubt the power of the stars. Worst of all, they doubt themselves, because they were trained to do so or suffered a heavy Saturn (structure principle) in their UCI. Doubt will destroy your life and your chances of success, if you don't correct yourself. It will empty your mind body and spirit and hurt your heart. Doubt is a serious enemy that must be removed from your mind.

The fourth enemy within is Worry: We all worry now and then, but don't let it conquer your entire life and neutralize your actions. Instead, be aware and work against it, however in certain situations, worry can be useful. If you are dumb enough to drive through a red light and another car is coming your way, I would suggest you to worry about it. But you can't let worry loose like a shy pet running away from the vacuum cleaner noise and hide away into a small corner of the house. Whatever worry is out to get you, trash it away and whatever is pushing on you, you've got to push back before it stops you.

The fifth enemy is Over-Caution: It is the timid approach to life in a very competitive world. Timidity is not a virtue (unlike humility - they are different); in fact, I see it more as an illness or numbness of the spirit. Like all other fears, left unchecked it will conquer and drown you. Timid people don't get promoted or get the goodies in an aggressive world. Over-caution leads to a blockage that must be removed all costs. You can't advance and become successful in life and the marketplace if you are timid, instead you must take chances. Forgive and forget is often the most difficult thing to do, but you can't forgive yourself for not trying to eliminate your fears and you will not be forgiven by them.

Do battle with your fears. Build your courage and fight what's holding you back and what's keeping you from your goals and dreams. Take all your misfortunes as a valuable lesson, because the painful experience will become an investment for your own pursuit of happiness. Be daring in your life and in your pursuit of happiness and the new person you want to become.

Planet and Souls

Mother Earth is a beautiful planet; she is our space ship, providing all that is needed for humanity to prosper. Greed and ignorance are destroying her beauty and vitality and she is giving us signs of distress with the damage inflicted to the ozone layer and the drastic weather changes taking place. It is the task of the children of tomorrow to stop the destruction and bring mother earth back to health again.

Everything on earth is under a constant process of changes as the world continues to evolve. Universal Laws are ignored and large greedy corporations suck her natural resources as if she was only a commodity. Man is still a child, while pain and suffering are the only painful way to learn and achieve spiritual growth. But, can it be peace without war? Plato wrote, "Only the dead will know the end of the war". We are the recipients of continuous changes and without wars there could be no appreciation for peace. It seems to be mankind's karma to endure eternal wars, as the painful lessons it carries are needed to reach balance, respect growth, and love for us all.

This is a hard physical world, where pain and tears are real while advanced souls aim to teach others to ascend and transform into better human beings. Some will use religious doctrines to make sense to a world gone mad and dangerously close to nuclear disasters. Other uninformed souls will blame God, the government's secret agenda, Harmonic Convergence, Solar Rain, nonsense or better yet, Aliens and their thirsty need to control the Earth.

How can mankind reach the higher rewards of the fourth dimension experiences and bring into play the archetypal realm of consciousness without proper education? The fate of making is sealed by its own ignorance of "The Universal Code" and disrespect of the celestial rules regulating its own existence. These Universal Laws are the eternal scriptures and must be heeded by all; instead many lost souls worship and die for deities. Man is simply paying the ultimate price of its own ignorance by mistakably following deceiving religious doctrines and trusting an infantile science. We are all born in a third dimension realm of consciousness and working hard to decipher the fourth dimensional world.

In time and space today's souls will get a glimpse of the fifth dimensional world, where the spirit of man will merge and become co-creator with God. Advanced souls are endowed by birth to conceive and handle higher dimensions, while others have more spiritual work to do. This is a karmic world and a decision made by the spirit itself well before entering this level of consciousness. Education can only produce bright people conscious of "The Universal Code" embedding all rules to reach peace and harmony. Man has a long way to go before perceiving the 4th and 5th dimensional worlds and his eternal fate. Some people believe in the body ascending to a higher form, unable to accept the limitation of the laws of physics, condemning us in a physical shelf. We are slowly reassigning ourselves towards the conception of the humongous transforming forces of 'The Cosmic Code" above. My Astro-Psychology students and I are the wise teachers of future spiritual teachers and true advocates of this new dimensional understanding. Let go of the past and live in the now, cherish those you love and respect, release all anger, and judgment from your consciousness. Above and below there is only eternity, we are immortal spirits and our greatness starts in the whole galaxy. Raise and ascend spiritually towards the stars, because as a child of the universe, this is where you came from.

The Power of Visualization and the Soul's Ascension

Like a responsible driver you must respect the laws of the road and wear your seat belt. The same apply for the spiritual world, if you are not prepared or well protected; the chance of possession by low entities is very real. Always call on your Guardian Angel before doing any incantations in your spiritual work, perform a Cabalistic Candle Ritual, and always stay in your circle of salt for safety. Your pet can and will protect you from demonic forces, so have the animals in the room and trust him to alert you of any nefarious energy by watching his behavior. Psychic accidents do happen and low entities are always on the outlook for a healthy body or a naive soul to invade. Any form of chemicals or drugs must be avoided at all cost. In this realm of supreme consciousness, a pure spirit can only operate safely in an untainted body. Follow the rules, don't allow Neptune to grasp the essence of your spirit into possession and get lost in the depths of any astral planes.

Once the spiritual and physical surrounding is cleaned off with the ritual, you are safe and ready to start your incantations. Remind yourself of all the laws you have learned in my book and thoughtfully acknowledge your U.C.I. If you ordered a taped Full Life reading and inherited a Pisces Dragon's Tail, I will strongly advise you to stay clear from any and all psychic séances. It is your responsibility to heed my warnings and I hope you can handle the true gift or limitations of your divinity. I often overstate my findings in my readings to make sure you get the "message" to avoid any hazardous situations. Most of us are too sensitive or unwilling to accept the facts and even though you will enjoy learning about your U.C.I. you must be ready to take the undiluted truth from me. I did not write the celestial rules and will not alter "The Universal Code" for anyone, I simply use my God given gifts to translate them for your benefit, so that you can lead a safe and more productive life.

Practice Concentration

The western culture is one that says that we should be very confident, but teaches that modesty and humility are proper at all times and humbleness is a virtue above all others. Well, we have learned and exaggerated these "virtues" so well that they became poison to the self-esteem and the soul. These "virtues" build insecurity, inferiority complex, and a lack of confidence in one's self. So get ready to clean out all those unworthy habits and put some worthwhile components in your subconscious. There are many ways to build self-love and self-confidence; there is no short cut, you will have to start right from the bottom and then build it all the way up. Once you have a full understanding of your U.C.I.'s strengths or defaults, you will be ready for your next step. The more effort you put into these exercises, the faster you will get out of any mental restriction. Realize also, you cannot just put a small amount of time on this project and expect great results right away. You need to be persistent and dedicate yourself and expect the incredible results in due time.

Step 1 - Find a peaceful room in your home and sit comfortably in a chair, avoid hard floor and do not cross your legs. Do not do this particular exercise in your bed, to avoid fire. Use a lit candle and secure it in front of you on a table. Keep all flammable materials away from it, in case it falls on the table and rolls onto the floor. No noise or distraction is allowed. (Only your pet if you have one, may be allowed in your space). You need to concentrate on only the candle flame for two minutes and then close your eyes and keep the image of the flame in your mind's eye for as long as you can hold on to it. The first time you will try to do this, you may not succeed at all. Do not worry; just continue trying and the results will be there. While you are sitting and meditating on the candle flame do not let your mind wander and concentrate on improving your power of visualization.

You will be surprised at how the mind tries to wander away from concentration, your nose will itch and small noises that you never heard before will try to occupy your attention. The dark force is about to lose power over your soul and will manifest in various ways, so do not fear as you are under the protection of your guardian angel and the watchful spiritual eye of your pet at all times. Discipline yourself and keep your mind only on the dancing flame. As you pave the way to succeed in building concentration, always remember to come back to the basics for reinforcement. Keep in mind to accomplish a great goal and reaffirm your wish to achieve, no matter what. It all starts with knowing thy self and the will to bring about spiritual miracles and with perseverance you will succeed.

When you first begin, be gentle on yourself and develop more focusing power with time. After one week of practice, you should be able to hold the picture of the flame in your mind for a longer period of time. After a few weeks of training, you will be ready to try this mind power technique outside of yourself. Go out into the world and practice your new skill carefully and observe other peoples reactions. Concentrate on any individual and call their spirit to acknowledge your thoughts and presence from a distance. When this process of mental power is performed properly the recipient's reaction will be obvious. The person will look around quickly as if someone called his or her name. You may try in the theater also and hold on to your power thoughts and look down at the back of someone's head. You will soon realize your power on this world and how easy it is to influence others at your discretion. As with everything, practice makes perfect. You will amaze yourself and do magic, but you must put in the physical work first. Manipulating the atomic molecules of this physical world to your advantage through your subconscious is a real thing and you did it since you were born. Managing to do the same on a higher plane through the force of your subconscious is also a reality. This will allow you to borrow the power to make drastic changes in your life and heal others. However, remember also that using this power selfishly or negatively will bring you serious karma into your life. With your request to master and handle Supra-knowledge comes also, the heavy responsibility of managing those forces to the well being of mankind.

Step 2 - After you have perfected your concentration, move on to visualization. This is a technique by which you picture in your mind the thing that you would like to attain as a finished product. It can be anything from a new car, to a promotion, even a person. Spend ten minutes every day sitting quietly and envision your goal. Get a picture of someone you care about and freeze your memory thought on that person and start sending messages. Make it a movie where you are the main actor and where the possibilities are endless. Use your God given gift of imagination for your good cause. This relaxing technique will also help you to get over any stress you may experience in your life. Avoid polluting your thought process with anything stressful before any session and concentrate on the spiritual task at hand. Build a beacon of light, by keeping your imagination full of life.

"I am enough of an artist to draw freely upon my imagination. Imagination is more important than knowledge. Knowledge is limited. Imagination encircles the world."
--Albert Einstein

Affirmations are another way to build self-love and reach your subconscious creative forces. Never put negative words within the framework of an affirmation, like: "I will not be fat!" Your subconscious mind does not dwell too well on affirmation and negation simultaneously, thus it gets confused. This type of mixed affirmation could defeat the purpose, entirely. One of the best ways to put these affirmations into practice is to say them in front of your mirror every morning with faith and vigor. Do not apologize or feel shy about your aims or wishes, not even to yourself. Be firm and convinced in your power to do all that is needed for you to reach the vast and glorious knowledge, for transformation and abundance. Let me give you a worst example that would undoubtedly confuse and neutralize your subconscious creative forces.

Just imagine a limousine driver (your subconscious) ready to take you anywhere you want to go. He has all addresses and all directions to take you the faster and safer way to your destination. The only difference with this driver is that he is endowed with magical power to bring all your dearest wishes. He knows every single possible ways to take you anywhere you want to go, so you can meet all the wonderful people that can bring about all your dreams. The driver opens the door for you and goes back to his seat, he then asks you "Where do you want me to drive you to today?"

Then you would answer, "Okay, I want to go and see my mother". The driver would then start the car and get it in motion. Just before the first corner you decide to change your mind and tell him "Excuse me driver, I have changed my mind, can we go to visit my sister, first?" the driver would certainly agree with you and change direction, per your request. Another block later, you call on him again and say "Excuse me Sir, but I do not feel too good about visiting my sister just yet, can I instead ask you to drive me to a movie theater?" The driver would begin to scratch his head, but would politely agree to do what ever you request him to do.

On the way to the best theater in town, where the people the driver has set for you to meet to explore your deepest wishes, you again call on him and ask. "I am sorry driver, but I don't think I want to see a movie today, instead I'd rather go to the zoo. Can you please change directions and take me there?" "Of course" the driver says and begins to turn the limo around. After driving all night long, you finally decide to go back home to rest and you simply ask the driver, and he does so without complaint.

The very next day, you start the same unnerving process and finally the limousine driver stops the car and tells you. "Well, I am trying so hard to fulfill all your wishes, but you seem to enjoy wasting my time and yours. Thus, I have decided to stop the limousine until you know what and where your needs are all about." The driver gets out of the car and adds, "I am here for your service and will always be. I have the power to drive and guide you to all that you really want, even to your craziest wish. But, before I start pointing you in the right direction, you immediately stop the wonderful creative forces I can use for you to benefit you. So, I am simply asking you to make up your mind before I start the limousine again."

Do you get the message? Avoiding confusion and adapting to a solid mental process is all you need. The right state of mind will take you to the right direction to use constructively your subconscious creative forces. The more that you work on your own psyche, the better you will be able to form your own affirmations. Anyone can achieve much success with affirmations alone and when faced with any situation, start affirming what you need to the universe. Put it out there and firmly announce your will to yourself and your subconscious. I have witnessed incredible metamorphosis with so many people in my life. Any woman can and will change her physical appearance and attract love with affirmations alone. She would tell herself every morning, "I am beautiful and no man can resist me!" and then go on with her day, dressed with this incredible magnetism. Adding time and efforts for mental and physical cardiovascular exercise, among other things would make her feel more confident and more beautiful. Remember, physical achievement will add to your affirmation for these results to come about. Here are some affirmations that you can try yourself.

I AM Safe. My life is full of love and the spirit of God within, keeps me safe.

I AM Love. I learn daily to grow, expanding my knowledge in a clean body. I express myself from within love. I am sensitive, full of understanding for all situations that I have to deal with. I share freely the loving good I AM.

I AM a child of the Universe. I have faith and the pathway to the stars leading me to wisdom. I see universal forces as a pathway to love. I see value in the beliefs of all people of all cultures. We are all working and growing together to find love, peace, and harmony.

I AM a child of the Infinite. The divine spirit of devotion flows through me, extending to all that I come in contact with. God is love. God is light. God is peace. I dwell in God's creation and radiate like a star of love and peace.

I AM a child of Light and Love. I am a part of a magnificent scheme of things.

I AM a blooming star in God's creation.

I AM Learning to Love without conditions and expectations. My life is filled with joy and love. I love openly and I am lovingly open as I express myself freely, easily, and lovingly.

I AM all that is Life. My purpose in life is to learn to love and grow. I know I have the spirit of love, which is life for me. My life is eternal. I cherish my gift of life and express it with love, peace, and faith. I now feel harmony with the universe and my life's purpose is fulfilled.

I AM Successful. All good is coming into my life from the divine celestial energy now. I accept the good now. I make wise decisions for the highest and best good of all concerned. I open my life in faith to the infinite and all my desires are fulfilled.

I AM full of the Light of God and my life is full of abundance. My life is overflowing with prosperity that comes to me from the universe. I am learning to release all my feelings of lack. These feelings exist no more. I AM rich with life and power.

I AM Happy and joy fills my life. My life is worth living; I pray for God's supreme universal guidance I asked for. There is warmth, understating, and compassion. I receive everything that I ask for.

Fighting Depression

Your zodiacal sign represents your specific soul's purpose, work with me and let's investigate your mission as intended by the stars. Realize this is a very generic insertion of a huge research, where vital elements cannot be taken in consideration. Your natal Dragon's Head and Tail in your chart may support or reject my general message to you.

APRIL SOULS: Need for actions. Regeneration takes place with words and actions. Since you have a hard time completing projects, you tend to feel guilty until all tasks have been completed. Give yourself one or two new small things to complete each day to build stamina. Fear of failures or not being loved or appreciated by others, may bring depression.

MAY SOULS: Need for financial security. Since you are cautious by nature, you work better in tandem with someone else. Your desire for security, food, and home is often in your mind. Fear of not having or getting the right education may jeopardize your foundation for building a solid future. Depression may come from your sense of insecurity for those you care about.

JUNE SOULS: Need for mental stimulation. Since you are overly gifted with mental energy, your attention can be scattered. Find a way to use this gift through communication and the arts. Fear of boredom may put at risk your decision for a good career. Depression may come from nurturing thoughts of never reaching love, fame, or power.

JULY SOULS: Need for emotional security. Since you are extremely sensitive to others, you imagine hurt, where none was intended. You need to have strong family relationships. Fear of old age may emphasize over concern with health. Depression may come from not being able to nurture and care properly for others.

AUGUST SOULS: Need for expressions. You are naturally gifted with a shining personality and a sense of justice. You work hard for your goals and you need a solid career. Fear of failures and death may poison your mind and health. Depression may come from not being able to build a stage of light and shine.

SEPTEMBER SOULS: Need for perfection. Attention to detail makes you an uncompromising worker and very critical to others. You need to relax more and enjoy life out of the office. You are an investigator and sarcastic at times. Fear of not giving less than perfection to others affects your life and health. Depression may come from thinking of not being able to build a good service to the world.

OCTOBER SOULS: Need for justice. You are natural peacemakers, ready to fight with anyone at all times. You have a natural abhorrence for lies and live your life by a strict moral code. You cultivate knowledge and you fear of wasting valuable information for the world. Depression may come from not being able to see other forms of mental exploration than religion and a strong desire to enforce rules into this world.

NOVEMBER SOULS: Need for control. You are intense and deeply emotional, which you hide well from others. You nurture a deep lack of trust and you fear of losing control in every area of yours and others life. Depression may come from not being able to investigate the incredible and miss the incredible power over others that it would bring into yours and others life.

DECEMBER SOULS: Need to teach. You have a natural desire to travel physically and spiritually into the incredible and you live your life in a busy mental state. You cultivate knowledge at all times and you fear of not being able to establish revenue with it. Depression may come from not being able to let go of the past and make a good use of your mystical knowledge.

JANUARY SOULS: Need to achieve. You were born an engineer and an astute politician with a natural ability to climb all the way up to the mountain of success. You may also deny anything not related to science, religion, or the use of your goat's fish tail and miss all rules involving the Moon's fluctuations. Your fears are based upon not receiving respect and recognition, which can lead to depression.

FEBRUARY SOULS: Need for freedom. You are unusual and naturally gifted in communications. Your need to explore anything under the Sun is unsurpassed and your genius mind is rarely at rest. Your downfall is to refuse to listen to others. You fear commitments. Depression may come from your realization of the spiritual limits imposed on mankind, jailing his latent spirit.

MARCH SOULS: Need for compassion. You can be either very spiritual or very religious, depending on your karmic load. You pick up energy like a sponge and integrate them into your own world. Your downfall is to daydream and seek refuse in religion or chemicals. Depressions may come from direction or your lack of mental and physical strengths. However, Einstein, George Washington, and Michael Angelo were born in March!

Rocks for the Soul

In order to increase your vibrations and attract your wishes, you need to magnetize yourself and rocks are naturally designed by nature to do so. Depression, guilt, and bad habits are your enemy and a powerful mind can only reside in a healthy body. Healthy habits and exercises bring about more magnetism, but Mother Earth has also things to offer you if you learn about her secret healing powers. Each one of us vibrates at a very specific level, some faster, some slower. If you are in need for a specific energy field, take the time to investigate the natural rocks and carry the needed specific stone with you at all times.

AGATE

The best stone for healing serpent or scorpion bites. Agate aids in building strength and courage. Compels truth, promotes good manners, happiness, intelligence, prosperity, longevity, fertility, and good health. -- Brownish-layered swirls.

AMBER

Amber is a powerful aid to furthering ambitions and for healing throat diseases. Creates magnetism. Electrically alive with solidified golden light. Emits a powerful amount of heat and light. Powerful healing stone with large amount of organic energy. In ancient times, it was ground to a powder and mixed with honey or oil of roses for various physical problems. Filters germs and infections and has the power to disinfect. Worn around the neck to help fight infection and respiratory diseases. Lifts the spirits. --Golden yellow stone.

AMETHYST

Stone of Venus. Assists those to maintain faithfulness, gives wearer the gift of tongues, increases spiritual awareness, has a calming and soothing influence, has ability to transmute negative into positive, very effective as a healing stone. Has ability to assist in prophecy, and wards off drunkenness. Warmed and placed on the forehead and temples, it is good for headaches. Has the ability to draw through it forces directed towards the body and repels vibrations which the body doesn't need, thus releasing only the energy patterns beneficial to the body. Best worn in healing near the heart center. Calming and protective, it aids meditation. It also aids in purification and regeneration on all levels of consciousness. Calming, grounding, a cleanser and spiritual stimulator, strengthens heart, cleanses liver of toxins, excellent for lung problems. -- Purple ranging from light to dark.

AQUAMARINE

Assists inspiration, favorable for travelers; helps to protect against accidents. Calms nervous tension. Calming effects of the sea. Used to help banish fears and phobias. It's soothing and cleansing. It is also a powerful aid to happiness in marriage. --Light blue clear stone.

ADVENTURINE

Increases perception and creative insight. Stimulates opportunity and motivation. Soothes emotions, used for the heart and heartache, for acceptance of self and others, for inner peace. --Green Layered.

AZURITE

Powerful healing stone, invokes spiritual guidance, opens psychic eye. Good for dreams and improving psychic ability. Liberates the etheric body for astral travel. --Sky blue.

BLOODSTONE

A favorite for healing and strength. Soldiers of old wore it in battle, believing it had the power to stop bleeding. Stimulates flow of energy for healing blood circulation, stops hemorrhaging. Removes emotional blockages. It's a great talisman for warding off all accidents and disease, especially suitable for men. --Greenish quartz with spots of red jasper.

CARBUNCLE

Worn to increase the feeling of self-confidence and the ability to fight through difficulties. --Coal like red garnet, cut without facets.

CHRYSOPRASE

Emits steady serene flow of light. Tranquilizing. Soothes emotions, will help tranquilize many forms of neurosis, used to absorb or deflect unwanted energies. --Translucent apple green stone.

CITRINE

Enables self-esteem. Stimulates openness and awakening of the mind. Aid to the digestive system. Helps eliminate toxins. Encourages tremendous healing on the emotional and mental levels, helps unblock subconscious fears, and serves as a natural relaxant. --Pale yellow clear stone.

CORAL

Promises a long and happy married life, protects a child from evil influences, and safeguards the teenager during the highly emotional period. Balances physical energy and relaxes tensions. Carries the creative vibrations of the sea. --Various colors.

CORNELIAN

Wish Stone is highly favorable to health, long life, and good fortune. Its special virtue is the fulfillment of one's wishes if the stone is worn near the heart. --

Shades of red.

DIAMOND

A symbol of bravery and strength and also one of the emblems of innocence. It is an antidote against pestilence. --Crystallized carbon.

EMERALD

Helps women attract a true love, and men to attract a loving wife. Promotes creativity, stimulates perception and insight, and strengthens memory. It has a beneficial effect on the eyes. Also an excellent preservative against decay, arrests dysentery, and heals bites from venomous animals. --Green clear stone with a hint of blue.

FLUORITE

It is considered a good luck piece. Also called Fairy Gem. Manifests innermost wishes. Promotes well-being, enhances concentration and meditation. Powerful spirit guide. Opens and softens the way for the use of other stones. Excellent used in aquariums-provides needed minerals. Charge on windowsill at night. --Varies in different shades of purples and greens. Identified by the bands of color seen within the stone.

GARNET

Wards off inflammatory diseases, promotes healthy and cheery disposition. Balances hormones, good for mental depression, enhances self-esteem, alleviates bad dreams, and encourages success in business. Thought to assist in seeing into past incarnations. Will ensure consistency in friendship and love, preserve health, and is generally fortunate. Vitality and passion. Stimulates happiness, peace, balance, patience, inspiration, persistence, good for rebirthing, menstruation and life passages, disorders, fertility, eases arthritis pain. --Ranges from orange-red to pink-red.

HEMATITE

Very strong stone; absorbs negativity. Gives optimism and courage. Calming to the emotions. Worn as an amulet confers strength and procures favorable legal judgments. In Egypt, used to reduce inflammation and treat hysteria. Considered to be a grounding stone. Helps maintain balance between body, mind, and spirit. Use for fevers, alleviates worry and anxiety as it allows for mental clarity, known as the "worry stone". --Heavy black metallic stone.

HERKIMER

Balancing special variety of quartz crystal. "Diamond" works with yin/yang energies, known as the "Dream Crystal", aids in bringing teachings of the dream state into conscious awareness, very highly attuned spiritually.

JACINTH

Renders the wearer extremely fascinating and strengthens the heart. Used for melancholy. --Reddish orange or brown zircon.

JADE

A most sacred stone and a symbol of divine revelation. Brings good fortune and health to its owner. Stimulates practicality, wisdom, and universal attunement. Thought to provide a link between the spiritual and the mundane. Most revered by the Chinese. --Creamy green stone.

JASPER

Safeguard personal independence, said to bring inspirational warnings when there is danger of unfair domination from others. Balance emotions and stress. For aid and comfort during periods of female distress. One stone is worn about the neck and another around the waist. --Opaque colored quartz.

LAPIS LAZULI

Prized for its prophetic virtues. Stimulates wisdom, truthfulness, & psychic experiences, healing and strengthening when worn next to the kin. Strengthens mind and body to spiritual awareness. --Royal blue in color with flecks of real gold.

LEOPARDSKIN – JASPER

Powerful healer of many known and unknown physical ailments.

MALACHITE

Called a magic stone, favorable for travelers, missionaries, and other adventurers. Used as a child's talisman to sleep soundly & protect from bad dreams. Stimulates clear vision and insight, represents hope and inner peace, believed to protect from danger. Increases abundance in all areas of life. This stone supposedly has equal amounts of negative and positive forces, thereby adding to the balance of physical and spiritual life. Used to release repressed emotions and for physical detoxifying. --Brilliant shades of green, very apparent in bands of shades.

MOONSTONE

Aids in bringing forth memories of past lives, carried as a good luck piece. Brings good fortune. Reflects the wearers being and feelings. Promotes unselfishness. Opens the heart to humanitarian love and hope. Good for protection while traveling on water. Gives clarity to spiritual understanding. Good for pre-menstrual symptoms and balancing the reproductive system. Used to ease childbirth. Sometimes called the Queen of the Heavens stone. Calming effect on emotions. Eases menstrual pain, alleviates many degenerative conditions in the skin, hair, eyes, and body fluids (tears, digestive juices). --Translucent milky stone with color tints ranging from white-yellow to blue-gray.

MOSS AGATE

Assists in making and keeping friends, helpful to farmers and those interested in growing plants. Moss Agates is considered to be most powerful. Aid in restoration of energy, used in healing, and believed to bring wearer happiness, wealth, health, and long life. Increases ability to ward off self-induced anger and inner bitterness. Moss green-balances emotional energy. Moss red-balances physical energy. Blue lace gives tranquility. --Translucent stone with flecks of green.

OBSIDIAN

Used to sharpen both the internal and external. --Black.

ONYX

Preserves against the bites of snakes and venomous insects, and assists in bringing marital happiness. When certain persons wear it, may bring on terrible shapes to a dreamer, from which the future can be divined. Will ground spiritual energy to physical plane. --Deep black color.

OPAL

An unlucky stone which can interfere with love and marriage, unless one was born between September 23rd and November 21. To these people it will give second sight, or clairvoyance, and prevent contagion from the air. --Generally white but various color ranges depending on variety. Identified by brilliant sparkling effect.

PEARLS

Worn as a necklace, makes the wearer chaste. Stimulates feminine qualities, used to focus attention, helps pull together mental and spiritual forces, peace of mind. Represents purity, modesty, & gentleness. A very lucky stone for those born in June. --White gray with a tinge of blue.

PERIDOT

Dispels fears, guilt, and depression. Used to counteract negative emotions and healing of the spirit. Once worn as a means of gaining foresight and divine inspiration. Protection, prosperity, emotional calming, purifies, balances. --Light green clear stone.

PHANTOM

Powerful tool for the New Age. Used to ground and center while attuning to higher spiritual energies, in healing work used to disperse congested energies. --Clear.

PYRITE

Enhances mental capacity and attracts money to owner. Has protecting, shielding aspect for physical, mental, emotional levels. Shields from negative energy, strengthens circulatory system, clears oxygen in the blood. --Brass yellow, also known as fool's gold.

QUARTZ

Amplifies healing energy. Used to help draw out pain. Enables the soul to tap into energies of the universe. Good stone for meditating on. Very potent and often worn to protect from negative vibrations. Cleanse regularly. --Rutilant-rutile needles help focus attention.

RAINBOW PYRITE

Strengthens the will. --Same as Pyrite in rainbow coloration.

RHODOCHROSITE

Adds courage, will, and passion to the loving heart vibration. Represents the love of God. --Milky pink stone with definition.

RHODONITE

Used to activate love. Attracts or keeps a loving partner. --Pink stone with black highlights - very defined.

ROSE QUARTZ

Worn or carried for love, fidelity, peace, and happy marriage. Aids intuition and emotional balance. Reduces stress and tension - cools hot tempers. Vibrations of universal love & inner serenity. Comforts heart from all wounds, helps heal emotional pain, enhances love, self-love, positive outlook, joy and oneness. --Light to medium milky pink color.

RUBY

The stone of freedom, charity, dignity and divine power. Increases vigor, renews vitality and cleanses the blood. The stone of courage. Helps banish grief for those in mourning. --generally deep red with orange or pink undertone.

SMOKY QUARTZ

Good for calming the mind. Eases depression, fear and panic.

SNOWFLAKE OBSIDIAN

Teaches one the truth of oneself in relation to ones ego, depicts the contrasts of life-day and night, darkness and light, truth and error. Grounds spiritual energy to the physical plane and absorbs negativity. --Black stone with lacy highlights of white.

SODALITE

Alleviates fears, Clears the mind. --Blue with white flecks.

TIGER EYE

Calms emotions, protects against external stresses. Worn to restore physical energy & quiet emotional nature. --Golden brown.

TOPAZ

Will make melancholy vanish, when worn or carried in the left hand. Calms emotions, protects against external stresses. Worn to restore physical energy & quiet emotional nature. Protects against insomnia and depression, mood elevator, revitalizes, stimulates creative thinking processes, eases death. -- Clear gold stone, deeper color than amber.

TOURMALINE

Supercharged with magnetic and electric energy. Lifts fears and negative conditions. Causes the wearer to be flexible, understanding and more objective in purpose and reason. Works as protective shield, consumes negative energy without releasing into atmosphere, has to do with visions and "seeing" with compassion, teaches to expand limited concepts of thinking, relates to aspirations for higher love, very complete stone. --Various shades of pink and green. Some stones will have both colors.

TURQUOISE

Helps ward off danger and clears one's path of pitfalls. Protector against evil. Self-love stone. Primary holy stone of Native Americans. Vibrates calming radiations, protective, and restores healthy mental attitude. Stone of friendship. Balancing and healing. Great strength and vitality. Takes on characteristics of the wearer. It is unwise to wear a turquoise formerly worn by one who has died. Excellent for both Spiritual attunement and healing of the energy centers and the physical body, valuable for grounding as well as for vision quests and astral travel, purifies all levels of being and is capable of handling strong negativity, also used for wounds and for damage to bones. --Shades of blue, ranging from deep sky blue to greenish Chinese turquoise.

Colors for the Soul

Your vibrations can also be increased with colors and bring more magnetism to yourself. Bad habits are the enemy of a great mind while a positive attitude brings about more drawing power to your wishes. Colors are tied to our emotions and can also increase your inner influence, if you learn about their powers. Colors are therefore easier for us to transmit since we already feel them on an intuitive level. Some correctional facilities paint their walls pink, because it has been scientifically proven to have a calming effect on the inmates.

Each colors vibrates at a very specific level, some faster, some slower. If you are in need for a specific energy field take the time to investigate and wear the cocktail of colors available to you.

WHITE: Moon - Spirituality, Faith, Purity, Truth, Safety, and Completeness. Whenever you use the color white you are actually using all colors in the spectrum and their reflection from the sun. This is always a positive energy and also has healing properties. Whenever you are feeling fear, mentally surround yourself with a bright white light so that no negativity can touch you and move on to another area.

PINK: Venus - Self-affection, Love, Friendship, Morality, General Success, and Honor. Whenever you are feeling unsure of yourself, choose to wear something pink and it will help to lift your self-esteem. Pink has a very calming effect and it's one of the innocent colors like white. That is why it is featured as a baby color.

RED: Mars - Aggression, Passion, Desire, Impatience, Gain through Marriage, Vitality. Red is a very powerful and aggressive energy representing blood. Red also means desire in its rough basic form; this can be a very positive energy when channeled in the right direction, or a very negative energy when allowed to destroy. Whenever using or working with the color red, be careful that your ends are good and wholesome.

ORANGE: Jupiter - Encouragement, Education, Communication, Philosophy, Luck, and Flexibility. Orange is part of the sunny group of colors along with yellow and white; they all have very positive energy. It transmits happiness in all areas. It also helps in areas of philosophy and deeply held beliefs, especially if you feel persecuted or estranged from loved ones because of religious differences. This color also gives the wearer a sense of luck. (Luck is when preparation meets with opportunity)

YELLOW: Sun - Persuasion, Charm, Adaptability, Curiosity, Intelligence, and Duality. Part of the sunny group of colors dealing directly with positivism. Whenever you take on a new study, it is best to surround yourself with the color yellow, as this will stimulate memory, as well as your ability to be curious and interested in the material. If you need to be extra persuasive, wear a touch of yellow and you will find yourself being extra charming, as well as full of confidence.

GREEN: Mercury - Prosperity, Fertility, Organization, Cooperation, Patience, Concentration, and Health. This color deals directly with the earth and the building of new things. If you need more impetus to finish things that you start and have good follow through, then the color green is for you. It is also great for dealing with financial situations, so if you find yourself in negotiations or talking to our taxman, then dress in some conservative greens for level headed decisions. This is also a great color to concentrate on when starting something new, as it instills patience and deals with fruition and fertility.

LIGHT BLUE: Venus - Perception, Protection, Inspiration, Tranquility, Understanding, and Innocence. This color is very useful when working on artistic endeavors, as well as spiritual ones. Its calming influence is very great and aids in cleansing the mind of mundane thoughts. It also aids in perception and will give you more ability to understand the messages that you receive from the universe, as well as the people who are sending you messages with ESP.

DARK BLUE: Uranus - Intelligence, Philanthropy, Universal Love, Nobility, Ingeniousness, and Friendship. This is one of the regal colors and it aids in learning to share the world with others, as well as material possessions. It has a stimulating effect on your mind and will help you to assimilate information more quickly, as well as the ability to tap into the supra-conscious, which is the big storehouse of all human thought. This gives people the ability to "channel" information, as well as aiding in psychic phenomena. It is the "all for one and one for all" color. It cares nothing for convention and tradition; its energy is quite magnetic and has the ability to bring groups together for a common purpose.

PURPLE: Saturn/Sun. Ambition, Progress, Power, Influence, Will Power, and Ego. Another of the regal, jewel tone family, this is a very strong color that radiates power and strength. If you need to overcome an obstacle, concentrate on the color purple and you will find inspired answers coming your way. It also will help you to become single minded in the attaining of a goal. When you become more advanced, concentrate on this color before beginning your ESP exercises, it will clear your mind of extraneous thoughts, and help you tap right into your psychic ability.

BROWN: Saturn – Jupiter. Grounding, Fertility, Growth, Tradition, Sincerity and Truth. If you are a very artistic person and need help bringing all your ideas to fruition, then wear something brown when you sit down to work, or meditate on the color brown before beginning your work. It is a very calming color and will aid in letting you auto-analyze yourself in a brutally honest manner. If you have devoted a great deal of time to this color, some people may not appreciate your total honesty in all things, so remember to be diplomatic in your dealings with others.

DEEP BLUE: Neptune. Intuition, Imagination, Spirituality, Devotion, and Care. If you are involved in homeopathic healing or need extra creativity and need help bringing all your ideas to fruition, wear something deep blue before starting the project. It is a very soothing and spiritual color and will aid in taping in the subconscious for all your creative purpose. This color supports all psychic and artistic endeavors and brings intuition to the fore in dealing with others.

BLACK: Pluto. Power, Mourning, Loss, Restructure, Regeneration, Magic, and the Unknown. Black can be used positively as well as negatively, so you should be very aware of what you are doing before you decide to meditate on the color black. If you are about to go through a major change in your life, it is a perfect color to wear and meditate on. It has connotations of mystery and will add sexiness to your wardrobe. It deals with the unknown and beyond corporeal death, and if you are very adept at meditation and psychic phenomena, you will be able to garner many answers from the great beyond. However, it is also associated with negativity and depression, so for beginners, I would relegate it to your closet for those nights out when you need a little extra magnetism, sensuality and mystery.

Extra Sensory Perception

Knowing that the future is nothing more than the reincarnation of your own thoughts, you should pay more attention to your ways of thinking. Cleansing the mind from poisonous thoughts is not an easy task, but there are ways in which we can train and discipline the mind to do so. ESP or Extra Sensory Perception uses this same phenomenon. ESP is nothing more than "that little voice within" that we call intuition or "the sixth sense". It is the art of using the subconscious constructively and we all possess this ability. Science reckons that man uses less than ten percent of its brain's capacity; I know this is a largely accepted theory, but again what the majority accepts, does not mean it to be a true statement. The reasoning is simply based upon a total emancipation of the Universal Mind's interaction with man's psyche. Sounds to me like a computer not being used with its screen saver on! As soon as a person sits in front of the electronic tools, life is again ingested by the machine, which will not and cannot perform, unless a higher power (you) is connected. The same process takes place while asleep, but your subconscious mind is never resting and your body functions are fully operational. If you were to use only ten percent of your brain capacity alive or sleeping, chances are you would be largely limited in all your physical and mental functions. Try to shut down a few programs on your computer and see its performances! More reliable powerful computers are designed and created everyday and with it numerous new programs facilitating a myriad of tasks. Limitation is based upon a lack of knowledge, while success is measured by progressive changes.

Changes can only come about with curiosity, inventiveness, and education. Life is a constant process of transformation and like old computer electronics, what we were yesterday is already obsolete. The only difference between a solid computer and man's brain is that the building and upgrading process of the latter takes place constantly. The windfall of information and experience allows more knowledge on the hard drive, or the subconscious. The Superconscious acts as God's interaction from the Universal Mind. Imagine what type of computer will be produced 500 years from today or imagine how advanced will be man's awareness of its cosmic legacy. Separating man's psyche from its Universal inherited code will be a story of the past. I can really relate to Einstein's quote "A human being is part of a whole, called by us the 'Universe,' a part limited in time and space. He experiences himself, his thoughts and feelings, as something separated from the rest--a kind of optical delusion of his consciousness". The real reason why people won't reach great success in their life is not because they have no talent, but because they have no reasoning skills. You must want more, to have more.

Wouldn't you like to develop more of your own brainpower, to achieve peace of mind and success? This is what will happen to you, if you coach your mind's incredible capacities and develop your own ESP. I am sure you already experienced this phenomenon in your own life. Have you ever been thinking of a friend and then the telephone rings and here he or she is talking to you? You are amazed and before the person says anything, you say "Oh, my God! I was thinking of you just now, and here you are!" Well you just unconsciously practiced your telepathic powers. The same applies, when you know who was on the phone before you picked it up. Have you ever wished that a certain person would notice you, but they had their back to you, and then as you wished, they turned around and came over to talk to you? Have you ever bought something for someone, just to find out it was the very thing that they wanted? These are just a few examples that most of us are familiar with and we all, are in constant emissions and receptions of each other's thoughts.

Some people are better with emissions than reception and you should first establish what you are. Then, work on the weaker side of your psyche, to improve your ESP powers. We are symmetrical and the duality in all things in life is quite obvious. There is an identical opposite in everything that was ever created, either by man or by God. A month is made of four weeks, a year is twice six months, there is a front and a back, and a man couldn't exist without a woman. There would be no night without a day and the positive, without the negative. Simply acknowledge, that all in this world is balanced with its corresponding opposite parameter. Realize also, "the Temple of God" or your body uses both sides of the brain, breathes with two lungs, sees with two eyes, uses two arms, walks on two legs and two feet, etc., the list is endless. Thus, like a battery, we were all born with an inborn polarity. Once you recognize the dualistic factor in all that makes up the world around us, your second challenge will be to acknowledge that without opposites there couldn't be life. Questions like: Could there be a God without a devil? If God is the ultimate creator and that powerful, then why did he create the devil and what for? Without opposite forces, there would be no tangible way to perceive good from bad or the negative from positive. Your own creative power is based upon a reaction between the positive and negative or a form of yin and yang principles interacting with both the physical and the spiritual world. The very principle or creation also uses those laws thus, the engineer will have to plan (create spiritually) a bridge first in the spiritual realm of consciousness using his creative imagination, then investigate the limits and rules of the palpable world, where "his dream" will slowly but surely take its physical form. We communicate with each other on a physical level (vocal chords, throat/words etc.) But "The Law Of Opposite" is also operational and we are communicating at a spiritual or subconscious level. Like a radio station emitting a program, the idea is to become a powerful transmitter and project enough thoughts to imprint the psyche on the receiver. I have done this "trick" thousands of time successfully and impressed many people in the process.

Remember those simple "guessing" games such as "I'm thinking if a number between __ and __", or "I spy, with my eye", even "charades" These "guessing games" are actually ESP practice, you are literally picking up the other person's thoughts. Of course clues are added to make it easier, but you'll find within time and practice, the clues won't be needed. You can start with these simple games and work your way up to "I'm thinking of a color, or animal, or country, etc." with out any clues. The stronger you can picture what you wish the other person to pick up, the easier it will be transmitted. If you have trouble visualizing, memory games are great for practice. There are plenty of games in the stores or online, or you can even create your own at home, such as self made memory cards or remembering and removing objects with someone else, to recall what's missing. There are dozens of "mental exercises" you can enjoy with someone, be creative.

Reverse the process and let your partner become the sender and you the receiver. Put feelings in your thoughts and remember your imagination will fuel the picture and will make it more vivid and more discernable to your subconscious. I have done this process successfully hundreds of time to many people and if I can do it, so can you. Share these activities with those whom you care about to support stronger connections; perfect for family game night, parties, and company gatherings.

Do not get discouraged, if at first you do not succeed and remember this is not a guessing game, you must concentrate and be in the right frame of mind to perform. Your mind is like any muscle of the body and need exercises every day to get stronger. (After 25 tries, give your companions the option to continue for another 25 tries or to view their accuracy score.)

A score of 5-7 has the same percentages of chance, so practice. Practice makes perfect!

A score of 8-13 is great sign of ability with chances of quick improvement!

A score of 14-19 shows fantastic perception and ability for you can alter your future!

A score of 20-25 means that you are an adept and amazing psychic and should be using your skills to help others. You also have the ability to manifest what ever you think about, quite quickly. Enjoy the rich rewards of your positive thought! (After viewing your mate's score give them the option to play again or move on to the next game.)

Numbers

We work with numbers every day and numerology has always played an important part in the mind of spiritualists. Even the days of the weeks have certain energies attached to them by virtue of a particular celestial body. The legacy of the hidden message is found in the day of the Sun (Sunday) the day of Saturn (Saturday) the day of the Moon (Monday) etc. My yearly publication book Moon Power is based upon the daily influence on each day of the year and serves as a very reliable source of guidance and predictions for many of my faithful readers worldwide. Check this fact by investigating your daily and monthly forecast on www.drturi.com. There are numerous methods of divination and using numbers is one of them. You are going to be working with the numbers one through twelve. (As the text for each number goes up, perhaps you can surround each explanation with a parade of that number or maybe a parade of a group of objects that represent the particular number)

ONE: The number one represents the oneness of life, the connection to the all that is. Beginnings. Initiator of action, a pioneering spirit, inventive ideas, strong leadership skills, independent, drives to attain, individualistic style, executive abilities, extraordinary will and determination, courageous.

TWO: The number two represents the duality of life, or the yin and yang that surrounds us every day. It is the completion of the forces of life, without opposites, life could not exist. It is the number of communication, and deals with selling and flexibility. People with a lot of this number attached to them will be able to blend into any crowd and easily gets along with people.

THREE: The number three deals with karma, which is why we say, "Trouble always happen in bunches of three". Karma can be positive or negative, depending on your thoughts and/or actions of the past. When you are trying to kick a bad habit or start a good habit, it happens in three portions of three. That is why it takes 90 days or three months to achieve these types of goals. A person who has a lot of this number attached to them will be quite diligent and methodical, though life may seem quite rough through the first half, the second half will see them with much success and reward for their hard work.

FOUR: The number four deals with stability and has connotations to your home life, because home is where you feel the most secure and stable. That is why your first teachers or your parents play an important role in developing self-esteem. It is important that you always feel the most comfortable in your home area. People who have a lot of this number attached to them will quite love and nurturing, however, they must guard against moodiness and insecurity. These people are usually born with some gifts in the culinary arts as well good business

FIVE: The number five deals with creativity and romance and has connotations to your children. This number also deals with good times and why people look forward to Friday the 5th day of the week. People with a lot of this number attached to them are very romantic and positive, however, they must guard against ego and boredom. These people are usually born with artistic ability and many organize large creative endeavors.

SIX: The number six deals with health matters as well as work habits. That is why on Saturday (the sixth day) we all have lists of chores that need to be done, and men especially get the "Honey-Do!" lists from their wives and sweethearts. It is our last day to work before resting and then getting on with the workweek again. People who have a lot of this number attached to them are very diligent, hard working, and detailed. They must guard against nit picking and an overwhelming perfectionist attitude.

SEVEN: The number seven is the number of perfection; it deals with completion, harmony, and partnership. God rested on the seventh day and was pleased with all that He saw. This is the energy of fruition and pay-off for a job well done. This is why even after people are retired or leave the work-a-day world they still feel as if Sunday is the day of resting and leisure. People who have a lot of the number seven attached to them are wise and usually are looked up to as mentors and teachers. This is the number of high evolution in the spiritual world, and means that you are ready to move on to new lessons. These people must guard against impatience and spiritual pride.

 EIGHT: The number eight deals with transformation and regeneration. Although these are high principals, they come about at great personal cost. This is a powerful number with magical properties of change. It also deals with will power, investment, sex, and metaphysics. People with a lot of this number attached to them will be very intense and magnetic. People will be drawn to them like moths to a flame. But these people must guard against bone chilling sarcasm and hunger for control. The intensity found in this number brings difficult for the bearer himself and demand caution in all endeavors.

NINE: The number nine deals with the search for truth, religions of all kinds, foreign places, nature, and animals. This number encompasses all the identicalness in the religious idiosyncrasies of the human race. It is the number that makes us ask, "Why are we here, God?" It keeps us constantly searching and learning the truth every day, leading the soul to breakthroughs in comprehension. People with a lot of this number attached them, have a serious amount of luck in the promotion of dogmatic teachings. They are quite philosophical and eager to share, even impose the book on others. They must guard against narrowness, induced fears, and explore other's values with respect.

TEN: The number ten deals with winning, success, career, and personal attainment. Accomplishments have a powerful effect on our psyche and self esteem and we should pay great attention to this number. It is the last number in a sequence before we begin again, therefore if we follow the one, two, three's of a situation, we will then be rewarded with success!! People who have a lot of this number attached to them are great leaders and quite adept at logical, linear thought. They are so practical that they must guard against manipulation once in power. Politicians, engineers, architects, lawyers, lawmakers and businessmen in position of authority share the values found in the number 10.

ELEVEN: The number eleven deals with friendships, world fraternity, the future and the power of wishing. This is the number of world peace and deals also with the breaking down of worn out traditions. It is an idealistic, utopian number and one to meditate on when dealing with the universal mind, new age matters and large fraternal groups. It brings together inventive ideas for a common futuristic goal. People born with a lot of this number attached to them will be quite original, ahead of time, ingenious, and intelligent. This is the number of a true and rare world leader with extraordinary vision. They must guard against their limit of sharing true knowledge with feeble minded. Trouble may come from deadly enemies such as jealousy, foolishness, inferiority, and insecurity complexes.

TWELVE: The number twelve deals with the subconscious mind, a secret hidden place where all of our mystical powers are from. This is also the seat of all our fears and wishes and the deadly trap of illusions energized by an incontrollable poisoned imagination. This is a very sophisticated area where the imagination can be of great help or great hindrance, depending on how we harness this energy. This is the theater of your pre-and after life where you are allowed to create your own movie. You are locked into the energy of the number twelve until you leave the theatre, by becoming a real actor in a real world. This is a great number to meditate on for artistic inspiration or to spur your intuitional faculties. People born with a great deal of this number attached to them are artistic, imaginative and have amazing intuitions. Prophets and healers such as Nostradamus, Edgar Cayce, and Madame Vladasky are good examples. "Belief is half of being." They must guard against drugs, chemicals, religions and self-pity. They must also learn to let go of the past and guilt.

Remember again, some people are better with emissions than reception and you should first establish what you are, in dealing with ESP. Then, keep working on the weaker side of your psyche to improve your ESP powers.

Let's now begin to practicing receiving and sending the correct number. Get a friend to pick a number and ask him to keep that number thought alive and strong in the back of his mind. Warm up your ESP and do 25 trial tries before noting your score.

Reverse the process and start practicing sending the chosen numbers. Tell your friend to empty his mind and to become the receptor of your thought number. Keep the picture of this number alive and strong in the back of your mind then, let your friend to tell you what he sees. Warm up your ESP and do 25 trial tries before noting your score.

It is also important for both parties to agree on a time limit when performing those spiritual gymnastics.

As always, do not give up if at first you do not succeed in picking the right number, you are not guessing anything. Simply concentrate and be in the right frame of mind to perform. Any muscle of the body needs exercises to keep strong and healthy, your legs and pumping heart will get you first at the end of the marathon. The same apply in your mind and spirit; keep working to develop your subconscious power. (After 25 tries, give your companion the option to continue for another 25 tries or to view their score.)

A score of 5-7 has the same percentages of chance, practice, practice makes perfect!
A score of 8-13 is great sign of ability with chances of quick improvement!
A score of 14-19 shows fantastic perception and ability, you are well on your way.
A score of 20-25 means that you are an adept and amazing psychic and should be using your skills to help others. You also have the ability to manifest what ever you think about, quite quickly. Enjoy the rich rewards of your positive thoughts! (After viewing your mate's score give them the option to play again or move on to the next game.)

Shapes

Now we are going to work with some simple shapes, and after the practice of the last two exercises, you should see some improvement. After doing this exercise evaluate your progress and see if sending a thought is easier than receiving. Here are the shapes we will be working with to improve your own power: (Have the shapes ready in a red or black solid color, not in just an outline.)

1) Circle

2) Triangle

3) Square

4) Rectangle

5) Star

6) Heart

7) Octagon

8) Pentagon

As always, get your partner to perform with you and reverse the process to stimulate the receiving and sending process. You must concentrate very hard, clearing your mind of all things and allowing it to become as a blank screen for you to receive or send the shape thought form. Now choose which shape from the list, check on your scores separately and remember practice makes perfect!

Images

Now you will get a chance to use all the skills you have learned together. You may choose one of the five categories; they are: People, Nature, Animals, Food and Furniture. There will be eight choices for each category. (For each category you will have to practice holding a graphic memory.)

(For People: you will need to stretch your imagination power to its limits and hold in your mind two babies, one a boy and one a girl, A young boy and a young girl, An adult man and woman, and finally an elderly man and woman.)

(For Nature: you will need to create and hold in your mind a sunset, a seascape, a green meadow, a forest, a mountain, a field of multi-colored flowers, a stream surrounded by green banks).

(For Animals: you will need to create and hold in your mind a dog, a cat like, a bird, a Giraffe, An Elephant, a Fish, a Snake and a Horse.)

(For Food: you will need to create and hold in your mind an apple, a loaf of bread, a bottle of wine, a pie, a round of cheese, a bunch of carrots, a carton of eggs, a mug of steaming coffee).

(For Furniture: you will need to create and hold in your mind a big stuffy easy chair, a large ornate sofa, a four poster bed, a large oak desk, a perfectly set up dinner table complete with center piece, a large well filled book case, a grandfather clock, a sparkling chandelier.)

After you have made your choice, you will begin to practice sending and receiving complete images. This ESP is also known as remote viewing and is practiced by some secret branches of the government for national security purpose.

For People: you will begin by making a choice of a person and then you must also create and decide which part of the house your person is in. Remember to concentrate very hard on that person if you are the sender or let your mind become completely blank if you decide to become a recipient.

Now, reverse the process with your mate and concentrate on sending the images. Create and hold the image of your choice and concentrate with all your will on sending to the recipient. This procedure is quite advanced and requires much patience to develop, because you are working with complicated imagery. Give yourself a lot of time to master this remote viewing process, with time you can only succeed. You will begin by receiving shadows of images, but if you practice, the pictures will come as clear as the sender can send them. Remember that these mental exercises are extremely complex in nature and require time and practice to become a real master. Your mind's eye is very real and very powerful, you were born with it and you can use it at will. Your next step will take place automatically and naturally and may scare some unaware people. This process is designed to lead you into your own subconscious in a conscious state and will lead to the astral projection in your etheric body in time and space.

This dense physical world can only operate safely if solid rules are established and respected by all of us. No one in his right mind would cross the street when the light is red or take a chance at a stop sign. Our system and ruling authorities, including the police force are there to reinforce all the rules for our safety. In every department of the human life, rules are to be found everywhere and those who ignore the rules found in the "signs" will pay a heavy price to themselves and society at large. The young soul's frame of mind neutralizes the visible expressions of the Divine; but in time, mankind will further its own cosmic consciousness and perceive the celestial rules.

As above, so below, meaning if those harsh physical rules are set for a tangible world, the same rules apply for the intangible world. Man made laws are set for our physical world and inserted in books, while God Universal Laws (the stars) are perceivable only through the archetypal realm of consciousness, when the soul has reached cosmic consciousness. These laws are inflexible and must be assimilated and respected at all times. This lack of knowledge or the reluctance to expand the mind is usually the result of religious poisoning and anyone breaking any physical or spiritual law will have to pay the heavy penalty of ignorance.

Sir Isaac Newton wrote, "For every action there will be a reaction." If this law applies for this physical world, common sense dictates that there are laws in action in the subtle spiritual world. Your first challenge is to realize the duality of all things in life and accept this fundamental, yet simplistic principle. The ultimate coordination between the physical and spiritual manifestation has been in action since forever. In the arena of life the struggle between the bull (earth/ rationale) and the matador (air/spirit) is unfolding daily. The bull (Taurus) is a solid representation of the rational and logical approach to life and represents its Earthy boundaries, laws and limitation. The matador (Gemini) exemplifies the element of Air curiosity, critical thinking, inventiveness, originality and intelligence. Earthy souls are grounded and indisposed to change their stubborn logical mind and earthy ways of life. The lesson is, to realize that life is a constant process of changes and that an inflexible intellect will not bring wisdom. Only donkeys do not change their mind! Those people simply need to grow and realize that rules written two thousands years ago for a bunch of smelly, dirty, God fearing uneducated peasants do not apply anymore for the busy modern man. There is such a thing as evolution in all departments of the human reasoning and its learning process.

"The stars are the elixir of life."
--Albert Einstein

Everything including the positive and negative polarity thought process, is based upon the law of relativity. In time and space, there are no limits; above and below and forever there is only space and eternity. Realize that your wish has to take its very existence first, in the spiritual realm of your own Superconscious. Nourished by the intensity released by your desire, your faith, and the use of your will, sooner or later manifest. Your aspiration was a dream that turns into a solid reality in this tangible world. The idea behind this theory is to understand the spiritual principle involved and willingly, stimulate your subconscious creative forces to perform by creating a form of chain reaction, in both the spiritual and physical worlds. Once more, simply illustrated, one must realize that the future (personal or as a whole) is nothing else than the reincarnation of the own positive or negative thought process. This subtle "modus operandi" does also affect the atomic particles and structure of the mind, body and spirit. This awareness and appropriate techniques can be used to generate a super flux of revitalizing energy, to prevent or heal parts of the body, straight from the Supraconcious in time and space.

Never forget the biblical phrases "Ask and you shall receive" and "God created man in his image." Without basic curiosity, there is no chance for mental exploration and the exceptional form of spiritual expansion. I also know that the truth is not within, but outside of oneself. I could be sitting for the next few years on top of a desolated mountain in Peru or India "meditating" in my research for the undiluted truth, as promised to me by a well known, half dead, longhaired bearded guru who spent last 40 days fasting to purify his body and spirit. Words of love and light would pour out of his mouth and prayers and songs would flow down incessantly from our mountains top. Well, five years later, I would probably find myself brainless, lacking wisdom and certainly be lost, spiritually.

Remember that people can only relate to you, because of their own experiences and education. Over the years, I came to realize that dealing with others in our daily life teaches the harsh reality about oneself and this truth is to be found outside of oneself, not inside. After reading these materials, simply ask this question. Did I learn anything in Dr. Turi's book so far? And if you did you simply picked it up in my world, not yours. With extraordinary experiences and sufferings, you will fast become a recipient of true wisdom to those willing to enter your world. Your mission then will be, to pass on your very valuable knowledge to those in need. There are so many lessons to be learned and sharing this knowledge is a part of your existence. Children are the future and as they learn love and wisdom from wiser souls, the world will become a safer place for them. Nothing will change until you decide to change and improve your own consciousness. What steps will you take to rise to a higher level of awareness and expand your knowledge and what will be the price? What must you learn to reach this goal? What must you do, or stop doing? If your dreams and goals are truly important to you, do one thing different in your life, and take new steps and try new ways. You may also because of induced fears, refuse to be curious and grow. You may decline critical thinking against what your first teachers have taught you to be the truth. In many cases this means a traditional religious or scientific education and unless you ask, you will not receive and upgrade your own personal vibrations.

Religion and Astrology

"But it's against my religion!" some people say. The majority of us have no choice, but to explore their fundamental relationship with the spiritual world, through their first teachers and traditional religious values. The amount of information received does not refer to the use of the subconscious in a safe or extraordinary way. Controlling the amount of information leads to a censured form of education and is also a sure way to manipulate the psyche of the masses for the financially concerned organized institutions. The option to do otherwise for millions of souls is out of the question, due to over 875 different denominations established world wide during the last 2000 years. Trying to free the troubled spirit from its own fears and limitation is also a long process and in some cases it's simply impossible. Using rocks, plants, and stars to heal the body, mind or spirit may sound like evil to some young souls. Again, evil is ignorance and a lack of knowledge breeds fears of the unknown and stops any form of mental development This is a very sensitive area and I want to approach it carefully, so the fear of "evil or devil" does not resonate negatively in the subconscious mind and freeze the critical attitude needed for spiritual exploration. A little history would certainly benefit the reader on certain facts involving this research.

Nearly 400 years after the Roman Catholic Church condemned Nicholas Copernicus's discovery that the Earth revolved around the sun as heresy, Pope John Paul II visited the astronomer's birthplace and praised his scientific achievements. "The discovery made by Copernicus, and its importance for history and science, remind us of the ever-present tension between reason and faith," the pope told officials of the University in Torun named after the astronomer. The pontiff is on the third day of 13-days trip to his homeland. The church condemned Copernicus' theory in 1616 and later condemned Galileo for supporting his findings. The Church banned Copernicus' book "De Revolutionibus Orbium Coelestium", until 1822. In 1992, John Paul proclaimed that the Vatican had erred when it condemned Galileo. In praising Copernicus' achievements, the pope noted that new scientific breakthroughs were "growing at a dizzying rate." "This progress gives rise to both wonderment and fear," he said. "Man is becoming ever more fearful of the products of his own intelligence and freedom … Concern for the moral conscience and the sense of moral responsibility has today become a fundamental imperative for men and women of science." The pope has warned of moral dangers associated with recent breakthroughs in cloning and artificial fertilization.

"*I want to know all of Gods thoughts; all the rest are just details.*"
--Albert Einstein

In the audience, modern Polish astronomer Alexander Wolszczan praised the pope's call for defining the relationship between faith and science. "They complement each other, though it is not always evident," said Wolszczan. "They are both directed at man and especially now … we are absorbed with so many problems, their cooperation is necessary." In 1992, Wolszczan discovered the existence of planets outside our solar system.

Note: Incidentally both Copernicus and Galileo before being astronomers were astrologers and it is from the work of those wise men, that astronomy was born. This rational science of the stars is a by-product of astrology and it is important for the readers to be aware of this fact. Astrological clay tablets made by the Babylonians over 35000 years ago were stolen and used by early "scientists" to depict the exact date of eclipses. Man then began to challenge Gods celestial order by the use a more scientific approach to his creation and began investigating the physical aspect of the stars only. Man's arrogance produced this fatalistic error and the loss of supra knowledge and ultimately, a heavy penalty to mankind. Science was born, with the downfall of man's spiritual faculties. It must never be forgotten that the Babylonians were also a nation of stargazers, and that they kept a body of men to do nothing else but report eclipses, appearances of the lunar phases, and sunspots, etc. The Atlantis, Sumerians, Incas, and many disappeared civilizations did the same and used the knowledge, so man could lead a more productive life and work in harmony with nature.

Sad enough, much of the valuable mystical knowledge has been cast aside during the "Dark Ages" and confiscated by the Vatican and stored in its well-guarded seven miles of secret library. Consequently, many advanced souls had to pay the ultimate price by burning on the stake. The truth is that the Universal message and religion are one, but keeping this fact away from the uneducated masses would give more power to the literati's government officials and its financial enterprises.

"Only two things are infinite, the universe and human stupidity, and I'm not sure about the former."
--Albert Einstein

My friend Jordan Maxwell, a reputable scholar on Genesis, gave me some information on the "Appendixes" from the structure of the books of the Old Testament according to the Hebrew canon. His findings are quite extraordinary and I decided to share his knowledge with you. Neptune is the planet regulating all deception and all poisons. This misleading Neptunian legacy, created eight hundred and seventy five different religious denominations since the "Dark Ages" where humankind's spirit surrendered and drowned irreversibly into the quick sands of this planet. You will never be taught in Sunday schools that the Pope was enthroned under the royal sign of Leo and the Vatican Council was teaching the Pope astrology.

**Enthronement of the Pope Under
The Zodiacal Sign of Leo (The King)**

The Vatican Counsil Teaching the Pope Astrology

3 Genesis Finds Its Complements In The Apocalypse

GENESIS

Genesis the book of the beginning
The Earth created (1.1).
Satan's first rebellion
Sun, Moon and Stars for Earth's government (1.14-16)
Sun to govern the day (1.16).

Note: They are great truths, which are taught from the position, symbols, and names of the heavenly bodies. When God created them and set them in the firmament of heaven, He said, in Gen. i. 14--"Let them be for signs and for seasons."

Note - Gen. i. 14 is very clear and therefore, "They (heavenly bodies, Moon, Sun and the Stars) were conceived by the Creator to be used as signs (that is things to come/predictions) and for specific cycles (periodicity)." Nothing can more articulate in reference to this biblical passage from God. The heavenly bodies contain not only a specific Revelation (predictions) involving "the things to come" to be learned in the "signs" of the Zodiac, but also in reference to the "appointed" times in his unyielding celestial will.

6. Darkness called night (1.5).
7. Water called seas (1.10).
8. A river for Earth's blessings (2.10.14).
9. Man in God's image (1.26).

APOCALYPSE

Apocalypse the book of the end
The Earth passed away (21.1.).
8. Satan's final rebellion (20.7.10).
Sun, Moon and Stars connected with Earth's judgment (6.13; 8.12; 16.8).

The bearing of the Sun, Moon and distant stars are so organized that towards the end of a specific period in time they "divinely" proceed, almost exactly in the same position, in harmony with each other, around the earth. Consequently, we have seasons and Eclipses Cycles on a regular basis.

Gen. xviii. 21, "At this set time in the next year."
Gen. xviii. 14, "At the time appointed I will return."
Gen. xvii. 2, "At the set time of which God has spoken."

In the old days, Astronomy commingled with astrology. The Babylonian libraries refer to the following - Isaiah, xlvii. 13, "Thou art wearied in the multitude of thy counsels. Let now, thy astrologers (wise men), the star-gazers, the monthly prognosticators stand up." The tremendous astrological work of the Babylonians accommodates seventy tablets, and was gathered by the command of Sargon of Agade thirty-eight hundred years BC. This is referred as the "Illumination of Bel."

This celestial memorandum was made daily in high towers called "ziggurats." Those cleverly build lookouts were erected in all large cities and their 'celestial" narration were sent regularly to their Masters for further explanations before reaching the King. Well before we were able to do so, the "wise men" calculated eclipses and heavenly motion. They also knew about the sun's spots and all known comets. Incredibly, famous writer, Zacharia Sitchin, one of the rare scholars able to do accurate Babylonian tablets translations, reported a full scale of our solar system, including, Uranus, Neptune and Pluto, well before the first telescope was invented. The Babylonians were the creators of the Zodiac, and in the British Museum, (fifth Creation Tablets) there are clay tablets fragments of two planispheres with incredible figures and astrological calculations impressed on them. Incidentally, the months were named after the signs of the Zodiac.

It reads as follow:

"Anu (God) made excellent the mansion (i.e. the celestial houses) of the great gods (twelve Greek mythology gods) in number (i.e. the twelve signs or mansion of the sun).

The stars he placed in them. The lumasi (i.e. groups of stars or figures) he fixed.

Note: Babylonian Life and History - Fragments of these colored glazed bricks are to be seen in the British Museum.

"My religion consists of a humble admiration of the illimitable superior spirit who reveals himself in the slight details we are able to perceive with our frail and feeble mind. I do not believe in the God of theology who rewards good and punishes evil."
  Albert Einstein

Doubt

The Bible speaks of these important truths uncovering in an holy way, how the Universal Laws operates: The immortal "Soul" is nothing else than a reflection of the Subconscious Mind and is "designed" as an intrinsic part of " The Universal Code"

"Marvelous are thy works, and that my soul knoweth right, well." -- Psalm 139:14

Disbelief is a dominant vibration, which tells the Subconscious Mind that your conscious Mind, or your ego, does not believe in the possibility to reach your wishes, which is more your reality. Note also your personal UCI interacting with "The Universal Code" may or may not support your wish. This indeed becomes the real reason why "The Universal Laws" does not appear to work for some people. However, with education you will be able to "counteract" or avoid the celestial opposition and become the creator of your aims.

Religion is all about prayers and like thoughts; prayers are powerful things or another means to liberate your subconscious' creative forces. However, never forget its direct relationship with your UCI (souls) and "The Universal Code" or "The Universal Laws" or the "Universal Mind" or "The Subconscious Mind" which are all one manifestation.

"So God created man in his own image, in the image of God he created him; male and female he created them" -- Genesis 1:27

"In that day you will know that I am in my Father, and you in me, and I in you" -- John 14:20

You must differentiate the UCI (your celestial program) and the Subconscious Mind or "The Universal Code" acting, as one in the larger scheme of things.

I have to remind you once more that your brain or your (UCI) has been "programmed" by the "Universal Mind" or "The Universal Code" or God, to perceive your physical reality and contain all your vices, virtues, gifts and karma. The human brain is not the Universal Mind, but interacts with it and is pre-programmed by your karma and turns out to be your UCI, or your astrological chart. Within this highly spiritual scheme of things, your senses allow for your perceptions and then become your reality.

Through "The Law Of Repetition" and your prayers, your Subconscious Mind will accept persistent thoughts, especially those energized by powerful emotion or fears. Your "enemy" is the lack of awareness of your UCI and your karmic limitations. You may pray night and day or affirm your wishes forever, if your UCI is "limited" or if you cannot bypass the limitation, you will never able to activate the force for your benefit. You may be told otherwise, but the fact is very real; only a minority of people will be able to stir the subconscious creative forces and bring about realizing their best dreams. Of course it's easier to be in denial and discard thirty-five years of my research, instead of working diligently to bring forth your cosmic consciousness. I can guarantee you, understanding and using a multitude of Universal Laws will steer your subconscious and "The Universal Code" in your favor.

The same regulations apply looking for true love, if regardless of your constant efforts to find the right partner; nothing or no one worthwhile of your interest will be attracted to you. You may pray, wish or hope for a miracle, but knowing that Saturn (constriction) is in your 7th house (marriage) or the Tail of the Dragon is in your 5th house (seat of attraction) would seriously help to realize your timed limitation. Instead, knowing when Venus (love) is transiting your 7th (partnerships) or 5th house (sweet heart) would become a major contribution to reach your wishes. But again, to make a good use of the celestial energy one must build enough cosmic consciousness to understand and handle "The Universal Code" and your subconscious creative forces. And that is the difference between a 60-minute DVD entitled "The Secret" and many hours of study uncovering "The Rest of the Secret!

In the future, the awareness of the thought power and the celestial rules will be understood, taught, and accepted as a solid discipline in our colleges and universities. The power within each one of us will be practiced by millions of people around the globe, bringing unlimited creative possibilities for future generations. 2012, the dawning of the golden age, shows its first ray of light, hope, and happiness for all. Mankind recognizes the creative forces of the subconscious and finally understood that All Men Are Gods.

"When men realize that the church is the universe and the twelve apostles are a reflection of the twelve signs of the zodiac, God's commandments written in light will bring true love and peace to the world"
--Dr. Turi

Closing Thoughts

The Last Frontier

Beyond the year 2012 man will perceive "The Universal Code" and unite with a hierarchy of ET's from the infinite amount of solar system surrounding his own. Due to a serious increase in UFO visitations, congress will be forced to release all pertinent information about this incredible phenomenon. Frequent Extraterrestrials visitations will compel a deep spiritual revolution in the consciousness of humanity. Specific purpose involving the evolution of mankind and our solar system will be fully endorsed by future generations while unlimited cosmic frontiers will be exposed to us all. Interstellar travel from end to end dimensions will open a new range of possibilities to visit parallel worlds in association with supremely advanced extraterrestrial beings.

Religious faith as practiced today, won't serve any progressive purpose for mankind. No Earth resident will ever die for a doctrine, a deity or a religion. Led by advanced spiritual leaders, the Golden Universal Truths will be offered to all. The children of the new millennium will benefit from an inborn cosmic consciousness and bear the common goal for universal love and widespread peace with the space brothers.

Those light teachers will provide all of mankind with a solid understanding of the dynamics of our solar system and the subtle spiritual values found in the stars. Some of my youngest students will become the pillars to advance future generations universal resolutions. This wisdom will assure the vital balance for peace and spiritual substance to all the world residents. A wonderful productive society will reign, furthering higher education, love, and respect for us all. Harmony and wisdom will replace man's ignorance and its worst animalistic destructive instincts.

The children of the future will be conscious of their unique spiritual heritage and will interact with the cosmic brothers, where love and respect will own the center stage. God's divine aims will shine under an atypical intrinsic light, producing well-balanced human beings. Strength, creativity, physical and spiritual potential for greatness, will be advocated as the main goal for all the children of this world. The best qualities found in "The Universal Code" will be cultivated to produce geniuses capable of incomparable achievements. Guided by wise spiritual masters, the children of the future will understand and avoid the destructive potential of every planet's potential. Knowledge will constrict ignorance and cosmic consciousness will advance the celestial energy in a beneficial way. The transcendental forces of the Universe interacting with the creative forces of the Superconscious, will be understood and wisely used by us all. Man is at the firmament of his greatest accomplishment, while uncovering unlimited creativity and his immortality.

ARIES - The aggressive tone of Mars will be channeled in constructive endeavors for all mankind - Wars will be part of the past and man's potential to destroy any world will be eliminated. Man's potential to achieve greatness will be allowed in each of us, supporting Man's powerful desire to succeed in all its constructive enterprises.

TAURUS - The lovely heart of Venus will promote a genuine love and a pure spiritual and physical beauty for all. Compassion will replace indolence, insecurity and manipulation. A higher form of art based on universal love will be expressing itself and blessing all worlds. Spiritual wealth will be guaranteed and available to all men.

GEMINI - The critical thinking power of Mercury will be applied to further investigate the future of mankind in relationship to others cosmic brothers. The challenge will be met successfully with all the questions that God's has enslaved man to search for. Intellectual notoriety based on universal exploration, will be a graduation for all existence.

CANCER – The Moon is the pulsing heart of the earth and will be wisely adjusted into man's hearty fruitful endeavors. The cycle of the Moon and her interaction on the bodies' minds and spirits on earth will be fully understood and used by us all. Creativity, sensitivity security and protection of man's celestial neighboring star families will be a reality for all.

LEO - The creative forces of the Sun will generate an infinite golden light to sustain harmony and pure love within the spiritual and physical realm of consciousness. Creativity and praiseworthiness of collective light will be geared towards the all-embracing welfare of love to the interstellar beings of all the worlds above.

VIRGO – The Mercurial energy will be used for the purification principle and duties to keep all worlds clean of negative energy. Men of the future will support all efforts to establish purity in its entire splendor. Service through all physical and spiritual levels of consciousness will be customary for the well being of the cosmos and its celestial residents.

LIBRA – The caring energy of Venus will achieve peace and harmony in all worlds. All earth and extraterrestrials hierarchies' goals will maintain and promote serenity and synchronization in all levels of consciousness. Mankind will ascend towards the true essence of love and respect for life itself.

SCORPIO – The powerful rebirthing supremacy of Pluto will be channeled prolifically towards a resurrection of man and its super enlightened spirit, where the Phoenix in its reincarnation principle will raise all souls above passions destruction and death. Men realize its immortality and safely ascend towards its own Godly powers.

SAGITTARIUS – The Lord of philosophy will unbolt mans aptitude to tap successfully into the realm of star consciousness and upgrade his spirit to a higher spiritual level. All the essence of the religions of the past will be no more. Man spirit will be free from deceiving doctrines and will discover the conception of time and space. The undiluted truth and intuitional domain of the stars will become a universal teaching.

CAPRICORN – The universal government will aim for a solid security, based upon values and universal order. Regulations and laws will be promoted with a strong sense of responsibility to all worlds and its inhabitants. Man's judgment will be based upon the higher celestial rules on which all spirits depend. All living souls will become essential parts of the process of electing and respecting the wiser soul in the universe.

AQUARIUS – Uranus' genius futuristic power will reign in its entire splendor. His universal message for love and respect in all creations will create its universal religion. Men realize the universe as the church of god and the twelve signs, as the apostles' commandments. The fundamental nature of universal brotherhood, universal freedom and universal love for all existence, will bring the ascensions of all souls to the illumination of oneness.

PISCES - The Apocalypse did not happen! Many young souls have grown by eliminating all denominations and the controls of information. California is still intact and people are still fishing on the coastlines of the great west, the Middle East is a peaceful, productive land – Jesus or Elvis never came back and organized religions and abusive corporations financial empires collapsed. Science has grown drastically and turned to technology and cold fusion, to replace empty oil reserves. The deceiving influence of Neptune is no more and Uranus is the new ruler of the world. The transcendental forces of the Supraconcious are used with the Universal Code on a daily basis and peace reigns on this world. Human and extraterrestrials communion is achieved, all for a greater purpose in neighboring worlds.

"God created the stars and the heaven for more than the sake of beauty; He gave them to us for interpretation, so that we may live a more productive life. Man is superior to the stars if he lives in the power of superior wisdom. Such a person, being the master over heaven and earth, by means of his will, is a magus, and magic is not sorcery but supreme wisdom.
~ Paracelsus

Bring Dr. Turi to Your City

Dr. Turi, a "Prophet for Modern Times"

If you are a radio or Television professional broadcaster or a group in need of Dr. Turi's exclusive wisdom and matchless presentation will change your entire conception of life and bring many answers we all have been enslaved to uncover on this dense physical world. A phenomenal guest speaker you cannot afford to miss for your audience!

Lecture title: "Beyond The Secret"

Dr. Turi was recognized in the 2003 Marquis "Who's Who in America" as an accomplished leading Clinical Hypnotherapist, Astropsychologist and Cabalistic Healer. Dr. Turi has appeared in numerous newspapers, magazines and with George Noory on Coast-To-Coast radio and numerous television programs worldwide. He spent the last 25 years mastering and teaching the mighty secrets of the Superconscious in time and space and its interaction with the "Universal Code". Dr. Turi will put the audience in a safe light trance and open the door to your subconscious' creative forces accordingly. The inserted suggestion will undoubtedly bring about one of your most cherished wish and open the gate to "Beyond The Secret". Dr. Turi requires a good PC and will bring a CD of the Dalai Lama Chanting For Healing.

Workshop title: "Nostradamus Cabalistic Healing"

Dr. Turi will teach the audience how to perform a rare Nostradamus Cabalistic Healing to improve your immune system, raise your vibrations build magnetism and increase the seat of attraction with the opposite sex. Be ready for incredible information pertaining to the spirit, health, love and career. Don't miss this great opportunity to work with your subconscious while enjoying deep spiritual and physical cleansing. Bring a large towel or a blanket at the event.

You may reach Dr. Turi at (602) 265-7667

Services http://drturi.com
http://cherrytap.com/drturi
http://www.myspace.com/drturi

❧ Books ❦

I Know All About You

Asia Dragon Predictions

Moon Power 2007 (Yearly)

Power of the Dragon

And God Created the Stars

CPSIA information can be obtained
at www.ICGtesting.com
Printed in the USA
BVHW072128110720
583438BV00001B/40